Lecture Notes in Computer Science 3933

Commenced Publication in 1973
Founding and Former Series Editors:
Gerhard Goos, Juris Hartmanis, and Jan van Leeuwen

Editorial Board

Francesco Bonchi   Jean-François Boulicaut (Eds.)

Knowledge Discovery in Inductive Databases

4th International Workshop, KDID 2005
Porto, Portugal, October 3, 2005
Revised Selected and Invited Papers

 Springer

Volume Editors

Francesco Bonchi
Pisa KDD Laboratory, ISTI - C.N.R.
Area della Ricerca di Pisa
Via Giuseppe Moruzzi, 1 - 56124 Pisa, Italy
E-mail: francesco.bonchi@isti.cnr.it

Jean-François Boulicaut
INSA Lyon, LIRIS CNRS UMR 5205
Bâtiment Blaise Pascal, 69621 Villeurbanne Cedex, France
E-mail: jean-francois.boulicaut@insa-lyon.fr

Library of Congress Control Number: 2006922625

CR Subject Classification (1998): H.2, I.2

LNCS Sublibrary: SL 3 – Information Systems and Application, incl. Internet/Web
and HCI

ISSN   0302-9743
ISBN-10   3-540-33292-8 Springer Berlin Heidelberg New York
ISBN-13   978-3-540-33292-3 Springer Berlin Heidelberg New York

Springer is a part of Springer Science+Business Media

springer.com

© Springer-Verlag Berlin Heidelberg 2006
Printed in Germany

Typesetting: Camera-ready by author, data conversion by Scientific Publishing Services, Chennai, India
Printed on acid-free paper   SPIN: 11733492   06/3142   5 4 3 2 1 0

Preface

The 4th International Workshop on Knowledge Discovery in Inductive Databases (KDID 2005) was held in Porto, Portugal, on October 3, 2005 in conjunction with the 16th European Conference on Machine Learning and the 9th European Conference on Principles and Practice of Knowledge Discovery in Databases.

Ever since the start of the field of data mining, it has been realized that the integration of the database technology into knowledge discovery processes was a crucial issue. This vision has been formalized into the inductive database perspective introduced by T. Imielinski and H. Mannila (CACM 1996, 39(11)). The main idea is to consider knowledge discovery as an extended querying process for which relevant query languages are to be specified. Therefore, inductive databases might contain not only the usual data but also inductive generalizations (e.g., patterns, models) holding within the data. Despite many recent developments, there is still a pressing need to understand the central issues in inductive databases. Constraint-based mining has been identified as a core technology for inductive querying, and promising results have been obtained for rather simple types of patterns (e.g., itemsets, sequential patterns). However, constraint-based mining of models remains a quite open issue. Also, coupling schemes between the available database technology and inductive querying proposals are not yet well understood. Finally, the definition of a general purpose inductive query language is still an on-going quest.

This workshop aimed to bring together database, machine learning and data mining researchers/practitioners who were interested in the numerous scientific and technological challenges that inductive databases offers. The workshop followed the previous three successful workshops organized in conjunction with ECML/PKDD: KDID 2002 held in Helsinki, Finland, KDID 2003 held in Cavtat-Dubrovnik, Croatia, and KDID 2004 held in Pisa, Italy. Its scientific program included seven regular presentations and four short communications, an invited talk by Carlo Zaniolo, and an invited "workshop-closing talk" by Arno Siebes. During the workshop, only informal proceedings were distributed. Most of the papers within this volume have been revised by the authors based on the comments from the initial referring stage and the discussion during the workshop. A few are invited chapters.

We wish to thank the invited speakers, all the authors of submitted papers, the Program Committee members and the ECML/PKDD 2005 Organization Committee. KDID 2005 was supported by the European project IQ "Inductive Queries for Mining Patterns and Models" (IST FET FP6-516169, 2005-2008).

December 2005

Francesco Bonchi
Jean-François Boulicaut

Organization

Program Chairs

Francesco Bonchi
Pisa KDD Laboratory
ISTI - C.N.R.
Italy
http://www-kdd.isti.cnr.it/~bonchi/

Jean-François Boulicaut
INSA Lyon
France
http://liris.cnrs.fr/~jboulica/

Program Committee

Hendrik Blockeel, *K.U. Leuven, Belgium*
Toon Calders, *University of Antwerp, Belgium*
Sašo Džeroski, *Jozef Stefan Institute, Slovenia*
Minos N. Garofalakis, *Bell Labs, USA*
Fosca Giannotti, *ISTI-C.N.R., Italy*
Bart Goethals, *University of Antwerp, Belgium*
Dominique Laurent, *LICP, Université de Cergy-Pontoise, France*
Giuseppe Manco, *ICAR-C.N.R., Italy*
Heikki Mannila, *University of Helsinki, Finland*
Rosa Meo, *University of Turin, Italy*
Taneli Mielikäinen, *University of Helsinki, Finland*
Katharina Morik, *University of Dortmund, Germany*
Céline Robardet, *INSA de Lyon, France*
Sunita Sarawagi, *KR School of Information Technology, IIT Bombay, India*
Arno Siebes, *University of Utrecht, The Netherlands*
Mohammed Zaki, *Rensselaer Polytechnic Institute, USA*
Carlo Zaniolo, *UCLA, USA*

Table of Contents

Invited Papers

Contributed Papers

Data Mining in Inductive Databases

Arno Siebes

Universiteit Utrecht,
Department of Computer Science,
Padualaan 14, 3584CH Utrecht, The Netherlands
arno@cs.uu.nl

Abstract. Ever since the seminal paper by Imielinski and Mannila [11], inductive databases have been a constant theme in the data mining literature. Operationally, such an inductive database is a database in which models and patterns are first class citizens.

In the extensive literature on inductive databases there is at least one consequence of this operational definition that is conspicuously missing. That is the question: if we have models and patterns in our inductive database, how does this help to discover other models and patterns? This question is the topic of this paper.

1 Introduction

Ever since the start of research in data mining, it has been clear that data mining, and more general the KDD process, should be merged into DBMSs. Since the seminal paper by Imielinski and Mannila [11], the so-called *inductive databases* have been a constant theme in data mining research, with its own series of workshops.

Perhaps surprisingly, there is no formal definition of what an inductive database actually is. In [30] it is stated that it might be too early for such a definition, given the issues I raise in this paper, I tend to agree with this opinion. Still, we need some sort of shared concept of an inductive database.

Mostly, people think of inductive databases in analogy with *deductive databases;* an analogy that is not without its weaknesses as we will see later. I take a slightly different angle, viz., an inductive database is a database in which the discovered models and patterns are first class citizens. That is, we should be able to treat models and patterns as any other data object. This very operational definition of an inductive database is our guiding principle in this paper.

Research in inductive databases is mainly focused on two aspects:

1. The integration of data mining and DBMSs, which itself encompasses two, not necessarily disjunct, main topics,
   (a) database support for data mining, or, the integration of data mining algorithms into a DBMS and
   (b) integrating data mining into standard query languages like SQL.
2. Querying models and patterns.

F. Bonchi and J.-F. Boulicaut (Eds.): KDID 2005, LNCS 3933, pp. 1–23, 2006.

These are clearly important aspects of an inductive database and surprisingly hard to do well to boot. However, they are not all there is for an inductive database. This alone doesn't make models and patterns first class cizitizens. In fact, the most important aspect of an inductive database is missing: the data mining!

This might seem a strange statement since both main topics are deeply concerned with data mining. The first one is all about making data mining no different from other, more standard, queries in, e.g., SQL. The second one is about storing the models and patterns that result from mining queries in the database and querying those results with constraints.

This is very much in line what would would expect for inductive databases, especially if one compares with deductive databases [23]. For, except for the architectural issues of integration, these topics can be nicely formalised in first order logic [30]. Moreover, pushing the query constraints into the mining algorithm is a natural extension of standard relational query optimisation.

So, the analogy of inductive databases and deductive databases is certainly a fruitful one. However, this analogy doesn't tell the whole story.

> In deductive databases, the Intentional Database (the rules) is a static component. Queries result in new facts, not in new rules.

In data mining, however, we are not interested in new facts, we want to discover new models and patterns. If we already have models and patterns in our database, a natural question is: does this help? So, a central question for data mining in inductive databases that is not covered by the analogy with deductive databases is:

> How do the models and patterns we have already discovered help us in discovering other models and patterns?

This question is the topic of this paper. Given that it is an invited paper, I feel free to raise more questions than I answer. The goal is to point to new research questions, not to answer them.

I discuss three aspects of this question in this paper:

Relational Algebra: Models and patterns are tightly connected to the data tables they have been induced from. In a DBMS we can construct new tables from existing ones using relational algebra. It would be useful if these algebraic manipulations could be *lifted* to the models and patterns. It would give us models and patterns for free.

Models for Models: If we have already induced models and/or patterns from a data table, does this help us in the induction of other models and/or patterns from that same table?

Models on Models: If models and patterns are first class citizens in our database, we should be able to mine a collection of models or a collection of patterns. How can we do this and, perhaps more importantly, does this make sense?

The questions are discussed both from a pattern and from a model perspective. The patterns used are mostly frequent item sets, the models mostly Bayesian networks.

This paper is not meant to be a survey paper, i.e., it is in no way complete. For some if not all off the (sub-)questions the paper discusses there is far more published literature than is mentioned or discussed. The choices made are mostly based on what I thought would nicely illustrate my point. Moreover, there is a clear bias to papers I have been involved in[1].

The road map of this paper is as follows. In Section 2, some preliminaries are introduced. The next three sections discuss the three sub-questions introduced above. Finally, in the final section concludes the paper by formulating a couple of research topics I feel are important for inductive databases.

2 Preliminaries

In order to keep our discussion simple, we assume a binary database. In fact, in general we assume the database contains one binary table. Only in the case of relational algebra we assume multiple tables when the operators require more than one input table.

In the case of frequent item sets, we use the standard terminology of items and transactions. In the Bayesian networks case, we will mostly call them variables and tuples. Given the simple relationship between a binary table and a set of transactions, this should not confuse the reader. We discuss both contexts briefly.

2.1 Models and Patterns

In the introduction we already used both the terms *model* and *patterns*. Both terms are probably familiar to all data miner, although I wouldn't know a formal definition of either. The goal of this subsection is not to present such a definition, but to point out the most important difference between the two.

Models describe the whole database, they are *global*. Patterns describe *local* phenomena in the database. In [8], a pattern is defined by:

$$data = model + patterns + random$$

In [22] this definition extended with three characteristics, viz.,

- Local patterns cover small parts of the data space.
- Local patterns deviate from the distribution of which they are part.
- Local patterns show some internal structure.

In other words, while a model tries to capture the whole distribution, patterns describe small sub-spaces were this distribution differs markedly from the global picture.

Given this distinction, it seems obvious that models that have been discovered offer more aid in the discovery of other models and patterns than discovered patterns can. While most of the examples in this paper agree with this observation, this is not true for all of them.

---

[1] In other words, this paper is blatant self promotion!

2.2 Frequent Item Sets

The problem of frequent item set mining [1] can be described as follows. The basis is a set of items $\mathcal{I}$, e.g., the items for sale in a store; $|\mathcal{I}| = n$. A transaction $t \in \mathcal{P}(\mathcal{I})$ is a set of items, e.g., representing the set of items a client bought at that store. A database over $\mathcal{I}$ is simply a set of transactions, e.g., the different sale transactions in the store on a given day. An item set $I \subset \mathcal{I}$ occurs in a transaction $t \in db$ iff $I \subseteq t$. The *support* of I in db, denoted by $supp_{db}(I)$ is the number of transactions in the database in which t occurs. The problem of frequent item set mining is: given a threshold *min-sup*, determine all item sets I such that $supp_{db}(I) \geq min\text{-}sup$. These *frequent item sets* represent, e.g., sets of items customers buy together often enough.

Association Rules are generated from these frequent item sets. If X is a frequent item set and $Y \subset X$,

$$X \setminus Y \to Y$$

is an association rule. Its *confidence* is defined as $\frac{supp_{db}(X)}{supp_{db}(X \setminus Y)}$. For association rule mining, one has the *min-sup* threshold for support and a *min-conf* threshold for the confidence of a rule. The problem is to find all rules that satisfy both minimal thresholds.

Often there are other interestingness measures used to reduce the number of discovered association rules. The one that is most often used is the *lift*. The lift of a rule $X \to Y$ is defined as $\frac{conf_{db}(X \to Y)}{supp_{db}(Y)}$.

If the database consists of a set of *sequences of events*, we can define analogous concepts [20]. An episode is simply a sequence of events. An episode E occurs in a sequence S if deleting events from S yields E; note that an episode E may occur multiple times in S. The support of an episode is the number of times an episode occurs in the database. With a minimal support threshold, the problem is: find all frequent episodes.

2.3 Bayesian Networks

Bayesian networks by now are widely accepted as powerful tools for representing and reasoning with uncertainty in decision-support systems. A Bayesian network is a concise model of a joint probability distribution over a set of stochastic variables [29]; it consists of a directed acyclic graph that captures the qualitative dependence structure of the distribution and a numerical part that specifies conditional probability distributions for each variable given its parents in the graph. Since a Bayesian network defines a unique distribution, it provides for computing any probability of interest over its variables.

A *Bayesian network* is a concise representation of a joint probability distribution over a set of stochastic variables $\mathbf{X} = (X_1, \ldots, X_n)$. The network consists of a directed acyclic graph in which each node corresponds with a variable and the arcs capture the qualitative dependence structure of the distribution. The network further includes a number of conditional probabilities, or *parameters*, $p(X_i \mid \mathbf{X}_{\pi(i)})$ for each variable X_i given its parents $\mathbf{X}_{\pi(i)}$ in the graph.

The graphical structure and associated probabilities with each other represent a unique joint probability distribution $\Pr(\mathbf{X})$ over the variables involved, which is factorised according to

$$\Pr(\mathbf{X}) = \prod_{i=1}^{n} p(X_i \mid \mathbf{X}_{\pi(i)})$$

There are numerous algorithms that induce Bayesian networks from data, see, e.g., [24].

3   Lifting Relational Algebra

The question is: can we extend the relational operators to models and patterns? By focusing on the relational algebra, we have already a syntax. How about the semantics? For example, what is the join of two models? Obviously there are many ways in which this can be defined and the choice for a particular semantics is perhaps the most important factor for our practical view on inductive databases. Our choice is to *lift* the standard operators to models. Lifting means that we want our new operator to construct a new model or a new collection of patterns from the input models or patterns only. That is, without consulting the database.

Note, we use the *bag* semantics for relational algebra rather than the *set* semantics that are more standard in database theory. The reason is that the databases we want to mine adhere to the bag semantics since this is the underlying principle of each available DBMS.

3.1   Select

The relational algebra operator σ (select) is a mapping:

$$\sigma : \mathcal{B}(D) \to \mathcal{B}(D)$$

in which $\mathcal{B}(D)$ denotes all possible bags over domain D.

Lifting means that we are looking for an operator $\sigma_{(D,\mathcal{A})}$ that makes the diagram in figure 1 commute: Such diagrams are well-known in , e.g., category theory [3] and the standard interpretation is:

$$\mathcal{A} \circ \sigma = \sigma_{(D,\mathcal{A})} \circ \mathcal{A}$$

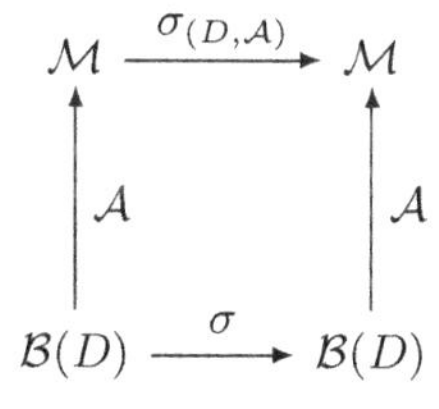

$$
\begin{array}{ccc}
\mathcal{M} & \xrightarrow{\;\sigma_{(D,\mathcal{A})}\;} & \mathcal{M} \\[2pt]
\Big\uparrow{\scriptstyle\mathcal{A}} & & \Big\uparrow{\scriptstyle\mathcal{A}} \\[2pt]
\mathcal{B}(D) & \xrightarrow{\;\sigma\;} & \mathcal{B}(D)
\end{array}
$$

Fig. 1. Lifting the selection operator

In other words, first inducing the model using algorithm $\mathcal{A}$ followed by the application of the *lifted* selection operator $\sigma_{(D,\mathcal{A})}$ yields the same result as first applying the *standard* selection operator σ followed by induction with algorithm $\mathcal{A}$.

For algorithms that do compute the optimal result, such a strict interpretation of the diagram seems reasonable. However, many algorithms rely on heuristic search. In such cases, it doesn't seem reasonable at all to require this strict reading of the diagram. Rather we settle for a *reasonably good approximation*. That is, the lifted selection operator doesn't have to result in a locally optimal model, but it should be close to one[2]. If not explicitly stated otherwise, we will use commutation in this loose sense.

Frequent Item Sets. The three basic selections are $\sigma_{I=0}$, $\sigma_{I=1}$, and $\sigma_{I_1=I_2}$. More complicated selections can be made by conjunctions of these basic comparisons. We look at the different basic selections in turn.

First consider $\sigma_{I=0}$. If it is applied to the database, all transactions in which I occurs are removed from the database. Hence, all item sets that contain I get a frequency of zero in the resulting database. For those item sets in which I doesn't occur, we have to compute which part of their support consists of transactions in which I does occur and subtract that number. Hence, we have:

$$freq_{\sigma_{I=0}(db)}(J) = \begin{cases} 0 & \text{if } I \in J, \\ freq_{db}(J) - freq_{db}(J \cup \{I\}) & \text{else.} \end{cases}$$

If we apply $\sigma_{I=1}$ to the database, all transactions in which I doesn't occur are removed from the database. In other words, the frequency of item sets that contain I doesn't change. For those item sets that do not contain, the frequency is given by those transactions that also contained I. Hence, we have:

$$freq_{\sigma_{I=1}(db)}(J) = \begin{cases} freq_{db}(J) & \text{if } I \in J, \\ freq_{db}(J \cup \{I\}) & \text{else.} \end{cases}$$

If we apply $\sigma_{I_1=I_2}$ to the database, the only transactions that remain are those that either contain both I_1 and I_2 or neither. In other words, for frequent item sets that contain both the frequency remains the same. For all others, the frequency changes. For those item sets J that contain just one of the I_i the frequency will be the frequency of $J \cup \{I_1, I_2\}$. For those that contain neither of the I_i, we have to correct for those transactions that contain one of the I_i in their support. If we denote this by $freq_{db}(J \neg I_1 \neg I_2)$ (a frequency that can be easily computed) We have:

$$freq_{\sigma_{I_1=I_2}(db)}(J) = \begin{cases} freq_{db}(J \cup \{I_1, I_2\}) & \text{if } \{I_1, I_2\} \cap J \neq \emptyset, \\ freq_{db}(J \neg I_1 \neg I_2) & \text{else.} \end{cases}$$

Clearly, we can also "lift" conjunctions of the basic selections, simply process one at the time. So, in principle, we can lift all selections for frequent item sets.

---

[2] Given the nature of this paper, I am not going to attempt to formalise this notion. I hope the reader has some idea of what I mean.

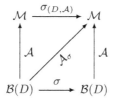

Fig. 2. Lifting selections for succinct constraints

But only in principle, because we need the frequency of item sets that are *not necessarily frequent.* Frequent item sets are a lossy model (not all aspects of the data distribution are modelled) and that can have its repercussions: in general the lifting will *not* be commutative. In our loose sense of "commutativity", the situation is slightly better. For, we can give bounds for the resulting frequencies.

We haven't mentioned constraints [25] so far. Constraints in frequent item set mining are the pre-dominant way to select a subset of the frequent item sets. That is exactly, why we haven't mentioned them so far. In general the constraints studied do not correspond to selections on the database. The exception is the class of *succinct anti-monotone constraints* introduced in [26]. For these constraints there is such a selection (that is what succinct means) and the constraint can be pushed into the algorithm. This means we get the commutative diagram in figure 2. Note that in this case we know that the diagonal arrow makes the bottom right triangle commute in the strict sense of the word. For the upper left triangle, as well as the square, our previous analysis remains true.

Bayesian Networks. The selections $\sigma_{A=0}$ and $\sigma_{A=1}$ in Bayesian networks are a simple example of *partial knowledge*: if we know that variable A has value 1, what can we infer about the values of the other attributes? There are standard inference algorithms [24] for this problem that allow us to propagate this partial knowledge. After that, we can remove the variables that are now fixed, such as A. For example:

$$B \leftarrow A \rightarrow C \text{ transforms to } B \quad C$$

That is, in this example B and C become independent after the selection. In the case of induced dependencies, we have to be careful to add the necessary induced arcs, such as:

$$B \rightarrow A \leftarrow C \text{ transforms to } B \rightarrow C$$

Note that for this simple case, the inference algorithms are polynomial.

The selection $\sigma_{A=B}$ is slightly more complicated. There are three cases we need to consider.

Firstly, if A and B are in disconnected components of the graph, we can simply add an arc from A to B[3]. Furthermore, we have to update the (conditional) probability table of B such that it gives probability zero to those cases were

---

[3] Or from B to A, without a causal interpretation this doesn't matter.

the configuration gives different values to A and B. Moreover, for the configurations that give equal values to A and B, we the probability-assignment should such that the marginal $P(B|A) = 1$. Given that the other marginals should not change, this completely specifies the probability table.

Secondly, if there is an arrow from A to B, the selection $\sigma_{A=B}$ is again a case of partial knowledge. We simply update the conditional probability table of B and propagate this knowledge through the network as before.

Thirdly, and finally, if there exists a path between A and B, we have to be careful not to introduce a cycle in the network. However, it will always be possible to either add an arc from A to B or the other way around without introducing such a cycle. Then we update the tables as before and propagate.

Note that given the heuristic nature of Bayesian network discovery, we cannot expect the diagram to commute in the strict sense. However, there is every reason to believe that we will end up with a good approximation. For the simple reason that we mostly rely on inference, which is a pretty accurate procedure. Hence, if the original network is a good representation of the underlying distribution, the derived network should be a good representation of the restricted distribution.

3.2   Project

For the projection operator π we have a new domain D_1 such that $D = D_1 \times D_2$. Projection on D_1 has thus as signature:

$$\pi_{D_1} : \mathcal{B}(D) \to \mathcal{B}(D_1)$$

Hence, we try to find an operator $\pi_{D_1}^{\mathcal{A}}$ that makes the diagram in figure 3 commute. Note that D_1 is spanned by the set of variables (or items) we project on.

Frequent Item Sets. We project on a set of items $\mathcal{J} \subseteq \mathcal{I}$, let $J \subseteq \mathcal{I}$ be a frequent item set. There are three cases to consider:

1. If $J \subseteq \mathcal{J}$, then all transactions in the support of J will simply remain in the database, hence J will remain frequent.
2. If $J \cap \mathcal{J} \neq \emptyset$, then $J \cap \mathcal{J}$ is also frequent and will remain in the set of frequent item sets.
3. If $J \cap \mathcal{J} = \emptyset$, then its support will vanish.

In other words, if $\mathcal{F}$ denotes the set of all frequent item sets, then:

$$\pi_{\mathcal{J}}(\mathcal{F}) = \{J \in \mathcal{F} | J \subseteq \mathcal{J}\}$$

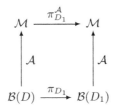

Fig. 3. Lifting projections

Clearly, this method of lifting will make the diagram commute in the strict sense if we use an absolute minimal frequency. In other words, for projections, frequent item sets do capture enough of the underlying data distribution to allow lifting.

Bayesian Networks. A Bayesian network represents a probability distribution. For probability distributions, projections are known as *marginalizations*. For example, if we have a distribution $P(A, B, C)$, we get the corresponding distribution on A and B by:

$$P(A, B) = \sum_C P(A, B, C)$$

Basically, this is what we do for each node in the network. All variables have their conditional probability tables marginalised on parents *not* in the domain projected on. So, again we get lifting in the approximation sense easily.

3.3 Cartesian Product

For the Cartesian product, we have two tables R_1 and R_2 with domains D_1 and D_2 and its signature is:

$$\times : \mathcal{B}(D_1) \times \mathcal{B}(D_2) \to \mathcal{B}(D_1 \times D_2)$$

In other words, we are looking for an operator that makes the following diagram in figure 4 commute.

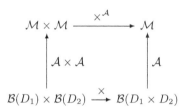

Fig. 4. Lifting the Cartesian product

Frequent Item Sets. Let J_1 be a frequent item set for the first database and J_2 for the second. The frequency of the pair on the Cartesian product of the two database is simply given by:

$$freq_{db_1 \times db_2}(J_1, J_2) = freq_{db_1}(J_1) \times freq_{db_2}(J_2)$$

While this is easy to compute, it means again that in general we will not be able to compute all frequent item sets on the Cartesian product without consulting the database. Even if we set the minimal frequency to the product of the two minimal frequencies, the combination of an infrequent item set on one database with a frequent one on the other may turn out to be frequent.

In other words, we cannot even make the diagram commute in the approximate sense of the word. The reason is that frequent item sets do not capture enough of the underlying data distribution. This shouldn't come as a surprise, patterns are not supposed to capture too much of the distribution.

Bayesian Networks. For Bayesian networks, the situation is completely different. In fact, the Cartesian product is the easiest operator imaginable for Bayesian networks. For, in $db_1 \times db_2$, a tuple in db_1 is combines with each tuple in db_2 and vice versa. That is knowledge about the db_1 part doesn't convey any information about the db_2 part and vice versa. That is, the two components are completely independent.

In other words, if BN_1 is the Bayesian network induced from db_1 and BN_2 that for db_2, the Bayesian network for $db_1 \times db_2$ simply consists of two disconnected components: BN_1 and BN_2.

Note that this also implies that we can lift the Cartesian product for Bayesian networks in the strong sense. Since the induction algorithm $\mathcal{A}$ works, for all practical purposes, independently on the two components one would expect the diagram to commute strictly.

3.4   EquiJoin

The equijoin is defined as $\bowtie = \pi \circ \sigma \circ \times$, it has as signature:

$$\bowtie: \mathcal{B}(D_1) \times \mathcal{B}(D_2) \to \mathcal{B}(D_1 \bowtie D_2)$$

In other words, we want to make the diagram given in figure 5 distribute.

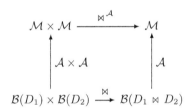

Fig. 5. Lifting the equijoin

Frequent Item Sets. Given the fact that lifting is not completely possible for both selections and Cartesian products for frequent item sets, there is little hope that one can lift the equijoin.

Bayesian Networks. Given that we already know hoe to lift all three basic operations, lifting the equi-join is a straight-forward procedure. The details are left as an exercise to the reader.

3.5   Set Operations

For so-called union compatible relations, i.e. two relations with the same scheme, the standard set operations $\{\cup, \cap, \backslash\}$ are also defined. Each $\theta \in \{\cup, \cap, \backslash\}$ has as signature:

$$\theta : \mathcal{B}(D) \times \mathcal{B}(D) \to \mathcal{B}(D)$$

In other words, we want to make the diagram in figure 6 commute.

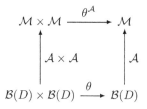

Fig. 6. Lifting set operators

Frequent Item Sets. The union for frequent item sets is a well studied topic as it is a central issue in distributed data mining. A survey of this area is far beyond the scope of the present article, the reader is referred to [13] instead.

The intersection is a far harder problem. The reason is that frequent item sets only code frequent parts of transactions. It is very well possible that each transaction contains one or more items that are not covered by any frequent item set. In other words, we only have partial knowledge about the transactions. If we compute the intersection of two sets of transactions on the other hand, we do employ complete information about the transactions: only those that occur in both remain. This means that we cannot compute the frequent item sets that hold for the intersection. In fact it is possible that an item sets J is frequent on both database while it has no support at all on the intersection.

Set difference, like the intersection, depends on complete knowledge of the transactions. Hence, like for intersection, we cannot lift this operator.

Bayesian Networks. As for frequent item sets, the union of Bayesian networks is a well studied problem. Clearly, if both database are sufficiently large, both BN's should be a good approximation of the generating probability distribution. Ideally they should be the same network. In practice, of course, they rarely are. There are various ways to unify the different networks, the LinOP bases algorithm in [10] presents a good example.

Again, the intersection presents a far harder problem. The basic question is: what network would we have learned if we had used less data? There doesn't seem to be a reasonable answer to this question. An observation that equally holds for set difference.

3.6   Conclusions

In this section we have investigated how the operators from relational algebra can be lifted for both frequent item sets and for Bayesian networks. The two main conclusions from this exercise are as follows.

1. In many cases frequent item sets simply do not capture enough of the underlying distribution to allow a "database-free" combination.
2. Bayesian networks on the other hand are meant to capture this underlying distribution, which is born out by the fact that lifting seems[4] to be possible

---
[4] "Seems" because I have only provided arguments, no formal proofs.

in most cases. The cases were it doesn't work are those were the underlying distribution may be changed in unforeseen ways, i.e., intersection and set difference.

My guess is that Frequent Item Sets are a typical example for any pattern class. Since the goal of pattern mining is to discover interesting local behaviour, most if not all patterns will not capture essential characteristics of the underlying distribution. In other words, lifting will only be possible in sporadic cases, like the projection for frequent item sets.

For models it is less straight forward to generalise from Bayesian networks. Bayesian networks are in a sense a-typical, unlike many other model classes there are no dependent variables. When there is a dependent variable, such as for classification, the quality of models is determined by how good they classify new data. For this task it is not necessary, or even detrimental, to model the complete underlying distribution. The difference between Bayesian networks and Baysian classifiers is a good illustration of this point. In other words, I do suspect that lifting will be more complicated for model classes with dependent variables.

In any case, our brief investigation in this section has barely scratched the surface of the lifting problem. A formal definition of relational algebra operators in inductive databases still requires a lot of research.

4 Models for Models

The second question we address is: do the models and patterns we have discovered help in the discovery of other models or patterns? This seems a reasonable requirement for an inductive database. One would expect some reward for storing these earlier results as first class citizens in the database.

There has been no systematic research effort in this direction that I am aware of, but there are examples in the literature. We discuss a few of these in this section.

4.1 In the Same Class

The first examples we briefly discuss remain in the same class of models. First we look at *condensed representations* for frequent item sets. Next we look at combining classifiers.

Frequent Item Sets. One example that remains in the same class of patterns is *condensed representations*. That is, a subset C of the set F of all frequent item sets for a given minimal support such that all elements of F and their support can be computed from the elements of C and their support. In other words, F can be generated from C.

Condensed representations have some potential advantages over the complete set of frequent item sets. Firstly, one expects the condensed representation to be, far, smaller than the complete set. One of the major problems in frequent item set mining is the size of the result set. Condensed representations make this problem far more manageable.

A second advantage is computationally. If the total costs of computing C and generating F from C is lower than the costs for directly computing F, the advantage is clear.

Perhaps the best known example of condensed representations is closed item sets. A frequent item set is closed iff all its supersets have a lower support [27]. The fact that closed item sets form a condensed representation is straight forward [6]. For an arbitrary item set, find the smallest closed item set that is a superset of this set. If such a closed item set exists, the support of this closed item set is the support of the given set. If no such closed item set exists, the given item set is not frequent.

In many experiments is has been shown that closed item sets do exhibit both potential advantages of condensed representations.

Combining Classifiers. Creating classifiers from sets of classifiers is a hot topic in both pattern recognition and in machine learning. It even has its own workshop series called Multiple Classifier Systems. In other words, there is far too much research in the area to even attempt an overview in this paper. Rather we point the reader to a recent survey article [37] and a recent book [17].

The result of the plethora of methods and algorithms is invariably a new classifier that performs better than the underlying, base, classifiers.

4.2   From Local to Global

In the previous subsection, we stayed in the same model class, i.e. frequent item sets and classifiers. A more general problem is whether we can use results from one model class to discover models from another class.

Classification by Association. Probably the best known example of computing a global model from local patterns is the construction of a classifier from association rules [19]. To built a classifier, we need a class attribute, hence, we assume that our database of transactions contains such an attribute C. Clearly, we can mine the set of all association rules that have (only) the class attribute as their right hand side:

$$J \rightarrow c_i \text{ where } J \subseteq \mathcal{I} \wedge c_i \in C$$

The two main problems in using the set of such association rules as a classifier are:

- as always, overfitting; the solution is to prune the set
- different rules may fit a transaction, the solution is to built an ordered decision list.

For pruning, we can use, e.g., pessimistic error rate pruning. If an association rule covers N transactions and makes E mistakes in classifying these transactions, E/N is an estimate of the error rate of that rule as a classifier. The "true" error rate can be higher, of course, we can bound the true error through *confidence intervals*:

$$P(m \notin CFI_\delta(N, E)) \leq \delta$$

If we denote the upper border of $CFI_\delta(N, E)$ by $U_\delta(N, E)$, we "know" with $100 - \delta/2\%$ certainty that the "true" error rate will be less than $U_\delta(N, E)$.

Now consider the two association rules

$$J_1 \to c_1$$
$$J_1 \wedge J_2 \to c_2$$

It seems reasonable to prune $J_1 \wedge J_2 \to c_2$ if it has a higher pessimistic error rate than $J_1 \to c_1$. In other words, we prune a rule r, if it has a subrule r' with *one item less* that has a *lower pessimistic error rate*.

For the second problem, define an order on the association rules by: for two rules r_1 and r_2, define $r_1 \succ r_2$ (r_1 precedes r_2) if:

- $conf(r_1) > conf(r_2)$;
- $conf(r_1) = conf(r_2) \wedge s(r_1) > s(r_2)$;
- $conf(r_1) = conf(r_2) \wedge s(r_1) = s(r_2)$ and r_1 is generated before r_2.

So, we prefer rules on confidence (first) and support (second), the third criterion is arbitrary and only necessary to define a complete order.

The algorithm considers each element of the pruned set of association rule in this order. This element is added to the decision list of there is at least one transaction left for it to classify and it classifies at least one of these transactions correctly; see [19] for the details.

Densities from Frequent Sets. The collection of frequent item sets gives us the support of all item sets that are frequent. It doesn't tell us anything about the support of an item set that is not frequent, except that this support is less than the minimal support. However, the *selectivity* of a query is an important measure for query optimisers in (relational) DBMSs. Hence, it is important to estimate that selectivity. In other words, can we estimate the support of an arbitrary item set based on the set of frequent item sets?

The key observation in [28] is that the frequent item sets can be seen as constraints on the probability distribution that underlies the database. Indeed, each frequent item set with its count gives a marginal distribution of this underlying distribution. In general, the constraints are not sufficient to completely determine the probability distribution. In other words, we need a criterion to pick one of the possible distributions. The authors in [28] use the *maximum entropy* principle [12] for this. That is, the choice is the least informative distribution that satisfies the constraints.

In other words, for an arbitrary item set J, the estimated marginal distribution is given by:

$$P_M(J) = arg \max_{p \in P} H(p)$$

in which $H(p)$ denotes as usual the entropy of p. The next step is the observation that the max-ent distribution is a Markov Random Field [32]:

$$P_M(J) = \mu_0 \prod_{J_i \subseteq J} \mu_i$$

The iterative scaling algorithm can be used to determine the parameters of this distribution subject to the constraints mentioned above; see [28] for full details.

Note that while we phrased the problem and the solution in terms of item sets, the authors actually solve the problem for an arbitrary query; i.e., one can ask for items that should not appear in the transaction.

4.3   Global to Local

In the previous subsection we looked at two examples in which local patterns were used for the construction of global models. In this section we turn this around, we take a global method and use it for local patterns.

Frequent Sets from EM. Frequent item sets are by definition local patterns, that is, they describe only those transactions in which they occur. In other words, it is very well possible that the database consists of different components such that different collections of frequent item sets hold in the different components. These different components could, e.g., be different days of the week or different groups of customers. In [9] this possibility is investigated, first the transactions are clustered using EM and then the frequent item sets are computed in each of the clusters.

For the clustering, the data is seen as generated by a mixture of multivariate Bernoulli distributions, i.e.,

$$P(\mathbf{x}|\Theta) = \sum_{j=1}^{k} \pi_i \prod_{j=1}^{n} \theta_{kj}^{x_j}(1 - \theta_{kj})^{(1-x_j)}$$

The parameters are estimated using the EM algorithm. The EM algorithm [21] is a well-known algorithm for dealing with missing data. It is an iterative algorithm with two main steps:

1. The E-step in which the expected value of the missing data is computed using the current set of parameters.
2. The M-step: in which the maximum likelihood of the parameters is computed using the current estimated value of the missing data items.

The missing data in this problem is, of course, the information to which cluster each data point belongs.

After the clusters are determined, the authors compute the frequent item sets in each of the clusters. In [9] it is shown that on some experimental data sets the different clusters have markedly different collections of frequent item sets.

Association Rules from Bayesian Networks. A well-known problem of association rule mining is that with high thresholds one only finds well-know results and with low thresholds, the number of results is amazingly large. In [7] we proposed to use Bayesian networks to generate far fewer association rules. More precisely, MAMBO discovers all association rules $X \to Y$ such that Y is a singleton and X is a subset of a Markov Blanket of Y.

To motivate this idea, recall the definition of conditional independence. Let $\mathbf{X}, \mathbf{Y}, \mathbf{Z}$ be subsets of a set of random variables $\mathbf{A}$ on which a probability distribution $P(\mathbf{A})$ is defined. Moreover, let $\mathbf{X}, \mathbf{Y}$ be disjoint and non-empty. We say that $\mathbf{X}$ is *conditionally independent* of $\mathbf{Y}$ given $\mathbf{Z}$, denoted by $\mathbf{X} \perp\!\!\!\perp \mathbf{Y} | \mathbf{Z}$, if $\forall \mathbf{x} \in D_{\mathbf{X}}, \mathbf{y} \in D_{\mathbf{Y}}, \mathbf{z} \in D_{\mathbf{Z}}$:

$$p(\mathbf{Y} = \mathbf{y}, \mathbf{Z} = \mathbf{z}) > 0 \Rightarrow p(\mathbf{X} = \mathbf{x} | \mathbf{Y} = \mathbf{y}, \mathbf{Z} = \mathbf{z}) = p(\mathbf{X} = \mathbf{x} | \mathbf{Z} = \mathbf{z})$$

In other words, conditional independence is a form of irrelevance. If we know $\mathbf{Z}$, any further information about $\mathbf{Y}$ cannot enhance the current state of information about $\mathbf{X}$, i.e. given $\mathbf{Z}$, $\mathbf{Y}$ becomes irrelevant to $\mathbf{X}$.

If we reformulate association rules in the context of random variables and probability distributions, the support of the rule $\mathbf{Y} = \mathbf{y} \rightarrow \mathbf{X} = \mathbf{x}$ becomes $p(\mathbf{Y} = \mathbf{y}, \mathbf{X} = \mathbf{x})$, the confidence becomes $p(\mathbf{X} = \mathbf{x} | \mathbf{Y} = \mathbf{y})$, and the lift becomes $p(\mathbf{X} = \mathbf{x} | \mathbf{Y} = \mathbf{y}) / p(\mathbf{X} = \mathbf{x})$.

If we know that $\mathbf{X} \perp\!\!\!\perp \mathbf{Y} | \mathbf{Z}$, we have that:

$$p(\mathbf{X} = \mathbf{x} | \mathbf{Y} = \mathbf{y}, \mathbf{Z} = \mathbf{z}) / p(\mathbf{X} = \mathbf{x}) = p(\mathbf{X} = \mathbf{x} | \mathbf{Y} = \mathbf{y}) / p(\mathbf{X} = \mathbf{x})$$

In other words, the lift doesn't rise by adding knowledge about $\mathbf{Y}$, $\mathbf{Y}$ is irrelevant to $\mathbf{X}$ given $\mathbf{Z}$. Or, if we have an association rule for $\mathbf{X}$ with $\mathbf{Y}$ and $\mathbf{Z}$ on the lefthand side, we might as well filter $\mathbf{Y}$ out.

This is interesting if $\mathbf{Z}$ *shields* $\mathbf{X}$ from all other variables, i.e., if $\mathbf{X} \perp\!\!\!\perp \mathbf{A} \setminus (\mathbf{Z} \cup \mathbf{X}) | \mathbf{Z}$. Because then we only have to consider association rules whose lefthand side is within $\mathbf{Z}$. All of this is even more interesting if $\mathbf{Z}$ is *minimal*, i.e, if we remove an element from $\mathbf{Z}$ it no longer shields $\mathbf{X}$ from the rest. Such a minimal set is called a *Markov Blanket* of $\mathbf{X}$.

There are two obstacles to use this idea to discover association rules. Firstly, we have a database rather than a probability distribution. Secondly, $\mathbf{X}$ may have many Markov Blankets. In [7], we solve these problems using MCMC. The MAMBO algorithm generates the k most likely Markov blankets of a variable Y and computes all association rules $X \rightarrow Y$, in which X is a subset of one of these k likely Markov blankets.

4.4   Conclusions

As already stated in the introduction, there is as of yet no structured approach, let alone a theory, for this problem. For frequent item sets and constraints there is a large body of work and a definite theory is in the making; see, e.g., [5]. For all other cases the work is mainly anecdotal, i.e., there are papers that address a particular instance of the problem but no concerted effort. This is not too surprising given the vast amount of different model classes and algorithms to induce such models.

Still, the problem is obviously relevant for inductive databases, if not for data analysis in general. Moreover, not all combinations of different model classes make sense. For example, the link between regression models and frequent item sets seems weak[5]. So, a first step towards a theory for this problem may lie in a systematic study: which combinations could be fruitful?

When the area has been charted in this way, the most promising combinations could be studied systematically. Given that patterns are the most fundamental contribution of the data mining field to data analysis, I would give preference to combinations that involve patterns.

5   Models on Models

If models and patterns are to be first class citizens in an inductive database, i.e., data, then we should be able to mine collections of models and patterns. I first discuss two examples, then I'll put this in the wider perspective of *feature construction.*

5.1   Mining Models and Patterns

Bayesian Networks. I am not aware of any research on mining collections of Bayesian networks, yet it is not too difficult to think of an application. Bayesian networks are an increasingly popular tool in the analysis of micro-array data [15]. The goal of this application is the, partial, reconstruction of, e.g., regulatory networks in a cell.

The number of micro-array studies is growing fast, and so will the resulting Bayesian networks. Given that micro-array data is rich in features (genes), poor in data (relatively few arrays compared to the number on an array per experiment) and high in variation these networks encode lots of uncertainty. Hence, it makes sense to mine such a collection of networks. For example for interactions that occur frequently in these networks.

Episodes. In one of our projects the aim is to infer phylogenetic knowledge form developmental biology data [4]. In [4], the data is a sequence of events, like the start of the development of the heart, in the development of an embryo of a given species; see figure 7 for an example of the data.

The question is whether the different sequences for different species reflect the evolutionary relationships between these species.

The evolutionary relationships are usually represented in *phylogenetic trees.* Two species are children of the same node in that tree if both are evolutionary descendents of the same species, which is represented by that node [33]. A common way to construct these trees is by clustering.

To cluster the developmental sequences, we needed a similarity measure on such sequences. To define this measure, we first computed the frequent episodes in the sequences. Next, we used these episodes as binary features of the species. The similarity between two species was now defined using the *Jacquard* measure on these binary features.

---

[5] Now that I have given a particular example, I fully expect to be pointed to a paper in which this link is exploited.

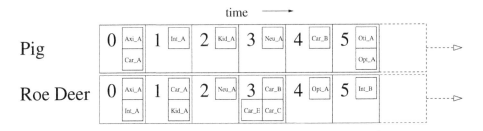

Fig. 7. Developmental sequences

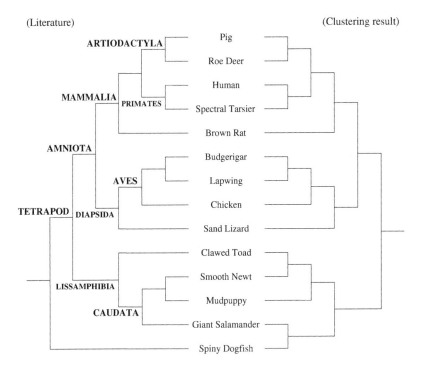

Fig. 8. The result tree in comparison

Simple hierarchical clustering using this similarity measure resulted in a tree that was almost an exact copy of the accepted phylogenetic tree for the species in our experiments; see figure 8 and [4] for further details.

5.2 Feature Construction

The episode example in the previous subsection used patterns as features. That is, pattern discovery is used as a feature construction mechanism. Feature construction has a long tradition in data analysis. Even in something simple as regression it is standard to add *mixture terms* like $x_1 x_2$ for a better fit.

One of the major reasons for feature construction in data mining is the, almost exponential, rise of new data types. Mostly, these types do not fit automatically the input requirements of the data mining algorithms we love and cherish. Hence, the data is transformed to some feature space that does meet these requirements. For example,

Text: Is often turned into a vector of keywords [38]. Standard algorithms can be applied to this new representation.

Pictures: As pioneered by *multi-media information retrieval*, features such as colour histograms and textures are computed for further processing [39].

Time Series: Represent a huge area of research [18]. Examples of features are Fourier coefficients [2] and wavelet coefficients [36].

Relational Mining: Aggregates are a popular way to incorporate the data from related tables, whether as a means to propostionalize or on the fly [16, 14]. In both cases, the aggregates are, of course, newly constructed features.

Note that this kind of feature construction is in a sense ad hoc. The features are hand-crafted for the job; the data analyst decides what the useful features are. This is not, of course, to say that they are not grounded in solid theory.

The other big boost in feature construction is due to the rapid rise of *kernel methods* [34]. For, a kernel is nothing less than a smart way to transform the data into a Hilbert space for no other purpose than to allow processing with standard analysis approaches. This kernel approach is to a lesser extend just as ad hoc as the examples mentioned above. Still kernels have to be constructed. It is less ad hoc, however, since there is, e.g., theory that allows one to construct kernels from other kernels. Moreover, after the kernel has been designed, the rest of the toolbox carries over automatically.

5.3   Patterns as Features

Using data mining for feature construction is a completely different approach. It is not the data analyst who decides what the good features are, the algorithms discover these features from the data. One could argue that this approach is not that different from the others. For, the data analyst still has to decide for which kind of patterns to mine.

However, I argue that it is rather different for two reasons:

- Firstly, there is no a priori reason to prefer one kind of pattern over the other. One can simply try all kinds of patterns and let the *data decide whichever fits best*.
- Secondly, this approach sees feature construction as data mining. Not as a separate phase that has to precede the actual mining of the data.

There is, of course, one major potential drawback of this approach to feature construction, viz., the sheer number of patterns that are usually discovered.

Given that it is not unusual in frequent item set mining to discover more frequent item sets than there are transactions in the database, this may seem an insurmountable problem. However, this only means that we have to single out those patterns that describe the data best. In a recent paper [35] we used MDL to achieve this: the best set of frequent item sets is that one that compresses the database best.

The potential advantages of this approach are possibly as big as the potential drawback, if not bigger. Firstly because many of the existing approaches ultimately treat the data as numeric data. Patterns on the other hand work as well, if not better, for non-numeric data. Secondly, patterns as features seems to offer so much more than aggregates for relational data mining. The number of bank accounts is just a very simple pattern. More expressive pattern languages should allow for better results.

Finally, this approach seems unavoidable in an inductive database context. If one has a large collection of models and/or patterns in a database they have to be mined. Just as data mining started because there were large amounts of data available.

5.4   Conclusions

Like in the previous section, there is only some scattered research in this area. Developing a theory for these kinds of problems is going to be hard. However, it is an undeniable necessity for an inductive database. Moreover, within a restricted area, viz., mining on patterns progress may be simpler than for the whole problem.

6   Future Research

Clearly, all questions I discussed in this paper pertain to problems I feel have to be solved before we have a truly inductive database. This doesn't mean, however, that all of them are equally urgent or difficult (nor does it mean that they are all there is). Given the conclusions I formulated I rank their urgency as follows:

Mining on Models and Patterns: Firstly because this has to be supported if models and patterns are supposed to be first class citizens. Secondly because of its potential role in relational data mining. As an aside, I haven't discussed the role of relational data mining in inductive databases. Clearly, this is a very important aspect. Databases have more than one table, inductive databases have to deal with this reality. In other words, inductive databases should include relational data mining.

Within this domain, I rank mining on patterns as the most promising field. It is relatively small and the potential benefit is large.

Models for Models: Ranked only second because it is a far harder problem. Firstly, because it requires a *probabilistic framework*. Many models are probabilistic, so if we want to use those models to discover other models, we have to deal with the probabilistic aspects. So, combined with our previous point, it means we need a probabilistic relational model. While there is some good work in this area [31], it hasn't been solved.

The second reason why this is a hard problem is the sheer size of the problem. There are many different kinds of models and patterns. The number of combinations is, of course, far larger again! But, as already stated, not all combinations make sense.

Like for the previous point, I would rank combinations that involve patterns highest. The reason is the complementarity of models and patterns in our "definition" of patterns. If patterns are deviations from a model, the interaction between models and patterns requires deep understanding.

Lifting the Algebra: This is only ranked third because after the initial analysis in this paper I am afraid that there are not too many positive results for this problem.

Perhaps more progress is possible if we view the third problem as a special case of the second one. For example, does knowledge of the frequent items sets on tables R_1 and R_2 help in computing the frequent item sets on table $R_1 \bowtie R_2$?

Clearly, for this simple example, the answer is affirmative. For, if we know that the item set with the largest support on R_i has support L_i, we need to find all item sets with support $\frac{min\text{-}sup}{L_i}$ on the "other" table. Given that L_i comes from the already discovered set of frequent item sets and that this already discovered set can be used as a starting point for the lower support computation, the gain is clear. Again, an interesting area for further research.

So, where does this leave us? I hope that research in inductive databases will go beyond constraints; however useful constraints are! For me, mining on patterns seems the most interesting direction. Together with my group I will certainly continue working in this area.

Acknowledgements. For the help in writing the "lifting" section, I am grateful for discussions with and help from Pedro Larañaga, Linda van der Gaag and Ad Feelders. Many of the thoughts in this paper have been shaped by numerous discussions with equally numerous colleagues, to many to name I am afraid. Both the current and previous members of my group and the members of the Cinq consortium are certainly among them.

Furthermore, I am grateful to the editors for their invitation and for the useful comments they gave me on the draft version of this paper. Finally, I thank Paul Taylor for his commutative diagram package that made producing the diagrams in this paper into a very simple exercise.

References

1. R. Agrawal, T. Imielinski, and A. Swami. Mining association rules between sets of items in large databases. In *Proc. ACM SIGMOD conference*, pages 207–216, 1993.
2. Rakesh Agrawal, Christos Faloutsos, and Arun N. Swami. Efficient similarity search in sequence databases. In D. Lomet, editor, *Proceedings of the 4th International Conference of Foundations of Data Organization and Algorithms*, pages 69–84. Springer Verlag, 1993.
3. Andrea Asperti and Giuseppe Longo. *Categories, Types, and Structures*. MIT Press, 1991.
4. Ronnie Bathoorn and Arno Siebes. Discovering (almost) phylogentic trees from developmental sequences data. In *Knowledge Discovery in Databases, PKDD2004*, volume 3202 of *Lecture Notes in AI*.

5. Francesco. Bonchi and Claudio Lucchese. On closed constrained frequent pattern mining. In Rajeev Rastogi, Katharina Morik, Max Bramer, and Xindong Wu, editors, *Proceedings of the Fourth IEEE International Conference on Data Mining (ICDM'04)*, pages 35–42, 2004.

6. Jean-François Boulicaut and Artur Bykowski. Frequent closures as a concise representation for binary data mining. In *Knowledge Discovery and Data Mining, Current Issues and New Applications, 4th Pacific-Asia Conference, PADKK 2000*, pages 62–73, 2000.

7. Robert Castelo, Ad Feelders, and Arno Siebes. Mambo: Discovering association rules based on conditional independencies. In *Advances in Intelligent Data Analysis, 4th International Conference, IDA 2001*, pages 289–298. Springer Verlag, 2001.

8. David J. Hand. Pattern detection and discovery. In *Pattern Detection and Discovery*, volume 2447 of *Lecture Notes in AI*, pages 1–12. Springer Verlag, 2002.

9. Jaakko Hollmén, Jouni K. Sepp anen, and Heikki Mannila. Mixture models and frequent sets: Combining global and local methods for 0-1 data. In *Proc. SIAM Conference on Data Mining (SDM) 2003*, 2003.

10. Pedrito Maynard-Reid II and Urszula Chajewska. Aggregating learned probabilistic beliefs. In *Proceedings of the 17th Conference in Uncertainty in Artificial Intelligence*, pages 354–361. Morgan Kaufmann, 2001.

11. Tomasz Imielinski and Heikki Mannila. A database perspective on knowledge discovery. *Communications of the ACM*, 39(11):58–64, 1996.

12. E.T. Jaynes. *Probability Theory: The Logic of Science*.

13. Hillol Kargupta and Philip Chan, editors. *Advances in Distributed and Parallel Knowledge Discovery*. MIT Press, 2000.

14. Arno J. Knobbe, Marc de Haas, and Arno Siebes. Propositionalisation and aggregates. In Luc De Raedt and Arno Siebes, editors, *Principles of Data Mining and Knowledge Discovery (PKDD)*, volume 2168 of *Lecture Notes in Computer Science*, pages 277–288. Springer Verlag, 2001.

15. Isaac S. Kohane, Alvin T. Kho, and Atul J. Butte. *Microarrays for an Integrative Genomics*. Computational Molecular Biology. MIT Press, 2003.

16. . Krogel, S. Rawles, F. Zelezny, P. Flach, N. Lavrac, and S. Wrobel. Comparative evaluation of approaches to propositionalization. In Tamas Horvath and Akihiro Yamamoto, editors, *Proceedings of the 13th International Conference on Inductive Logic Programming (ILP'2003)*, pages 194–217. Springer-Verlag, October 2003.

17. Ludmila Kuncheva. *Combining Pattern Classifiers: Methods and Algorithms*. John Wiley & Sons, 2004.

18. Mark Last, Abraham Kandel, and Horst Bunke, editors. *Data Mining in Time Series Databases*. World Scientific, 2004.

19. Bing Liu, Wynne Hsu, and Yiming Ma. Integrating classification and association rule mining. In *Proc. of the ACM KDD conference*, pages 80–86, 1998.

20. H. Mannila, H. Toivonen, and A.I. Verkamo. Discovery of frequent episodes in event sequences. volume 1, pages 259–289, 1997.

21. Geoffrey J. McLachlan and Thriyambakam Krishnan. *The EM Algorithm and Extensions*. Wiley Series in Probability and Statistics. John Wiley & Sons, 1997.

22. Katharina Morik, Jean-François Boulicaut, and Arno Siebes. Preface. In *Local Pattern Detection*, volume 3539 of *Lecture Notes in AI*. Springer Verlag, 2005.

23. S. Naqvi and S. Tsur. *A Logical Language for Data and Knowledge Bases*. Computer Science Press, 1989.

24. Richard E. Neapolitan. *Learning Bayesian Networks*. Prentice Hall, 2003.

25. Raymond T. Ng, Laks V. S. Lakshmanan, Jiawei Han, and Alex Pang. Exploratory mining and pruning optimizations of constrained associations rules. In *Proc. ACM SIGMOD conference*, 1998.

26. Raymond T. Ng, Laks V. S. Lakshmanan, Jiawei Han, and Alex Pang. Exploratory mining and pruning optimizations of constrained associations rules. In *Proceedings of 1998 ACM SIGMOD International Conference Management of Data*, pages 13–24, 1998.

27. Nicolas Pasquier, Yves Bastide, Rafik Taouil, and Lotfi Lakhal. Discovering frequent closed itemsets for association rules. In *Proceedings of 7th ICDT*, pages 398–416, 1999.

28. Dmitry Pavlov, Heikki Mannila, and Padhraic Smyth. Beyond independence: Probabilistic models for query approximation on binary transaction data. Technical Report UCI-ICS TR-01-09, UC Irvine, 2001.

29. Judea Pearl. *Probabilistic Reasoning in Intelligent Systems: Networks of Plausible Inference*. Morgan Kauffman, 1997.

30. Luc De Raedt. A perspective on inductive databases. *SIGKDD Explorations*, 4(2):69–77, 2000.

31. Luc De Raedt and Kristian Kersting. Probabilistic logic learning. *SIGKDD Explorations*, 5(1):31–48, 2003.

32. Håvard Rue and Leonhard Held. *Gaussian Markov Random Fields*, volume 104 of *Monographs on Statistics and Applied Probablity*. Chapman & Hall/CRC, 2005.

33. Charles Semple and Mike Steel. *Phylogenetics*, volume 24 of *Oxford Lecture Series in Mathematics and its Applications*. Oxford University Press, 2003.

34. John Shaw-Taylor and Nello Cristianini. *Kernel Methods for Pattern Analysis*. Cambridge University Press, 2004.

35. Arno Siebes, Jilles Vreeken, and Matthijs van Leeuwen. Item sets that compress. In *Proceedings of the SIAM conference on Data Mining (SDM)*, 2006.

36. Zbyszek Struzik and Arno Siebes. The haar wavelet transform in the time series similarity paradigm. In Jan M. Zytkow and Jan Rauch, editors, *Principles of Data Mining and Knowledge Discovery (PKDD)*, volume 1704 of *Lecture Notes in AI*, pages 12–22. Springer Verlag, 1999.

37. Giorgio Valentini and Francesco Masulli. Ensembles of learning machinesensembles of learning machines. In *Proceedings of the 13th Italian Workshop on Neural Nets-Revised Papers*, pages 3–22. Springer Verlag, 2002.

38. Shalom M. Weiss, Nitin Indurkhya, Tong Zhang, and Fred J. Damerau. *Text Mining*. Springer Verlag, 2005.

39. Osmar R. Zaiane, Simeon Simoff, and Chabane Djeraba, editors. *Mining Multimedia and Complex Data*, volume 2797 of *Lecture Notes in AI*. Springer Verlag, 2003.

Mining Databases and Data Streams
with Query Languages and Rules

Carlo Zaniolo

Computer Science Department,
UCLA, Los Angeles, CA 90095
zaniolo@cs.ucla.edu

Abstract. Among data-intensive applications that are beyond the reach
of traditional Data Base Management Systems (DBMS), data mining
stands out because of practical importance and the complexity of the
research problems that must be solved before the vision of Inductive
DBMS can become a reality. In this paper, we first discuss technical developments that have occurred since the very notion of Inductive DBMS
emerged as a result of the seminal papers authored by Imielinski and
Mannila a decade ago. The research progress achieved since then can be
subdivided into three main problem subareas as follows: (i) language (ii)
optimization, and (iii) representation. We discuss the problems in these
three areas and the different approaches to Inductive DBMS that are
made possible by recent technical advances. Then, we pursue a language-
centric solution, and introduce simple SQL extensions that have proven
very effective at supporting data mining. Finally, we turn our attention
to the related problem of supporting data stream mining using Data
Stream Management Systems (DSMS) and introduce the notion of Inductive DSMS. In addition to continuous query languages, DSMS provide support for synopses, sampling, load shedding, and other built-in
functions that are needed for data stream mining. Moreover, we show
that Inductive DSMS can be achieved by generalizing DSMS to assure
that their continuous query languages support efficiently data stream
mining applications. Thus, DSMS extended with inductive capabilities
will provide a uniquely supportive environment for data stream mining
applications.

1   Introduction

Data Base Management Systems (DBMS) and their enabling technology have
evolved successfully to deal with most of the data-intensive application areas
that have emerged anew during the last twenty years. For instance, in response
to the growing importance of decision-support applications, relational DBMS
and SQL were quickly extended to support OLAP queries—a remarkable exploit
from both technical and commercial viewpoints. On the other hand, there have
also been significant failures, with data mining applications representing the
most egregious of such failures. Therefore, databases today are still mined using
primarily a cache-mining approach, whereby the data is first moved from the

F. Bonchi and J.-F. Boulicaut (Eds.): KDID 2005, LNCS 3933, pp. 24–37, 2006.

database to a memory cache, which is then processed using mining methods written in a procedural programming language. Indeed, most mining functions cannot be expressed efficiently using SQL:2003, which represents the standard query language of DBMS.

Research on Inductive Inductive DBMS aims at changing this state of affairs and make it easy to mine databases by their query languages. The emergence of Inductive DBMS as a well-defined research area can be traced back to the seminal papers by Imielinski and Manilla [1, 2] who introduced the lofty notion of a DBMS where complex mining tasks can be expressed with ease using the query language of the system[1]. According to [2], Inductive DBMS should also assure efficient execution of such high-level mining queries via powerful query optimization techniques—although the enabling technology for such a task was not available at the time[2].

Early attempts to realize the lofty notion of Inductive DBMS have produced mining languages such as MSQL[3], DMQL[4] and the Mine Rule [5]. These projects propose SQL extensions to specify the data to be mined and the kind of patterns to be derived, along with other parameters needed for the task, such the support and confidence required. As discussed in a comprehensive comparative study [6], these projects have made a number of contributions, by exploring and demonstrating some of the key features required in a Inductive DBMS, including

(i) the ability of specifying constraints, meta-patterns, and concept hierarchies to sharpen the search process,
(ii) the ability to apply the derived rules to the original data for verification and analysis (crossing over),
(iii) the closure property whereby the query language can be used to operate on the results produced by the mining query.

The research contributions brought by these approaches have not led to significant commercial deployments, because of practical limitations. A first limitation is that these approaches are primarily intended for association rule mining, although DMQL consider other patterns besides association rules.

A second and more serious concern is that of performance: the projects discussed in [3, 4, 5] do not claim to have achieved performance levels that are comparable to those achievable with the cache-mining approach, nor they claim to have identified a query-optimization approach that can be reasonably expected to take them there. This in line with the view of Imielinski and Manilla[2] that sophisticated optimizers are needed to achieve good performance and developing such technology represents a long-term research challenge for which no quick solution should be expected. Furthermore, experience with query optimizers has shown that it is very difficult to extend relational optimizers to handle more powerful constructs, such as recursive queries, or richer data models and their query

---

[1] 'There is no such thing as real discovery, just a matter of the expressive power of the query languages' [2].
[2] 'KDD query optimization will be more challenging than relational query optimization ... It took more than 20 years to develop efficient query optimization and execution methods for relational query languages' [2].

languages, i.e., XML and XQuery. Therefore, optimizers for data mining queries require novel techniques, not just extensions of relational optimizer technology. Such a task could take many years, although progress on this difficult problem has been achieved in the last few years [7, 8, 9, 10]. Once these techniques will be incorporated into systems supporting declarative mining queries, the lofty vision of [2] will then be realized, at least for associative rule mining.

In order to provide data mining functions to their users, commercial database vendors are instead taking a quite different approach. Typically, vendors have been implementing a suite of data mining functions on top of their DBMS, along with graphical interfaces to drive these packages [11, 12, 13]. While only providing a predefined set of built-in mining functions, the Microsoft DB serve is however achieving a closer integration and better interoperability of the mining task with the SQL query task, by using the descriptive+predictive mining model of OLE DB DM [13]. Thus the descriptive task generates an internal representation (a mining model) as a special table that is populated (learned) by executing the mining task on the training data. Then, a special operator called prediction join is provided that can be used to predict unknown attribute values for new data [13]. It is also possible to inspect the descriptive model and export it into an XML-based representation called PMML (Predictive Model Markup Language). PMML is a markup language proposed to represent statistical and data mining information [14].

Therefore, OLE DB DM goes beyond the mining-language approach by addressing the need to support the multiple steps of the DM process with well-defined representations linking the various steps. Ideally, this should lead to the notion of open Inductive DBMS, where, for instance, descriptive models can be imported into the system and used for prediction (or exported and used for predictive tasks in a second system).

In addition to the mining-language approach and the DM approach of OLE DB, there is also a third approach that we will call the middle-road approach. This offers interesting promises both in terms of mining data bases and data streams, and is discussed in the next two sections.

2   Query Languages and Data Mining

The mining-language approach proposed in [3, 4, 5] defines a very ambitious high-road path toward Inductive DBMS, since users only need to provide high-level declarative queries specifying their mining goals. Then, the Inductive DBMS optimizer is left with the responsibility of selecting an algorithm to accomplish those goals—a task that, in general, exceeds the capabilities of current technology.

At the opposite end of the spectrum, we find the low-road approach discussed in the prize-winning paper presented in [15]. In said study, a task force of researchers with deep expertise on mining methods and the IBM DB2 O-R DBMS tried to implement efficiently the APriori algorithm, exploring several implementation alternatives that only use the DBMS as is, using the standard SQL version supported by DB2. An acceptable level of performance was achieved through the

Table 1. The relation **PlayTennis**

RID	Outlook	Temp	Humidity	Wind	Play
1	Sunny	Hot	High	Weak	No
2	Sunny	Hot	High	Strong	Yes
3	Overcast	Hot	High	Weak	Yes
...	...	...	...	..	...

Table 2. A Column-oriented representation for **PlayTennis**

RID	Column	Value	Dec
1	1	Sunny	No
1	2	Hot	No
1	3	High	No
1	4	Weak	No
2	1	Sunny	Yes
2	2	Hot	Yes
2	3	High	Yes
2	4	Strong	Yes
...	...	...	...

use of specialized join techniques and user-defined functions (UDFs), at the price of excessive difficulties in programming and debugging [15]. We will characterize the approach taken in [15] as a 'low-road' path toward Inductive DBMS. While the work presented in [15] established the inadequacy of SQL in supporting complex data mining algorithms such as Apriori, it provided no clear indication how to proceed to overcome these inadequacy.

Once we compare the high-road approach against the low road we see that the first makes unrealistic demands upon the system, while the second makes unrealistic demands on the users. Given this situation, it is only natural to pursue middle-road approaches that explore extensions of SQL and DBMS that are realizable with current technology and make the task of writing mining algorithms simple for common mortals. We next describe the ATLaS system that is taking such middle-road path to Inductive DBMS.

As described by Arno Siebes in his invited talk [16], data mining success stories in the real world, frequently employ the simplest mining methods, e.g., Naive Bayesian Classifiers (NBCs). NBCs are also significant for the very subject of this paper, since they provide a unique example of on data mining algorithm that current DBMS can support as well as full-fledged Inductive DBMS would.

Take for instance the well-known Play-Tennis example of Table 1: we want to predict the value of **Play** as a 'Yes' or a 'No' given a training set consisting of tuples similar to the three shown in Table 1.

The first step is to convert the training set into column/value pairs whereby the first two tuples in Table 1 are now represented by the eight tuples shown in Table 2.

This verticalization can be implemented using a table function, which is a very useful SQL:2003 construct now supported by most DSMS. From this representation, we can now build a Bayesian classifier by simply counting the occurrences of Yes and No with a statement as follows:

Example 1. *Disassemble a relation into column/value pairs.*

```
SELECT Column, Value, Dec, count(Dec) as mycount
       FROM traningset
       GROUP BY Col, Value, Dec
```

We can then add up the counts for each column, and use it to normalize the values of **mycount** (by dividing by the total number of 'Yes' and 'No'). Finally, we take the absolute value of the log of the results and thus obtain a descriptor table as follows:

DescriptorTbl(Col: int, Value: int, Dec: int, Log: real)

Now, the set of tuples submitted for prediction will also be collected in a table called, say **TestTuples** having the same format as Table 2, except that the column **Dec** is missing. Then, the Naive Bayesian classifier is implemented using the results of the following query:

Example 2. *Probabilities for each tuple to be predicted*

```
SELECT t.RID, d.Dec, sum(d.Log)
FROM DescriptorTbl AS d, TestTuples AS t
WHERE d.Val=t.Val AND d.Col=t.Col
       GROUP BY t.RID, d.Dec
```

Thus, for each test tuple, and each class label we multiply (sum the logs of) the relative frequencies for each column value supporting this class label. The final step would consist in selecting for each RID the class label with the least sum, a step that in SQL requires finding first the min value and then the columns where such min value occurs (such a min maximizes the probability since we use absolute values of logarithms).

Observe that so far, we have only described the core descriptive and predictive tasks and not discussed other tasks such as data preparation, testing the model accuracy, and boosting it. However, these tasks can normally be expressed by rather simple SQL queries on our basic relational representation. For instance, if we want to build an ensemble of classifiers, we only need to add to the descriptor table a new column containing the classifier name: then voting operations can be reduced to counting the number of individual classifiers for each (i.e., grouped by each) **Dec** value and then selecting the decision supported by most votes. Here again relational tables are used to describe both the data and the induced model.

The example of Naive Bayesian Classifiers illustrates the superior computational environment that DBMS can bring to the data mining process once their query languages are capable of expressing such applications. Therefore, a very natural middle-road approach can be that of preserving the basic relational representation for the data sets and the induced models, but providing extensions to SQL:2003 to turn it into a more powerful language—one that is capable of expressing complex mining algorithms. In the past, aggregates extended with more general GROUP BY constructs enabled SQL-compliant DSMS to support decision support functions via OLAP and data cubes. More recently, in our ATLaS project, we have shown that User-Defined Aggregates (UDAs) natively defined in SQL can turn SQL into a powerful (Turing-complete [17]) language for data mining applications [18].

The ATLaS middle-road approach allows users to write data mining algorithms in SQL extended with natively defined UDAs. For instance, we will now write a simple UDA that computes the correct classification from a table storing the results of Example 2. If we were restricted to standard SQL, things would be more complex, since we would need to nest a statement that finds the minimum into another statement that finds all the points where this occur. Moreover, to break ties, we will have to find again the min (or max) among the such points (ordered by lexicographically). Alternatively, we can use the following UDA:

Example 3. *Defining the standard aggregate minpoint*

```
AGGREGATE mincol(inCol Int, inValue Real) : Int
{    TABLE current( CrCol Int, CrValue Int);
     INITIALIZE : {
        INSERT INTO current VALUES (inCol, inValue);
     }
     ITERATE : {
        UPDATE current SET CrCol=inCol, CrValue=inValue;
        WHERE CrValue <= inValue
     }
     TERMINATE : {
        INSERT INTO RETURN SELECT CrCol FROM current;
     }
}
```

In this case, we have an internal table which only contains one tuple that is always updated to the incoming **inCol**, **inValue** pair when **inValue** is less or equal to the current minimum (but in a situation where we want to find the top K values/points our table would instead contain K tuples). Observe the stream-oriented computation is specified in the three steps: (i) when the first tuple arrives (initialize), (ii) when the successive tuples arrive (iterate), and (iii) after the input is exhausted (terminate). A number of commercial DBMS support UDAs where the computations in these three states can be defined in an external procedural language. However, as shown by our simple example, these computations can be naturally defined in SQL itself, an approach that has three important advantages:

- UDAs can be invoked from other UDAs,
- UDAs can access the database tables besides their internal tables, and
- any impedance mismatch problem is eliminated.

In a nutshell, we obtain a rich programming environment, which brings native extensibility and Turing-completeness to SQL [17] which can be used in a number of other applications besides data mining. For data mining, however, UDAs afford the ability of expressing concisely and efficiently all data mining methods, including Apriori [18].

For instance, a basic-decision tree classifier might start by computing the gini index (or entropy gain) instead of the probabilities used for NBCs. Then, to decide where to split, we will have to find where a minimum occurs. For instance, for a multiway split we will count for each column and each value in the column the number of Yes and No, and we use those to compute a gini index. If store the pairs (column, gini-value) in a temporary table, the next step consists in selecting the column where we have the least gini index by calling the UDA of Example 3, above.

This would generate the first level of nodes in our decision tree. We can now partition the training set according to these node numbers, and then we can call the same UDA grouped by this node number. Thus, a classifier can be written as a UDA consisting of fourteen ATLaS-SQL lines [18].

Not surprising, given the experience described in [15], writing an efficient implementation of Apriori proved a tougher test, one that required forty-five lines of ATLaS-SQL code. In terms of performance, the key issue proved to be the support for data structures such as prefix trees, which we were able to support via the use of in-memory tables and SQL reference data types that, for in-memory tables, can be used to point to other tuples [18]. The performance and scalability so obtained are comparable to those obtainable with the cache-mining approach, and normally better than those of java-based data mining libraries [19].

The ability of working directly with SQL represents a practical advantage of this approach over others using new special algebras [20]. Moreover, the stream-oriented definition mechanism of UDAs makes them particularly effective at mining data streams, as discussed next.

3   Inductive Data Stream Management Systems

There is a great deal of interest in managing high volumes of information that is exchanged as data streams that, because of high arrival rates or immediate response requirements, cannot be managed via DBMS. Therefore, Data Stream Management Systems (DSMS) are being developed to manage streaming information by supporting data streams applications via continuous queries [21]. In particular, data stream mining applications have been the focus of much recent interest [22, 23, 24] raising the issue of designing the best DSMS to support such applications. Therefore, in this section, we introduce the notion of an Inductive DSMS which falls naturally at the intersection of the two research areas. In most general terms, we will define Inductive DSMS as DSMS designed to supports and facilitate the task of data stream mining.

While many approaches are possible to the design of management systems that support publish & subscribe OR data streams, a very popular research approach consists in using query languages and operators similar to those of databases [21, 25, 26, 27, 28] and extend them with operators and constructs specifically designed for data streams. Typical extensions include windows or other synoptic structures, sampling, and load shedding [21, 25]. Moreover, Inductive DSMS are often used to support mining algorithms that are similar to those of Inductive DBMS, as demonstrated by the fact that stream mining algorithms are often fast&light, one-pass adaptation of the original algorithms designed to work on stored data. Therefore, approaching Inductive DSMS and Inductive DBMS as two closely related technical topics is natural and likely to be beneficial from a research viewpoint. In terms of practical issues, however, we see that the two areas are different and face somewhat complementary concerns, which are briefly discussed next.

The fact that DSMS are far from the level of maturity and standardization achieved by DBMS represents a clear disadvantage for Inductive DSMS, which however, also enjoy major advantages, because of the number of built-in functions they support, and because cache mining might no longer represent an appealing alternative for data streams. For instance, the typical approach used for mining data streams consists in dividing the incoming data into windows. By comparing the statistics of successive windows we can (i) detect concept shift/drift, and when none is detected (ii) use bagging and boosting techniques to improve the predictive accuracy of our model [23, 24]. DSMS support a rich assortment of window constructs that can be utilized very effectively in these tasks [29, 27, 21].

Sampling represents another basic function that is useful for mining data streams [30] and is well-supported in DSMS [26]. For instance, sampling can be used to find the center of clusters [31] or frequent item sets for mining association rules [32]. Moreover, building classifier ensembles via multiple samples of the data can result in improved accuracy [33]. Also, interesting techniques have been proposed to improve the accuracy of aggregates and mining methods on sample data using past information on the stream behavior [34]. In principle, a cache-mining programmer could code these sampling techniques or import them from some library, but in practice, an Inductive DSMS that supports windows and sampling as built-ins could be hard to resist for our opportunistic data stream miner.

The reasons for using an Inductive DBMS become even more compelling as we move from the language level to the system level, since DSMS provide unique functions such as load balancing, scheduling, and shedding, which are designed to assure quality-of-service and prompt response in the presence of multiple users and bursty arrivals [35]. By taking advantage of computing grids, or distributed computing platforms, DSMS can provide highly reliable, non-stop service [36]. Thus data mining applications seeking uninterrupted service, reliability, robustness, and sharing by multiple applications will need Inductive DSMS (unlike database mining applications that can live without the support for transaction, recovery, and data independence provided by DBMS).

In summary, Inductive DBMS can deliver to the data stream miner great practical benefits—possibly even greater than those of Inductive DBMS in traditional mining applications. Moreover this research area also offers interesting opportunities, since techniques and solutions developed for Inductive DBMS can be naturally transferred to Inductive DSMS and vice versa. In particular, we have extended the middle-road approach to Inductive DBMS described in the previous section and applied to Inductive DSMS, by extending the UDAs of ATLaS with powerful primitives for windows, sampling, and time-stamp management. The Expressive Stream Language (ESL) so obtained, can express every non-blocking function expressible by a Turing machine and it is supported efficiently in our Stream Mill prototype [37]. In data streams applications, windows are often used in conjunction with aggregates, to overcome their blocking behavior and to summarize the past history of the data stream. Unlike other DSMS that only support windows on built-in aggregates, ESL supports a vast assortment of windows on arbitrary UDAs. For instance, a classifier UDA can be called on tumbles, i.e., windows that partition the input stream into disjoint segment, and the results produced by few recent tumbles can be used to build a classifier ensemble [38]. A sliding window aggregate is instead one that recomputes the value of the aggregate when new tuples arrive or leave the window, using differential maintenance techniques. The development of such techniques for the various mining methods represent an interesting topic of ongoing research. In the following example we show how the DBscan algorithm can be concisely written in ESL and applied to an incoming stream partitioned into tumble windows.

Density-Based Clustering. In our application, we have a stream of points in a two-dimensional space. In order to study the data and distribution changes, we (i) partition the stream into windows of equal size, (ii) cluster the data in each window, and (iii) compare the sizes of the different clusters in successive windows, along with any appearance of new clusters or disappearance of old ones. For clustering, we employ the density-based clustering algorithm DBScan [39]. The density conditions is defined by the fact that within a radius of **eps**, we find at least **minPts** points; thus, points that occur in a dense area are assigned to the same cluster, while points that fall in a sparse area are instead classified as outliers.

The partition of the incoming stream into windows and the execution of DBscan on each window are accomplished by the following ESL statement that calls the **dbscan** aggregate on input data stream:

Stream_of_Points(Xvalue, Yvalue, TimeStamp).

Example 4. *Applying dbscan with minPts = 10 and eps = 50*

```
            /*call dbscan with minPts = 10 and eps = 50 */
    SELECT dbscan(Xvalue, Yvalue, 0, 10, 50)
            OVER(ROWS 999 PRECEDING SLIDE 1000 )
    FROM Stream_of_Points
```

Here 10 and 50 are the example values we assign to two important parameters for the DBScan Algorithm, **eps** and **minPts**, respectively. The third argument is for book-keeping purposes. Observe that since the size of the slide is the same as that of the window, this is known as a tumble. Therefore the Stream Mill system will use the base definition of DBscan, shown below. Given the two parameters **eps** and **minPts**, the DBScan algorithm works as follows: pick an arbitrary point **p** and find its neighbors (points that are less than eps distance away). If **p** has more than **minPts** neighbors then form a cluster and call DBScan on all its neighbors recursively. If **p** does not have more than **minPts** neighbors then move to other un-clustered points in the database. Note, this can be viewed as a depth-first search.

```
AGGREGATE dbscan(iX Real, iY Real, Flag Int, minPt Int, eps Int): Int
{        TABLE closepnts(X2 real, Y2 real, C2 Int) MEMORY;
         INITIALIZE: ITERATE: {
             /* Find neighbors of the given point */
             INSERT INTO CLOSEPNTS SELECT X1, Y1, C1 FROM points
             WHERE sqrt((X1-iX)*(X1-iX) + (Y1-iY)*(Y1-iY)) < eps;

             /* If there are more than minPt neighbors, form a cluster */
             UPDATE clusterno SET Cno= Cno+1  /* new cluster number*/
             WHERE Flag=0 AND SQLCODE=0 /* A new cluster */
             AND minPt < (SELECT count(C2) FROM closepnts);

             /* Assign these neighboring points to this cluster */
             UPDATE points SET C1 = (SELECT Cno FROM clusterno)
             WHERE points.C1=0 AND
             EXISTS (SELECT S.X1 FROM closepnts AS S
                 WHERE points.X1=S.X2 AND points.Y1=S.Y2 )
                 AND minPt < (SELECT count(C2) FROM closepnts);

             /* Call dbscan recursively */
             SELECT dbscan(X2, Y2, 1, minPt, eps)
             FROM  closepnts, points
             WHERE X1 = X2 AND Y1=Y2;
             DELETE FROM closepnts;
         }
};       /*end dbscan*/
```

This density-based clustering was part of a demo presented at the ACM SIG-MOD 2005 conference of the Stream Mill System that supports very powerful continuous queries on data streams and applications that span both data streams and databases using a client-server architecture [38]. Another data mining application demonstrated on that occasion, was an ensemble-based classifier where each window was used to build a separate classifier. Sliding windows that are recomputed after each new tuple arrives in the window, are suitable when incremental computation is feasible—as in the case of mining methods, such as Naive Bayesian Classifiers that are based on count or other algebraic aggregates. Two other important advantages of Stream Mill are (i) support for time series applications, and [40], and (ii) inclusion of streaming XML data along with relational streams [41], as needed e.g., to support PPML data. Indeed, Stream Mill has already taken the first important steps toward becoming an Inductive DSMS.

This example illustrates how the middle-road approach to data mining can be generalized to work with data streams, and in fact the simpler one-one pass algorithms that are prevalent with data streams can be expressed simply and concisely using UDAs. However, other approaches to Inductive DBMS, such as the mining-language approach, or the OLE DB DM approach, can also be extended naturally to support Inductive DSMS and such extensions provide an interesting topic for future research.

4   Conclusion

Ten years after being proposed in concept papers [1, 2], the notion of inductive databases is coming of age in terms of research advances and commercial systems with progress occurring along three largely parallel and independent paths. Progress along the high-road pathway, has been made with the introduction of the first generation of mining languages [6], and with techniques for the optimization of declarative mining queries based on association rules [9]. Progress along the middle-road has delivered SQL extensions based on natively defined UDAs that can be used to write data mining algorithms [18]. On the commercial front, DBMS can now support the combination of descriptive/predictive data mining via a predefined library mining methods [42].

Remarkably these advances are not mutually exclusive but they should instead be integrated to produce more powerful Inductive DBMS. In particular, the libraries of systems such as OLE DB DM should be made extensible, as to accommodate the inclusion of new declarative mining methods and procedural mining methods. As demonstrated by ATLaS, new mining methods can be added to DSMS as UDAs operating on tables. While these UDAs could be written in a foreign language, UDAs natively and concisely written in SQL are preferable, because they are safe, easier to modify, and free of 'impedance mismatch' problems.

In order to get synergy between these different approaches, we must assure their interoperability. Experience with data mining libraries [43, 19] indicates that for flexibility and interoperability, we need to establish well-defined representations between the various steps of the mining process. These representations must, e.g., support import/export of data, metadata and mining models, so that they can be cooperatively exchanged between different systems. The PMML-based approach of OLE DB [42] represents an important first step in the right direction, but it suffers from limitations in terms of power and generality. For instance, while a single classifier can be imported/exported using PMML, it is not clear how ensembles of such classifiers could be assembled and reimported to perform a predictive task. While more general approaches to the representation of mining artifacts are possible using XML, not all representations are equally desirable. For instance, for large data sets, relational tables have proven to be much more efficient than XML-based ones both in terms of data and query efficiencies. On the other hand, logical rules are clearly the representation of choice in dealing with knowledge. As describe in [44] logical rule are very effective at (i) bringing the domain knowledge to bear upon specific mining task, (ii) driving the mining process by calling procedurally defined UDAs to perform the specific mining tasks, and (iii) combining the results of knowledge extraction with application-expert rules. From a research viewpoint, the success obtained in [45] with a rule-based data mining environment suggests the need for two important enhancements that were not available in the framework of systems [46] originally used in those experiments. One is the ability of using induced rules as if they were deductive rules, and the other is ability of using deductive rules to define UDAs which compare in terms of efficiency with those written in ATLaS SQL which approach those of UDAs written in a procedural language.

Finally, we have shown that the problem of mining data streams is so close to that of mining databases that the two should be pursued together to exploit the considerable opportunities their close relationship offers both in terms of research and commercial applications.

Acknowledgements

I would like to thank Francesco Bonchi and Yan-Nei Law for their comments and suggested improvements on the first version of the manuscript. In addition to their many helpful comments, Haixun Wang, Yijian Bai and Hetal Thakkar must also be credited with building ATLaS and Stream Mill.

References

1. Tomasz Imielinski. A database perspective on knowledge discovery. In *The First International Conference on Knowledge Discovery and Data Mining (KDD-95)*, 1995.
2. Tomasz Imielinski and Heikki Mannila. A database perspective on knowledge discovery. *Communication ACM*, 39(11):58–64, 1996.
3. T. Imielinski and A. Virmani. MSQL: a query language for database mining. *Data Mining and Knowledge Discovery*, 3:373–408, 1999.
4. J. Han, Y. Fu, W. Wang, K. Koperski, and O. R. Zaiane. DMQL: A data mining query language for relational databases. In *Workshop on Research Issues on Data Mining and Knowledge Discovery (DMKD)*, pages 27–33, Montreal, Canada, June 1996.
5. R. Meo, G. Psaila, and S. Ceri. A new SQL-like operator for mining association rules. In *VLDB*, pages 122–133, Bombay, India, 1996.
6. Marco Botta, Jean-François Boulicaut, Cyrille Masson, and Rosa Meo. Query languages supporting descriptive rule mining: A comparative study. In *Database Support for Data Mining Applications*, pages 24–51, 2004.
7. Francesco Bonchi, Fosca Giannotti, Alessio Mazzanti, and Dino Pedreschi. Examiner: Optimized level-wise frequent pattern mining with monotone constraint. In *ICDM*, pages 11–18, 2003.
8. Sau Dan Lee and Luc De Raedt. An algebra for inductive query evaluation. In *ICDM*, pages 147–154, 2003.
9. Francesco Bonchi and Claudio Lucchese. Pushing tougher constraints in frequent pattern mining. In *PAKDD*, pages 114–124, 2005.
10. Baptiste Jeudy and Jean-François Boulicaut. Constraint-based discovery and inductive queries: Application to association rule mining. In *Pattern Detection and Discovery*, pages 110–124, 2002.
11. IBM. Db2 intelligent miner, http://www-306.ibm.com/software/data/iminer.

12. ORACLE. Oracle data miner release 10gr2, http://www.oracle.com/technology/ products/bi/odm.
13. Z. Tang, J. Maclennan, and P.P. Kim. Building data mining solutions with ole db for dm and xml for analysis. *SIGMOD Record*, 34(2):80–85, 2005.
14. Data Mining Group (DMG). Predictive model markup language (pmml), http://sourceforge.net/projects/pmml.
15. S. Sarawagi, S. Thomas, and R. Agrawal. Integrating association rule mining with relational database systems: Alternatives and implications. In *SIGMOD*, 1998.
16. Arno Siebes. Where is the mining in kdid? (invited talk). In *Fourth Int. Workshop on Knowledge Discovery in Inductive Databases (KDID 2005), Porto, Prtugal*, 2005.
17. Yan-Nei Law, Haixun Wang, and Carlo Zaniolo. Data models and query language for data streams. In *VLDB*, pages 492–503, 2004.
18. Haixun Wang and Carlo Zaniolo. Atlas: a native extension of sql for data minining. In *Proceedings of Third SIAM Int. Conference on Data Mining*, pages 130–141, 2003.
19. Weka 3—data mining with open source machine learning software in java http://www.cs.waikato.ac.nz.
20. Theodore Johnson, Laks V. S. Lakshmanan, and Raymond T. Ng. The 3w model and algebra for unified data mining. In *VLDB 2000, Proceedings of 26th International Conference on Very Large Data Bases*, pages 21–32. Morgan Kaufmann, 2000.
21. B. Babcock, S. Babu, M. Datar, R. Motawani, and J. Widom. Models and issues in data stream systems. In *PODS*, 2002.
22. G. Hulten, L. Spencer, and P. Domingos. Mining time-changing data streams. In *SIGKDD*, pages 97–106, San Francisco, CA, 2001. ACM Press.
23. Haixun Wang, Wei Fan, Philip S. Yu, and Jiawei Han. Mining concept-drifting data streams using ensemble classifiers. In *KDD*, pages 226–235, 2003.
24. Fang Chu, Yizhou Wang, and Carlo Zaniolo. An adaptive learning approach for noisy data streams. In *ICDM*, pages 351–354, 2004.
25. Lukasz Golab and M. Tamer Ozsu. Issues in data stream management. *ACM SIGMOD Record*, 32(2):5–14, 2003.
26. Theodore Johnson, S. Muthukrishnan, and Irina Rozenbaum. Sampling algorithms in a stream operator. In *SIGMOD Conference*, pages 1–12, 2005.
27. D. Abadi, D. Carney, U. Cetintemel, M. Cherniack, C. Convey, S. Lee, M. Stonebraker, N. Tatbul, and S. Zdonik. Aurora: A new model and architecture for data stream management. *VLDB Journal*, 12(2):120–139, 2003.
28. C. Cranor, Y. Gao, T. Johnson, V. Shkapenyuk, and O. Spatscheck. Gigascope: High performance network monitoring with an sql interface. In *SIGMOD*, page 623. ACM Press, 2002.
29. A. Arasu, S. Babu, and J. Widom. Cql: A language for continuous queries over streams and relations. In *DBPL*, pages 1–19, 2003.
30. Mohamed Medhat Gaber, Arkady B. Zaslavsky, and Shonali Krishnaswamy. Mining data streams: a review. *SIGMOD Record*, 34(2):18–26, 2005.
31. Sudipto Guha, Adam Meyerson, Nina Mishra, Rajeev Motwani, and Liadan O'Callaghan. Clustering data streams: Theory and practice. *IEEE Trans. Knowl. Data Eng.*, 15(3):515–528, 2003.
32. Hannu Toivonen. Sampling large databases for association rules. In T. M. Vijayaraman, Alejandro P. Buchmann, C. Mohan, and Nandlal L. Sarda, editors, *VLDB'96, Proceedings of 22th International Conference on Very Large Data Bases, September 3-6, 1996, Mumbai (Bombay), India*, pages 134–145. Morgan Kaufmann, 1996.

33. Kagan Tumer and Joydeep Ghosh. Error correlation and error reduction in ensemble classifiers. *Connect. Sci.*, 8(3):385–404, 1996.
34. Yan-Nei Law and Carlo Zaniolo. Improving the accuracy of continuous aggregates and mining queries. In *Submitted for Publication*, 2005.
35. Nesime Tatbul, Ugur Çetintemel, Stanley B. Zdonik, Mitch Cherniack, and Michael Stonebraker. Load shedding in a data stream manager. In *VLDB*, pages 309–320, 2003.
36. Yanif Ahmad, Bradley Berg, Ugur Çetintemel, Mark Humphrey, Jeong-Hyon Hwang, Anjali Jhingran, Anurag Maskey, Olga Papaemmanouil, Alex Rasin, Nesime Tatbul, Wenjuan Xing, Ying Xing, and Stanley B. Zdonik. Distributed operation in the borealis stream processing engine. In *SIGMOD Conference*, pages 882–884, 2005.
37. Stream mill home. http://wis.cs.ucla.edu/stream-mill.
38. Chang Luo, Hetal Thakkar, Haixun Wang, and Carlo Zaniolo. A native extension of sql for mining data streams. pages 873–875, 2005.
39. Hans-Peter Kriegel Martin Ester, J. Sander, and Xiaowei Xu. A density-based algorithm for discovering clusters in large spatial databases with noise. In *KDD 1996*, pages 226–231, 1996.
40. Y. Bai, L. Chang, H. Thakkar, X. Zhou, and C. Zaniolo. Efficient support for time series queries in data stream management systems. In K. Shaw N. Chaudhry and M. Abdelguerfi (eds), editors, *Stream Data Management" Kluwer: Chapter 6*. Kluwer Academic Publishers, 2005.
41. Xin Zhou, Hetal Thakkar, and Carlo Zaniolo. Unifying the processing of xml streams and relational data streams. The 22nd International Conference on Data Engineering April 3-7, Atlanta, GA, 2006, 2005.
42. ZhaoHui Tang, Jamie Maclennan, and Pyungchul (Peter) Kim. Building data mining solutions with ole db for dm and xml for analysis. *SIGMOD Record*, 34(2):80–85, 2005.
43. Clementine http://www.spss.com/clementine/index.htm.
44. F. Giannotti, G. Manco, D. Pedreschi, and F. Turini. Experiences with a logic-based knowledge discovery support environment. In *ACM SIGMOD Workshop on Research Issues in Data Mining and Knowledge Discovery (DMKD)*, 1999.
45. Fosca Giannotti, Giuseppe Manco, Dino Pedreschi, and Franco Turini. Experiences with a logic-based knowledge discovery support environment. In *AI*IA*, pages 202–213, 1999.
46. Faiz Arni, KayLiang Ong, Shalom Tsur, Haixun Wang, and Carlo Zaniolo. The deductive database system ldl++. *TPLP*, 3(1):61–94, 2003.

Memory-Aware Frequent k-Itemset Mining

Maurizio Atzori[1,2], Paolo Mancarella[1], and Franco Turini[1]

[1] Dipartimento di Informatica, University of Pisa, Italy
{atzori, paolo, turini}@di.unipi.it
[2] ISTI-CNR, Area della Ricerca di Pisa, Italy

Abstract. In this paper we show that the well known problem of computing frequent k-itemsets (i.e. itemsets of cardinality k) in a given dataset can be reduced to the problem of finding iceberg queries from a stream of queries suitably constructed from the original dataset. Hence, algorithms for computing frequent k-itemsets can be obtained by adapting algorithms for computing iceberg queries. In the paper we show that, for sparse datasets, this can be done directly, i.e. without generating frequent x-itemsets, for each $x < k$, as done in the most common algorithms based on a level-wise approach. We exploit a recent algorithm for finding iceberg queries and define an algorithm which requires only three sequential passes over the dataset to compute the frequent k-itemsets (even for $k > 3$). An important feature of the algorithm is that the amount of main memory required can be determined in advance, and it is shown to be very low for sparse datasets. Experiments show that for very large datasets with millions of small transactions our proposal outperforms the state-of-the-art algorithms. Furthermore, we sketch a first extension of our algorithm that works over data streams.

1 Introduction

The field of Data Mining concerns the extraction of useful information from raw data. This is usually done by generalizing data to induce models from datasets. Among the models considered important for decision making, association rules [1, 2] play an important role, in that they allow us to highlight relevant trends in the data and also to gain some improvements when dealing with other models, such as classification (see e.g. [3]) and clustering [4]. Roughly speaking, mining association rules from a given set of transactions (e.g. a given set of supermarket receipts) amounts at finding rules of the form $i_1, \ldots, i_n \Rightarrow i_{n+1}, \ldots, i_k$, where each i_j is an item (e.g. a supermarket good). The intended meaning of such a rule is that it is likely that a transaction containing the items in the premise contains also the items in the conclusion.

It is well known that the most expensive task in mining association rules is the extraction of frequent itemsets, i.e. sets of items which occur together in at least a given percentage of the whole set of transactions. Once frequent itemsets are produced from the dataset, the generation of the association rules is rather straightforward. Since the datasets we are interested in are typically huge, it is

F. Bonchi and J.-F. Boulicaut (Eds.): KDID 2005, LNCS 3933, pp. 38–54, 2006.
© Springer-Verlag Berlin Heidelberg 2006

important to devise algorithms which try to minimize both the time and the space required for the analysis. Most of the known proposals that solve this kind of problem for huge datasets are based on level-wise algorithms that compute frequent itemsets of increasing cardinality, up to a given one, thus requiring several passes through the dataset. This is done in order to maintain the main memory space usage acceptable. Non level-wise, depth-first algorithms also exist [5], but they usually require that the whole dataset (although in a compressed form) fits into main memory.

In this paper we will focus on the problem of finding itemsets of a given size directly, i.e. without generating smaller itemsets as done in level-wise approaches. This is particularly useful in the context of *Inductive Databases* since in order to answer some queries, it would be necessary to know the exact support or the number of the frequent k-itemsets. Mining all the frequent itemsets would reduce memory and time efficiency; on the other hand, maximal itemset mining could be not sufficient to answer the query (in fact maximal itemsets do not allow us to compute the exact support of smaller itemsets). As shown later in the experiment section, in very large datasets with thousands of items and millions of small transactions our proposal is able to compute frequent k-itemsets while the current state-of-the-art algorithms fail due to huge main memory requirements.

First we show that the problem of finding frequent k-itemsets addressed in this paper can be transformed into the problem of finding frequent symbols over a (huge) stream of symbols over a given alphabet, often referred to as the iceberg queries problem or the hot list analysis. Then, we exploit a recent algorithm for the iceberg queries problem which allows us to solve the original frequent itemset problem by only two sequential passes over the dataset plus a preprocessing step aimed at computing some statistics on the dataset (three passes in total). We will see that, for sparse datasets (i.e. datasets with few items per transactions w.r.t. the total number of possible items) the amount of main memory required by the proposed algorithm is very low and independent from both the number of items and the size of the dataset, as shown by some experiments we have conducted on a prototype implementation of the algorithm. Notice that, when looking for association rules of the form $i_1 \ldots i_n \Rightarrow i_{n+1} \ldots i_k$, with $k > n$, we need to determine frequent itemsets of cardinality n and k. Using standard level-wise algorithms such as *Apriori* [6], k passes through the dataset have to be performed. Using our approach, we can run two instances of the proposed algorithm in parallel, thus requiring three passes through the dataset overall. The main contribution of this paper is the development of an algorithm that, for sparse datasets, requires a limited amount of memory while keeping a (small) constant number of passes over the input. Furthermore, we sketch first extension of our algorithm that works over data streams. The contribution here is the development of an algorithm that, with limited memory consumption, is able to mine frequent k-itemsets over a window (a subset of the stream) with size proportional to the length of the stream read so far.

1.1   Paper Organization

The paper is organized as follows. In Section 2 we set up the notation used in the rest of the paper, formally defining both the frequent itemsets and the iceberg queries frameworks and we briefly recall some of the existing works related to these problems. Section 3 describes a new approach to the problem of finding frequent itemsets of size k, based on the reduction to the iceberg queries problem. In Section 4 we present an algorithm that computes the exact set of k-itemsets reading sequentially the dataset only three times, or even two. In Section 5 we study the space complexity and the number of passes over the dataset needed to compute the set of all frequent itemsets. Under reasonable assumptions we show that online (i.e. one pass) frequent itemset mining is not possible in the worst case. Section 6 is devoted to present some experiments we have conducted in order to show the effectiveness of our algorithm in terms of the amount of main memory needed. Section 7 sketches a possible extension of the algorithm to work over data streams. Finally, Section 8 contains some discussions on future work and directions we are planning to follow.

2   Preliminaries

In this section we set up the basic notations and terminology that we are going to adopt in the rest of the paper, and we formally define the so called *frequent itemset mining* problem and the *iceberg queries* problem.

2.1   Frequent Itemset Mining Problem

Let us first set up some notational conventions used in the sequel.

Set of items. A set of items is a finite set, denoted by $\mathcal{I}$. Elements of $\mathcal{I}$ will be denoted by $i, i', i_1, \ldots$ and are referred to as *items*.

Itemset. An itemset is a subset of $\mathcal{I}$. Itemsets will be denoted by $I, I', \ldots$.

k-itemset. An itemset I is called a k-itemset if $|I| = k$, where $|I|$ denotes the cardinality of I.

Transaction. A transaction T is an itemset, denoted by $T, T', \ldots$.

Dataset. A *dataset* $\mathcal{D}$ is a multiset (a bag) of transactions. Given $\mathcal{D}$, the *maximal transaction length* of $\mathcal{D}$ is

$$m_{\mathcal{D}} = \max\{|T| \mid T \in \mathcal{D}\}.$$

In order to show some properties and theorems in the next sections, let us formally define the frequent itemsets mining problem.

Definition 1 (FIM Problem). *Let $\mathcal{D}$ be a dataset and I be an itemset. I is called a* frequent *itemset with respect to $\mathcal{D}$ and a support σ, with $0 < \sigma \leq 1$ if:*

$$|\{T \in \mathcal{D} \mid I \subseteq I(T)\}| \geq \sigma|\mathcal{D}|.$$

Let $\mathcal{F}_k(\sigma, \mathcal{D})$ be the set of all k-itemset that are frequent w.r.t. σ and $\mathcal{D}$. Then, the FIM problem is defined as the task of determining $\mathcal{F}_k(\sigma, \mathcal{D})$ for each k such that $0 < k \leq m_{\mathcal{D}}$.

In the sequel we will often write simply $\mathcal{F}_k$ instead of $\mathcal{F}_k(\sigma, \mathcal{D})$, whenever the parameters σ and $\mathcal{D}$ are either clear from the context or irrelevant.

2.2   Iceberg Queries

Our approach is based on the reduction of the problem of frequent itemsets computation to the problem of finding iceberg queries. Let us define the so called *Iceberg Queries* problem (also known as *Hot List Analysis*).

Alphabet. By $\mathcal{Q}$ we denote a finite alphabet. Elements of $\mathcal{Q}$ are denoted by $q, q', q_1, \ldots$ and are referred to as *queries*.

Stream. A *stream of queries* is a sequence $s = \langle q_1, \ldots, q_n \rangle$, such that $q_i \in \mathcal{Q}$, for each $1 \leq i \leq n$; the length n of the stream is referred to as $|s|$.

Frequence. Given a stream s and a query q, $f_s(q)$ denotes the number of occurrences of q in s.

Definition 2 (IQ Problem). *Let $\mathcal{Q}$ be a set of queries, s be a stream of queries and ϑ be a real number such that $0 < \vartheta \leq 1$. The IQ problem is defined as the task of determining the subset $Q(\vartheta, s)$ defined as follows:*

$$Q(\vartheta, s) = \{ q \in \mathcal{Q} \mid f_s(q) > \vartheta |s| \}.$$

In the sequel, if a query q belongs to $Q(\vartheta, s)$ we will say that q is an *iceberg query* with respect to $\mathcal{Q}$, s and ϑ.

Before going on, it is worth pointing out that, in concrete applications of both FIM and IQ problems, the input ($\mathcal{D}$ and s, respectively) is usually huge and it can only be read sequentially (e.g. according to transaction identifiers in the first case and to the sequence order in the second case). Moreover, in FIM problems we usually have $|\mathcal{D}| \gg |\mathcal{I}|$ and in IQ problems we usually have $|s| \gg \mathcal{Q} \gg 1/\vartheta$.

2.3   The *KSP* Algorithm

A simple and exact algorithm to solve the IQ problem is described in [7], and we will refer to it as the *KSP*-algorithm (see Algorithm 1). Given a stream s and a real number ϑ (called the *threshold*), the algorithm in [7] requires one pass through the input stream in order to find a superset of the required $Q(\vartheta, s)$. A trivial second pass can be done to find exactly $Q(\vartheta, s)$, keeping the same performance characteristics. In particular, the authors show that their algorithm requires only $O(1/\vartheta)$ memory cells. As shown in Algorithm 1, the only data structures used by *KSP* is a set of queries K and a counter for each query in K.

Example 1. Suppose to have $s = \langle c, b, b, f, g \rangle$ and $\vartheta = 0.4$. This means that we are looking for queries that occur at least 2 times (40% of a stream of 5 queries) At the very beginning of the computation, the set K is empty. We first find c and insert it into K, and $count(c) = 1$. Since $|K| = 1 \not> 1/0.4 = 2.5$ we process the next query, b. Now we have $K = \{b, c\}$, $count(c) = 1$ and $count(b) = 1$. After the third query (another b) we have $K = \{b, c\}$, $count(c) = 1$ and $count(b) = 2$. With the fourth query, f, we first have $K = \{c, b, f\}$. But since $|K| = 3 > 2.5$ then

Algorithm 1. The *KSP*-algorithm

Input: s, ϑ
Output: a superset K of $Q(\vartheta, s)$ s.t. $|K| \leq 1/\vartheta$
1: **for all** $q \in s$ **do**
2:    **if** $q \notin K$ **then**
3:       $K \leftarrow K \cup q$;
4:       $count(q) \leftarrow 0$;
5:    $count(q) \leftarrow count(q) + 1$;
6:    **if** $|K| > 1/\vartheta$ **then**
7:       **for all** $a \in K$ **do**
8:          $count(a) \leftarrow count(a) - 1$;
9:          **if** $count(a) = 0$ **then**
10:            $K \leftarrow K \setminus a$;

---

every *count* has to be decremented: $count(f) = count(c) = 0$ while $count(b) = 1$. Every query in K with count equal to zero must be removed from K, so now we have $K = \{b\}$. By taking into account also the last query, g, we will have $K = \{b, g\}$. In fact, $\{b, g\}$ is a superset of the exact result $\{b\}$ with less than 2.5 elements. Another trivial pass through the stream s will show that $count(b) = 2$ and therefore it can be considered as a valid output while g is not frequent enough since $count(g) = 1$.

2.4 Related Work

Almost all the algorithms for finding frequent itemsets are based on the level-wise generation of candidates of the *Apriori* algorithm [6]. The level-wise approach is performed in order to maintain the search space small enough to fit into the main memory. This strategy necessarily leads to several passes through the dataset.

Some other papers present different approaches in order to keep the number of passes through the dataset constant. In [8] the authors show a partitioning technique that needs two passes through the database. First, the dataset is partitioned into several parts which are small enough to fit into the memory. Every partition is elaborated using a level-wise algorithm and then the results of each partition are merged. This leads to a superset of the solution. A second scan then removes the false positive elements of the superset. Unfortunately, if the dataset is very large then the resulting partitions can be too small with respect to the dataset, leading to a huge superset, and this can reduce the effectiveness of the algorithm.

Another important approach to reduce the number of passes through the dataset is the one proposed by Toivonen in [9] and then refined in [10, 11], based on the evaluation of a small random sample of the dataset. A set of patterns that are probably frequent in the whole dataset are generated, and then their exact frequencies are verified in the rest of the dataset. If a failure occurs in the generation of candidates (i.e., there are false negatives), a mechanism is provided which, in a second pass, computes the remaining frequent patterns.

By decreasing the support threshold the probability of failure can be decreased, but for low probabilities this drastically increments the number of candidates. Furthermore, if we are dealing with very large datasets, it is possible that the (small) sample is not very representative of the whole dataset, and this means that there is a high probability of failure. In this case the candidates to be verified in the second pass can be too many to be fitted into the main memory (i.e. more than two passes are needed). For a survey on frequent itemset mining algorithms, see [2].

Main memory usage of depth-first (i.e., non-levelwise) frequent pattern mining algorithms is discussed in [12]: two state-of-the-art algorithms, FP-Growth [5] and Eclat [13], are tested and shown to be very memory consuming even for medium-size datasets. A simple improvement of Eclat, named Medic, is proposed but it is empirically shown to reduce the amount of memory needed of $\approx 50\%$ in the best case: the memory requirements still depend on the size of the dataset, and this fact leaves the algorithm impractical when datasets are very large. Another confirmation of the scalability limitations of current state-of-the-art algorithms for frequent itemset mining came from the First IEEE ICDM Workshop on Frequent Itemset Mining Implementations, FIMI 2003 [14], where several well-known algorithms were implemented and independently tested. The results show that *"none of the algorithms is able to gracefully scale-up to very large datasets, with millions of transactions"*.

The approach presented in this paper computes frequent itemsets of size k directly (i.e. without computing smaller itemsets), performing two passes though the dataset. Moreover, the amount of main memory needed is known in advance and it is acceptable under the hypothesis that the given dataset is sparse.

Our technique is based on a novel approach to the Iceberg Queries problem, proposed in [7] and briefly summarized in the previous subsection. The authors present a (surprisingly) simple algorithm able to find all queries with frequency greater than or equal to a given threshold ϑ, from a given stream of queries (i.e., iceberg queries) by using $O(1/\vartheta)$ main memory cells and performing two passes through the stream. Notice that, in the worst-case, the output size is exactly $1/\vartheta$. Furthermore, the algorithm proposed in [7], that we call *KSP*, does $O(1)$ operations per query (under the reasonable assumption that hash tables make $O(1)$ operations for insertion, search and deletion).

3   Transforming FIM Problems into IQ Problems

In this section we show how a FIM problem can be transformed into an IQ problem. Roughly speaking, the idea is to associate to each k-itemset a query and to construct a suitable stream $s_\mathcal{D}$ of queries starting from the given dataset $\mathcal{D}$, in such a way that the problem of determining $\mathcal{F}_k(\sigma, \mathcal{D})$ is transformed into the problem of determining $Q(\vartheta, s_\mathcal{D})$, where ϑ is a function of $\sigma, m_\mathcal{D}$ and k. Once we have defined such transformation, we can adopt any algorithm for the IQ problem in order to solve the original FIM problem. In particular, we can adopt algorithms which keep the number of passes through the dataset as small as possible. In the next section, we will show such an algorithm which is based on the one proposed by [7] for the IQ problem.

In the sequel, given a finite set S and a natural number k, we denote by S^k the set of all the subsets $P \subseteq S$ such that $|P| = k$. Moreover, given two sequences $s = \langle x_1, \ldots, x_n \rangle$ and $s' = \langle y_1, \ldots, y_m \rangle$, we denote by $s :: s'$ the sequence $\langle x_1, \ldots, x_n, y_1, \ldots, y_m \rangle$.

We first define the transformation which, given a FIM problem, constructs a corresponding IQ problem.

Definition 3 (FIM to IQ). *Let $\mathcal{I}$ be an itemset, $\mathcal{D}$ be a dataset, and k be a natural number such that $k \leq m_{\mathcal{D}}$. Then:*

(i) *The alphabet $Q^{\mathcal{I}}$ is defined as the set $\mathcal{I}^k$ (each set in $\mathcal{I}^k$ is a symbol in the alphabet).*

(ii) *For each $T \in \mathcal{D}$, a stream associated with T is a sequence $s_T = \langle I_1, \ldots, I_{n_T} \rangle$ such that*

   - $\{I_1, \ldots, I_{n_T}\} = T^k$
   - *each $I_j \in T^k$ occurs in s_T exactly once.*

(iii) *If $\mathcal{D} = \{T_1, \ldots, T_n\}$, then a stream $s_{\mathcal{D}}$ associated with $\mathcal{D}$ is a sequence*

$$s = s_{T_1} :: s_{T_2} :: \ldots :: s_{T_n}.$$

Notice that, in the above definition, we do not define *the* stream associated with a transaction, but rather *a* stream associated with it. Similarly we talk about *a* stream associated with the dataset $\mathcal{D}$. Indeed, given a transaction T_i there are many ways of constructing a stream s_{T_i} corresponding to it, and consequently, there may be many ways of constructing $s_{\mathcal{D}}$. Actually, the choice of $s_{\mathcal{D}}$ is irrelevant as far as the correctness of the transformation is concerned.

In the next theorem we show that a FIM problem $\mathcal{F}_k(\sigma, \mathcal{D})$ can be mapped into an IQ problem $Q(\vartheta, s_{\mathcal{D}})$ where $s_{\mathcal{D}}$ is any stream constructed as in the previous definition and ϑ is a suitable function of σ, k and $m_{\mathcal{D}}$.

Theorem 1. *Let $\mathcal{I}$ be an itemset, $\mathcal{D}$ be a dataset, k be a natural number such that $k \leq m_{\mathcal{D}}$, and σ be a real number such that $0 < \sigma \leq 1$. Let $Q^{\mathcal{I}}$ and $s_{\mathcal{D}}$ be the alphabet and a stream of queries as in Definition 3. Let also $\bar{e} = \binom{m_{\mathcal{D}}}{k}$. If an itemset I is a frequent k-itemset with respect to σ and $\mathcal{D}$, then I is an iceberg query with respect to $Q^{\mathcal{I}}$, $s_{\mathcal{D}}$, and $\vartheta = \frac{\sigma}{\bar{e}}$. Formally:*

$$I \in \mathcal{F}_k(\sigma, \mathcal{D}) \Longrightarrow I \in Q(\vartheta, s_{\mathcal{D}}).$$

Proof. Let $|\mathcal{D}| = N$ and $\mathcal{D} = \{T_1, \ldots, T_N\}$. We observe:

(1) $|s_{\mathcal{D}}| = \sum_{i=1}^{N} \binom{|T_i|}{k} \leq \sum_{i=1}^{N} \binom{m_{\mathcal{D}}}{k} = \bar{e}N$

(2) By construction of $s_{\mathcal{D}}$, $|\{T \in \mathcal{D} | I \subseteq I(T)\}| = f_{s_{\mathcal{D}}}(I)$.

$$I \in \mathcal{F}_k(\sigma, \mathcal{D})$$

$\implies$ \hspace{2cm} \{By definition of $\mathcal{F}_k(\sigma, \mathcal{D})$\}

$$|\{T \in \mathcal{D} | I \subseteq I(T)\}| \geq \sigma N$$

$\iff$ \hspace{2cm} \{By observation (2)\}

$$f_{s_\mathcal{D}}(I) \geq \sigma N$$

$\iff$ \hspace{2cm} \{algebra\}

$$f_{s_\mathcal{D}}(I) \geq \frac{\sigma}{\bar{e}} N \bar{e}$$

$\implies$ \hspace{2cm} \{By observation (1) and definition of ϑ\}

$$f_{s_\mathcal{D}}(I) \geq \vartheta |s_\mathcal{D}|$$

$\implies$ \hspace{2cm} \{by definition of $Q(\vartheta, s_\mathcal{D})$\}

$$I \in Q(\vartheta, s_\mathcal{D}). \hspace{4cm} \square$$

The previous theorem suggests a new technique for finding frequent k-itemsets, which can be sketched as follows:

(1) Construct a stream $s_\mathcal{D}$ corresponding to $\mathcal{D}$;
(2) Find the set of Iceberg Queries $Q(\vartheta, s_\mathcal{D})$.

It is worth noting that, in our proposal, step (1) and (2) are not performed sequentially, but rather they are interleaved.

Example 2. Let us give a simple example of the above transformation. Let $\mathcal{I} = \{a, b, c, d, e, f\}$ be the underlying set of items and let $\mathcal{D}$ be the following set of transactions:

$$\mathcal{D} = \{\{a, b, d\}, \{a, c, e\}, \{a, d, f\}, \{b, c\}, \{b, d, e\}, \{c, d, f\}\}$$

Assume that we are interested in 2-itemsets which occur in at least $\sigma = 1/3$ of the transactions. It is easy to see that, among all possible 2-itemsets ($\binom{|\mathcal{I}|}{k}$) = $\binom{6}{2}$ = 15), only $\{a, d\}$, $\{b, d\}$ and $\{d, f\}$ appear at least twice.

It is worth noting that anti-monotonicity[1] here is not useful at all. In fact, every item (1-itemset) in this example is frequent: it means that 15 candidate 2-itemsets have to be tested by a levelwise algorithm (e.g. Apriori) in a second pass. Even constraint-based techniques (e.g. [15]) cannot be used here since there are no transactions containing less than 2 items (they would be removed since they do not generate any 2-itemset, possibly reducing the search space) and thus the constraint on the size of the itemsets cannot be exploited.

Let us consider now our *FIM-to-IQ* transformation. For each transaction T_i in $\mathcal{D}$, we build a stream s_i associated with it:

$$s_1 = \langle \{a, b\}, \{a, d\}, \{b, d\} \rangle$$
$$s_2 = \langle \{a, c\}, \{a, e\}, \{c, e\} \rangle$$
$$s_2 = \langle \{a, d\}, \{a, f\}, \{d, f\} \rangle$$
$$s_4 = \langle \{b, c\} \rangle$$
$$s_5 = \langle \{b, d\}, \{b, e\}, \{d, e\} \rangle$$
$$s_6 = \langle \{c, d\}, \{c, f\}, \{d, f\} \rangle$$

---

[1] The anti-motonicity property of the itemset frequency asserts that if I is frequent, then all the subsets of I have to be frequent.

The stream associated with $\mathcal{D}$ is then $s_{\mathcal{D}} = s_1 :: s_2 :: s_3 :: s_4 :: s_5 :: s_6$. Since $m_{\mathcal{D}} = 3$, in this case the threshold for the IQ problem is set to

$$\vartheta = \frac{\sigma}{\binom{m_{\mathcal{D}}}{k}} = \frac{\frac{1}{3}}{\binom{3}{2}} = \frac{1}{9}$$

Notice that in the stream $s_{\mathcal{D}}$, the "queries" $\{a, d\}$, $\{b, d\}$ and $\{d, f\}$ are the only ones occurring with a frequency of $1/8 \geq \vartheta$. In this case the *KSP* algorithm only requires $1/\vartheta = 9$ counters instead of the 15 needed by a levelwise algorithm for frequent itemset mining, and only two passes over the dataset (but we need to know $m_{\mathcal{D}}$ in advance). If $|I| > 10000$ and most of the items are frequent, then the number of candidate 2-itemsets can be too large to be fitted in main memory. In such a case an Apriori-like approach will lead to "out of memory errors", while our transformation approach is still effective (see Section 6).

4   The Proposed Algorithm

In this section we propose an instance of the technique based on the result of the previous section, which exploits the *KSP*-algorithm [7] showed in Section 2.3. Given a stream s and a threshold ϑ, the *KSP*-algorithm requires one pass through the input stream in order to find a superset of the required $Q(\vartheta, s)$. A trivial second pass can be done to find exactly $Q(\vartheta, s)$, keeping the same performance characteristics, using only $O(1/\vartheta)$ memory cells.

In order to exploit the *KSP*-algorithm, given a dataset $\mathcal{D}$, for each transaction $T \in \mathcal{D}$ we feed the *KSP*-algorithm by each k-itemset contained in $I(T)$, where k is the given size of itemsets we are interested in. The parameters for the *KSP*-algorithm are set as suggested in Theorem 1, i.e. the threshold is set to $\frac{\sigma}{\bar{e}}$ (recall that $\bar{e} = \binom{m_{\mathcal{D}}}{k}$, where $m_{\mathcal{D}}$ is the maximal length of a transaction in $\mathcal{D}$). In this way we obtain a two-passes algorithm, with the drawback of having to know the value of $m_{\mathcal{D}}$ in advance. If $m_{\mathcal{D}}$ is not known, a "preprocessing pass" is required. Thus, we obtain a three-passes algorithm that saves more memory (w.r.t the two-passes version) since the length of the stream $s_{\mathcal{D}}$ can be computed exactly in the preprocessing pass, instead of being roughly over-approximated in a pessimistic way by $\binom{m_{\mathcal{D}}}{k} |\mathcal{D}|$.

In the specification of our algorithm (see Algorithm 2), we will use the following notations:

- *KSP*.init sets up the data structures for the *KSP*-algorithm;
- *KSP*.threshold refers to the parameter ϑ of the *KSP*-algorithm;
- *KSP*.send(I) sends the itemset I to the *KSP*-algorithm as an element of the stream of queries;
- *KSP*.output denotes the set computed by the *KSP*-algorithm.

Notice that Pass 1 (lines 10–12) of Algorithm 2 basically corresponds to run *KSP* for computing a superset of the desired set of queries (itemsets in our case). The second, trivial pass of our algorithm (lines 15–22) filters out from this

---

Algorithm 2. Stream Mining Algorithm

Input: $\mathcal{D}, \sigma, k$
Output: $\mathcal{F}_k(\sigma, \mathcal{D})$, $count(I)$ $\forall I \in \mathcal{F}_k(\sigma, \mathcal{D})$
 1: //Pre-processing pass: some statistics on $\mathcal{D}$ are computed
 2: $streamLength \leftarrow 0$; $dbLength \leftarrow 0$;
 3: **for all** $T \in \mathcal{D}$ **do**
 4:     $dbLength \leftarrow dbLength + 1$;
 5:     $streamLength \leftarrow streamLength + \binom{|T|}{k}$;
 6: //Initialize the data structures for KSP
 7: $KSP.threshold \leftarrow \sigma \frac{dbLength}{streamLength}$;
 8: $KSP.init$;
 9: //Pass 1: a superset of $\mathcal{F}_k(\sigma, \mathcal{D})$ is computed
10: **for all** $T \in \mathcal{D}$ **do**
11:     **for all** $I \subseteq T$ s.t. $|I| = k$ **do**
12:         $KSP.send(I)$;
13: //assert: KSP.output is a superset of $\mathcal{F}_k(\sigma, \mathcal{D})$
14: //Pass 2: the actual counts of frequent k-itemsets are obtained
15: **for all** $T \in \mathcal{D}$ **do**
16:     **for all** $I \subseteq T$ s.t. $|I| = k$ **do**
17:         **if** $I \in KSP.output$ **then**
18:             $count(I) \leftarrow count(I) + 1$;
19: //infrequent k-itemsets are pruned
20: **for all** $I \in KSP.output$ **do**
21:     **if** $count(I) \geq \sigma \cdot dbLength$ **then**
22:         $\mathcal{F}_k(\sigma, \mathcal{D}) \leftarrow \mathcal{F}_k(\sigma, \mathcal{D}) \cup I$;

---

superset those itemsets which do not occur at least $\sigma \cdot |\mathcal{D}|$ times in the given dataset. In Pass 2, count is a data structure used to actually count the number of exact occurrences of an itemset in the given dataset. Notice that the same data structure used to represent the output of the KSP-algorithm (typically an hash table) can be used to implement the count data structure as well. This is indeed what we have done in our prototype implementation of the algorithm.

The correctness of the algorithm is guaranteed by the correctness of the KSP-algorithm and by Theorem 1. As far as space complexity is concerned, the following theorems can be easily proven.

Theorem 2. *Pass 1 of the proposed algorithm computes a superset of $\mathcal{F}_k(\sigma, \mathcal{D})$ in $O(\bar{e}/\sigma)$ space with one sequential pass through the dataset.*

Proof. The data structures used in Pass 1 of the algorithm are those used by KSP. The space complexity of the latter, given a threshold ϑ, is $O(1/\theta)$. Since KSP.threshold is set to $\sigma/\bar{e}$ the result follows trivially.   □

Trivially, Pass 2 of the algorithm computes the actual $\mathcal{F}_k(\sigma, \mathcal{D})$ reading once more the dataset, but without requiring further data structures. Hence we have the following corollary.

Corollary 1. *The proposed algorithm computes $\mathcal{F}_k(\sigma, \mathcal{D})$ in $O(\bar{e}/\sigma)$ space with two sequential passes through the dataset.*

5   Space Complexity of the Online Frequent Itemset Mining Problem

In this section we study the space complexity and the number of passes over the dataset needed to compute the set of all frequent itemsets. As we will show, there is a trade-off between the space complexity (memory needed) and the number of passes required. One of the main result is to prove that online (i.e. one pass) frequent itemset mining is not possible in the worst case (under the usual and reasonable assumption that the memory cannot contain all the couple of items). This theoretical result justifies the use of approximated algorithms for stream mining of frequent itemset.

We are going to prove the theorem, we need the following proposition, proved in [7]:

Lemma 1. *Any online algorithm for computing iceberg queries needs $\Omega(|\mathcal{A}|)$ space, where $\mathcal{A}$ is the alphabet (the set of all queries).*

Then we have:

Theorem 3. *Space complexity of online mining of σ-frequent 2-itemsets is $\Theta(|\mathcal{I}|^2)$.*

Proof. By contradiction. We prove that if the theorem is false then also online θ-frequent iceberg queries can be obtained in less than $O(|\mathcal{A}|)$, where $|\mathcal{A}|$ is the size of the alphabet, that is false as shown in [7].

The idea is based on datasets composed by exactly 2 items per transaction. The number of different 2-itemsets is

$$\binom{\mathcal{I}}{2} = \frac{|\mathcal{I}| \cdot (|\mathcal{I}| - 1)}{2} \in \Theta(|\mathcal{I}|^2)$$

Seeing the database as a stream of queries where each transaction is a query, then we have a stream of length N in the alphabet of 2-itemsets, of size $\binom{\mathcal{I}}{2}$ Note that, until now, we didn't fix any dataset nor stream in particular, but only the size of the alphabet. Among all possible such streams let us take the worst case stream (therefore, now we are fixing a specific dataset). In this case, according to Lemma 1, we need at least cardinality of the alphabet cells to compute (in one pass) the most frequent queries (i.e. 2-itemsets).   □

The following result trivially follows:

Corollary 2. *Space complexity of the exact online σ-frequent itemset mining problem is $\Omega(|\mathcal{I}|^2)$.*

6   Experiments

Even if our algorithm performs only two or three passes through the dataset (depending on whether we know $m_\mathcal{D}$ in advance or not, where $m_\mathcal{D}$ is the maximal transaction length of the dataset), both time and space complexity linearly

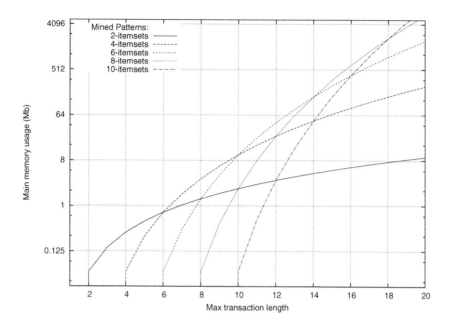

Fig. 1. Memory usage is a function of m_d and k (in this graph σ is fixed to $1/1000$)

depend on $\bar{e}$. The first thing to keep in mind is that, for the class of applications of the algorithm we have in mind, accessing the dataset is much more expensive than performing main memory operations, and if $\bar{e}$ is not too big, we can perform main memory operations while reading the dataset. For example, let us imagine a scenario in which a huge dataset is stored in different servers, and communications are encrypted (e.g., in the context of distributed data mining). It is easy to understand that, in this context, reducing the number of passes through the dataset is preferable, even at the cost of adding some more local main memory computations.

Anyway, we know that $\bar{e} = \binom{m_\mathcal{D}}{k}$ is polynomial in $m_\mathcal{D}$ (it is $\Theta(n^k)$, where $n = m_\mathcal{D}$). This can lead to huge memory requirements, which is obviously not acceptable. The graph in Fig. 1 shows the amount of memory needed by our algorithm, when varying both $m_\mathcal{D}$ and k (the size of the frequent itemsets we are looking for), and keeping σ fixed to $1/1000$ (be aware of the logarithmic scale used for the y axis). These results actually show the minimal requirements for the main hashtable structure used by our algorithm. Of course, a real implementation will use some more memory in order to store other runtime data, but since the hashtable is the only data structure in our algorithm, we can fairly expect to use such amount of memory by an actual implementation. As we will see later in this section, this is actually confirmed by experiments with our prototype implementation.

For example, the graph shows that if $m_\mathcal{D} = 16$ and $k = 4$ ($\sigma = 1/1000$) then we need less than 128 Mb. Notice that the space requirements are also linearly dependent on $1/\sigma$. Hence, in the previous example, if $\sigma = 1/100$ then we need only ≈ 13 Mb in order to compute the exact set of all frequent 6-itemsets. These results are obtained by using an hashtable for *KSP* which requires 40 bytes per cell and a load factor of 0.75 (it is the only data structure used in Algorithm 2).

We believe that these results are quite satisfactory. Notice that they *do not depend on the size of the dataset or the number of possible items* (except for a necessary logarithmic factor due to the number of bits required for the counters) but only on σ, $m_\mathcal{D}$ and k.

Furthermore, although the proposed algorithm scales polynomially in the size of the maximal transaction, if the dataset is sufficiently sparse it is possible to divide the transactions into two groups: a small group with the large transactions, and a large group where the proposed algorithm can be applied, containing short transactions. If the former group is small enough, the parameters of the iceberg algorithm would only need to be modified slightly, and the filtering pass would use the original parameter to select the actual frequent itemsets.

We also carried on a set of experiments in order to compare the scalability of our algorithm with the state-of-the-art algorithms FPGrowth [5], Eclat [13], Relim [16] and the well-known Apriori [6]. We generated an artificial dataset Retail-like, by replicating the Retail dataset (from the FIMI Repository [14]) and by inserting 2 different items in each transaction, with the following characteristics:

Number of Transactions	12,497,500
Number of Items	16,470
Size of Largest Transaction	78
Size of Dataset	722Mb

Then, we truncated the dataset in order to limit the number of transactions at 1, 2, 3, 4 and 5 millions. Results on main memory usage are showed in Fig. 2. On a 512Mb-Ram Pentium machine, Relim was able to find 2-frequent itemsets up to 3 millions of transaction before crashing, while Apriori, FPGrowth and Eclat went up to 4 millions. Only our three-passes algorithm was able to compute all the 2-frequent itemsets in the 5 millions dataset.

Memory requirements of almost all algorithms grow linearly with the size of the dataset. This is a big problem for huge datasets, as the one we used. Even Apriori algorithm, whose space complexity doesn't really depend on the number of transactions, show to be linearly growing. This happens because in our dataset new transactions often contain new (i.e., not seen so far) pairs of items (while the number of different items is fixed). Anti-monotonicity is not very exploitable since most of items are frequent, so almost every 2-itemset is a valid candidate. Our 3-passes algorithm shows a completely different behavior, actually being the only scalable algorithm with constant memory consumption.

With respect to time performance, our algorithm, in the current unoptimized Java implementation, is slower than the other algorithms (all implemented in-

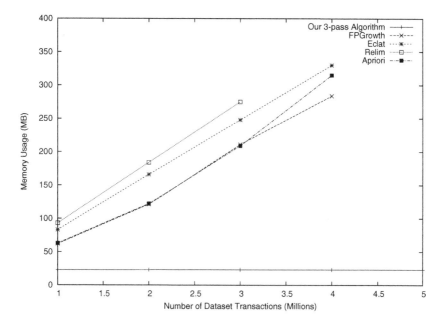

Fig. 2. Memory actually used by FIM Algorithms ($\sigma = 1/100$)

dependently in C), but it comes out to be very scalable, by requiring 21 minutes for the 1 million dataset, and 41 minutes for the 2 millions dataset. We also noted that in all FIM algorithms we tested running time are very related with memory used and available.

7 Frequent k-Itemset Mining over Streams

In this section we describe how to exploit the above results in the case of *Stream Mining*. We assume to have a stream of transactions and we want to compute k-itemset that appear at least $\sigma\%$ times over the stream. Once we access a transaction, we cannot access to the previous one; in other words, the stream can be read only once, sequentially. Every problem over streams can be trivially reduced to the non-stream version by assuming to have enough memory to store the whole stream. Unfortunately, this assumption is not acceptable in most of the practical stream problems, rather impossible in some cases, since the stream is potentially infinitely long. Therefore, in the case of frequent itemset mining over streams, only online (i.e., 1-pass) algorithms are acceptable. Another common requirement in data stream algorithms is the ability to show anytime partial results (computed over the part of stream analyzed so far).

In Section 5 we showed (Corollary 2) that space complexity of exact online σ-frequent itemset mining problems is $\Omega(|\mathcal{I}|^2)$. As we mentioned, this means that only approximated algorithms are good for online σ-frequent itemset mining problems. The last part of the stream is usually more interesting since it contains the most recent trends in the stream itself. Many online algorithms are based on sliding windows, i.e., they compute the frequent (k-)itemsets over the last l transactions read so far (i.e., windows of size l), where l is a constant that depends on the memory available.

The following is an adaptation of our Algorithm 2 presented in Section 4 that is able to mine frequent k-itemsets online (over a stream), with the guarantee to compute the results considering a window with size proportional to the length of the stream read so far (not only a window of constant size).

Algorithm 3. Online Stream Mining Algorithm

Input: $\mathcal{S}, \sigma, k, m_\mathcal{D}$
Output: $\mathcal{F}_k(\sigma, \mathcal{S})$, $count(I)$ $\forall I \in \mathcal{F}_k(\sigma, \mathcal{D})$
1: $KSP.threshold \leftarrow \frac{\sigma}{\binom{m_\mathcal{D}}{k}}$;
2: $KSP.init$;
3: $current \leftarrow 1$;
4: $window\_size \leftarrow 1$;
5: **while** true **do**
6:     **for** $i : 1$ **to** $window\_size$ **do**
7:         use $\mathcal{S}[current]$ with our Pass1;
8:         $current \leftarrow current + 1$;
9:     **for** $i : 1$ **to** $window\_size$ **do**
10:        use $\mathcal{S}[current]$ with our Pass2;
11:        $current \leftarrow current + 1$;
12:    $window\_size \leftarrow 2 \cdot window\_size$;

Our *Online Stream Mining Algorithm* (Algorithm 3) alternates *Pass 1* and *Pass 2* of Algorithm 3 over exponential growing windows. First, a window of size 1 (i.e., only one transaction is considered) is used, applying Pass 1. Then the second transaction is read, applying Pass 2. Now the window size is doubled, and Pass 1 is applied to the next two transactions (transactions 3 and 4), then Pass 2 to transactions 5 and 6.

8   Conclusions and Future Work

We presented an algorithm to compute the exact set of frequent k-itemsets (and their counts) on a given dataset, with reasonable space requirements under the hypothesis that the dataset is sparse. The algorithm is obtained by transforming the set of transactions into streams of k-itemsets and by using an algorithm for iceberg queries in order to compute the output. As far as space complexity is concerned, the algorithm requires an acceptable amount of main memory even for huge datasets, as shown in the paper. We have actually implemented a first, non-optimized version of the algorithm, i.e. without making use of specific (e.g., compressed) data structures. Some experiments on concrete (sparse) datasets are encouraging also as far as time complexity is concerned, showing the effectiveness of the algorithm.

We plan to implement an optimized version of our algorithm that is able to compute all the frequent itemsets with only two passes (having the maximum transaction length in input), running some instances of the current version of the algorithm for different values of k, but saving memory because of the redundancies among different instances (e.g., if the 3-itemset $\{(a, b, c)\}$ is frequent we do not need to store that also the 2-itemsets $\{(a, b), (a, c), (b, c)\}$ are frequent).

Moreover, we plan to study hybrid algorithms which exploit our approach for the first few steps of a level-wise algorithm à la *Apriori*. For example, we can determine in advance suitable bounds for k which ensure that the amount of memory required by our algorithm keeps reasonable in computing x-itemsets, for each level $x \leq k$. Then, we can continue the generation of frequent h-itemsets, for $h > k$, by using a standard level-wise approach. Notice that, for each $x < k$ we can even adopt a simpler version of our algorithm, which performs only the first pass through the dataset (i.e., computing supersets of frequent x-itemsets).

Finally, from the theoretical point of view, we believe that the FIM to IQ transformation presented in the paper can also be useful to get theoretical results on the trade-off between memory requirements and number of passes over the dataset in the FIM problem. Further work is still needed in this respect.

Acknowledgments. The authors wish to thank the three anonymous reviewers of *KDID05* for their useful comments and suggestions.

References

1. Hipp, J., Güntzer, U., Nakhaeizadeh, G.: Algorithms for association rule mining – a general survey and comparison. SIGKDD Explorations **2** (2000) 58–64
2. Goethals, B.: Survey on frequent pattern mining (2003)
3. Li, W., Han, J., Pei, J.: CMAR: Accurate and efficient classification based on multiple class-association rules. In: International Conference on Data Mining. (2001) 369–376
4. Han, E.H., Karypis, G., Kumar, V., Mobasher, B.: Clustering based on association rule hypergraphs. In: Research Issues on Data Mining and Knowledge Discovery. (1997)
5. Han, J., Pei, J., Yin, Y.: Mining frequent patterns without candidate generation. In Chen, W., Naughton, J.F., Bernstein, P.A., eds.: Proceedings of the 2000 ACM SIGMOD International Conference on Management of Data, May 16-18, 2000, Dallas, Texas, USA, ACM (2000) 1–12
6. Agrawal, R., Srikant, R.: Fast algorithms for mining association rules. In Bocca, J.B., Jarke, M., Zaniolo, C., eds.: Proc. 20th Int. Conf. Very Large Data Bases, VLDB, Morgan Kaufmann (1994) 487–499
7. Karp, R.M., Shenker, S., Papadimitriou, C.H.: A simple algorithm for finding frequent elements in streams and bags. In: Proceedings of the ACM PODS 2003. Volume 28., ACM (2003)
8. Savasere, A., Omiecinski, E., Navathe, S.B.: An efficient algorithm for mining association rules in large databases. In: The VLDB Journal. (1995) 432–444
9. Toivonen, H.: Sampling large databases for association rules. In Vijayaraman, T.M., Buchmann, A.P., Mohan, C., Sarda, N.L., eds.: In Proc. 1996 Int. Conf. Very Large Data Bases, Morgan Kaufman (1996) 134–145

10. Chen, B., Haas, P., Scheuermann, P.: A new two-phase sampling based algorithm for discovering association rules. In: Proceedings of the eighth ACM SIGKDD international conference on Knowledge discovery and data mining, ACM Press (2002) 462–468
11. B. Chen, P.J. Haas, P.S.: Fast: A new sampling-based algorithm for discovering association rules. In: 18th International Conference on Data Engineering. (2002)
12. Goethals, B.: Memory issues in frequent itemset mining. In: Proceedings of the 2004 ACM Symposium on Applied Computing (SAC'04), Nicosia, Cyprus, March 14 –17, 2004, ACM (2004)
13. Zaki, M.J.: Scalable algorithms for association mining. In: IEEE Transactions on Knowledge and Data Engineering, ACM Press (2000) 372–390
14. Goethals, B., Zaki, M.J., eds.: FIMI '03, Frequent Itemset Mining Implementations, Proceedings of the ICDM 2003, Workshop on Frequent Itemset Mining Implementations, 19 December 2003, Melbourne, Florida, USA. In Goethals, B., Zaki, M.J., eds.: FIMI. Volume 90 of CEUR Workshop Proceedings., CEUR-WS.org (2003)
15. Bonchi, F., Giannotti, F., Mazzanti, A., Pedreschi, D.: Examiner: Optimized level-wise frequent pattern mining with monotone constraint. In: International Conference on Data Mining 2003, Melbourne, Florida, USA. (2003) 11–18
16. Borgelt, C.: Keeping things simple: Finding frequent item sets by recursive elimination. In: Workshop Open Software for Data Mining, on Frequent Pattern Mining Implementations (OSDM05), Chicago, IL, USA. (2005)

Constraint-Based Mining of Fault-Tolerant Patterns from Boolean Data

Jérémy Besson[1,2], Ruggero G. Pensa[1], Céline Robardet[3],
and Jean-François Boulicaut[1]

[1] INSA Lyon, LIRIS CNRS UMR 5205, F-69621 Villeurbanne cedex, France
[2] UMR INRA/INSERM 1235, F-69372 Lyon cedex 08, France
[3] INSA Lyon, PRISMA, F-69621 Villeurbanne cedex, France
{Firstname.Name}@insa-lyon.fr

Abstract. Thanks to an important research effort during the last few years, inductive queries on local patterns (e.g., set patterns) and their associated complete solvers have been proved extremely useful to support knowledge discovery. The more we use such queries on real-life data, e.g., biological data, the more we are convinced that inductive queries should return fault-tolerant patterns. This is obviously the case when considering formal concept discovery from noisy datasets. Therefore, we study various extensions of this kind of bi-set towards fault-tolerance. We compare three declarative specifications of fault-tolerant bi-sets by means of a constraint-based mining approach. Our framework enables a better understanding of the needed trade-off between extraction feasibility, completeness, relevance, and ease of interpretation of these fault-tolerant patterns. An original empirical evaluation on both synthetic and real-life medical data is given. It enables a comparison of the various proposals and it motivates further directions of research.

1 Introduction

According to the inductive database approach, mining queries can be expressed declaratively in terms of constraints on the desired patterns or models [16, 10, 6]. Thanks to an important research effort the last few years, inductive queries on local patterns (e.g., set or sequential patterns) and complete solvers which can evaluate them on large datasets (Boolean or sequence databases) have been proved extremely useful. Properties of constraints have been studied in depth (e.g., monotonicity, succinctness, convertibility) and sophisticated pruning strategies enable to compute complete answer sets for many constraints (i.e., Boolean combination of primitive constraints) of practical interest. However, the more we use these techniques on intrinsically dirty and noisy real-life data, e.g., biological or medical data, the more we are convinced that inductive queries should return fault-tolerant patterns. One interesting direction of research is to introduce softness w.r.t. constraint satisfaction [1, 5]. We consider in this paper another direction leading to crispy constraints in which fault-tolerance is declaratively specified.

F. Bonchi and J.-F. Boulicaut (Eds.): KDID 2005, LNCS 3933, pp. 55–71, 2006.
© Springer-Verlag Berlin Heidelberg 2006

Table 1. A Boolean context $\mathbf{r}_1$

	g_1	g_2	g_3	g_4	g_5	g_6	g_7
t_1	1	0	1	0	1	0	0
t_2	1	1	1	1	0	1	0
t_3	0	1	1	1	1	1	1
t_4	0	0	0	1	1	1	0
t_5	1	0	0	0	0	1	0
t_6	1	1	1	1	1	0	0
t_7	1	1	1	1	1	0	0

Our starting point is the fundamental limitation of formal concept (i.e., connected closed sets) discovery from noisy data. Formal concept analysis has been
developed for more than two decades [24] as a way to extract knowledge from
Boolean datasets. Informally, formal concepts are maximal bi-sets/rectangles of
true values[1]. For instance, Table 1 is a toy example dataset $\mathbf{r}_1$ and the bi-set
$(\{t_6, t_7\}, \{g_1, g_2, g_3, g_4, g_5\})$ is a formal concept in $\mathbf{r}_1$.

Some algorithms are dedicated to the computation of complete collections of
formal concepts [17]. Since, by construction, formal concepts are built on closed
sets, the extensive research on (frequent) closed set computation (see [15] for a
survey) has obviously opened new application domains for formal concept discovery. When considering very large and/or dense Boolean matrices, constraint-
based mining of formal concepts has been studied [23, 4]: every formal concept
which furthermore satisfies some other user-defined constraints is computed. For
example, we can extract formal concepts with minimal size constraints for both
set components. Given our previous example, if we want formal concepts with
at least 3 elements in each set, the formal concept $(\{t_3, t_6, t_7\}, \{g_2, g_3, g_4, g_5\})$
satisfies the constraint whereas $(\{t_6, t_7\}, \{g_1, g_2, g_3, g_4, g_5\})$ does not.

A formal concept associates a maximal set of objects to a maximal set of
properties which are all in relation. Such an association is often too strong in real-
world data. Even though the extraction might remain tractable, the needed post-
processing and interpretation phases turn out to be tedious or even impossible.
Indeed, in noisy data, not only the number of formal concepts explodes but
also many of them are not relevant enough. It has motivated new directions
of research where interesting bi-sets are considered as dense rectangles of true
values [2, 14, 13, 3, 19].

In this paper, we consider a constraint-based mining approach for relevant
fault-tolerant formal concept mining. We decided to look for an adequate formalization for three of our recent proposals (i.e., CBS [2], FBS [19], and DRBS
[3]) which have been motivated by a declarative specification for fault-tolerance.
We do not provide the algorithms which have been recently published for solving
inductive queries on such patterns [2, 19, 3]. The contribution of this paper is to
propose a simple framework to support a better understanding of the needed

---

[1] We might say combinatorial rectangles since it is up to arbitrary permutations of
rows and columns in the Boolean matrix.

trade-off between extraction feasibility, completeness, relevance, and ease of interpretation of these various pattern types. This formalization enables to predict part of the behavior of the associated solvers and some formal properties can be established. An original empirical evaluation on both synthetic and real-life medical data is given. It enables to compare the pros and cons of each proposal. An outcome of these experiments is that fault-tolerant bi-set mining is possible. Used in conjunction with other user-defined constraints, it should support the dissemination of relevant local set pattern discovery techniques for intrinsically noisy data.

Section 2 provides the needed definitions. Section 3 presents a discussion on some important properties that fault-tolerant bi-set mining should satisfy. Section 4 provides not only experimental results on synthetic data when various levels of noise are added but also experiments on a real-life medical dataset. Section 5 is a short conclusion.

2   Pattern Domains

We now define the different classes of patterns to be studied in this paper. Assume a set of objects $\mathcal{O} = \{t_1, \ldots, t_m\}$ and a set of Boolean properties $\mathcal{P} = \{g_1, \ldots, g_n\}$. The Boolean context to be mined is $\mathbf{r} \subseteq \mathcal{O} \times \mathcal{P}$, where $r_{ij} = 1$ if property g_j is satisfied by object t_i, 0 otherwise. Formally, a bi-set is an element (X, Y) where $X \subseteq \mathcal{O}$ and $Y \subseteq \mathcal{P}$. $\mathcal{L} = 2^{\mathcal{O}} \times 2^{\mathcal{P}}$ denotes the search space for bi-sets. We say that a bi-set (X, Y) is included in a bi-set (X', Y') (denoted $(X, Y) \subseteq (X', Y')$) iff $(X \subseteq X' \wedge Y \subseteq Y')$.

Definition 1. *Let us denote by $\mathcal{Z}_l(x, Y)$ the number of false values of a row x on the columns in Y: $\mathcal{Z}_l(x, Y) = \sharp\{y \in Y | (x, y) \notin \mathbf{r}\}$ where $\sharp$ denotes the cardinality of a set. Similarly, $\mathcal{Z}_c(y, X) = \sharp\{x \in X | (x, y) \notin \mathbf{r}\}$ denotes the number of false values of a column y on the rows in X.*

Let us now give an original definition of formal concepts (see, e.g., [24] for a classical one). Sub-constraint 2.1 expresses that a formal concept contains only true values. Sub-constraint 2.2 denotes that formal concept relevancy is enhanced by a maximality property.

Definition 2 (FC). *A bi-set $(X, Y) \in \mathcal{L}$ is a formal concept in $\mathbf{r}$ iff*
(2.1) $\forall x \in X, \mathcal{Z}_l(x, Y) = 0 \ \wedge \ \forall y \in Y, \mathcal{Z}_c(y, X) = 0$
(2.2) $\forall x \in \mathcal{O} \setminus X, \mathcal{Z}_l(x, Y) \geq 1 \ \wedge \ \forall y \in \mathcal{P} \setminus Y, \mathcal{Z}_c(y, X) \geq 1.$

Example 1. *Given $\mathbf{r}_1$, we have $\mathcal{Z}_l(t_6, \{g_4, g_5, g_6\}) = 1$ and $\mathcal{Z}_c(g_5, \mathcal{O}) = 2$. $(\{t_3, t_4, t_6, t_7\}, \{g_4, g_5\})$ and $(\{t_3, t_4\}, \{g_4, g_5, g_6\})$ are FC patterns (see Table 2).*

Let us now define the so-called DRBS, CBS and FBS fault tolerant patterns.

Definition 3 (DRBS [3]). *Given integer parameters δ and ϵ, a bi-set $(X, Y) \in \mathcal{L}$ is called a DRBS pattern (Dense and Relevant Bi-Set) in $\mathbf{r}$ iff*

Table 2. A row permutation on $\mathbf{r}_1$ to illustrate Example 1

	g_1	g_2	g_3	g_4	g_5	g_6	g_7
t_3	0	1	1	1	1	1	1
t_4	0	0	0	1	1	1	0
t_6	1	1	1	1	1	0	0
t_7	1	1	1	1	1	0	0
t_1	1	0	1	0	1	0	0
t_2	1	1	1	1	0	1	0
t_5	1	0	0	0	0	1	0

(3.1) $\forall x \in X,\ \mathcal{Z}_l(x, Y) \leq \delta\ \wedge\ \forall y \in Y,\ \mathcal{Z}_c(y, X) \leq \delta$

(3.2) $\forall e \in \mathcal{O} \setminus X,\ \forall x \in X,\ \mathcal{Z}_l(e, Y) \geq \mathcal{Z}_l(x, Y) + \epsilon$
$\wedge\ \forall e' \in \mathcal{P} \setminus Y,\ \forall y \in Y,\ \mathcal{Z}_c(e', X) \geq \mathcal{Z}_c(y, X) + \epsilon$

(3.3) It is maximal, i.e., $\nexists (X', Y') \in \mathcal{L}$ s.t. (X', Y') is a DRBS pattern and $(X, Y) \subseteq (X', Y')$.

DRBS patterns have at most δ false values per row and per column (Sub-constraint 3.1) and are such that each outside row (resp. column) has at least ϵ false values plus the maximal number of false values on the inside rows (resp. columns) according to Sub-constraint 3.2. The size of a DRBS pattern increases with δ such that when $\delta > 0$, it happens that several bi-sets are included in each other. Only maximal bi-sets are kept (Sub-constraint 3.3). Notice that δ and ϵ can take different values on rows and on columns.

Property 1. When $\delta = 0$ and $\epsilon = 1$, DRBS $\equiv$ FC.

Example 2. If $\delta = \epsilon = 1$, $(X, Y) = (\{t_1, t_2, t_3, t_4, t_6, t_7\}, \{g_3, g_4, g_5\})$ is a DRBS pattern in $\mathbf{r}_1$. Columns g_1, g_2, g_6 and g_7 contain at least two false values on X, and t_5 contains three false values on Y (see Table 3).

Table 3. A row permutation on $\mathbf{r}_1$ to illustrate Example 2

	g_1	g_2	g_3	g_4	g_5	g_6	g_7
t_1	1	0	1	0	1	0	0
t_2	1	1	1	1	0	1	0
t_3	0	1	1	1	1	1	1
t_4	0	0	0	1	1	1	0
t_6	1	1	1	1	1	0	0
t_7	1	1	1	1	1	0	0
t_5	1	0	0	0	0	1	0

The whole collection of DRBS can be computed (in rather small datasets) by using the correct and complete algorithm DR-MINER described in [3]. It is a generic algorithm for bi-set constraint-based mining which is an adaptation of DUAL-MINER [9]. It is based on an enumeration strategy of bi-sets which enables efficient anti-monotonic and monotonic pruning (Sub-constraint 3.1 in conjunction with other user-defined constraints which have monotonicity properties), and partial pruning for Sub-constraint 3.2. Sub-constraint 3.3 is checked in a post-processing phase.

We now consider a preliminary approach for specifying symmetrical fault-tolerant formal concepts. Indeed, DRBS class has been designed afterwards.

Definition 4 (CBS [2]). *Given an integer parameter δ, a bi-set $(X, Y) \in \mathcal{L}$ is called a* CBS *pattern (Consistent Bi-Set) iff*

(4.1) $\forall x \in X,\ \mathcal{Z}_l(x, Y) \leq \delta \ \wedge \ \forall y \in Y,\ \mathcal{Z}_c(y, X) \leq \delta$

(4.2) No row (resp. column) outside (X, Y) is identical to a row (resp. column) inside (X, Y)

(4.3) It is maximal, i.e., $\nexists (X', Y') \in \mathcal{L}$ s.t. (X', Y') is a CBS pattern and $(X, Y) \subseteq (X', Y')$.

Notice that again, parameter δ can be chosen with different values on rows and on columns.

Example 3. *If $\delta = 1$, $(X, Y) = (\{t_1, t_2, t_3, t_6, t_7\}, \{g_1, g_3, g_5\})$ is a CBS pattern in $\mathbf{r}_1$. Columns g_6 and g_7 contain more than one false value on X, t_4 and t_5 contain more than one false value on Y. g_2 and g_4 contain only one false value, but as they are identical on X, either we add both or they are both excluded. As there are two false values on t_1, we do not add them (see Table 4).*

Table 4. A row and column permutation on $\mathbf{r}_1$ to illustrate Example 3

	g_1	g_3	g_5	g_2	g_4	g_6	g_7
t_1	1	1	1	0	0	0	0
t_2	1	1	0	1	1	1	0
t_3	0	1	1	1	1	1	1
t_6	1	1	1	1	1	0	0
t_7	1	1	1	1	1	0	0
t_4	0	0	1	0	1	1	0
t_5	1	0	0	0	0	1	0

Property 2. *When $\delta = 0$, CBS $\equiv$ FC. Furthermore, when $\epsilon = 1$, each DRBS pattern is included in one of the CBS patterns.*

In [2], the authors propose an algorithm for computing CBS patterns by merging formal concepts which have been extracted beforehand. The obtained bi-sets are then processed to keep only the maximal ones having less than δ false values per row and per column. This principle is however incomplete: every bi-set which satisfies the above constraints can not be extracted by this principle. In other terms, some CBS patterns can not be obtained as a merge between two formal concepts. CBS patterns might be extracted by a straightforward adaptation of the DR-MINER generic algorithm but the price to pay for completeness would be too expensive.

Let us finally consider another extension of formal concepts which is not symmetrical. It has been designed thanks to some previous work on one of the few approximate condensed representations of frequent sets, the so-called δ-free sets [7, 8]. δ-free sets are well-specified sets whose counted frequencies enable to infer the frequency of many sets (sets included in their so-called δ-closures) without further counting but with a bounded error. When $\delta = 0$, the 0-closure on a 0-free set X is the classical closure and it provides a closed set. The idea is to consider bi-sets built on δ-free sets with the intuition that it will provide strong associations between sets of rows and sets of columns. It has been introduced for the first time in [19] as a potentially interesting local pattern type for bi-cluster characterization.

Providing details on δ-freeness and δ-closures is beyond the objective of this paper (see [7, 8] for details). We just give here an intuitive definition of these notions. A set $Y \subseteq \mathcal{P}$ is δ-free for a positive integer δ if its absolute frequency in $\mathbf{r}$ differs from the frequency of all its strict subsets by at least $\delta + 1$. For instance, in $\mathbf{r}_1$, $\{g_2\}$ is a 1-free set. The δ-closure of a set $Y \subseteq \mathcal{P}$ is the superset Z of Y such that every added property ($\in Z \setminus Y$) is almost always true for the objects which satisfy the properties from Y: at most δ false values are enabled. For instance, the 1-closure of $\{g_2\}$ is $\{g_1, g_2, g_3, g_4, g_5\}$. It is possible to consider bi-sets which can be built on δ-free sets and their δ-closures on one hand, on the sets of objects which support the δ-free set on the properties on the other hand.

Definition 5 (FBS). *A bi-set $(X, Y) \in \mathcal{L}$ is a FBS pattern (Free-set based Bi-Set) iff Y can be decomposed into $Y = K \cup C$ such that K is a δ-free set in $\mathbf{r}$, C is its associated δ-closure and $X = \{t \in \mathcal{O} \mid \forall k \in K, (t, k) \in \mathbf{r}\}$. By construction, $\forall y \in Y, \mathcal{Z}_c(y, X) \leq \delta$ and $\forall y \in K, \mathcal{Z}_c(y, X) = 0$.*

Property 3. *When $\delta = 0$, FBS $\equiv$ FC.*

Example 4. *If $\delta = 1$, $\{g_2\}$ is a δ-free set and $(\{t_2, t_3, t_6, t_7\}, \{g_1, g_2, g_3, g_4, g_5\})$ is a FBS pattern in $\mathbf{r}_1$. Another one is $(\{t_3, t_4\}, \{g_2, g_3, g_4, g_5, g_6, g_7\})$. Notice that we get at most one false value per column but we have three false values on t_4 (see Table 5).*

Table 5. A row permutation on $\mathbf{r}_1$ to illustrate Example 4

	g_1	g_2	g_3	g_4	g_5	g_6	g_7
t_2	1	1	1	1	0	1	0
t_3	0	1	1	1	1	1	1
t_6	1	1	1	1	1	0	0
t_7	1	1	1	1	1	0	0
t_1	1	0	1	0	1	0	0
t_4	0	0	0	1	1	1	0
t_5	1	0	0	0	0	1	0

The extraction of FBS can be extremely efficient thanks to δ-freeness anti-monotonicity. The implementation described in [8] can be straightforwardly extended to output FBS patterns. Notice that FBS patterns are bi-sets with a bounded number of exception per column but every bi-set with a bounded number of exception per column is not necessarily a FBS pattern. An example of a bi-set with at most 1 false value per column which is not a FBS pattern in $\mathbf{r}_1$ is $(\{t_1, t_2, t_3, t_4, t_6, t_7\}, \{g_3, g_4, g_5\})$.

3 Discussion

This section discusses the desired properties for formal concept extensions towards fault-tolerant patterns. It enables to consider the pros and the cons of the available proposals and to better understand related open problems.

- **Fault tolerance:** Can we control the number of false values inside the bi-sets?
- **Relevancy:** Are they consistent w.r.t. the outside rows and columns? At least two views on consistency exist. We might say that a bi-set B is weakly consistent if it is maximal and if we have no row (resp. column) outside B identical to one row (resp. column) inside B. B is called strongly consistent if we have no row (resp. column) outside B with at most the same number of false values than one row (resp. column) of B.
- **Ease of interpretation:** For each bi-set (X, Y), does it exist a function which associates X and Y or even better a Galois connection? If a function exists which associates to each set X (resp. Y) at most a unique set Y (resp. X), the interpretation of each bi-set is much easier. Furthermore, it is interesting that such functions are monotonically decreasing, i.e., when the size of X (resp. Y) increases, the size of its associated set Y (resp. X) decreases. Such a property is meaningful: the more we have rows inside a bi-set, the less there are columns that can be associated to describe them (or vice versa). One of the appreciated properties of formal concepts is clearly the existence of such functions. If $f_1(X, \mathbf{r}) = \{g \in \mathcal{P} \mid \forall t \in X, (t, g) \in \mathbf{r}\}$ and $f_2(Y, \mathbf{r}) = \{t \in \mathcal{O} \mid \forall g \in Y, (t, g) \in \mathbf{r}\}$, (f_1, f_2) is a Galois connection between $\mathcal{O}$ and $\mathcal{P}$: f_1 and f_2 are decreasing functions w.r.t. set inclusion.
- **Completeness and efficiency**: Can we compute the whole collection of specified bi-sets, i.e., can we ensure a completeness w.r.t. the specified constraints? Is it tractable in practice?

The formal concepts satisfy these properties except the first one. Indeed, we have an explicit Galois connection which enables to compute the complete collection in many datasets of interest. These bi-sets are maximal and consistent but they are not fault-tolerant.

In a FBS pattern, the number of false values are only bounded on columns. The definition of this pattern is not symmetrical. They are not strongly consistent because we can have rows outside the bi-set with the same number of false values than a row inside (one of this false value must be on the δ-free set supporting set). On the columns, the property is satisfied. These bi-sets are however weakly consistent. There is no function from column to row sets (e.g., using $\delta = 1$ in $\mathbf{r}_1$, $(\{t_2, t_6, t_7\}, \{g_1, g_2, g_3, g_4, g_5\})$ and $(\{t_1, t_6, t_7\}, \{g_1, g_2, g_3, g_4, g_5\})$ are two FBS with the same set of columns, see Table 6 left). However, we have

Table 6. Illustration of the lack of function for FBS (left) and CBS (right)

	g_1	g_2	g_3	g_4	g_5	g_6	g_7
t_1	1	0	1	0	1	0	0
t_6	1	1	1	1	1	0	0
t_7	1	1	1	1	1	0	0
t_2	1	1	1	1	0	1	0
t_3	0	1	1	1	1	1	1
t_4	0	0	0	1	1	1	0
t_5	1	0	0	0	0	1	0

	g_2	g_3	g_4	g_1
t_1	0	1	0	1
t_2	1	1	1	1
t_3	1	1	1	0
t_4	0	0	1	0

a function between $2^\mathcal{O}$ to $2^\mathcal{P}$. In many datasets, including huge and dense ones, complete collections of FBS can be extracted efficiently. Further research is needed for a better characterization of more relevant FBS patterns which might remain easy to extract from huge databases, e.g., what is the impact of different δ-thresholds for the δ-free-set part and the δ-closure computation? how can we avoid an unfortunate distribution of the false values among the same rows?

CBS are symmetrical on rows and columns. Indeed, the number of exceptions is bounded on rows and on columns. CBS are weakly consistent but not strongly consistent (see Example 3). There are neither a function from $2^\mathcal{O}$ to $2^\mathcal{P}$ nor from $2^\mathcal{P}$ to $2^\mathcal{O}$ (e.g., $(\{t_1, t_2, t_3, t_4\}, \{g_1, g_3, g_4\})$ and $(\{t_1, t_2, t_3, t_4\}, \{g_2, g_3, g_4\})$ are two CBS with $\delta = 2$ having the same set of rows in Table 6 right). According to the implementation in [2], extracting these patterns can be untractable even in rather small datasets and this extraction strategy is not complete w.r.t. the specified constraints.

By definition, a DRBS has a bounded number of exceptions per row and per column and they are strongly consistent. Two new properties can be considered.

Property 4 (Existence of functions ϕ and ψ on DRBS ($\epsilon > 0$)). *For $\epsilon > 0$, DRBS patterns are embedded by two functions ϕ (resp. ψ) which associate to X (resp. Y) a unique set Y (resp. X).*

Property 5 (Monotonicity of ϕ and ψ on DRBS (δ fixed)). *Let $\mathcal{L}_{\delta,\epsilon}$ the collection of DRBS patterns and $\mathcal{L}'_{\tau\tau'}$ the subset of $\mathcal{L}_{\delta,\epsilon}$ s.t. $(X, Y) \in \mathcal{L}'_{\tau\tau'}$ iff (X, Y) contains at least a row (resp. column) with τ (resp. τ') false values in Y (resp. X), and such that no row (resp. column) contains more. Then, ϕ and ψ are decreasing functions on $\mathcal{L}'_{\tau\tau'}$.*

Unfortunately, the functions loose this property on the whole DRBS collection. Furthermore, we did not identified yet an intensional definition of these functions. As a result, it leads to a quite expensive computation of the complete collection. Looking for such functions is clearly one of the main challenges for further work.

4   Related Work

There are only few papers which propose definitions of set patterns with exceptions. To the best of our knowledge, most of the related work has concerned mono-dimensional patterns and/or the use of heuristic techniques. In [25], the frequent set mining task is extended towards fault-tolerance: given a threshold ϵ, an itemset P holds in a transaction X iff $\sharp(X \cap P) \geq (1-\epsilon)\sharp P$, where $\sharp X$ denotes the size of X. A level-wise algorithm is proposed but their fault-tolerant property is not anti-monotonic while this is crucially needed to achieve tractability. Therefore, [25] provides a greedy algorithm leading to an incomplete computation. [22] revisits this work and it looks for an anti-monotonic constraint such that a level-wise algorithm can provide every set whose density of 1 values is greater than δ in at least σ situations. Anti-monotonicity is obtained by enforcing that every subset of extracted sets satisfies the constraint as well. The extension of such dense sets to dense bi-sets is difficult: the connection which associates objects to properties and vice-versa is not decreasing while this is an appreciated property of formal concepts.

Instead of using a relative density definition, [18] considers an absolute threshold to define fault-tolerant frequent patterns: given a threshold δ, a set of columns P, such that $\sharp P > \delta$, holds in a row X iff $\sharp(X \cap P) \geq \sharp P - \delta$. To ensure that the support is significant for each column, they use a minimum support threshold per column beside the classical minimum support. Thus, each row of an extracted pattern contains less than δ false values and each column contains more true values than the given minimum support for each column. This definition is not symmetrical and the more the support increases, the less the patterns are relevant.

In [14], the authors are interested in geometrical tiles (i.e., dense bi-sets which involve contiguous elements given predefined orders on both dimensions). To extract them, they propose a local optimization algorithm which is not deterministic and thus can not guarantee the global quality of the extracted patterns. The hypothesis on built-in orders can not be accepted on many Boolean datasets.

Co-clustering (or bi-clustering) can be also applied to extract fault-tolerant bi-clusters [11, 20] from boolean data. It provides linked partitions on both dimensions and tend to compute rectangles with mainly true (resp. false) values. Heuristic techniques (i.e., local optimization) enable to compute one bi-partition, i.e., a quite restrictive collection of dense bi-sets. In fact, bi-clustering provides a global structure over the data while fault-tolerant formal concepts are typical local patterns. In other terms, these bi-sets are relevant but they constitute a quite restrictive collection of dense bi-sets which lack from formal properties.

5   Empirical Evaluation

In this section we investigate on the added-value of fault-tolerant pattern mining by considering experiments on both synthetic and "real world" data. For each experiment, we compare the formal concept mining algorithm output with the fault-tolerant approaches. The goal is not to assess the supremacy of a single class over the other ones, but to present an overview of the principal pros and cons of each approach in practical applications. First, we process artificially noised datasets to extract formal concepts and the three types of fault-tolerant bi-sets.

Then, we mine a "real world" medical dataset to get various collections of bi-sets for different parameters. Besides evaluating the performances and the size of the collections, we analyze the relevancy of the extracted bi-sets.

5.1 Experiments on Artificially Noised Data

Let us first discuss the evaluation method. We call $\mathbf{r}_2$ a reference data set, i.e., a dataset which is supposed to be noise free and contains built-in patterns. Then, we derive various datasets from it by adding some quantity of uniform random noise (i.e., for a X% noise level, each value is randomly changed with a probability of X%). Our goal is to compare the collection of formal concepts holding in the reference dataset with several collections of fault-tolerant formal concepts extracted from the noised matrices.

To measure the relevancy of each extracted collection $(\mathcal{C}_e)$ w.r.t the reference one $(\mathcal{C}_r)$, we test the presence of a subset of the reference collection in each of them. Since both sets of objects and properties of each formal concept can be changed when noise is introduced, we identify those having the largest area in common with the reference. Our measure, called σ, takes into account the common area and is defined as follows:

$$\sigma(\mathcal{C}_r, \mathcal{C}_e) = \frac{\rho(\mathcal{C}_r, \mathcal{C}_e) + \rho(\mathcal{C}_e, \mathcal{C}_r)}{2}$$

where ρ is computed as follows:

$$\rho(\mathcal{C}_1, \mathcal{C}_2) = \frac{1}{\sharp \mathcal{C}_1} \sum_{(X_i, Y_i) \in \mathcal{C}_1} \max_{(X_j, Y_j) \in \mathcal{C}_2} \frac{\sharp(X_i \cap X_j) + \sharp(Y_i \cap Y_j)}{\sharp(X_i \cup X_j) + \sharp(Y_i \cup Y_j)}$$

Here, $\mathcal{C}_r$ is the collection of formal concepts computed on the reference dataset, $\mathcal{C}_e$ is a collection of patterns in a noised dataset. When $\rho(\mathcal{C}_r, \mathcal{C}_e) = 1$, all the bi-sets belonging to $\mathcal{C}_r$ have identical instances in the collection $\mathcal{C}_e$. Analogously, when $\rho(\mathcal{C}_e, \mathcal{C}_r) = 1$, all the bi-sets belonging to $\mathcal{C}_e$ have identical instances in the collection $\mathcal{C}_r$. Indeed, when $\sigma = 1$, the two collections are identical. High values of σ, mean not only that we can find all the formal concepts of the reference collection in the noised matrix, but also that the noised collection does not contain many bi-sets that are too different from the reference ones.

In this experiment, $\mathbf{r}_2$ concerns 30 objects (rows) and 15 properties (columns) and it contains 3 formal concepts of the same size which are pair-wise disjoint. In other terms, the formal concepts in $\mathbf{r}_2$ are $(\{t_1, \ldots, t_{10}\}, \{g_1, \ldots, g_5\})$, $(\{t_{11}, \ldots, t_{20}\}, \{g_6, \ldots, g_{10}\})$, and $(\{t_{21}, \ldots, t_{30}\}, \{g_{11}, \ldots, g_{15}\})$. Then, we generated 40 different datasets by adding to $\mathbf{r}_2$ increasing quantities of noise (from 1% to 40% of the matrix). A robust technique should be able to capture the three formal concepts even in presence of noise. Therefore, for each dataset, we have extracted a collection of formal concepts and different collections of fault-tolerant patterns with different parameters. For FBS collection, we considered δ values between 1 and 6. Then we extracted two groups of CBS collections given parameter δ (resp. δ') for the maximum number of false values per row

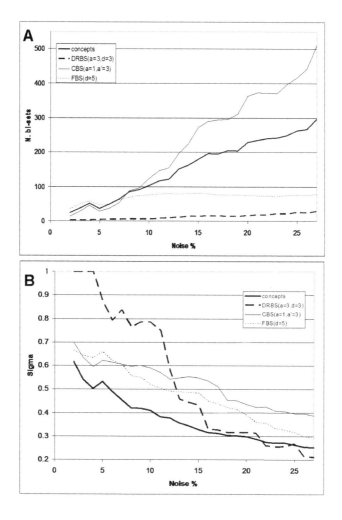

Fig. 1. Size of different collections of bi-sets and related values of σ w.r.t. noise level for all types of bi-sets

(resp. per column): one with $\delta = 1$ and $\delta' = 1\ldots3$ and the second with $\delta' = 1$ and $\delta = 1\ldots3$. Finally we extracted DRBS collections for each combination of $\delta = 1\ldots3$ and $\epsilon = 1\ldots3$.

In Fig. 1, we only report the best results w.r.t. σ for each class of patterns. Fig. 1A provides the number of extracted patterns in each collection. Fault-tolerant bi-set collections contain almost always less patterns than the collection of formal concepts. The only exception is the CBS class when $\delta = 1$. The DRBS class performs better than the other ones. The size of its collections is almost constant, even for rather high levels of noise. The discriminant parameter is ϵ. In Fig. 1B, the values of the σ measure for DRBS collections obviously decrease when the noise ratio increases. In general, every class of fault-tolerant bi-set

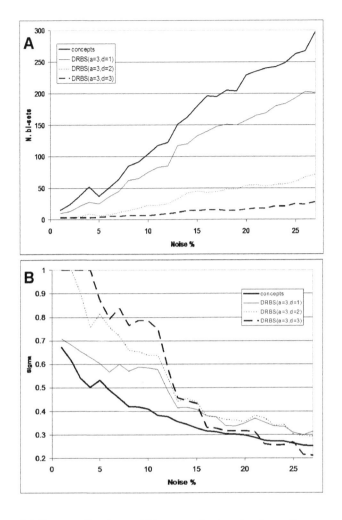

Fig. 2. Size of different collections of bi-sets and related values of σ w.r.t. noise level for different instances of DRBS collections

performs better than the formal concept one. In terms of relevancy, the DRBS pattern class gives the best results as well. Notice that the results for FBS and CBS classes are not significantly different when their parameters change. The parameter that has the greatest impact on σ value for the DRBS patterns is ϵ. For reasonable levels of noise ($< 15\%$), it makes sense to use DRBS. For higher levels, CBS and FBS perform slightly better.

In Fig. 2, we report the experiments on the extraction of DRBS collections with $\delta = 3$ and $\epsilon = 1 \dots 3$. Fig. 2A shows the number of extracted patterns. The size of the collections is drastically reduced when ϵ grows. Fig. 2B provides the σ measure for these collections. Using a higher ϵ value improves the quality of the results because less patterns are produced. When the noise level is smaller than 5%, the collection of DRBS, with $\epsilon = 2..3$, is the same as the three formal concepts holding in $\mathbf{r}_2$. This experiment confirms that fault-tolerant bi-sets are more robust to noise than formal concepts, and that the provided collection for the crucially needed expert-driven interpretation is considerably reduced.

5.2   Experiments on a Medical Dataset

It is important to get a qualitative feedback about fault-tolerant pattern relevancy in a real dataset. For this purpose, we have considered the real world medical dataset meningitis [12]. These data have been gathered from children hospitalized for acute meningitis over a period of 4 years. The pre-processed Boolean dataset is composed of 329 patients described by 60 Boolean properties encoding clinical signs (e.g., consciousness troubles), cytochemical analysis of the cerebrospinal fluid (e.g., C.S.F proteins) and blood analysis (e.g., sedimentation rate). The majority of the cases are viral infections, whereas about one quarter of the cases are caused by bacteria. It is interesting to look at the bacterial cases since they need treatment with suitable antibiotics, while for the viral cases a simple medical supervision is sufficient. A certain number of attribute-variable pairs have been identified as being characteristic of the bacterial form of meningitis [12, 21]. In other terms, the quality of the fault-tolerant patterns can be evaluated w.r.t. available medical knowledge. Our idea is that by looking for rather large fault-tolerant bi-sets, the algorithms will provide some new associations between attribute-value pairs (Boolean properties) and objects. If the whole sets of objects and properties within bi-sets are compatible (e.g., all the objects are of bacterial type, and all the properties are compatible with bacterial meningitis), then we can argue that we got new relevant information.

A straightforward approach to avoid some irrelevant patterns and to reduce the pattern collection size is to use size constraints on bi-set components. For this experiment, we enforce a minimal size of 10 for sets of objects and 5 for sets of properties. Using D-MINER [4], we computed the collection of such large enough formal concepts and we got more than 300 000 formal concepts in a

Table 7. Size and extraction time for FBS and DRBS in meningitis

Formal Concepts					
size	354 366				
time	5s				
FBS					
δ	1	2	3	4	5	6
size	141 983	67 898	39 536	25 851	18 035	13 382
time	19s	10s	6s	4s	3s	2s
DRBS (δ=1)					
ϵ	1	2	3	4	5	6
size	-	75 378	22 882	8 810	4 164	2 021
time	-	1507s	857s	424s	233s	140s

relatively short time (see Table 7). It is obviously hard to exploit such a quantity of patterns. For instance, we were not able to post-process this collection to produce CBS patterns according to [2].

Then, we tried to extract different collections of FBS and DRBS. For FBS, with $\delta = 1$ (at most one exception per column), we got a 60% reduction on the size of the computed bi-sets. Using values of δ between 2 and 6, this size is reduced at each step by a coefficient between 0.5 and 0.3. Finally, we used DR-MINER to extract different collections of DRBS. The δ parameter was set to 1 (at most one exception per row and per column) and we used the parameter ϵ to further reduce the size of the computed collection. Setting $\epsilon = 1$ leads to an untractable extraction but, with $\epsilon = 2$, the resulting collection is 80% smaller than the related formal concept collection. Moreover, with $\delta = 1$ and $\epsilon = 2$ the size of the DRBS collection is much smaller than the computed FBS collection for the same constraint (i.e., $\delta = 1$). On the other hand, computational times are sensibly higher.

We now consider relevancy issues. We have been looking for bi-sets containing the property "presence of bacteria detected in C.S.F. bacteriological analysis" with at least one exception. This property is typically true in the bacterial type of meningitis [12, 21]. By looking for bi-sets satisfying such a constraint, we expect to obtain associations between bacterial meningitis objects and properties characterizing this class of meningitis. We analyzed the collection of FBS when $\delta = 1$. We got 763 FBS that satisfy the chosen constraint. Among these, 124 FBS contain only one viral meningitis object. We got no FBS containing more than one viral object. Properties belonging to these FBS are either characteristic features of the bacterial cases or non discriminant (but compatible) features such as the age and sex of the patient. When $\delta = 2$, the number of FBS satisfying the constraint is 925. Among them, 260 contain at least one viral case of meningitis, and about 25 FBS contain more than one viral case. For $\delta = 5$ the obtained bi-sets are no longer relevant, i.e., the exceptions include contradictory Boolean properties (e.g., presence and absence of bacteria). We performed the same analysis on DRBS for $\epsilon = 2$. We found 24 rather large DRBS. Among them, 2 contain also one viral object. Only one DRBS seems irrelevant: it contains 3 viral and 8 bacterial cases. Looking at its Boolean properties, we noticed that they were not known as discriminant w.r.t. the bacterial meningitis. If we analyze the collection obtained for $\epsilon = 3$, there is only one DRBS satisfying the constraint. It is a rather large bi-set involving 11 Boolean properties and 14 objects. All the 14 objects belong to the bacterial class and the 11 properties are compatible with the bacterial condition of meningitis. It appears that using DRBS instead of FBS leads to a smaller number of relevant bi-sets for our analysis task (24 against 763). Notice however that DRBS are larger than FBS (for an identical number of exceptions): it means that the information provided by several FBS patterns might be incorporated in only one DRBS pattern. Moreover we got no DRBS pattern whose set of properties is included in the set of properties of another one. This is not the case for FBS.

To summarize this experiment, let us first note that using size constraints to reduce the size of the collection is not always sufficient. meningitis is a rather small dataset which leads to the extraction of several hundreds of thousands of formal concepts (about 700 000 if no constraint is given). By extracting fault-tolerant bi-sets, we reduce the size of the collection to be interpreted and this is crucial for the targeted exploratory knowledge discovery processes. In particular, for DRBS, the ϵ parameter is more stringent than the δ parameter. Then, the relevancy of the extracted patterns can be improved if a reasonable number of exceptions is allowed. For instance, extracting FBS with a low δ (1 or 2) leads to relevant associations while a high δ (e.g., 5) introduces too many irrelevant bi-sets. From this point of view, the DRBS class leads to the most interesting results and their quality can be improved by tuning the ϵ parameter. On the other hand, FBS are easier to compute, even in rather hard contexts, while computing DRBS remains untractable in many cases.

5.3   Post-experiment Discussion

Both experiments have shown the advantages of using a fault-tolerant bi-set mining technique in noisy data. Let us emphasize that adding minimal size constraints on both dimensions to fault-tolerance constraints is useful: it ensures that the number of false values is quite small w.r.t. the bi-set size. It enables to speed up the mining process as well because such constraints can be exploited for efficient search space pruning.

Using CBS might be a good choice when a relatively small collection of formal concepts is already available. When data are dense or significantly correlated, such as in meningitis, CBS mining fails even in relatively small matrices. In this case, we can use either FBS or DRBS. Experiments have shown that the second class gives more relevant results and that DRBS pattern collection sizes tend to be significantly smaller. Trigging the ϵ parameter enables to further reduce the collection size while preserving relevancy. The problem is however that this task turns out to be untractable for large matrices. On the other hand, FBS can be rather easily extracted but their semantics is not symmetrical and it affects their relevancy. A post-processing step might be used to eliminate all the bi-sets which do not satisfy the maximum error constraint on rows.

6   Conclusion

We have discussed a fundamental limitation of formal concept mining to capture strong associations between sets of objects and sets of properties in possibly large and noisy Boolean datasets. Relevancy issues are crucial to avoid too many irrelevant patterns during the targeted data mining processes. It is challenging to alleviate the expensive interpretation phases while still promoting unexpectedness of the discovered (local) patterns. The lack of consensual extensions of formal concepts towards fault-tolerance has given rise to several ad-hoc proposals. Considering three recent proposals, we have formalized fault-tolerant bi-dimensional pattern mining within a constraint-based approach. It has been useful for a better understanding of the needed trade-off between extraction feasibility, completeness, relevancy, and ease of interpretation. An empirical evaluation on both synthetic and real-life medical data has been given. It shows that fault-tolerant formal concept mining is possible and this should have an impact on the dissemination of local set pattern discovery techniques in intrinsically noisy Boolean data. DRBS pattern class appears as a well-designed class but the price to pay is computational complexity. The good news are that (a) the submitted inductive queries on DRBS patterns might involve further user-defined constraints which can be used for efficient pruning, and (b) one can look for more efficient data structures and thus a more efficient implementation of the DR-MINER generic algorithm. A pragmatic usage of available algorithms is indeed to extract some bi-sets, e.g., formal concepts, and then select some of them (say $B = (X, Y)$) for further extensions towards fault-tolerant patterns: it becomes, e.g., the computation of a DRBS pattern (say $B' = (X', Y')$) such that the constraint $B \subseteq B'$ is enforced. Also, a better characterization of FBS pattern class might be useful for huge database processing.

Acknowledgements. The authors thank P. François and B. Crémilleux who provided meningitis. J. Besson's work is funded by INRA. This research is partly funded by ACI CNRS MD 46 Bingo and by EU contract IQ FP6-516169 (FET arm of the IST programme).

References

1. C. Antunes and A.L. Oliveira. Constraint relaxations for discovering unknown sequential patterns. In *Revised selected and invited papers KDID'04*, volume 3377 of *LNCS*, pages 11–32. Springer-Verlag, 2005.
2. J. Besson, C. Robardet, and J-F. Boulicaut. Mining formal concepts with a bounded number of exceptions from transactional data. In *Revised selected and invited papers KDID'04*, volume 3377 of *LNCS*, pages 33–45. Springer-Verlag, 2004.
3. J. Besson, C. Robardet, and J-F. Boulicaut. Approximation de collections de concepts formels par des bi-ensembles denses et pertinents. In *Proceedings CAp 2005*, pages 313–328. PUG, 2005. An extended and revised version in English is submitted to a journal.
4. J. Besson, C. Robardet, J-F. Boulicaut, and S. Rome. Constraint-based concept mining and its application to microarray data analysis. *Intelligent Data Analysis*, 9(1):59–82, 2005.
5. M. Bistarelli and F. Bonchi. Interestingness is not a dichotomy: introducing softness in constrained pattern mining. In *Proceedings PKDD'05*, volume 3721 of *LNCS*, pages 22–33. Springer-Verlag, 2005.
6. J-F. Boulicaut. Inductive databases and multiple uses of frequent itemsets: the cInQ approach. In *Database Technologies for Data Mining - Discovering Knowledge with Inductive Queries*, volume 2682 of *LNCS*, pages 1–23. Springer-Verlag, 2004.
7. J-F. Boulicaut, A. Bykowski, and C. Rigotti. Approximation of frequency queries by mean of free-sets. In *Proceedings PKDD'00*, volume 1910 of *LNAI*, pages 75–85. Springer-Verlag, 2000.
8. J-F. Boulicaut, A. Bykowski, and C. Rigotti. Free-sets: a condensed representation of boolean data for the approximation of frequency queries. *Data Mining and Knowledge Discovery journal*, 7 (1):5–22, 2003.

9. C. Bucila, J. E. Gehrke, D. Kifer, and W. White. Dualminer: A dual-pruning algorithm for itemsets with constraints. *Data Mining and Knowledge Discovery journal*, 7 (4):241–272, 2003.
10. L. De Raedt. A perspective on inductive databases. *SIGKDD Explorations*, 4(2):69–77, 2003.
11. I. S. Dhillon, S. Mallela, and D. S. Modha. Information-theoretic co-clustering. In *Proceedings ACM SIGKDD 2003*, pages 89–98, Washington, USA, 2003. ACM Press.
12. P. François, C. Robert, B. Cremilleux, C. Bucharles, and J. Demongeot. Variables processing in expert system building: application to the aetiological diagnosis of infantile meningitis. *Med Inform*, 15(2):115–124, 1990.
13. F. Geerts, B. Goethals, and T. Mielikäinen. Tiling databases. In *Proceedings DS'04*, volume 3245 of *LNAI*, pages 278–289. Springer-Verlag, 2004.
14. A. Gionis, H. Mannila, and J. K. Seppänen. Geometric and combinatorial tiles in 0-1 data. In *Proceedings PKDD'04*, volume 3202 of *LNAI*, pages 173–184. Springer-Verlag, 2004.
15. B. Goethals and M. Zaki. *Proceedings of the IEEE ICDM Workshop on Frequent Itemset Mining Implementations FIMI 2003*. CEUR-WS, Melbourne, USA, 2003.
16. T. Imielinski and H. Mannila. A database perspective on knowledge discovery. *Communications of the ACM*, 39(11):58–64, 1996.
17. S. O. Kuznetsov and S. A. Obiedkov. Comparing performance of algorithms for generating concept lattices. *Journal of Experimental and Theoretical Artificial Intelligence*, 14 (2-3):189–216, 2002.
18. J. Pei, A. K. H. Tung, and J. Han. Fault-tolerant frequent pattern mining: Problems and challenges. In *SIGMOD wokshop DMKD*. ACM workshop, 2001.
19. R. Pensa and J-F. Boulicaut. From local pattern mining to relevant bi-cluster characterization. In *Proceedings IDA'05*, volume 3646 of *LNCS*, pages 293–304. Springer-Verlag, 2005.
20. R. G. Pensa, C. Robardet, and J.-F. Boulicaut. A bi-clustering framework for categorical data. In *Proceedings PKDD'05*, volume 3721 of *LNCS*, pages 643–650. Springer-Verlag, 2005.
21. C. Robardet, B. Crémilleux, and J.-F. Boulicaut. Characterization of unsupervized clusters by means of the simplest association rules: an application for child's meningitis. In *Proceedings IDAMAP'02 co-located with ECAI'02*, pages 61–66, Lyon, F, 2002.
22. J. K. Seppänen and H. Mannila. Dense itemsets. In *Proceedings ACM SIGKDD'04*, pages 683–688, Seattle, USA, 2004. ACM Press.
23. G. Stumme, R. Taouil, Y. Bastide, N. Pasqier, and L. Lakhal. Computing iceberg concept lattices with TITANIC. *Journal of Data and Knowledge Engineering*, 42 (2):189–222, 2002.
24. R. Wille. Restructuring lattice theory: an approach based on hierarchies of concepts. In I. Rival, editor, *Ordered sets*, pages 445–470. Reidel, 1982.
25. C. Yang, U. Fayyad, and P. S. Bradley. Efficient discovery of error-tolerant frequent itemsets in high dimensions. In *Proceedings ACM SIGKDD'01*, pages 194–203. ACM Press, 2001.

Experiment Databases: A Novel Methodology for Experimental Research

Hendrik Blockeel

Katholieke Universiteit Leuven, Department of Computer Science,
Celestijnenlaan 200A, 3001 Leuven, Belgium
Hendrik.Blockeel@cs.kuleuven.be

Abstract. Data mining and machine learning are experimental sciences: a lot of insight in the behaviour of algorithms is obtained by implementing them and studying how they behave when run on datasets. However, such experiments are often not as extensive and systematic as they ideally would be, and therefore the experimental results must be interpreted with caution. In this paper we present a new experimental methodology that is based on the concept of "experiment databases". An experiment database can be seen as a special kind of inductive database, and the experimental methodology consists of filling and then querying this database. We show that the novel methodology has numerous advantages over the existing one. As such, this paper presents a novel and interesting application of inductive databases that may have a significant impact on experimental research in machine learning and data mining.

1 Introduction

Data mining and machine learning are experimental sciences: much insight in the behaviour of algorithms is obtained by implementing them and studying their behaviour on specific datasets. E.g., one might run different learners using different algorithms to see which approach works best on a particular dataset. Or one may try to obtain insight into which kind of learners work best on which kind of datasets, or for which parameter settings a parametrized learner performs best on a certain task.

Such experimental research is difficult to interpret. When one learner performs better than another on a few datasets, how generalizable is this result? The reason for a difference in performance may be in the parameter settings used, it may be due to certain properties of the datasets, etc. Similarly, when we vary one parameter in the hope of understanding its effect on the learner's performance, any effect we notice might in fact be specific for this dataset or application; it might be due to interaction with other, uncontrolled, effects; and even if we eliminate this interaction by keeping the values for other parameters fixed, perhaps the effect would have been different with other values for those parameters.

As a consequence of this complex situation, overly general conclusions are sometimes drawn. For instance, it has recently been shown [5] that the relative performance of different learners depends on the size of the dataset they are used

F. Bonchi and J.-F. Boulicaut (Eds.): KDID 2005, LNCS 3933, pp. 72–85, 2006.

on. Consequently, any comparative results obtained in the literature that do not take dataset size explicitly into account (which is probably the large majority) are to be interpreted with caution.

Clearly, the methodology usually followed for experimental research in machine learning has its drawbacks. In this paper we present a new methodology that avoids these drawbacks and allows a much cleaner interpretation of results. It is based on the concept of *experiment databases*. An experiment database can be seen as a kind of inductive database, and the methodology we propose essentially consists of querying this database for patterns. As such, this paper presents a novel and potentially interesting application of inductive databases that may have a significant impact on how experimental research in machine learning and data mining is conducted in the future.

We present the basic ideas of the approach, but many details are left open and there remain several interesting questions for further research.

We will first give an overview of the shortcomings and caveats of the classical experimental methodology (Section 2), then we introduce informally the concept of experiment databases and show how they can be used (Section 3). We summarize our conclusions in Section 4.

2   The Classical Experimental Methodology

Let us look at a typical case of an experimental comparison of algorithms. A realistic setup of the experiments is:

- A number of datasets is chosen; these may be existing benchmarks, or synthetic datasets with specific built-in properties (for instance, one may want to control the skewness of the class distribution in the dataset).
- On all of these datasets, a number of algorithms are run. These algorithms may have different parameter settings; typically they are run with "suitable" (not necessarily optimal) parameters.
- Certain performance criteria are measured for all these algorithms.

The above methodology, while very often followed, has two important disadvantages: the generalizability of the findings is often unclear, and the experiments are not reusable.

2.1   Unclear Generalizability

The conclusions drawn from experiments may not hold as generally as one might expect, because the experiments typically cover a limited range of **datasets** as well as **parameter settings**.

Comparisons typically happen on a relatively small number of datasets, in the range of 1-30. Imagine describing all datasets using a number of properties such as the number of examples in the dataset, the number of attributes, the skewedness of the class distribution, the noise level, level of missing values, etc. Many such properties can be thought of, leading to a description of these datasets in a high-dimensional space, let us call it D-space (D for datasets). Clearly, in such a high-dimensional space, a sample of 1-30 points (datasets) is extremely sparse. As a consequence, any experimental results obtained with such a small number of datasets, no matter how thoroughly the experiments have been performed, are necessarily limited with respect to their generalizability towards other datasets.

This is not a purely theoretical issue; as we already mentioned, recent work [5] has shown how the relative performance of different learning algorithms in terms of predictive accuracy may depend strongly on the size of the dataset. This sheds a new light on hundreds of scientific papers in machine learning and data mining. Indeed, many authors implicitly assume the predictive accuracy of algorithms, relative to each other, to be independent of data set size (or any other data set parameters, for that matter).

A second possible cause for limited generalizability is that many algorithms are highly parametrized. Let us call an algorithm with completely instantiated parameters a ground algorithm. Then typically, a limited number of ground algorithms is used in the experiments. If, similar to D-space, we define for each parameterized algorithm or class of algorithms its parameter space (P-space), then again the experiments involve a very sparse sample from this space, and the results may not be representative for the average or optimal behaviour of the algorithm.

An additional problem here is that authors presenting new algorithms often understand their own algorithm better and may be better at choosing optimal parameter values for their own approach, putting the existing algorithm at a small disadvantage.

The above discussion was from viewpoint of comparing algorithms, but the generalizability problem also occurs when, for instance, the effect of a single parameter of the algorithm or dataset on the performance of the system is investigated. For instance, to study the robustness of an algorithm to noise, one would typically run it on a variety of data sets with increasing noise levels. Using synthetic datasets in which the noise level can be controlled, it makes sense to increase the noise level while keeping all other parameters of the data set and the algorithm constant, and plot performance as a function of the noise level.

Here, too, generalizability is problematic. If we look at such approaches in $D \times P$-space or P-space, it is clear that by varying one parameter of the dataset or algorithm, one constructs a sample that lies in a one-dimensional subspace of the high-dimensional space. The sample is typically dense within this subspace, but still located in a very limited area of the overall space, so, again, the generalizability of the results may be low due to this. For instance, one might conclude that a certain parameter has a large influence on the efficiency of an algorithm, when in fact this holds only for datasets having certain specific properties.

2.2   No Reusability

In the classical methodology, the experimental setup is typically oriented towards a specific goal. The above example regarding the study of the effect of noise illustrates this: since the researcher knows that she wants to study the effect of noise, she varies the noise level and nothing else. Such an experimental setup is clearly goal-oriented. Each time the researcher has a new experimental hypothesis to be tested or wants to investigate a new effect, this will involve setting up and running new experiments. This obviously takes additional work. Moreover, there may be practical problems involved. For instance, if there is a large time span between the original experiments and the newly planned experiments, certain algorithm implementations may have evolved since the time of the original experiments, making the new results incompatible with the old ones.

2.3 Summary

The above problems can be summarized as follows:

1. Experimental results regarding the relative performance of different methods and the effect that certain parameters of the algorithm or properties of the dataset have, may have limited generalizability.
2. For each additional experimental hypothesis that is to be investigated, new experiments must be set up.

We will next show how the use of experiment databases can solve these problems.

3   Experiment Databases

An experiment database (in short, an ExpDB) is a database that contains results of many random experiments. The experiments in themselves are unfocused; the focused, goal-oriented experiments mentioned above will be replaced by specific queries to the database.

In the following, we first describe how the database can be created, and next, how it can be mined to obtain useful knowledge. For simplicity, we start with the case where we are interested in the behaviour of a single algorithm. The extension towards a comparison of multiple algorithms is non-trivial but will briefly be discussed afterwards.

3.1   Creating an Experiment Database

Assume we have a single algorithm A with a parameter space P. Assume furthermore that some fixed method for describing datasets is given, which gives rise to a D-space D. (Note that there is a difference between the dataset space and the D-space; the D-space is an n-dimensional space containing *descriptions* of datasets, not the datasets themselves). Finally, we denote with M a set of performance metrics; M may include runtime, predictive accuracy, true and false positive rates, precision, recall, etc.

We further assume that a dataset generator G_D is given. G_D generates datasets at random, according to some distribution over D. This distribution need not be uniform (this would be impossible if some parameters are un-bounded), but it should *cover* all of D, i.e., for each $d \in D$, the distribution must assign a non-zero probability to an element "sufficiently close to" d. For instance, the "dataset size" parameter is continuous but one could choose to use only the values 10^k with $k = 2, 3, 4, 5, 6, 7, 8, 9$. A dataset generator using these values could be said to "cover" datasets of a hundred up to a billion instances.

Finally, we assume we have a random generator G_P for parameter values of the algorithm; again this generator should generate values according to a distribution that covers, in the same sense as above, all of P.

Now we can create a table of experimental results, as follows:

Experiment Database Creation:
Input: A, D, G_D, P, G_P, M
Output: a table T
Create a table T with attributes from $D \times P \times M$.
for i = 1 **to** k:
    Generate a random data set DS using G_D
    Let d be the D-space description of DS
    Generate random parameter values p according to G_P
    Run A with parameter values p on DS
    Let m be the result of this run in terms of the performance metrics M
    Insert a new row containing d, p, m in the table.

The table now contains the results of k random experiments, that is, runs of algorithm A with random parameters on random datasets. We will discuss later how large k would need to be for this table to be useful.

A final note regarding the creation of the database: we have assumed that datasets and algorithm parameters are chosen at random, and we will continue our discussion under this assumption. However, total randomness is not required; we require only that the whole $D \times P$-space is covered. As several researchers have pointed out (personal communication), it may well be possible to do better, for instance, by filling the table according to experiment design principles. The analysis we further make on the required size of the table should therefore be considered a worst-case analysis.

3.2   Mining the Database

We have a database of "random" experiments, but we are in fact interested in testing specific hypotheses about the behaviour of the algorithm A, or investigating the influence of certain parameters or dataset properties on A's performance.

If the table is considered an inductive database and we can query for patterns in the table, then such knowledge is immediately obtainable in a very straight-forward way.

Suppose A is some frequent itemset discovery algorithm, and we want to see the influence of the total number of items in the dataset on A's runtime. Assuming NItems (number of items in the dataset) is one dimension of D and the attribute Runtime is included in M, the following simple SQL query

```
SELECT NItems, Runtime
FROM EXP
SORT BY NItems
```

gives us the results. (In practice we would of course graphically plot Runtime against NItems; such a plot can be readily derived from the result of the SQL query. In this text we are mainly concerned with how the results to be visualized can be obtained with a query language, rather than the visualization itself.)

The Runtime attribute is of course related to many other parameters, which vary randomly, and as a result the above query may result in a very jagged plot (e.g., Runtime for NItems=100 might be larger than Runtime for NItems=1000 just because lower values for the MinSupport parameter were used for the former). In the classical experimental setting, one would keep all other parameters equal when one is interested in the effect of the number of items only. For instance, knowing that the minimal support parameter of a frequent itemset mining algorithm typically has a large influence on the run time, one might keep this parameter fixed at, say, 0.05. This can easily be simulated with our approach:

```
SELECT NItems, Runtime
FROM EXP
WHERE MinSupport = 0.05
SORT BY NItems
```

Assuming that G_P generates 10 different values for MinSupport, uniformly distributed, the result of this query is based on roughly 10% of the database. Compared to the classical setting where the experimenter chooses in advance to use only MinSupport=0.05, we need to populate the database with 10 times as many experiments. Figure 1 illustrates how the WHERE constraint gives rise to fewer points with a clearer trend.

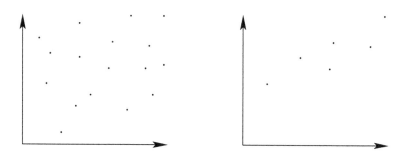

Fig. 1. An impression of what plots would typically look like under different constraints in the SQL query. The left plot shows a cloud obtained from all data points, the right plot shows a cloud obtained using MinSupport=0.05. The latter contains a subset of the former's points, but with a clearer trend.

Now, as said before, the influence of NItems on Runtime might be different if we vary other parameters, such as MinSupport. We can easily vary the MinSupport condition in the above query to check whether this is the case. For instance, using an ad-hoc scripting language that allows to plot query results, and where we use the notation $x inside an SQL query to refer to the value of a variable x defined outside the query, we could write

```
FOR ms = 0.001, 0.005, 0.01, 0.05, 0.1 DO
  PLOT
    SELECT NItems, Runtime
    FROM EXP
    WHERE MinSupport = $ms
    SORT BY NItems
```

and get a figure showing different curves indicating the effect of NItems, one for each value of MinSupport.

In the classical experimental setting, if the experimenter realizes that this would be a better approach only after having performed the experiments, she needs to set up new experiments. The total number of experiments will then be equal to the number of experiments in our database.

From the above discussion, two differences between the classical approach and the ExpDB approach become clear.

1. *In the classical approach, experiments are set up from the beginning to test a specific hypothesis; to test new hypotheses, new experiments are needed. With the ExpDB approach, many experiments are run once, in advance, independent of the goal; to test new hypotheses, new queries are run on the database.*

2. *Due to stronger randomization of the experiments, the experiment database approach tends to yield results in which fewer parameter values are kept constant. This may lead to less convincing (though more generalizable) results. To some extent, queries can be written so as to counter this effect.*

Looking at the above SQL queries, another advantage of the ExpDB approach becomes clear. As said before, the second query has the advantage of producing a less jagged curve, in other words, less variance in the results, but this comes at the cost of obtaining less generalizable results. It is immediately clear from the form of the second query that the obtained results are for MinSupport=0.05, whereas in the classical approach this is left implicit. In both queries, nothing is explicitly assumed about the unmentioned parameters, and indeed in the actual experiments these parameters get random values and we may assume that roughly the whole range of values is covered. Thus, these queries explicitly state how general a result is. The first query yields the most general results (and, as a consequence, the least conclusive results, as far as the detection of trends or rejection of hypotheses is concerned). The second query yields results for a more specific case; the results are more conclusive but may be less generalizable.

3. *The ExpDB approach explicitates the conditions under which the results are valid.*

What if, at some point, the researcher realizes that besides MinSupport, also the number of transactions NTrans in the database might influence the effect of NItems on Runtime? Now the researcher following the classical approach has several options. He may run new experiments, fixing MinSupport at 0.05 but now varying NTrans. He might also decide to combine each value of MinSupport with each value of NTrans, which would give a detailed account of the effect of both together on Runtime. Or he might randomize the MinSupport setting while controlling NTrans.

In each case, new experiments are needed. The original experiments are not usable because the NTrans parameter was not varied. Even if it was varied, the necessary statistics to test the new hypothesis have not been recorded in the original experiments because they were not needed for the goal of those experiments.

The situation is entirely different with the ExpDB approach. The experiment database was created to be as generally useful as possible; a large number of statistics, potentially useful for a variety of purposes, have been recorded. When the researcher wants to test a new hypothesis, he just needs to query the experiment database. In other words, a fixed set of experimental results is re-used for many different hypothesis tests or other kinds of investigations. This leads us to a fourth difference:

4. *The ExpDB approach is more efficient than the classical approach if multiple hypotheses will be tested.*

Clearly, the ExpDB approach makes controlled experimentation much easier. As a result, such experimentation can easily be performed in much more depth than with the classical approach. For instance, classically, higher-order effects are usually not investigated. Researchers vary one parameter P1 to investigate its effect, then vary another parameter P2 to investigate its effect. This leads to the discovery of only so-called marginal effects of the parameters. By varying P1 and P2 together, one can discover so-called higher order effects; for instance, one might discover that the effect of P1 on performance is large when P2 is low but not so large when P2 is high.

With the ad-hoc language introduced before, such interaction can be studied easily, for instance using the following SQL query:

```
FOR a=0.01, 0.02, 0.05, 0.1 DO
  FOR b = 1000, 10000, 100000, 1000000 DO
    PLOT
        SELECT NItems, Runtime
        FROM EXP
        WHERE MinSupport = $a AND $b <= NTrans < 10*$b
        SORT BY NItems
```

This shows that

5. *The ExpDB approach makes it easy to perform in-depth analyses of both marginal and higher-order effects of parameters and dataset properties.*

The inductive database approach, where mining is performed by querying for patterns using a special-purpose inductive query language [1], allows us to go further. While the above kind of queries amount to checking manually for the effects of specific parameters or dataset characteristics, or interactions between them, one can easily think of more sophisticated data mining approaches that allow the researcher to ask questions such as "what is the parameter that has the strongest influence on the predictive accuracy of my decision tree system", or "are there any dataset characteristics that interact with the effect of parameter P on predictive accuracy", etc. Clearly, inductive database query languages are needed for this purpose. A possible query would be

```
SELECT ParName, Var(A) / Avg(V) as Effect
FROM AlgorithmParameters,
     SELECT $ParName, Var(Runtime) as V, Avg(Runtime) as A
     FROM EXP
     GROUP BY $ParName
GROUP BY ParName
SORT BY Effect
```

This SQL-like query (it is not standard SQL)[1] requires some explanation. The inner SELECT query takes a parameter $ParName (e.g., $ParName = 'MinSupport') and computes the average A and variance V of the runtimes measured for specific values of $ParName. If $ParName = 'MinSupport', then the result of the inner query is a table with attributes MinSupport, A, V, and for each occurring value of MinSupport the corresponding average runtime is listed as well as the runtimes' variance.

The outer SELECT query takes a table AlgorithmParameters that is supposed to have an attribute ParName. For each value of ParName, the inner query is instantiated and run. We again use the convention that $ParName refers by definition to the *value* of ParName. The result of this construction is a "table" with attributes ParName, $ParName, A, V. (It is not a standard SQL table because the second attribute does not have a fixed name.) The SELECT part of the outer query projects this onto ParName and Effect, sorting the parameters according to their influence on runtime, where this influence is defined as the ratio of the variance of the averages of the different groups to the average variance within these groups.

6. *The ExpDB approach, if accompanied by suitable inductive querying languages, allows for a much more direct kind of questions, along the lines of "which parameter has most influence on runtime", instead of finding this out with repeated specific questions.*

A final advantage of the ExpDB approach is their reusability: experiment databases could be published on the web, so that other researchers can investigate the database in ways not thought of by the original researcher. Currently,

---

[1] The same query could be expressed in standard SQL if the parameter names listed in ParNames are hardcoded in the query, but this makes the query lengthy and cumbersome, and less reusable. We prefer this more compact and intuitive notation.

the tendency is to make available the datasets themselves, possibly also implementations of systems used, but the actual experiments and conclusions are described on paper (and sometimes the experimental settings are not described in sufficient detail for others to reconstruct the experiments exactly). By following the ExpDB approach and publishing the experiment database, a detailed log of the experiments remains available, and it becomes possible for other researchers to, e.g., refine conclusions drawn by previous researchers from these experiments. It is likely that such refinements would happen less frequently than is currently the case, exactly because the ExpDB approach enforces a much more diligent experimental procedure.

7. *The ExpDB approach leads to better reusability of experiments and better reproducibility of results.*

3.3   A Summary of the Advantages

We can summarize the advantages of the experiment database approach as follows:

- Efficiency. The same set of runs (of algorithms on datasets) is reused for many different goal-oriented experiments.
- Generalizability. The generalizability of experimental results in the original setting is often unclear. With the experiment database approach, due to randomization of all parameters not under investigation, it is always clear to what extent results are generalizable. Results are obtained from a relatively large sample in $P \times D$-space that covers the whole space, instead of from a small sample covering a small part of the space.
- Depth of analysis. It is easy to investigate the combined effect of two or more parameters on some performance metric, or, in general, to check for higher-order interactions (in the statistical sense) between algorithm parameters, dataset properties, and performance criteria.
- True data mining capacity. With a suitable query language, one can also ask questions such as "what algorithm parameters have the most influence on the accuracy of the algorithm?" (and hence are most important to tune).
- Reusability. Publishing an experimental database guarantees that a detailed log of the experiments is available. It makes it easier for other researchers to reproduce the experiments, and it makes it possible for them to investigate other hypotheses than the ones described by the authors of the experiment database.

3.4   Size of the Table

How large should the number of tuples in the experiment table, k, be? Assume that we want each point that we plot to be the average of at least e examples and no parameter or dataset characteristic has more than v values (continuous variables are discretized). $e = 30$ and $v = 10$ are reasonable values. Then we need to have $ve = 300$ experiments to measure the effect of any single parameter on any single performance metric. Measuring the effect while keeping the value of a single other parameter constant, may require up to v times more data to obtain equally precise results (e.g., averaged over 30 measurements); the same holds for measuring any second-order effects. In general, to measure mth-order effects, we need ev^m experiments. Thus, a table listing a few thousand experimental results is typically enough to perform more thorough experiments than what is typically done with the classical approach. Note that it is not problematic for the creation of this table to create hours or even days, as this can be done off-line, possibly as background computations, and subsequent experimentation will take require very little time. In this way, assuming the use of reasonably efficient algorithms, creation of a database of 10,000 to 100,000 experiments is quite feasible.

As mentioned before, this analysis holds for a method where the experiment database is filled randomly. Following experiment design principles, it may be possible to improve this number, but we have not looked into this issue yet. The main conclusion here is that even with the randomized approach, the number of experiments needed is not prohibitive.

Note that there is always the possibility of filling the database also in a goal-oriented way, by only generating tuples with specific values for certain attributes. This defeats part of the purpose of the ExpDB, but makes it possible to build an ExpDB with exactly the same number of experiments as would have been needed in the classical setting, while still allowing deeper analysis.

3.5   The Multiple-Algorithm Case

Up till now we have assumed that the experiments recorded in the ExpDB involve one single algorithm. In practice, it will be useful to build ExpDB's with information on multiple algorithms.

One problem that then arises, is that different algorithms typically have different sets of parameters. As a result, there exists no elegant schema for the single table we considered up till now.

A solution is to have multiple tables for describing parameter settings, where each class of algorithms has its own different table and schema. An example is shown in Figure 2. This necessitates a relational data mining approach [2]. The SQL-like "mining" approach that we have discussed before is not limited to querying a single experiment table, and hence simple queries can be asked to compare for instance the best-case, worst-case, average-case behaviour of different algorithms, possibly with constraints on the parameters of the algorithms and datasets. For instance, the query

```
SELECT AVG(s.Accuracy) - AVG(t.Accuracy),
       VAR(s.Accuracy), VAR(t.Accuracy)
FROM (ExpDB JOIN Alg1) s , (ExpDB JOIN Alg2) t
WHERE Alg1.C=0 and Examples < 1000
```

for the database schema shown in Figure 2 compares the average and variance of the accuracy of algorithms Alg1 and Alg2 under the constraint that Alg1's C parameter is 0 (e.g., the default), on datasets of less than one thousand examples.

An alternative to this approach could be to define a generic description of algorithms: a so-called A-space, in which any algorithm is described using algorithm-

ExpDB

ExpID	Attr	Examples	Target Complexity	Runtime	Accuracy

Alg1

ExpID	A	B	C	D

Alg2

ExpID	A	B	E	F

Fig. 2. Schema for an experiment database containing data for two algorithms Alg1 and Alg2 with different parameters

independent properties, similarly to the D-space that describes datasets without giving full information on the dataset. An advantage would be that one would be able to detect dependencies between algorithm-independent characteristics of learners, and the performance on certain kinds of datasets. It is unclear, however, what kind of characteristics those should be.

3.6   A Connection to Meta-learning

Meta-learning is a subfield of machine learning that is concerned with learning to understand machine learning algorithms by applying machine learning methods to obtained experimental results. While our ExpDB approach has been presented as a way to improve the experimental methodology typically followed by machine learning and data mining researchers, it is clear that the approach is very suitable for meta-learning:

- Working with synthetic datasets solves the problem of sparse data that is so typical of meta-learning. While the UCI repository, for instance, is a sizeable collection of machine learning problems, from the meta-learning point of view each UCI dataset yields a single example, so the meta-learning dataset derived from the UCI repository contains only a few dozen examples. This makes it difficult to derive any conclusions. A synthetic dataset generator, such as used in the ExpDB approach, appears crucial for the success of meta-learning.
- As explained, our approach allows thorough investigation of the interactions between algorithm parameters, dataset characteristics, and performance metrics, in addition to allowing a comparison between different kinds of algorithms.

Conversely, a lot of existing work in meta-learning is very useful for the concept of experiment databases. For instance, significant efforts have been invested in the description of datasets and algorithms [6, 4] and in methods for generating synthetic datasets (Soares, Džeroski, personal communication). All of these can be used to give the work on experiment databases a headstart.

4   Conclusions

We have presented a novel methodology for experimental research in machine learning and data mining. The methodology makes use of the concept of experiment databases. The idea behind this is that a database of random experiments is first created, then hypotheses can be tested ad libitum by just querying the database instead of repeatedly setting up new experiments. The experiment database approach has many advantages with respect to reusability, reproducibility and generalizability of results, efficiency of obtaining them, ease of performing thorough and sophisticated analysis, and explicitness of assumptions under which the obtained results are valid.

The current paper is obviously very preliminary; it presents the basic ideas and promises of experiment databases. There are many open questions, such as:

- *The format of the D-space*: it is easy to list some characteristics of datasets that might be useful, but difficult to ensure no important ones are missed. Some work has already been done on this in the meta-learning community [4], but we expect further efforts on this may yield more results.
- *The dataset generator*: such a generator generates data according to a certain distribution; how do we specify this distribution? For supervised learners a target concept must be included; how do we generate this target concept? Information on this concept (e.g., its complexity) is part of the D-space.
- *An inductive query language*: In the above we have used an ad hoc language for inductive queries. It is necessary to define a suitable inductive query language for the kind of patterns we are interested in. It is not clear if any of the existing query languages are suitable; for instance, languages for finding frequent itemsets or association rules [3] are not immediately applicable. It seems that a kind of standard SQL that allows the user to mix the meta and object level in a single query, would be useful.

We believe that further research along the proposed direction has the potential to lead to much better experimental research in machine learning and data mining, and to ultimately lead to a greatly improved understanding of the strengths and weaknesses of different approaches.

Acknowledgements

The author is a post-doctoral fellow of the Fund for Scientific Research of Flanders, Belgium (FWO-Vlaanderen). He thanks Sašo Džeroski, Carlos Soares, Ashwin Srinivasan, and Joaquin Vanschoren for interesting comments and suggestions.

References

1. L. De Raedt. A perspective on inductive databases. *SIGKDD Explorations*, 4(2):69–77, 2002.
2. S. Džeroski and N. Lavrač, editors. *Relational Data Mining*. Springer-Verlag, 2001.
3. R. Meo, G. Psaila, and S. Ceri. An extension to SQL for mining association rules in SQL. *Data Mining and Knowledge Discovery*, 2:195 – 224, 1998.

4. Y. Peng, P. Flach, C. Soares, and P. Brazdil. Improved dataset characterisation for meta-learning. In *Proceedings of the 5th International Conference on Discovery Science*, volume 2534 of *Lecture Notes in Computer Science*, pages 141–152. Springer-Verlag, 2002.
5. C. Perlich, F. Provost, and J. Siminoff. Tree induction vs. logicstic regression: A learning curve analysis. *Journal of Machine Learning Research*, 4:211–255, 2003.
6. B. Pfahringer, H. Bensusan, and C. Giraud-Carrier. Meta-learning by landmarking various learning algorithms. In *Proceedings of the 17th International Conference on Machine Learning (ICML 2000)*, pages 743–750. Morgan Kaufmann, 2000.

Quick Inclusion-Exclusion

Toon Calders and Bart Goethals

University of Antwerp, Belgium
{toon.calders, bart.goethals}@ua.ac.be

Abstract. Many data mining algorithms make use of the well-known Inclusion-Exclusion principle. As a consequence, using this principle efficiently is crucial for the success of all these algorithms. Especially in the context of condensed representations, such as NDI, and in computing interesting measures, a quick inclusion-exclusion algorithm can be crucial for the performance. In this paper, we give an overview of several algorithms that depend on the inclusion-exclusion principle and propose an efficient algorithm to use it and evaluate its complexity. The theoretically obtained results are supported by experimental evaluation of the quick IE technique in isolation, and of an example application.

1 Introduction

The inclusion-exclusion (IE) principle is well known as it is an important method for many enumeration problems [8]. Also in many data mining applications this principle is used regularly. Moreover, as is typical in many data mining applications, when the formula is used, then it is evaluated many times. Indeed, data mining algorithms typically traverse huge pattern spaces in which hundreds to millions of potential patterns are evaluated. In this paper, we consider frequent itemsets and give an overview of several methods to efficiently evaluate the Inclusion-Exclusion formulas in order to obtain the supports of itemsets containing negated items. This leads us to the Quick Inclusion-Exclusion (QIE) algorithm, that is based on the same principles as the ADTree structure [13], and of which we show its efficiency in theory as well as in practice.

First, we shortly revisit the IE-principle and how it connects to itemsets and data mining.

Let $A_1, \ldots, A_n$ be n finite sets. The inclusion-exclusion principle is the following equality:

$$\left| \bigcup_{i=1}^{n} A_i \right| = \sum_{1 \leq i \leq n} |A_i| - \sum_{1 \leq i < j \leq n} |A_i \cap A_j| + \ldots - (-1)^n \left| \bigcap_{i=1}^{n} A_i \right|$$

We can connect the IE principle with frequent set mining as follows. Let a *generalized itemset* be a conjunction of items and negations of items. For example, $G = \{a, b, \bar{c}, d\}$ is a generalized itemset; a, b, and d are the positive items, and $\bar{c}$ denotes the negation of c. We will often denote a generalized itemset $X \cup \overline{Y}$, where X is the set of positive items, and Y the set of items that are

F. Bonchi and J.-F. Boulicaut (Eds.): KDID 2005, LNCS 3933, pp. 86–103, 2006.
© Springer-Verlag Berlin Heidelberg 2006

$$support(\overline{abcd}) = support(\emptyset) - support(a) - support(b) - support(c) - support(d)$$
$$+ support(ab) + support(ac) + support(ad)$$
$$+ support(bc) + support(bd) + support(cd)$$
$$- support(abc) - support(abd) - support(acd) - support(bcd)$$
$$+ support(abcd)$$

$$support(a\overline{bcd}) = support(a) - support(ab) - support(ac) - support(ad)$$
$$+ support(abc) + support(abd) + support(acd) - support(abcd)$$

$$support(\overline{a}b\overline{cd}) = support(b) - support(ab) - support(bc) - support(bd)$$
$$+ support(abc) + support(abd) + support(bcd) - support(abcd)$$

$$support(\overline{ab}c\overline{d}) = support(c) - support(ac) - support(bc) - support(cd)$$
$$+ support(abc) + support(acd) + support(bcd) - support(abcd)$$

$$support(\overline{abc}d) = support(d) - support(ad) - support(bd) - support(cd)$$
$$+ support(abd) + support(acd) + support(bcd) - support(abcd)$$

$$support(ab\overline{cd}) = support(ab) - support(abc) - support(abd) + support(abcd)$$

$$support(a\overline{b}c\overline{d}) = support(ac) - support(abc) - support(acd) + support(abcd)$$

$$support(a\overline{bc}d) = support(ad) - support(abd) - support(acd) + support(abcd)$$

$$support(\overline{a}bc\overline{d}) = support(bc) - support(abc) - support(bcd) + support(abcd)$$

$$support(\overline{a}b\overline{c}d) = support(bd) - support(abd) - support(bcd) + support(abcd)$$

$$support(\overline{ab}cd) = support(cd) - support(acd) - support(bcd) + support(abcd)$$

$$support(abc\overline{d}) = support(abc) - support(abcd)$$

$$support(ab\overline{c}d) = support(abd) - support(abcd)$$

$$support(a\overline{b}cd) = support(acd) - support(abcd)$$

$$support(\overline{a}bcd) = support(bcd) - support(abcd)$$

$$support(abcd) = support(abcd)$$

Fig. 1. The IE formulas for the itemset $abcd$

negated. For example, for the generalized itemset $\{a, b, \overline{c}, d\}$, $X = \{a, b, d\}$ and $Y = \{c\}$. A transaction T is said to *contain a general itemset* $G = X \cup \overline{Y}$ if $X \subseteq T$ and $T \cap Y = \emptyset$. The *support of a generalized itemset G in a database $\mathcal{D}$* is the number of transactions of $\mathcal{D}$ that contain G.

We say that a general itemset $G = X \cup \overline{Y}$ is *based* on itemset I if $I = X \cup Y$. From the IE principle [8], we can now derive that for a given general itemset $G = X \cup \overline{Y}$ based on I,

$$support(G) = \sum_{X \subseteq J \subseteq I} (-1)^{|J \setminus X|} support(J) \ . \tag{1}$$

Indeed; for all $y \in Y$, let A_y denote the set of transactions that contain $X \cup \{y\}$. Then, $\bigcup_{y \in Y} A_y$ denotes the set of transactions that contain X, and at least one item of Y. Hence, $|\bigcup_{y \in Y} A_y|$ equals $support(X) - support(G)$. This observation in combination with IE leads to the equation (1). The collection of formulas to compute the supports of all generalized itemsets based on $abcd$ can be seen in Figure 1.

Note, if the supports of all strict subsets of I are known, from the support of one generalized itemset based on I, the support of all other generalized itemsets can be derived.

In the next section, we explain the uses of the IE principle within several frequent set mining tasks. Then, we present several algorithms that compute the supports of all generalized itemsets at once and show that the QIE algorithm is the most efficient algorithm to solve this problem. Several experiments illustrate the theoretically obtained results in Section 4 after which Section 5 ends with conclusions and future work.

2   Multiple Uses of IE

2.1   Support Estimation and Bounding

Recently, several techniques have been developed to estimate the support of an itemset or the confidence of an association rule, based on the given supports of some sets [10, 11, 12, 14, 16]. The motivation for these techniques comes from the fact that the traditional support-confidence framework is well-suited to the market-basket problem, but is less appropriate for other types of transactional datasets. See, e.g., [16] for an extensive argumentation of this claim. Therefore, other interestingness measures have been developed.

The main idea is that interesting itemsets are ones that are both frequent (have required support) and have dependencies between the items. For example, consider items a and b. Assume that support measures are translated to probabilities (by dividing absolute support by number of database records). For example, $P(a)$ is the percentage of records with item a. To determine whether items a and b are independent (and hence not correlated), we need to check if the following 4 equations hold. Measures of correlation are based on the degree to which these equations are violated.

$$P(a,b) = P(a)P(b) \quad P(a,\overline{b}) = P(a)P(\overline{b})$$
$$P(\overline{a},b) = P(\overline{a})P(b) \quad P(\overline{a},\overline{b}) = P(\overline{a})P(\overline{b})$$

Observe that standard frequent itemset mining algorithms (e.g., Apriori) only provide information needed to check the first of these equations. However, all is not lost. Given $P(a)$, $P(b)$, and $P(a,b)$, we can derive exact values for $P(\overline{a},b)$, $P(a,\overline{b})$, and $P(\overline{a},\overline{b})$ by evaluating the Inclusion-Exclusion formulas for these terms without taking any additional counts.

The following four approaches are examples of similar measures, that also require the supports of itemsets with negations, and hence for which a quick inclusion-exclusion algorithm is useful:

- The dependency estimate of Silverstein et al., based on the χ^2 test [16].
- The dependence value of Meo, based on maximal entropy [12].

- The non-derivable itemsets (NDIs), based on tight support bounding [6].
- The support quota of Savinov [15], combining the dependency values of [12] and the tight support bounding of [6].

In this paper we will show a method to compute the IE sums in time $\mathcal{O}(n2^n)$. This exponential cost may seem unrealistically high for real applications. In reality, however, in the applications we describe, the IE sums need to be computed mostly for relatively small itemsets. For an empirical proof of the feasibility of computing IE sums, we refer to the experimental section, where it is shown that for the computation of NDIs, the exponential cost is reasonable.

We now discuss the four approaches in more detail.

Dependency Estimate. In [16], a χ^2-test is used to test the (in)dependence of items in an itemset. An itemset is only considered interesting if the items are dependent at a given significance level. The test of dependence is as follows. First, a contingency table for the itemset is constructed. This contingency table contains an entry for every combination of occurence/absence of the items in the itemset. Hence, the cells in the contingency table are exactly the supports of every generalized itemset based on the set. This contingency table is then compared to the estimates for the cells under the assumption of statistical independence. For the cell holding the support of $X \cup \overline{Y}$, this independence estimate is

$$E(X \cup \overline{Y}) := |\mathcal{D}| \cdot \prod_{x \in X} \frac{support(\{x\})}{|\mathcal{D}|} \cdot \prod_{y \in Y} \frac{|\mathcal{D}| - support(\{y\})}{|\mathcal{D}|} \ .$$

Then, the χ^2-score is used to quantify the difference between the observed counts and the estimated counts. This degree of independence for a set I is:

$$\chi^2(I) := \sum_{X \cup \overline{Y} \text{ based on } I} \frac{(support(X \cup \overline{Y}) - E(X \cup \overline{Y}))^2}{E(X \cup \overline{Y})} \ .$$

The set is then called *dependent at significance level* α if $\chi^2(I)$ exceeds the cut-off value χ^2_α.

In [16], an algorithm to find all dependent itemsets that also satisfy a support constraint is given. In this algorithm, the contingency tables are constructed by scanning the complete database. Because scanning the transaction database for every candidate separately can be very costly, in [16], the contingency tables of all candidates at the same level are constructed in one pass over the database.

The construction of the contingency tables in the algorithm of [16], however, has two big disadvantages: first, scanning the database can be very costly, especially for large datasets. Second: the contingency tables grow exponentially with the size of the itemset. Therefore, maintaining all contingency tables in memory simultaneously results in gigantic memory requirements. Therefore, we propose the use of the inclusion-exclusion principle for the construction of the contingency tables instead. Indeed, the cells in the contingency table are exactly the supports of the generalized itemsets, and, as was shown in the introduction, for a given set, the support of all its generalized itemsets based can be computed, based solely on the supports of all its subsets.

Notice that this use of the inclusion-exclusion principle goes far beyond the algorithm of [16] alone; every algorithm using contingency tables can benefit from it, and many statistical measures use contingency tables.

Dependency Values. In [12], Meo addresses the following problem with the estimate of [16]. A major drawback of the framework proposed in [16] is that in the estimation of the support of the contingency table entries, only the supports of the singleton itemsets are used. In this way, it is possible (and even often the case) that the estimated supports are inconsistent with the supports of itemsets of higher length. Meo addresses this problem by adopting a maximal entropy model to estimate the support of an itemset. Let I be an itemset for which we want to estimate the support, based on the supports of all its strict subsets. First, the notion of the entropy of a transaction database is defined. In general, entropy is defined as a measure on probability distributions. Let $\Omega = \{\omega_1, \ldots, \omega_m\}$ be a set of possible outcomes of an experiment. Let X be a probability distribution that assigns probability p_i to ω_i, for $i = 1 \ldots m$. The entropy of X is then defined as $\sum_{i=1}^n p_i \cdot \ln(p_i)$.

To define the entropy of a transaction database, it suffices to regard the database as a probability distribution. When we are interested in the itemset I, we can view the database as a probability structure assigning probabilities to the generalized itemsets based on I. That is, the different generalized itemsets are the "events", and their probability is their support divided by the total number of transactions in the database. From this viewpoint, the entropy of the database when restricted to the itemset I, denoted $\mathcal{E}_I(\mathcal{D})$, is defined as

$$\sum_{X \cup \overline{Y} \text{ based on } I} \frac{support(X \cup \overline{Y})}{|\mathcal{D}|} \cdot \ln \left(\frac{support(X \cup \overline{Y})}{|\mathcal{D}|} \right) .$$

Remember from Section 1, that if we know the supports of all strict subsets of I, then from the support of I, the support of all generalized itemsets based on I can be derived. The maximal entropy estimate for the support of I now is the one that maximizes the entropy $\mathcal{E}_I(\mathcal{D})$. In [12], based on the maximal entropy estimate, the notion of *Dependence Values* of an itemset is defined as the difference of this estimated support and the actual support of the itemset. For the exact details on the computation, we refer to [12], but for here it suffices that again all IE formulas need to be computed. In [12], these IE sums are calculated in isolation. This will correspond to our brute force evaluation method which we improve upon significantly in this paper. As the experiments will show, the gain of the quick inclusion-exclusion is large, which implies that the application of our quick IE-computation improves the performance of determining dependence values significantly.

2.2   Non-derivable Itemsets

In [6], tight bounds for an itemset are given for the case in which the supports of all its subsets are known. That is, from the supports of the strict subsets of

I, a lower bound l and an upper bound u are calculated, such that the support of I must be in the interval $[l, u]$. A set is considered uninteresting if its lower bound equals its upper bound, because this equality implies that the support of the itemset is completely determined by the supports of its subsets. Such a set is called a derivable itemset. In [6], an algorithm is given to find all non-derivable itemsets.

The bounds in [6] are based on the inclusion-exclusion principle. Recall the equality

$$support(X \cup \overline{Y}) = \sum_{X \subseteq J \subseteq I} (-1)^{|J \setminus X|} support(J) \ .$$

Since $support(X \cup \overline{Y})$ is always positive, we get

$$0 \leq \sum_{X \subseteq J \subseteq I} (-1)^{|J \setminus X|} support(J) \ . \tag{2}$$

In [6], this observation was used to calculate lower and upper bounds on the support of an itemset I, by isolating $support(I)$ in (2). For each set I, let l_I (u_I) denote the lower (upper) bound we can derive using these deduction rules. That is,

$$l_I = \max\{-\sum_{X \subseteq J \subset I} (-1)^{|J \setminus X|} support(J) \mid X \subseteq I, |I \setminus X| \text{ odd}\},$$

$$u_I = \min\{\sum_{X \subseteq J \subset I} (-1)^{|J \setminus X|} support(J) \mid X \subseteq I, |I \setminus X| \text{ even}\}.$$

Notice that these sums only differ little from the IE-sums we are optimizing. In fact, the sums coincide when we set $support(I)$ equal to 0. Therefore, our quick inclusion-exclusion technique directly leads to an efficient procedure for computation of bounds on the support of an itemset.

Notice that for the bounds in [6], the supports of all subsets of I must be known. This is often the case (e.g. in levelwise algorithms), but not always. In these cases, approximate inclusion-exclusion techniques can be used to find bounds on the support of an itemset. In [7], e.g., bounds on the support of an itemset are given when the support of all subsets up to a certain size only are known. These bounds are based on the so-called Bonferoni inequalities, which are an extension of the inclusion-exclusion principle.

Support Quotas. In [15], Savinov proposes the use of *support quotas* to improve the performance of mining the dependence rules of [12]. The support quota of an itemset is defined as the size of the bounding interval for its support as in [6]. Let $[l, u]$ be the bounds on the support of I. The support of I must always be in this interval. If the estimate $e(I)$ is consistent with the supports of the subsets of I, there must exist a database that is consistent with the supports of all subsets of I, and with $support(I) = e(I)$. For example, the maximum entropy estimate of [12] is in this case. Therefore, the difference between $e(I)$ and the actual support of I can maximally be $u - l$. If $u - l$ is smaller than the minimal dependence value, the difference between the estimate and the actual support will be smaller than this threshold as well and hence can be pruned. Moreover, since the interval width decreases when going from sub- to superset, all supersets of I can be pruned as well. This is a very interesting situation, as the dependence value is non-monotonic and thus not allows for pruning supersets. By using support bounding, however, an upper bound on the dependence values can be found that is monotonic. Even though Savinov's technique was introduced specifically for the dependence rules of [12], it can be extended to improve every estimate that is consistent with given supports, leading to yet another important application of quick IE.

2.3   Condensed Representation

The use of the quick inclusion-exclusion technique goes beyond advanced interesting measures for itemsets. In [11], for example, Mannila et al consider the collection of frequent sets as a condensed representation that allows to speed up support counts of arbitrary Boolean expressions over the items. In this context, the inclusion-exclusion principle can be used as a mean to estimate the support of arbitrary Boolean formulas based on the support of the frequent itemsets alone. Our quick IE method can here be used to quickly find the support of all conjunctive Boolean formulas with negations.

Also when we are only interested in the frequent itemsets, condensed representation are very useful, since the collection of all frequent itemsets can already be far too large to store. In the literature, many different condensed representations have been studied. In [5], the free sets [3], disjunction-free sets [4], generalized disjunction-free sets [9], and the non-derivable sets [6] are all shown to be based on the same support bounding technique which is based on the inclusion-exclusion formulas. For the exact details of this connection we refer to [5]. Because of this connection, improving the efficiency of the inclusion-exclusion computation results in performance gains when constructing one of these condensed representations.

3   QIE: The Algorithm

We first start with a formal problem definition.

Definition 1. *Let I be an itemset. Suppose that of every subset of I its support has en given. The* IE *problem is to compute for every subset X of I, the sum*

$$\sum_{X \subseteq J \subseteq I} (-1)^{|J \setminus X|} support(J) \ .$$

Obviously, efficiently computing IE is crucial for the success of all previously discussed methods. Nevertheless, for a given itemset I, there exist $2^{|I|}$ rules, and every such rule, with $I = X \cup Y$, consist of $2^{|Y|}$ terms, resulting in a total number of terms equal to

$$\sum_{X \subseteq I} 2^{|I \setminus X|} = \sum_{i=0}^{|I|} \binom{|I|}{i} 2^i = 3^{|I|} \ .$$

In what follows, we present several techniques to evaluate these rules efficiently. To compare their costs, we assume all itemsets are stored in a trie-like data structure [2]. Finding the support of a single itemset of size k in such a trie requires exactly k lookup operations. The cost model we use, assigns a cost of 1 to every lookup operation, and thus a cost of k for the retrieval of the support of an itemset of size k. In theory, however, this cost is in worst case as high as $\log(|\mathcal{I}|)$, but in practice, and with the use of advanced indexing techniques such as hash tables, the cost of 1 for every lookup operation is realistic. Notice that we could also hash the itemsets directly, and thus have a cost of $\mathcal{O}(1)$ per *itemset* that needs to be looked up. Nevertheless, the computation of any reasonable hash-key will be linear in the size of the set. For one computation this linearity does not matter and can be omitted from the complexity analysis. In our case, however, we need to incorporate the fact that this computation needs to be done for many itemsets.

3.1   Brute Force IE

A brute force algorithm would simply evaluate all rules separately and fetch all supports one at a time, as shown in Fig. 2.

The total cost of this algorithm is captured in the following Lemma.

Lemma 1. *For a given itemset I, with $|I| = n$, computing the supports of all generalized itemsets $X \cup \overline{Y}$, with $X \cup Y = I$, using the brute force algorithm, comes down to a cost of $2n3^{n-1}$.*

Proof. Computing the support of $X \cup \overline{Y}$ requires the retrieval of $\binom{|Y|}{0}$ sets of size $|X| = k$, $\binom{|Y|}{1}$ sets of size $|X| + 1$, ..., $\binom{|Y|}{|Y|}$ sets of size $|X \cup Y| = |I| = n$, which amounts to

$$\sum_{i=0}^{n-k} \binom{n-k}{i}(i+k) \ = \ (n+k)2^{n-k-1} \ .$$

Require: $I \subseteq \mathcal{I}$, $support(J)$ for all $J \subseteq I$
Ensure: $support(X \cup \overline{Y})$ for all $X \dot\cup Y = I$
1: **for all** $X \subseteq I$ **do**
2:    $support(X \cup \overline{Y}) := 0$
3:    **for all** $J \supseteq X$ **do**
4:       find $support(J)$
5:       $support(X \cup \overline{Y}) += (-1)^{|J \setminus X|} support(J)$
6:    **end for**
7: **end for**

Fig. 2. BFIE: Brute Force IE

Thus, evaluating the supports for all $X \cup \overline{Y}$ comes down to

$$\sum_{k=0}^{n} \binom{n}{k}(n+k)2^{n-k-1} = 2n3^{n-1} .$$

3.2 Combined IE

Instead of retrieving the support of all supersets of X separately, this can be done in a single large retrieval operation combined with the computation of the support of $X \cup \overline{Y}$. Indeed, the items in X occur in all itemsets we retrieve, while the items in Y are "optional". This observation is reflected in the recursive procedure illustrated in Figure 3.

Initially, the procedure starts in the root node, and scans over the items in $X \cup Y$. If the current item is in X, then it is found among the children of the

Require: Root node n, $X \cup \overline{Y}$
Ensure: $support(X \cup \overline{Y})$
1: **if** $X \cup \overline{Y}$ is empty **then**
2:    **return** $n.support$;
3: **end if**
4: {Let i be the first item in $X \cup \overline{Y}$}
5: **if** i in X **then**
6:    $X := X \setminus \{i\}$;
7:    **return** $CIE(n \rightarrow i, X \cup \overline{Y})$;
8: **else**
9:    $Y := Y \setminus \{i\}$;
10:   **return** $CIE(n, X \cup \overline{Y}) - CIE(n \rightarrow i, X \cup \overline{Y})$;
11: **end if**

Fig. 3. CIE: Combined IE for a single $support(X \cup \overline{Y})$

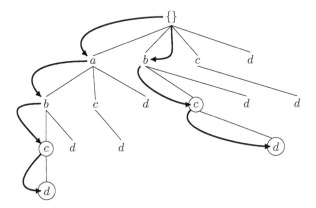

Fig. 4. Example trace of combined IE algorithm for a single $\overline{a}bc\overline{d}$

current node and the procedure recursively continues from this node for the remaining items. If the current item is in Y, then the computation is split into
two paths; on one path, the item is ignored, and the procedure recursively continues from the current node for the remaining items; on the other path, the
item is found among the children of the current node and the procedure recursively continues from this node for the remaining items. In this way, the different
computation paths end up in exactly the supersets of X, the supports are re-
turned and, depending on their cardinality, added or subtracted. In Figure 4,
this procedure is illustrated for the set $\overline{ab}c\overline{d}$. The arrows indicate the recursion,
the encircled nodes the itemsets that are summed.

Lemma 2. *For a given itemset I, with $|I| = n$, computing the supports of all
generalized itemsets $X \cup \overline{Y}$, with $X \cup Y = I$, using the combined IE algorithm,
comes down to a cost of $2(3^n - 2^n)$.*

Proof. The total cost of computing the supports of all generalized itemsets consists of the total number of visits to non-root nodes in the itemset trie.

Consider a node in the trie associated with itemset J. This node is visited
in the computation of the support for all generalized itemset $X \cup \overline{Y}$, such that
there is a superset of X that is in the trie below the node for J. Because the
trie below J contains all sets with J as prefix, this means that there must be
a superset of X such that J is a prefix of this superset. Let j be the last item
in the set J. The trie below J contains the supports of all sets $J \cup J'$ with J'
a subset of $\{i \in I \mid i > j\}$. Hence, there exists a superset of X that is below
J in the itemset trie, if and only if X is a subset of $J \cup \{i \in I \mid i > j\}$. Let
$m = |\{i \in I \mid i < j, i \notin J\}|$ be the number of so-called "missing items" in J.
The number of times J is visited during the combined IE algorithm depends on
this number of missing items m, and is 2^{n-m}.

To make the total sum of visits, we still need to determine the number of
nodes with m missing items. This number equals $\binom{n}{m+1}$. Indeed, consider an
itemset with m missing items. This itemset is completely characterized by the
list of the m missing items, and its last item. Therefore, the number of itemsets
with m missing items is exactly the number of combinations of $m + 1$ out of n.

Combining these two results, the total number of visits to nodes in the trie
can be obtained:

$$\sum_{m=0}^{n-1} \binom{n}{m+1} 2^{n-m} = 2(3^n - 2^n) \ .$$

3.3   Direct Access

Although the previous method already combines the retrieval of the supports of
several itemsets in a single scan through the itemset trie, this still needs to be
done for every possible subset of I. Fortunately, it is also possible to collect the
support of all subsets of I once, store it in a specialized storage structure, and
access this structure for every set X. Preferably, the specialized structure does
not introduce too much overhead, and allows for fast access to the supports of

the supersets of a set X. These requirements can be met with a simple linear array, and an indexing pattern based on the bit-pattern of the itemsets. From now on, we assume that the items of $\mathcal{I}$ are ordered.

To store the supports of the subsets of an itemset I, we create an array of size $2^{|I|}$, denoted by A, and the ith entry of A is denoted by $A[i]$. Then, the *bitpattern* of an itemset $X \subseteq I$, denoted by X_b, is simply the sequence $x_1 \ldots x_{|I|}$, where $x_j = 1$ if $i_j \in X$, and $x_j = 0$ otherwise. The *index* of X is the number represented by the bitpattern of X. Hence, this index can be used to directly access the entry in A storing the support of X.

The array structure, and the bitpattern access method have several interesting properties.

1. Enumerating all subsets of I comes down to a for loop from 0 to $2^{|I|}$.
2. The indices of the supersets of a set X can be enumerated by switching some of the 0-bits to 1 in the bitpattern of X.
3. The order in which the subsets are stored is also known as the *reverse pre-order*. This order has the interesting property that, given two sets X, X', such that $X \subseteq X' \subseteq I$, the index of X will be smaller than the index of X'. Therefore, we compute the support of $X \cup \overline{Y}$ in ascending order of the index of X. After that, we can simply replace the entry containing the support of X with the support of $X \cup \overline{Y}$ as we do not need its support anymore anyway.

Given this array containing the supports of all subsets of I, we automatically obtain the naive algorithm that sums for each $X \subset I$, the supports of all supersets of X. The exact algorithm is shown in Fig. 5 and illustrated in Figure 6. The arrows in the figure represent all necessary additions or subtractions.

The first three lines store the support of each subset of I in the array. Then, in line 4, a for-loop traverses each subset X in ascending order of its index. In the nested for-loop, all supports of all supersets of X are added (subtracted) to the support of X, resulting in the support of $X \cup \overline{I \setminus X}$, stored at index X_b of the array.

Lemma 3. *For a given itemset I, with $|I| = n$, computing the supports of all generalized itemsets $X \cup \overline{Y}$, with $X \dot{\cup} Y = I$, using the naive IE algorithm with direct access to the itemset supports, comes down to a cost of 3^n.*

> **Require:** $I \subseteq \mathcal{I}$, $support(J)$ for all $J \subseteq I$
> **Ensure:** $support(X \cup \overline{Y})$ for all $X \dot{\cup} Y = I$
> 1: **for all** $X \subseteq I$ **do**
> 2: $A[X_b] := support(X)$;
> 3: **end for**
> 4: **for** $i := 1$ to $2^{|I|}$ **do**
> 5:   {Let X be the itemset for which $X_b = i$}
> 6:   **for all** $J \subseteq I$, such that $J \supset X$ **do**
> 7: $A[i] := A[i] + (-1)^{|J \setminus X|} A[J_b]$;
> 8:   **end for**
> 9: **end for**

Fig. 5. NIE: Naive IE algorithm using direct access to the itemset supports

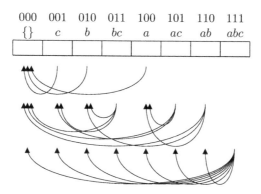

Fig. 6. Illustration of the naive IE algorithm using direct access to the itemset supports, for the generalized itemsets based on *abc*

Proof. Retrieving the supports of all subsets of I has a cost of $2^{|I|}$. For each generalized itemset $X \cup \overline{Y}$, the IE formulas consist of $2^{|Y|} - 1$ operations, resulting in a total of exactly $3^{|I|} - 2^{|I|}$ operations over all generalized itemsets. Hence, the total cost equals $2^{|I|} + 3^{|I|} - 2^{|I|} = 3^{|I|}$.

Until now, we have mainly concentrated on optimizing the number of costly retrievals in the itemset trie by introducing an array for the itemset supports with an efficient indexing structure. In this way, the number of retrieval operations could be lowered from 3^n to 2^n. The number of additions, however, remains $3^n - 2^n$. Even though the cost of *one* addition is negligible compared to the cost of one retrieval operation, the cost of $3^n - 2^n$ additions quickly grows far beyond the cost of 2^n retrieval operations.

3.4 Quick IE

The retrieval of the supports of all subsets is not the only operation that can be shared among the different inclusion-exclusion computations. Indeed, many of the inclusion- exclusion sums share a considerable number of terms. Therefore, by sharing part of the computation of the sums, a considerable number of additions can be saved. For example, consider the sums for $ab\overline{cd}$ and $\overline{abcd}$:

$$ab\overline{cd} = ab - abc - abd + abcd$$
$$\overline{abcd} = a - \mathbf{ab} - ac - ad + \mathbf{abc} + \mathbf{abd} + acd - \mathbf{abcd}$$

Hence, if we first compute $support(ab\overline{cd})$, and then use

$$\overline{abcd} = a\overline{cd} - ab\overline{cd} = a - ac - ad + acd - ab\overline{cd}$$

we save 3 additions. In general, for a generalized itemset G, and an item a not in G, the following equality holds:

$$support(\overline{a}G) = support(G) - support(aG) .$$

This fact can now be exploited in a systematic manner as in Fig. 7.

Require: $I \subseteq \mathcal{I}$, $support(J)$ for all $J \subseteq I$
Ensure: $support(X \cup \overline{Y})$ for all $X \dot\cup Y = I$
1: **for all** $X \subseteq I$ **do**
2:      $A[X_b] := support(X)$;
3: **end for**
4: **for** $l := 2; l < 2^{|I|}; l := 2l$ **do**
5:      **for** $i := 1; i < 2^{|I|}; i{+} = l$ **do**
6:          **for** $j := 0$ to $l - 1$ **do**
7:              $A[i + j] := A[i + j] - A[i + l/2 + j]$;
8:          **end for**
9:      **end for**
10: **end for**

Fig. 7. QIE: Quick IE algorithm

Again, the algorithm starts by filling an array with the supports of all subsets of I. In the end, the entry for X in the array will contain the support of $X \cup \overline{Y}$, with $X \dot\cup Y = I$. To get to this support, the entries of A are iteratively updated. Let $I = \{i_1, \ldots, i_n\}$. After the jth iteration, the entry for X will contain the support of the generalized set $X \cup \overline{\{i_{n-j+1}, \ldots, i_n\} \setminus X}$. In other words, in the jth iteration, the entries for all X that do not contain item i_{n-j+1} are updated by adding $\overline{i_{n-j+1}}$ to it, and updating its support accordingly.

For example, let I be the itemset $\{a, b, c\}$. Before the procedure starts, array A contains the following supports:

000	001	010	011	100	101	110	111
{}	c	b	bc	a	ac	ab	abc

In the first iteration, item c is handled. This means that in this iterations, the entries of all sets X that do not contain c are updated to contain the support of $X \cup \overline{c}$. Hence, after the first iteration, the array contains the following supports:

000	001	010	011	100	101	110	111
$\overline{c}$	c	$b\overline{c}$	bc	$a\overline{c}$	ac	$ab\overline{c}$	abc

In the second iteration, item b is handled. Thus, after the second iteration, the array contains the following supports:

000	001	010	011	100	101	110	111
$\overline{bc}$	$\overline{b}c$	$b\overline{c}$	bc	$a\overline{bc}$	$a\overline{b}c$	$ab\overline{c}$	abc

In the third and last iteration, item a is handled, giving the final array:

000	001	010	011	100	101	110	111
$\overline{abc}$	$\overline{ab}c$	$\overline{a}b\overline{c}$	$\overline{a}bc$	$a\overline{bc}$	$a\overline{b}c$	$ab\overline{c}$	abc

Lemma 4. *For a given itemset I, with $|I| = n$, computing the supports of all generalized itemsets $X \cup \overline{Y}$, with $X \dot\cup Y = I$, using the Quick IE algorithm, comes down to a cost of $2^n + n2^{n-1}$.*

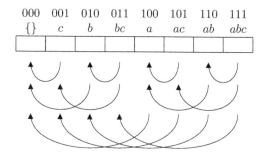

Fig. 8. Visualization of the QIE algorithm

Proof. The first term comes from filling the array with all subsets of I. Then, for every item $i \in I$, we update all itemsets not containing i, i.e. exactly 2^{n-1}.

Notice that the principle used in QIE, is also used in ADTrees [13], in the more general context of relations with categorical attributes, in order to speed up the computation of contingency tables. An ADTree is a datastructure that stored the counts of some queries over the relation. If now a transaction database is considered as a relation with binary attributes, and the construction of the ADTree is slightly modified such that only counts of itemsets are stored, the computation of a contingency table in ADTree, and the computation of the supports of all general itemsets by QIE will become very similar.

3.5 Summary

The memory and time requirements of the different methods discussed in this section are summarized in the following table. n denotes the number of items in an itemset I, for which the supports of all generalized itemsets based on it are computed. For the space requirement, we only report the memory required for the computation, not the input-, or the output size. This choice is motivated by the fact that the frequent itemsets and their supports can be stored in secondary storage, and the output can either directly be filtered for patterns meeting a support threshold, or be written to a database. Hence, the space requirement is the amount of main memory needed to compute the inclusion-exclusion. Notice also that reporting the total memory requirement instead would be far less informative, as it would yield a lower bound of $\mathcal{O}(2^n)$ for all methods.

Method	Space	Time	
Brute force	constant	$2n3^{n-1}$	$= \mathcal{O}(n3^n)$
Combined, no direct access	constant	$2(3^n - 2^n)$	$= \mathcal{O}(3^n)$
Combined, direct access	$\mathcal{O}(2^n)$	3^n	$= \mathcal{O}(3^n)$
QIE	$\mathcal{O}(2^n)$	$2^n + n2^{n-1}$	$= \mathcal{O}(n2^n)$

From this table we can conclude that, if the itemset is small, the QIE method is clearly the best. In the case, however, that the itemsets are stored in secondary storage, n is large, and memory is limited, the combined method without direct access is preferable.

4   Experiments

We implemented the well known Apriori algorithm [1] and adapted it to incorporate all proposed techniques for computing the supports of all generalized
itemsets. The experiments were ran on a 1.2 GHz Pentium IV using 1GB of
memory. More specifically, for every candidate itemset, we recorded the amount
of time needed to compute the supports of all generalized itemsets. The results
of this experiment are shown in Figure 9. In this figure, the average running time
per itemset length has been given. The dataset we used for this experiment was
the BMS-Webview-1 dataset donated by Kohavi et al. [17]. We experimented on
several datasets as well, but only report on BMS-Webview-1, as these figures are
independent of the dataset used. As expected, the algorithms behave as shown
in theory. (Note the logarithmic y axes.)

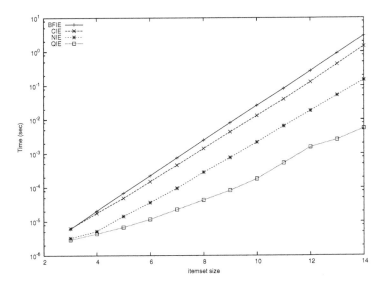

Fig. 9. Time needed to compute the generalized itemsets

For further evaluation, we also implemented the presented techniques in our
NDI implementation to see what the effect would be in a real application.
We performed our experimented on the BMS-Webview-1 and BMS-Webview-
2 datasets [17], and the results turned out to be very nice. The results are
shown in Figure 10 for BMS-Webview-1 and in Figure 11 for BMS-Webview-2.
We only show the results for the NIE and QIE algorithm as these are the two
fastest.

Although Non-Derivable Itemsets are shown to be small in general [6], and
the computation of the IE formulas in the candidate generation phase is only a
small part of the total cost of the algorithm, we observe remarkable speedups

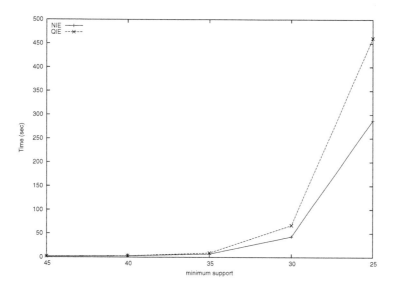

Fig. 10. Peformance improvement of the NDI algorithm for BMS-Webview-1

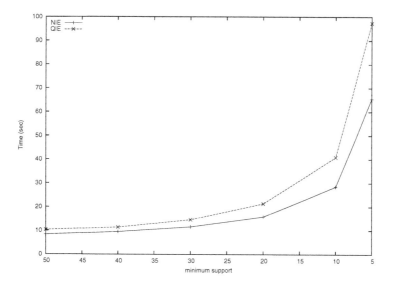

Fig. 11. Peformance improvement of the NDI algorithm for BMS-Webview-2

showing the applicability for the proposed QIE algorithm. For example, in BMS-Webview-1, for the lowest threshold, a speedup of more that 200 seconds was obtained.

5   Conclusion

We presented an overview of algorithms to compute the supports of so called generalized itemsets, i.e. itemsets in which items are allowed to be negated. We explained how this can be done without going back to the database, using the principle of Inclusion-Exclusion. We showed that many data mining applications could benefit from this principle in case an efficient algorithm existed. The QIE algorithm is theoretically and experimentally shown to be extremely efficient compared to several other techniques.

References

1. R. Agrawal and R. Srikant. Fast algorithms for mining association rules. In J.B. Bocca, M. Jarke, and C. Zaniolo, editors, *Proceedings 20th International Conference on Very Large Data Bases*, pages 487–499. Morgan Kaufmann, 1994.
2. C. Borgelt and R. Kruse. Induction of association rules: Apriori implementation. In W. Härdle and B. Rönz, editors, *Proceedings of the 15th Conference on Computational Statistics*, pages 395–400, `http://fuzzy.cs.uni-magdeburg.de/~borgelt/software.html`, 2002. Physica-Verlag.
3. J.-F. Boulicaut, A. Bykowski, and C. Rigotti. Approximation of frequency queries by means of free-sets. In *Proc. PKDD Int. Conf. Principles of Data Mining and Knowledge Discovery*, pages 75–85, 2000.
4. A. Bykowski and C. Rigotti. A condensed representation to find frequent patterns. In *Proc. PODS Int. Conf. Principles of Database Systems*, 2001.
5. T. Calders and B. Goethals. Minimal k-free representations of frequent sets. In *Proc. PKDD Int. Conf. Principles of Data Mining and Knowledge Discovery*, pages 71–82, 2002.
6. T. Calders and B. Goethals. Mining all non-derivable frequent itemsets. In *Proc. PKDD Int. Conf. Principles of Data Mining and Knowledge Discovery*, pages 74–85. Springer, 2002.
7. S. Jaroszewicz and D. A. Simivici. Support approximations using bonferroni-type inequalities. In *Proc. PKDD Int. Conf. Principles of Data Mining and Knowledge Discovery*, pages 212–224, 2002.
8. D.E. Knuth. *Fundamental Algorithms*. Addison-Wesley, Reading, Massachusetts, 1997.
9. M. Kryszkiewicz and M. Gajek. Why to apply generalized disjunction-free generators representation of frequent patterns? In *Proc. International Syposium on Methodologies for Intelligent Systems*, pages 382–392, 2002.
10. H. Mannila. Local and global methods in data mining: Basic techniques and open problems. In *ICALP 2002, 29th International Colloquium on Automata, Languages, and Programming*, 2002.
11. H. Mannila and H. Toivonen. Multiple uses of frequent sets and condensed representations. In *Proc. KDD Int. Conf. Knowledge Discovery in Databases*, 1996.
12. R. Meo. Theory of dependence values. *ACM Trans. on Database Systems*, 25(3):380–406, 2000.
13. A. Moore and M.S. Lee. Cached sufficient statistics for efficient machine learning with large datasets. *Journal of Artificial Intelligence Research*, 8:67–91, 1998.

14. D. Pavlov, H. Mannila, and P. Smyth. Beyond independence: Probabilistic models for query approximation on binary transaction data. *IEEE Trans. on Knowledge and Data Engineering*, 15(6):1409–1421, 2003.
15. A. Savinov. Mining dependence rules by finding largest support quota. In *ACM Symposium on Applied Computing*, pages 525–529, 2004.
16. Craig Silverstein, Sergey Brin, and Rajeev Motwani. Beyond market baskets: Generalizing association rules to dependence rules. *Data Mining and Knowledge Discovery*, 2(1):39–68, 1998.
17. Z. Zheng, R. Kohavi, and L. Mason. Real world performance of association rule algorithms. In *Proc. KDD Int. Conf. Knowledge Discovery in Databases*, pages 401–406. ACM Press, 2001.

Towards Mining Frequent Queries
in Star Schemes

Tao-Yuan Jen[1], Dominique Laurent[1], Nicolas Spyratos[2], and Oumar Sy[1,3]

[1] LICP, Université de Cergy-Pontoise, 95302 Cergy-Pontoise Cedex, France
{tao-yuan.jen, dominique.laurent}@dept-info.u-cergy.fr
[2] LRI, Université Paris 11, 91405 Orsay Cedex, France
spyratos@lri.fr
[3] Université Gaston Berger, Saint-Louis, Senegal
oumar.sy@ugb.sn

Abstract. The problem of mining *all* frequent queries in a database is
intractable, even if we consider conjunctive queries only. In this paper,
we study this problem under reasonable restrictions on the database,
namely: (*i*) the database scheme is a star scheme; (*ii*) the data in the
database satisfies a set of functional dependencies and a set of referential
constraints.

We note that star schemes are considered to be the most appropriate
schemes for data warehouses, while functional dependencies and referential constraints are the most common constraints that one encounters in
real databases. Our approach is based on the weak instance semantics
of databases and considers the class of selection-projection queries over
weak instances. In such a context, we show that frequent queries can be
mined using level-wise algorithms such as Apriori.

1 Introduction

The general problem of mining *all* frequent queries in a (relational) database,
i.e., all queries whose answer has a cardinality above a given threshold, is known
to be intractable, even if we consider conjunctive queries only [9].

However, mining all frequent queries from a database allows for the generation
of rules that cannot be easily obtained, even by approaches dealing with multiple
tables, such as in [4, 6, 7, 11, 15, 16]. This is so because, in these approaches, for
a given mining query, frequent queries are mined over the *same* scheme in one
single table. The following example, that serves as a running example throughout
the paper, illustrates this point.

Example 1. Let Δ be a database containing the tables *Cust*, *Prod* and *Sales*,
concerning customers, products and sales, respectively, and suppose that:

- the table *Cust* is defined over the attributes *Cid*, *Cname* and *Caddr*, standing respectively for the identifiers, the names and the addresses of customers,
- the table *Prod* is defined over the attributes *Pid* and *Ptype*, standing respectively for the identifiers and the types of products,

F. Bonchi and J.-F. Boulicaut (Eds.): KDID 2005, LNCS 3933, pp. 104–123, 2006.

– the table *Sales* is defined over the attributes Cid, Pid and Qty where Qty stands for the numbers of products bought by customers, characterized by their identifiers Pid and Cid, respectively.

If all frequent queries in Δ can be mined, then it is possible to mine a "rule" such as: *At least* 80% *of the customers living in Paris buy at least* 75% *of products of type beer*, or in other words: *At least* 80% *of all Parisian customers buy beer, and at least* 75% *of all beers have at least one Parisian customer.*

Denoting respectively by S and S' the selection conditions $Caddr = Paris$ and $Ptype = beer$, this is stated by the facts that the queries

– $q_1 = \pi_{Cid}(\sigma_S(Cust))$, $q_2 = \pi_{Cid}(\sigma_{S \wedge S'}(Cust \bowtie Prod \bowtie Sales))$,
– $q_3 = \pi_{Pid}(\sigma_{S'}(Prod))$, $q_4 = \pi_{Pid}(\sigma_{S \wedge S'}(Cust \bowtie Prod \bowtie Sales))$

are frequent (*i.e.*, the cardinalities of their answers are greater than or equal to a given threshold), and that the confidences of the rules (*i.e.*, the ratios of the supports of the right-hand sides over the supports of the left-hand sides) $q_1 \Rightarrow q_2$ and $q_3 \Rightarrow q_4$ are greater than or equal to 80% and 75%, respectively.

Note that since q_1 and q_2 (respectively q_3 and q_4) involve different tables over different schemes, customers (respectively beers) with no transactions are taken into account, which is not possible if only the join is considered.   □

In this paper, we study the problem of mining all frequent queries in a database under restrictions that are met in data warehousing. Indeed, data warehouses are generally organized according to *star schemes*, over which constraints such as functional dependencies and referential dependencies hold. We show that for databases over star schemes, all frequent projection-selection-join queries can be computed based on any level-wise algorithm such as Apriori [1].

In our formalism, a database Δ satisfying a set FD of functional dependencies is represented by its *weak instance*, denoted by Δ_{FD} [17]. Roughly speaking, Δ_{FD} is a table defined over the set U of all attributes, whose tuples may contain null values. We consider all queries q of the form $\sigma_S(\pi_X^{\downarrow}(\Delta_{FD}))$, where S is a conjunction of selection conditions, X is any set of attributes and $\pi_X^{\downarrow}(\Delta_{FD})$ is the *total* projection of Δ_{FD} over X (the total porjection over X is defined as the set of all restrictions of tuples containing no null values).

Given such a query q, the *answer in* Δ, denoted by $ans_\Delta(q)$, is the set of all tuples in $\pi_X^{\downarrow}(\Delta_{FD})$ that satisfy the selection condition S. We define the *support of* q *in* Δ, denoted by $sup_\Delta(q)$, to be the cardinality of $ans_\Delta(q)$.

Example 2. Referring back to Example 1, assume that the table $Cust$ satisfies the functional dependencies $Cid \rightarrow Cname$ and $Cid \rightarrow Caddr$, $Prod$ satisfies $Pid \rightarrow Ptype$ and $Sales$ satisfies $Cid, Pid \rightarrow Qty$. Then, Cid (respectively Pid) is the key of the table $Cust$ (respectively $Prod$), and the key of the table $Sales$ is the union of the keys of the tables $Cust$ and $Prod$. Thus, the scheme of Δ is a star scheme in which the fact table is $Sales$, the measure is Qty and the two dimension tables are $Cust$ and $Prod$.

Denoting by FD the set of functional dependencies given above, we consider the weak instance Δ_{FD} of Δ and we "adapt" the queries q_1, q_2, q_3 and q_4 of Example 1 to this setting. The resulting queries q'_1, q'_2, q'_3 and q'_4 are the following:

- $q'_1 = \sigma_S(\pi^{\downarrow}_{Cid,Caddr}(\Delta_{FD}))$, $q'_2 = \sigma_{S \wedge S'}(\pi^{\downarrow}_{Cid,Caddr,Ptype}(\Delta_{FD}))$,
- $q'_3 = \sigma_{S'}(\pi^{\downarrow}_{Pid,Ptype}(\Delta_{FD}))$, $q'_4 = \sigma_{S \wedge S'}(\pi^{\downarrow}_{Caddr,Pid,Ptype}(\Delta_{FD}))$,

where S and S' are as in Example 1.

We note that, although the four queries above involve the same table Δ_{FD}, they involve different projections. Hence, the computation of the supports (and thus of the confidences) takes into account the fact that there may exist customers (respectively beers) whose identifiers occur in the table $Cust$ (respectively $Prod$) but not in the table $Sales$. □

As we shall see, if the scheme of Δ is a star scheme, then the problem of mining all frequent conjunctive queries can be treated according to the following two steps, each of them being based on a level-wise algorithm such as Apriori [1]:

Step 1: compute all frequent queries of the form $\pi^{\downarrow}_X(\Delta_{FD})$.

Step 2: for each relation scheme X such that $\pi^{\downarrow}_X(\Delta_{FD})$ is frequent, compute all frequent queries of the form $\sigma_S(\pi^{\downarrow}_X(\Delta_{FD}))$, where S is a conjunction of selection conditions of the form $A = a$ with A in X and a is in $dom(A)$.

In this paper, we provide the theoretical framework for achieving the previous two steps, and in particular, we show that by taking the functional dependencies into account, queries with the same support can be characterized independently from the database instance. Moreover, we give algorithms and experimental results for Step 1, whereas the implementation of Step 2 is left to future work.

The paper is organized as follows: In Section 2, we briefly review previous work dealing with the problem of mining frequent queries in a relational database, and in Section 3, we recall the basics of weak instance semantics and of star schemes. Section 4 deals with the queries that are of interest in our approach. In Section 5, algorithms for the computation of Step 1 above are presented and experiments are reported. In Section 6 further issues are discussed, and Section 7 concludes the paper and presents some issues for future work.

2   Related Work

To our knowledge, except in [9, 10], no other work addresses the general problem of computing all frequent queries in a given database. The work in [9] considers *conjunctive* queries, as we do in this paper and points out that considering no restrictions on the database scheme and no functional dependencies leads to a non tractable complexity. Although some hints on possible restrictions are mentioned in [9], no specific case is actually studied.

We note that in [10], the authors consider restrictions on the frequent queries to be mined using the formalism of rule based languages. Restrictions are put mainly on the number of atoms in the body of the rules and on variables occurring in the heads of the rules. Although we do not consider such restrictions, we note that, in our approach, a query cannot involve more than one occurrence of every table present in the database. On the other hand, restrictions on variables in [10] roughly correspond to joins, projections and selections, as we do in this paper. Although more queries than in our approach are considered in [10], it should be pointed out that:

1. In [10], equivalent queries can be generated, which can not be tested efficiently and which does not happen in our approach.
2. Constraints such as functional dependencies and referential constraints are not taken into account in [10], as we do in this paper.

In [4], a set of attributes, called the key, provides the set of values according to which the supports are to be counted. Then, using a bias language, the different tables involving the key attributes are mined, based on a level-wise algorithm. Our approach (as well as that of [10]) can be seen as a generalization of the work in [4], in the sense that we mine all frequent conjunctive projection-selection-join queries for *all* keys. Notice that, in [4], joins are performed during the mining phase, whereas, in our approach, joins are somehow pre-computed in the weak instance. In this respect, it is important to note that, in our approach, functional dependencies are used to compute the joins, as well as to optimize the computation of frequent queries.

The work of [7] follows roughly the same strategy as in [4], except that joins are first performed in a level-wise manner, and for each join, conjunctive selection frequent queries are mined, based also on a level-wise algorithm.

All other approaches dealing with mining frequent queries in multi-relational databases [6, 11, 15, 16] consider a fixed set of "objects" to be counted during the mining phase and only one table for a given mining task. For instance, in [16], objects are (eventually partially) characterized by values over given attributes, whereas in [6], objects are characterized by a query, called the reference. Then, frequent queries are mined in one table that is defined by a query. We also note that, except for [16], all these approaches are restricted to conjunctive queries, as is the case in the present paper.

We refer to [5] for a more detailed comparison of the approaches presented in [4, 6, 7, 11, 15, 16]. The important thing to note is that all these works mine frequent queries according to a *fixed* set of "objects". Consequently, in order to mine rules as in Example 1 in these approaches, several minig queries are necessary, since such rules refer to different sets of "objects". In our approach, all frequent projection-join queries referring to any set of "objects" are mined through one single mining query, and then these queries are used as a basis for the computation of all frequent conjunctive projection-selection-join queries.

The approach of [3] is also related to our work because data cubes and star schemes both deal with multi dimensional data. However, the frequent queries considered in [3] involve the fact table only. Thus, contrary to our approach, it is not possible to mine frequent queries defined on any set of attributes. However, hierarchies are taken into account in [3], which is not the case in our approach.

3   Background

In this section, we recall briefly some basic notions related to the relational model of databases, universal relation scheme interfaces and star schemes.

Following [17] we consider a universe of attributes U, in which every attribute A is associated with a set of values called its domain and denoted by $dom(A)$; a relational database scheme consists of a set S of tables $\tau_1, \dots, \tau_n$, where each table τ_i is associated with an attribute set, called the scheme of τ_i and denoted by $sch(\tau_i)$; a relational database over S associates each table τ_i with a finite set of tuples over $sch(\tau_i)$.

3.1   Universal Relation Scheme Interfaces

Universal relation scheme interfaces were introduced in the early 80s in order to provide logical independence to the relational model. Given a database Δ over a universe of attributes U and a set of functional dependencies FD over U, logical independence is achieved by associating the pair (Δ, FD) to a *single* table over U, denoted by Δ_{FD}, and called the *weak instance* of Δ.

Without loss of generality ([2]), we assume that all functional dependencies in FD are of the form $X \to A$ where X is a relation scheme and A is an attribute of U not in X. The table Δ_{FD} is computed using the following procedure, called the *chase* procedure [17]:

1. *Initialization.* Build a table Δ_U over universe U as follows:
   For every tuple t over X appearing in Δ, define a tuple t_U over U such that for every A in U, $t_U.A = t.A$ if $A \in X$ and $t_U.A = w_i$ otherwise, where w_i is a null value not appearing in Δ_U; insert t_U into Δ_U.
2. *Iteration.* While Δ_U changes do the following:
   For every $X \to A$ in FD, for all tuples t_U and t'_U in Δ_U such that $t_U.X = t'_U.X$ do
   (a) if $t_U.A$ and $t'_U.A$ are two distinct constants, then stop (in this case, (Δ, FD) is inconsistent)
   (b) if $t_U.A$ is the constant a and $t'_U.A$ the null value w_i then replace w_i by a in t'_U
   (c) if $t_U.A$ is the null value w_i and $t'_U.A$ the null value w_j and if $w_i \neq w_j$ then replace w_j by w_i in t'_U.

If (Δ, FD) is consistent (*i.e.,* case (a) above did not occur), then the output of this procedure, denoted by Δ_{FD}, is called the *weak instance of Δ and FD*.

Following the weak instance model, the table Δ_{FD} is the only table to which queries on Δ are addressed. More precisely, for every relation scheme X, let $\pi_X^{\downarrow}(\Delta_{FD})$ denote the set of all tuples t over X such that (i) t contains no null value, and (ii) there exists t' in Δ_{FD} such that $t'.A = t.A$ for every A in X. Then it is possible to consider all queries of the form $\sigma_S(\pi_X^{\downarrow}(\Delta_{FD}))$ where S is a selection condition involving only attributes in X. If q is such a query, then we denote by $ans(q)$ the set of all tuples in $\pi_X^{\downarrow}(\Delta_{FD})$ that satisfy S.

In this paper, we consider only queries whose selection condition is a conjunction of elementary selection conditions of the form $A = a$ where A is an attribute in X and a a constant in $dom(A)$. We refer to [13, 17] for more details on the construction of Δ_{FD}.

3.2 Star Schemes

An N-*dimensional star scheme* consists of a distinguished table φ with scheme F, called the *fact table*, and N other tables $\delta_1, \ldots, \delta_N$ with schemes $D_1, \ldots, D_N$, called the *dimension tables*, such that:

1. If $K_1, \ldots, K_N$ are the (primary) keys of $\delta_1, \ldots, \delta_N$, respectively, then $K = K_1 \cup \ldots \cup K_N$ is the key of φ;
2. For every $i = 1, \ldots, N$, $\pi_{K_i}(\varphi) \subseteq \pi_{K_i}(\delta_i)$ (Note that each K_i is a foreign key in the fact table φ).

The attribute set $M = sch(\varphi) \setminus K$ is called the *measure* of the star scheme.

Example 3. The scheme of the database (Δ, FD) in our running example is a 2-dimensional star scheme $\{\delta_1, \delta_2, \varphi\}$ where the two dimension tables are $\delta_1 = Cust$ and $\delta_2 = Prod$, the fact table is $\varphi = Sales$ and the measure is $\{Qty\}$. Moreover:

- Cid is the key of δ_1, Pid is the key of δ_2, and $\{Cid, Pid\}$ is the key of φ,
- $\pi_{Cid}(\varphi) \subseteq \pi_{Cid}(\delta_1)$ and $\pi_{Pid}(\varphi) \subseteq \pi_{Pid}(\delta_2)$. ☐

In order to consider the weak instance of an N-dimensional star scheme Δ, we associate Δ with a set of functional dependencies FD defined as follows:

- for every $i = 1, \ldots, N$ and every attribute A in $D_i \setminus K_i$, $K_i \rightarrow A \in FD$,
- $K_1 \ldots K_N \rightarrow M \in FD$.

If (Δ, FD) is a database over an N-dimensional star scheme, we "simplify" its weak instance Δ_{FD} by removing from it all tuples t' for which there exists t in Δ_{FD} such that $t'.A = t.A$ for every attribute A over which t' is not null. We feel justified in performing this simplification because doing so does not change the answers to queries. From now on, the symbol Δ_{FD} will denote the simplified table. The following proposition gives a characterization of the tuples in the simplified table.

Proposition 1. *Let (Δ, FD) be a database over an N-dimensional star scheme. The (simplified) weak instance Δ_{FD} of (Δ, FD) contains two kinds of tuples:*

- *either total tuples, i.e., tuples containing no null value, and there is a one-to-one mapping between these tuples and the tuples of the fact table,*
- *or tuples t containing constants over the attributes of a single dimension, say i, such that the key value $t.K_i$ does not occur in the fact table.*

Proof. At the initialization step, the table under construction contains either rows having no null values only over attributes in F (those tuples come from the fact table φ), or rows having no null values only over attributes in D_i, for some i in $\{1, \ldots, N\}$ (those tuples come from the dimension table D_i).

Due to the fact that each K_i is a foreign key in φ, during the iteration step every row r having no null values over attributes in F is combined with exactly one row r_i having no null values over attributes in D_i, for every i in $\{1, \ldots, N\}$. This produces a row having no null value, and the rows $r_1, \ldots, r_N$ are removed according to the simplification assumption.

Therefore, in Δ_{FD}, the rows having no null value come from exactly one tuple in φ, and for every $i = 1, \ldots, N$, all tuples in D_i whose key value does not appear in φ are unchanged by the chase procedure; and this completes the proof.

We denote by Δ_{FD}^{φ} the set of all total tuples in Δ_{FD} and by Δ_{FD}^{i} the set of all tuples in Δ_{FD} containing constants only over attributes of dimension i, for $i = 1, \ldots, N$.

In the remainder of this paper, we consider a *fixed N-dimensional star scheme*, with fact table φ and dimension tables $\delta_1, \ldots, \delta_N$, and a *fixed* database Δ over that scheme. Moreover, for the sake of simplification, we assume that for every $i = 1, \ldots, N$, the key of dimension i is reduced to a single attribute K_i.

On the other hand, it is well-known that in practice, the cardinality of the fact table is much higher than that of any dimension table. In order to take this situation into account, we assume that for every $i = 1, \ldots, N$, $|\delta_i| \leq |\varphi|$.

Example 4. Referring back to Example 1, the universe of attributes is $U = \{Cid,$ $Cname, Caddr, Pid, Ptype, Qty\}$ and the functional dependencies are $FD = \{Cid \rightarrow Cname, Cid \rightarrow Caddr, Pid \rightarrow Ptype, CidPid \rightarrow Qty\}$.

Let us consider a database (Δ, FD) consisting of the following three relations:

Cust	Cid	Cname	Caddr
	c_1	John	Paris
	c_2	Mary	Paris
	c_3	Jane	Paris
	c_4	Anne	Tours

Prod	Pid	Ptype
	p_1	milk
	p_2	beer

Sales	Cid	Pid	Qty
	c_1	p_1	10
	c_2	p_2	5
	c_2	p_1	1
	c_1	p_2	10

The simplified weak instance Δ_{FD} is the following (where null values are represented by the empty character):

Δ_{FD}	Cid	Pid	Cname	Caddr	Ptype	Qty
	c_3		Jane	Paris		
	c_4		Anne	Tours		
	c_1	p_1	John	Paris	milk	10
	c_2	p_2	Mary	Paris	beer	5
	c_2	p_1	Mary	Paris	milk	1
	c_1	p_2	John	Paris	beer	10

Note that in this example, Δ_{FD}^{φ} consists of the last four tuples of Δ_{FD}, Δ_{FD}^{1} of the first two tuples, and Δ_{FD}^{2} is empty. □

4   Frequent Queries

4.1   Queries

Definition 1. *Let Δ be a database over an N-dimensional star scheme, and let X be a relation scheme. Denoting by $\perp$ and $\top$ the false and true conditions, respectively, let $\Sigma(X)$ be the following set of conjunctive selection conditions:*

$$\Sigma(X) = \{\perp, \top\} \cup \{\, (A_1 = a_1) \wedge \ldots \wedge (A_k = a_k) \mid$$
$$(\forall i = 1, \ldots, k)(A_i \in X \text{ and } a_i \in dom(A_i)) \text{ and}$$
$$(\forall i, j \in \{1, \ldots, k\})(i \neq j \Rightarrow A_i \neq A_j)\}.$$

Selection conditions of $\Sigma(X)$ are called selection conditions over X. *Moreover, we denote by $\mathcal{Q}(X)$ the set of all queries of the form $\sigma_S(\pi_X^{\downarrow}(\Delta_{FD}))$ where $S \in \Sigma(X)$, and by $\mathcal{Q}(\Delta)$ the union of all sets $\mathcal{Q}(X)$ for all relation schemes X.*

According to Definition 1, we have $\sigma_{\top}(\pi_X^{\downarrow}(\Delta_{FD})) = \pi_X^{\downarrow}(\Delta_{FD})$. To simplify the notations, we denote $\sigma_S(\pi_X^{\downarrow}(\Delta_{FD}))$ by $\sigma_S(X)$ with the convention that when $S = \top$, $\pi_X^{\downarrow}(\Delta_{FD})$ is denoted by (X). We define frequent queries as in [9]:

Definition 2. *Let Δ be a database over an N-dimensional star scheme. For every query q in $\mathcal{Q}(\Delta)$, the* support *of q in Δ, denoted by $sup_\Delta(q)$ (or by $sup(q)$ when Δ is understood), is the cardinality of the answer to q in Δ.*

Given a support threshold min-sup, a query q is said to be frequent *in Δ (or simply* frequent *when Δ in understood) if $sup_\Delta(q) \geq$ min-sup.*

Referring back to Example 4, it is easy to see that $sup(q_1') = 3$, $sup(q_2') = 2$ and $sup(q_3') = sup(q_4') = 1$. Thus, for a support threshold equal to 3, q_1' is frequent whereas q_2', q_3' and q_4' are not.

As shown in [6], for every X, $\mathcal{Q}(X)$ has a lattice structure, which implies that frequent queries of $\mathcal{Q}(X)$ can be computed using any level-wise algorithm such as Apriori ([1]). However, the main difficulty in the present approach is that such a computation should be processed for every relation scheme X.

We notice in this respect that for every relation scheme X and for every query q in $\mathcal{Q}(X)$, we have $sup((X)) \geq sup(q)$. Therefore, if (X) is not frequent, then no exploration of $\mathcal{Q}(X)$ is needed. Based on this observation, in the next section, we focus on the computation of all frequent queries of the form (X).

4.2   Equivalent Relation Schemes

Our approach for the efficient computation of frequent queries is based on the following remark: if X and Y are two schemes having the same key, then for every selection condition S over X and Y we have $|\sigma_S(X)| = |\sigma_S(Y)|$ (see Proposition 2 below). Moreover, as stated by the following lemma, in the case of a star scheme, every relation scheme X has only one key.

Lemma 1. *Let Δ be a database over an N-dimensional star scheme. For every relation scheme X, let key(X) be defined as follows:*

- $if\ for\ every\ i = 1, \ldots, N,\ K_i \in X\ then\ key(X) = K_1 \ldots K_N$
- $else\ key(X) = X \setminus \{A \in X \mid (\exists i \in \{1, \ldots, N\})(K_i A \subseteq D_i \cap X\ and\ A \neq K_i)\}.$

Then $(i)\ key(X)$ *is a key of* X, *and* $(ii)\ key(X)$ *is the only key of* X.

Proof. Let X be a relation scheme. Clearly, the functional dependency $key(X) \to X$ holds and thus, $key(X)$ is a super key of X. In order to show that $key(X)$ is minimal, let A be an attribute in $key(X)$ and let us show that the dependency $key(X) \setminus A \to A$ cannot be obtained from FD:

- This holds if $A = K_i$, because FD contains no functional dependency has K_i in its right hand side.
- If A is a measure attribute in M, by definition of $key(X)$, this implies that there exists i_0 in $\{1, \ldots, N\}$ such that $K_{i_0} \notin X$. Since the only functional dependency having A in its right hand side contains all K_is in its left hand side, K_{i_0} has to be obtained using FD and the attributes in $key(X) \setminus A$. However, this not possible because FD contains no dependency having K_{i_0} in its right hand side.
- Otherwise, A is an attribute in some D_i different than K_i. In this case, by definition of $key(X)$, $K_i \notin X$. Since the only functional dependency having A in its right hand side contains K_i in its left hand side, it can be seen as above that $key(X) \setminus A \to A$ cannot be derived from FD.

Therefore, $key(X)$ is a key of X. Now, let us assume that K is another key of X. It can be shown as above that there cannot exist an attribute A in $key(X) \setminus K$. Thus $key(X) \subseteq K$, which implies that $key(X) = K$. Therefore, the proof is complete.

We define the following equivalence relation between relation schemes, based on the functional dependencies in FD and their properties ([2, 17]).

Definition 3. *Given two relation schemes* X *and* Y, X *is said to be* less than or equal to Y, *denoted by* $X \preceq Y$, *if* $X \to Y$ *can be derived from* FD.

It is easy to see that the relation $\preceq$ as defined above is a pre-ordering. We can extend this preordering to a partiel ordering over equivalence classes of schemes as usual, *i.e.*, by defining

$$X \equiv Y \text{ if and only if } X \preceq Y \text{ and } Y \preceq X.$$

We denote by $[X]$ the equivalence class of X and by $\mathcal{K}$ the set of all equivalence classes of schemes. We note that this partial ordering can also be defined using closures: $X \preceq Y$ if $Y^+ \subseteq X^+$, where X^+ is the closure of X under FD, *i.e.*, the set of all attributes A such that $X \to A$ can be derived from FD ([2, 17]).

Example 5. Let us consider again the database (Δ, FD) and its weak instance shown in Example 4. For $X = \{Cid, Caddr\}$, by Lemma 1, we have $key(X) = \{Cid\}$, since Cid is the key of the table $Cust$ and $\{Cid, Caddr\} \subseteq \{Cid, Cname, Caddr\}$. Moreover, using the functional dependencies in FD, it easy to see that $X^+ = \{Cid, Cname, Caddr\}$.

Similarly, for $Y = \{Cid, Caddr, Qty\}$, we have $key(Y) = \{Cid, Qty\}$ and $Y^+ = \{Cid, Cname, Caddr, Qty\}$. Moreover, as $X \subseteq Y$, $Y \to X$ can be derived from FD, and thus, $[Y] \preceq [X]$ holds. $\qquad\square$

In the following proposition, we state basic properties of equivalence classes.

Proposition 2. *1. For every relation scheme X, $[X] = [key(X)] = [X^+]$.*
2. For all relation schemes X and Y such that $[X] = [Y]$, if S is a selection condition over $X \cap Y$, then we have: $sup(\sigma_S(X)) = sup(\sigma_S(Y))$.

Proof
1. The result follows from the definition of the equivalence relation $\equiv$ and from the fact that $X^+ = (key(X))^+$.
2. For every X, we have $|ans((X))| = |ans(key(X))|$. Since $[X] = [Y]$, X and Y have the same keys. By Lemma 1, we obtain $key(X) = key(Y)$. Hence, $[X] = [Y]$ implies that $sup((X)) = sup((Y))$, and thus, if S is a selection condition over $X \cap Y$, then $sup(\sigma_S(X)) = sup(\sigma_S(Y))$; which completes the proof.

Proposition 2(1) states that every class $[X]$ has two distinguished representatives, namely $key(X)$ and X^+. In fact for every relation scheme X, since $key(X)$ is the only key of X, it can be seen that $[X] = \{X' \mid key(X) \subseteq X' \subseteq X^+\}$.

Moreover, Proposition 2(2) suggests that only one computation is necessary to know the supports of frequent queries over *all* relation schemes from the same class. The following corollary states this important property of our approach.

Corollary 1. *Let X be a relation scheme and min-sup a support threshold. For every selection condition S in $\Sigma(X)$, $\sigma_S(X)$ is frequent if and only if $\sigma_S(X^+)$ is frequent.*

Proof. Since $X \subseteq X^+$, we have $\Sigma(X) \subseteq \Sigma(X^+)$. Thus, S is in $\Sigma(X^+)$, and the corollary follows from Proposition 2(2) above.

In order to state a property of monotonicity of the support with respect to $\preceq$, we introduce the following two exclusive kinds of relation schemes:

1. Schemes X for which there exists i in $\{1, \ldots, N\}$ such that $X \subseteq D_i$. These schemes are called *D-schemes*.
2. Schemes X such that, for all i in $\{1, \ldots, N\}$, $X \not\subseteq D_i$. These schemes are called *F-schemes*.

In our running example, if we consider $X = \{Cid, Caddr\}$ and $Y = \{Cid, Caddr, Qty\}$, then X is a D-scheme (because $X \subseteq \{Cid, Cname, Caddr\}$) and Y is an F-scheme (because $Y \not\subseteq \{Cid, Cname, Caddr\}$ and $Y \not\subseteq \{Pid, Ptype\}$).

The following lemma shows that all schemes in a given equivalence class modulo $\equiv$ are of the same kind.

Lemma 2. *For every relation scheme X, if X is a D-scheme (respectively an F-scheme) then, every X' in $[X]$ is a D-scheme (respectively an F-scheme).*

Proof. We first note that, for every X and every X' in $[X]$, we have $X' \subseteq X^+$. Moreover, let X be a D-scheme such that $X \subseteq D_i$. Then $X^+ \subseteq D_i$, and thus $X' \subseteq D_i$. On the other hand, if X is an F-scheme, then assuming that X' is a D-scheme such that $[X] = [X']$ implies that X is also a D-scheme, which is a contradiction. Thus, the proof is complete.

Proposition 3. *If X and Y are both D-schemes or both F-schemes and if S is a selection condition over $X \cap Y$, then:* $[Y] \preceq [X] \Rightarrow sup(\sigma_S(X)) \leq sup(\sigma_S(Y))$.

Proof. We first show that under the hypotheses of the proposition, if $[Y] \preceq [X]$ then $sup((X^+)) \leq sup((Y^+))$. To this end, let t be in $ans((X^+))$. Then, there exists a row r in Δ_{FD} such that $r.(X^+) = t$, and since t contains no null values, such is the case for $r.(X^+)$. Moreover, as $[Y] \preceq [X]$, we have $X^+ \subseteq Y^+$.

If X and Y are D-schemes, then there exist i and j in $\{1, \ldots, N\}$ such that $X^+ \subseteq D_i$ and $Y^+ \subseteq D_j$. As $X^+ \subseteq Y^+$, we have $i = j$. Therefore, by Proposition 1, $r.(Y^+)$ contains no null values, and thus, we have that $r.(Y^+) \in ans((Y^+))$.

If X and Y are F-schemes, then by Proposition 1, r contains no null values, which implies that $r.(Y^+)$ contains no null values, and thus that $r.(Y^+) \in ans((Y^+))$.

In other words, we have just shown that $|ans((X^+))| \leq |ans((Y^+))|$, thus that $sup((X^+)) \leq sup((Y^+))$. Moreover, based on Proposition 2, we have $sup((X^+)) = sup((X))$ and $sup((Y^+)) = sup((Y))$, and the proof follows from the fact that the selection operator with conjunctive selection conditions is monotonic.

The following example illustrates Proposition 3.

Example 6. Let us consider again the database (Δ, FD) and its weak instance shown in Example 4. We recall that, for $X = \{Cid, Caddr\}$ and $Y = \{Cid, Caddr, Qty\}$, we have $key(X) = \{Cid\}$, $X^+ = \{Cid, Cname, Caddr\}$, $key(Y) = \{Cid, Qty\}$ and $Y^+ = \{Cid, Cname, Caddr, Qty\}$.

Proposition 2 shows that $sup((X)) = sup((X^+)) = sup((Cid))$ and that $sup((Y)) = sup((Y^+)) = sup((Cid\,Qty))$. However, although $[Y] \preceq [X]$, we have $sup((X)) > sup((Y))$, because $sup((X)) = 4$ and $sup((Y)) = 3$. This shows that Proposition 3 does not hold if, for instance, X is a D-scheme and Y is an F-scheme.

On the other hand, denoting by S the selection condition $Caddr = Paris \wedge Ptype = beer$, recall that for a support threshold equal to 3, the query $q_2' = \sigma_S(Cid\,Caddr\,Ptype)$ is not frequent. Therefore, when computing the frequent queries of $Q(Y')$, where $Y' = \{Cname, Caddr, Ptype\}$, by Proposition 3, we know, *without any computation*, that $\sigma_S(Y')$ is not frequent, because Y^+ and Y' are two F-schemes such that $[Y^+] \preceq [Y']$. $\square$

Now, in order to show that the set $\mathcal{K}$ of equivalence classes has a lattice structure, we define the following operations.

Definition 4. *Let $\otimes$ and $\oplus$ be two binary operations over $\mathcal{K}$ defined for every $[X]$ and $[Y]$ in $\mathcal{K}$ by:* $[X] \otimes [Y] = [X^+ \cup Y^+]$ *and* $[X] \oplus [Y] = [X^+ \cap Y^+]$.

Proposition 2(1) implies that the operators given above are independent from the repensentatives of the classes. In other words, if $[X] = [X']$ and $[Y] = [Y']$, then $[X] \otimes [Y] = [X'] \otimes [Y']$ and $[X] \oplus [Y] = [X'] \oplus [Y']$.

Moreover, it is easy to see that, for all $[X_1]$ and $[X_2]$ in $\mathcal{K}$, we have:

1. $[X_1] \otimes [X_2] \preceq [X_i]$ and $[X_i] \preceq [X_1] \oplus [X_2]$, for $i = 1, 2$,
2. $[X_1] \otimes [X_2] = \max_{\preceq} \{[Y] \in \mathcal{K} \mid [Y] \preceq [X_1] \text{ and } [Y] \preceq [X_2]\}$, and
   $[X_1] \oplus [X_2] = \min_{\preceq} \{[Y] \in \mathcal{K} \mid [X_1] \preceq [Y] \text{ and } [X_2] \preceq [Y]\}$.

As a consequence, $\langle \mathcal{K}, \preceq \rangle$ with the operators $\otimes$ and $\oplus$ is a lattice. Based on these results, given a support threshold *min-sup*, all frequent queries can be computed according to the following two steps:

1. *Step 1:* Computation of all frequent classes, *i.e.*, all classes $[X]$ such that, for all $X \in [X]$, $sup((X)) \geq$ *min-sup*. Minimal representatives of classes (*i.e.*, $key(X)$) are used, in order to manipulate schemes as small as possible.
2. *Step 2:* Computation of all frequent queries. For each frequent class $[X]$, all frequent queries of the form $\sigma_S(X^+)$ are computed. Then, based on Corollary 1, for all X' in $[X]$, the frequent queries of the form $\sigma_{S'}(X')$ can be obtained *without any access to the data.*

Regarding Step 1 above, based on Proposition 3 and our assumption $|\varphi| \geq |\delta_i|$ for every $i = 1, \ldots, N$, it turns out that the support of $(K_1 \ldots K_N)$ is maximal among the supports of all classes of $\mathcal{K}$. We also note that the computation of $sup((K_1 \ldots K_N))$ requires no access to the database, since $sup((K_1 \ldots K_N)) = |\varphi|$, which is assumed to be known in advance.

Moreover, due to Lemma 1, starting from $[K_1 \ldots K_N]$, the lattice $\langle \mathcal{K}, \preceq \rangle$ is built up level by level as follows:

- Level 1 consists of the single class $[K_1 \ldots K_N]$.
- At every level l, given a class $[X]$, let us assume that $X = K_{i_1} \ldots K_{i_p} X'$ where X' contains no key attributes. Then, all successors of $[X]$ at level $l+1$ are obtained by applying one of the transformations below:
  1. choose j in $1, \ldots, p$ and replace K_{i_j} in X by all non key attributes in D_{i_j}, or
  2. remove from X an attribute A of X'.
  Moreover, if $l = 1$ then add the set M of measure attributes to every scheme computed by the previous two steps.

Example 7. In our running example, level 1 of the lattice $\langle \mathcal{K}, \preceq \rangle$ contains the class $[\{Cid, Pid\}]$, and as Qty is the only measure attribute, level 2 contains $[\{Cname, Caddr, Pid, Qty\}]$ and $[\{Cid, Ptype, Qty\}]$. Then, the successors of $[\{Cid, Ptype, Qty\}]$ at level 3 are $[\{Cname, Caddr, Ptype, Qty\}]$, $[\{Cid, Qty\}]$ and $[\{Cid, Ptype\}]$. □

5   Computation of Frequent Classes

5.1   Algorithms

In the following algorithm, C is meant to contain all candidate classes for a given iteration step. As in Apriori, C is generated from the set L of frequent classes computed during the previous iteration step. Moreover, the function **prune** performs the pruning of candidates, based on Proposition 3.

Algorithm 1

Input: The simplified weak instance Δ_{FD} associated to a database Δ over an N-dimensional star scheme $\{D_1, \ldots, D_N, F\}$. The cardinalities $|\varphi|, |\delta_1|, \ldots, |\delta_N|$ of all tables in Δ. A support threshold $min\text{-}sup$.

Output: All frequent classes.

Method:

```
if |φ| < min-sup then //no computation because for every q ∈ Q(Δ), |φ| ≥ sup(q)
    Freq = ∅
else //the computation starts with [K₁...Kₙ] which is frequent
    Freq = {[K₁...Kₙ]}; L = {[K₁...Kₙ]}; toDo = {1,...,N}
    while L ≠ ∅ do
        C = generate(L) ; prune(C, L, toDo)
        L = L ∪ {[X] ∈ C | sup((X)) ≥ min-sup}
        if L = ∅ then
            L = {[Kᵢ] | i ∈ toDo and |δᵢ| ≥ min-sup}
            toDo = ∅
        end if
        Freq = Freq ∪ L
    end while
end if
return Freq
```

We note that the last if-statement in Algorithm 1 is due to the fact that even if, due to prunings, some D-schemes have not been processed, this processing has to be done. This is so because Proposition 3 implies that the supports of D-schemes cannot be compared with those of F-schemes. This remark is also taken into account in the algorithms **generate** and **prune** (see Figure 1).

We note that, in algorithm **prune**, we consider separately the cases of a D-scheme and of an F-scheme as follows:

– If X is a D-scheme such that $X \subseteq D_i$, then we know that either $X = K_i$ or $X \subseteq D_i \setminus K_i$. In the first case, $[X]$ has to be processed because no other scheme contained in D_i has been encountered in the previous computations. Since the cardinality of δ_i is assumed to be known, $[X]$ is removed from C and the sets L' and $ToDo$ are modified accordingly. If $X \subseteq D_i \setminus K_i$, the pruning is achieved as usual: if there is some A in D_i different than K_i such that $[XA]$ is not in L, then we know that X and XA are two D-schemes such that $[XA] \preceq [X]$ and (XA) is not frequent. Therefore, according to Proposition 3, $[X]$ is not frequent and thus, can be removed from C.

– If X is an F-scheme, in the first if-statement of this case, A is a non key attribute not in X' and not in $D_{i_1} \cup \ldots \cup D_{i_p}$. Then, by construction of $\langle \mathcal{K}, \preceq \rangle$, $[X]$ has been generated from $[XA]$. Therefore, $[XA] \preceq [X]$, and as $[XA]$ is not in L, $[X]$ is not frequent and so, can be removed from C.

In the second if-statement, we consider the case where X contains all non key attributes of a dimension D_i. Then, $i \notin \{i_1, \ldots, i_p\}$ and thus, by construction of $\langle \mathcal{K}, \preceq \rangle$, $[X]$ has been generated from $(X \setminus D_i) \cup K_i$. Therefore, $[(X \setminus D_i) \cup K_i] \preceq [X]$, and as $[(X \setminus D_i) \cup K_i]$ is not in L, $[X]$ is not frequent and so, can be removed from C.

Algorithm generate

Input: A set L of frequent classes $[X]$ at the same level l in $\langle \mathcal{K}, \preceq \rangle$.
Output: The set C of all candidate classes $[X]$ obtained from L at level $l+1$ in $\langle \mathcal{K}, \preceq \rangle$.
Method:
if $L = \{[K_1 \ldots K_N]\}$ then
    //for every $i = 1, \ldots, N$ replace K_i with all non-key attributes of D_i and add M
    $C = \{[(K_1 \ldots K_N \setminus K_i) \cup (D_i M \setminus K_i)] \mid i = 1, \ldots, N\}$
else
    $C = \emptyset$
    for each $[X] \in L$ do
        for each attribute A in X do
            if A is the key attribute K_i then
                //replace K_i in X with all non-key attributes of D_i to get a candidate
                $C = C \cup \{[(X \setminus K_i) \cup (D_i \setminus K_i)] \mid D_i \neq K_i\}$
            else //remove A from X to get a candidate
                $C = C \cup \{[X \setminus A] \mid X \neq A\}$
            end if
        end for each
    end for each
end if
return C

Algorithm prune

Input: A set L of frequent classes $[X]$ at the same level l in $\langle \mathcal{K}, \preceq \rangle$, the set C of candidate classes $[X]$ for level $l+1$ and the current value of $toDo$.
Output: The pruned set C, the initial value of the set L of frequent classes at level $l+1$ in $\langle \mathcal{K}, \preceq \rangle$, and the modified value of $toDo$.
Method:
$L' = \emptyset$
for each $[X] \in C$ do
    if X is a D-scheme such that $X \subseteq D_i$ then
        if $X = K_i$ then
            if $|\delta_i| \geq min\text{-}sup$ then $L' = L' \cup \{[K_i]\}$ end if
            $toDo = toDo \setminus \{i\}$; $C = C \setminus \{[X]\}$
        else //$X \neq K_i$
            if $(\exists A \in D_i \setminus K_i)(A \notin X$ and $[XA] \notin L)$ then $C = C \setminus \{[X]\}$ end if
        end if
    else //X is an F-scheme
        Assume $X = K_{i_1} \ldots K_{i_p} X'$ where X' contains no K_i
        if $(\exists A)(A \notin X'$ and $A \in D_i \setminus K_i$ for $i \neq i_1, \ldots, i_p$ and $[XA] \notin L)$ then
            $C = C \setminus \{[X]\}$
        end if
        if $(\exists i)(D_i \setminus K_i \subseteq X'$ and $[(X \setminus D_i) \cup K_i] \notin L)$ then $C = C \setminus \{[X]\}$ end if
    end if
end for each
$L = L'$;
return L, C and $toDo$

Fig. 1. Algorithms for Generating and Pruning Candidates

5.2   Implementation of Algorithm 1

The main difficulty in implementing Algorithm 1 is counting the supports of
the candidates, because a tuple over a given scheme can appear in several rows
of Δ_{FD}. Since we have to consider several classes at the same time (*i.e.*, the
candidates at a given level in $\langle \mathcal{K}, \preceq \rangle$), it is not possible to sort Δ_{FD} accordingly,
as done in [4, 6]. Note also that this remark shows that an FP-growth technique
([12]) can not be efficiently used in our appoach, since it would require that the
database be sorted for each candidate.

To cope with this problem, the table Δ_{FD} is stored as a two-dimensional array
of booleans, denoted by B, as follows: each tuple t is stored as a vector of booleans,
whose length L is the total number of constants appearing in Δ. Assuming that
all these constants are ordered, the vector associated to t has value *true* at each
position corresponding to a constant occurring in t, and *false* at any other position.

Similarly, every relation scheme X is seen as a vector of booleans, denoted
by B_X, the length of which is the cardinality of the universe U. To this end, we
order the attributes in such a way that all key attributes K_i are smaller than any
non-key attribute. Based on this ordering, the algorithms generate and prune
above can be implemented efficiently.

At each level of $\langle \mathcal{K}, \preceq \rangle$, the rows of B are scanned and for each of them, the
following actions are performed: Let $r_i = [b_1, \ldots, b_M]$ be the ith row in B, then

- For every $j = 1, \ldots, L$ such that $b_j = true$, consider the vector $[B(1, j), \ldots,$
  $B(i - 1, j)]$. All these vectors build a two dimensional array, denoted by
  B_{aux}. Note that B_{aux} can be stored in main memory, since it contains at
  most $|U| \times (|B| - 1)$ booleans, where $|B|$ is the number of rows in B.
- B_{aux} is used for the computation of the support counts of the current candidates as follows: For each candidate $[X]$, compute the boolean AND of all
  columns of B_{aux} corresponding to an attribute in X. Denoting by V the
  resulting boolean vector, the support of (X) is computed as follows:
  - If V contains at least one value *true*, then do not increment the support
    count of (X) (because in this case, the subtuple over X of the current
    tuple represented by r_i has been counted previously).
  - Otherwise increment the support count of (X) (because in this case, the
    subtuple over X of the current tuple represented by r_i has not been
    counted previously).

5.3   Experimental Results

The algorithms given previously have been implemented in C, and our first experiments have been processed on a Pentium 2.8 GHz PC with 496 MB main
memory running FreeBSD. The randomly generated data sets that we have considered are denoted by $NDRRAAX$ where N is the number of dimensions, R is
the number of rows in the fact table, A is the total number of attributes in U
and X is the maximum number of descriptive attributes (attributes other than
the key) in the dimensions. We report below our results on the following data
sets, for which R has been set successively to 500, 1,000, 1,500 and 2,000:

- 4D*RR*25A06. In this case, we have 4 dimensions, with 7, 6, 6 and 5 attributes, respectively, resulting in 25 attributes including the measure.
- 4D*RR*25A08. This case is the same as above except that we have 9, 8, 4 and 3 attributes in the dimensions.
- 6D*RR*25A04. In this case, we have 6 dimensions, with 5, 5, 4, 4, 3 and 3 attributes, respectively, resulting in 25 attributes including the measure.
- 6D*RR*25A07. This case is the same as above except that we have 8, 4, 4, 3, 3 and 2 attributes in the dimensions.

In our tests, the support threshold has been set to 70% of the number of rows in the fact table. For every data set, the following tables show on the one hand the number of frequent classes (F-classes), and on the other hand the total computation time (T-time) and the time spent for counting (C-time), both given in seconds. It turns out from our first experiments that the computation of frequent classes *is tractable,* even though it can take up to 5.5 hours (see 4D2000R25A08).

Data set	F-classes	T-time	C-time
4D0500R25A06	2,399,888	1,487	1,450
4D1000R25A06	2,375,011	4,884	4,847
4D1500R25A06	2,368,956	10,236	10,200
4D2000R25A06	2,368,429	17,574	17,535
4D0500R25A08	2,960,332	1,802	1,755
4D1000R25A08	2,824,546	5,632	5,585
4D1500R25A08	2,818,652	11,724	11,680
4D2000R25A08	2,818,202	20,002	19,955

Data set	F-classes	T-time	C-time
6D0500R25A04	1,168,371	599	583
6D1000R25A04	1,164,123	1,884	1,867
6D1500R25A04	1,162,506	3,866	3,849
6D2000R25A04	1,162,060	6,560	6,542
6D0500R25A07	1,562,568	813	788
6D1000R25A07	1,546,520	2,468	2,444
6D1500R25A07	1,544,035	5,047	5,026
6D2000R25A07	1,543,850	8,545	8,522

It is important to note that we tried to compute frequent schemes for the data set 4D0500R25A06 by running our algorithm on the power set of the universe U, *i.e., without considering equivalence classes.* Considering one single level in the corresponding lattice, the ratio of frequent *schemes* over frequent *classes* is about 40 (27,105 frequent classes and 1,081,575 frequent schemes). This shows that considering equivalence classes instead of single schemes is an important issue in our approach and leads to significant computational savings. Moreover, it can be seen from the tables above that most of the computation time is used for counting the supports.

We are currently investigating optimizations for this computation. As a first issue in this respect, we note that, in practice, repeated measure values in a fact table are not common, meaning that the scheme (M) is in general frequent. This implies that, in Algorithm 1, the lattice is explored down to its lowest level, which is costly.

On the other hand, for every class $[X]$ such that $M \not\subseteq X$, M and XM are F-schemes such that $[XM] \preceq [M]$. Thus, if (M) is frequent then, based on Proposition 3, (XM) is frequent. Hence, the computation of frequent classes can be achieved as follows:

1. Compute the support of (M). Assuming that Δ_{FD} is sorted according to the values over M, this computation requires a single pass over Δ_{FD}.
2. Compute frequent classes over $\pi^{\downarrow}_{D_1...D_N}(\Delta_{FD})$.

The tests we ran based on this policy have shown computation times about half of those reported above. However, the price to pay for this important optimization is that the supports of all frequent schemes of the form (XM) are unknown, therefore, this issue must be investigated further.

6   Further Issues

In this section, we first consider the problem of mining all frequent queries, and not only the frequent classes. Then, the problem of charactizing frequent queries through a *frequency* threshold, instead of a support threshold is discussed.

6.1   Computation of Frequent Queries

Although our approach is only partially implemented, we argue that our work leads to a tractable computation of all frequent queries. First, since we consider star schemes only, it is easy to see that the table Δ_{FD} can be computed in only one step, without iterations. Moreover, as shown above, the computation of all frequent classes can be effectively achieved.

On the other hand, it is likely that all frequent queries are not of interest for each user. Instead, some users can be interested in some schemes while other users would like to focuss on other schemes. Therefore, in such an environment, every user should not have to compute *all* frequent queries. In order to take this point into account, we propose the following policy:

- Algorithm 1 can be run against the database once for all users, as a pre-processing phase. Storing all frequent queries of the form (X) with their supports could then serve as a basis for queries issued by the different users.
- Assuming that all frequent queries computed so far are stored with their supports, when users ask for frequent queries on different schemes (but rarely all of them), additional prunings are possible. Note that this point is related to the iterative computation of frequent patterns of [8].

The following example illustrates the second item just above.

Example 8. Referring to our running example, let us assume that all frequent queries of the form (X) have been computed and stored, and that a first user asks for all frequent queries of $\mathcal{Q}(X_1)$ where $X_1 = \{Cid, Caddr, Ptype, Qty\}$. Let Q_1 be this mining query.

In this case, we first notice that if $key(X_1) = \{Cid, Ptype, Qty\}$ is not stored as a frequent class, then the answer to Q_1 is empty. Let us now assume that $key(X_1)$ is frequent.

Then, based on Corollary 1, we can consider $X_1^+ = \{Cid, Cname, Caddr, Ptype, Qty\}$ instead of X_1, and compute all frequent queries of the form $\sigma_S(X_1^+)$ where $S \in \Sigma(X_1^+)$. If all these frequent queries are stored, then:

1. The answer to Q_1 is computed without any further access to the database. Indeed, the answer to Q_1 is the set of all queries of the form $\sigma_S(X_1)$ such that $\sigma_S(X_1^+)$ is frequent.

2. For any other mining query Q'_1 asking for all frequent queries of the form $\sigma_S(X'_1)$ where $key(X_1) \subseteq X'_1 \subseteq X_1^+$, the answer to Q'_1 can be obtained as above, *i.e.*, without any access to the database.

Assume now that after this computation, a user issues the mining query Q_2 asking for all frequent queries of $\mathcal{Q}(X_2)$ where $X_2 = \{Cid, Ptype\}$. Since $X_1 \preceq X_2$, we also have $X_1^+ \preceq X_2^+$. Thus, based on Proposition 3, when computing the frequent queries of the form $\sigma_S(X_2^+)$ where $S \in \Sigma(X_2^+)$, a candidate query $\sigma_{S_0}(X_2^+)$ cannot be frequent if $\sigma_{S_0}(X_1^+)$ has not been found frequent in the previous computation (because we know that $sup(\sigma_{S_0}(X_2^+)) \leq sup(\sigma_{S_0}(X_1^+))$). This point illustrates a case of additional pruning when iteratively computing mining queries. □

6.2 Frequency Threshold vs. Support Threshold

In the present approach, we have defined frequent queries based on the cardinality of the answers to the queries, *i.e.*, we have defined frequent queries based on a *support* threshold. However, one may argue that it might be interesting to define the threshold as a ratio, *i.e.*, as a *frequency* threshold.

Indeed, in the context of our running example, assume that we have 10^6 transactions in the fact table φ and 10^2 products in the dimension table *Prod*. In this case, choosing a support threshold *min-sup* might be difficult for the following reasons:

1. If *min-sup* $\geq 10^2$, then no query involving only products can be frequent.
2. If *min-sup* $\leq 10^2$, then too many queries involving transactions could be frequent.

On the other hand, it is clear that this problem does not occur when considering a frequency threshold *min-freq* of say 10%, meaning that a query involving only products (respectively transactions) is frequent if its answer contains at least 10% of the total number of pruducts (respectively of the total number of transactions).

More generally, let us consider that a query $q = \sigma_S(X)$ is said to be frequent if $freq(q) = \frac{sup(\sigma_S(X))}{sup((X))}$ is greater than or equal to a frequency threshold *min-freq*. It turns out that, in this case, the property of monotonicity of the frequency with respect to $\preceq$ does not hold, *i.e.*, given two queries $q = \sigma_S(X)$ and $q' = \sigma_S(Y)$,

$$X \preceq Y \Rightarrow freq(q) \geq freq(q')$$

does not hold even if X and Y are either both F-schemes or both D-schemes.

This is so, because if X and Y are two F-schemes or two D-schemes such that $X \preceq Y$, by Proposition 3, we have $sup(q) \geq sup(q')$ and $sup((X)) \geq sup((Y))$, and this does *not* imply that $\frac{sup(q)}{sup((X))} \geq \frac{sup(q')}{sup((Y))}$.

To cope with this problem, we recall that in Proposition 3, monotonicity holds only when the two schemes involved in the comparison are either F-schemes or D-schemes. Therefore, given a minimal frequency threshold *min-freq*, a query $q = \sigma_S(X)$ can be said to be frequent if:

- $\frac{sup(q)}{|\varphi|} \geq$ *min-freq*, when X is an F-scheme, or
- $\frac{sup(q)}{|\delta_i|} \geq$ *min-freq*, when X is a D-scheme included in the relation scheme of the dimension table δ_i.

It can be shown that, with this definition of frequency, Algorithm 1 is still correct if we replace the support threshold *min-sup* by *min-freq* $\times |\varphi|$ (respectively *min-freq* $\times |\delta_i|$) in case of an F-scheme (respectively a D-scheme included in D_i).

7   Conclusion and Further Work

In this paper, we have considered the weak instance model of relational databases, in order to design level-wise algorithms for the computation of *all* frequent queries in a database over an N-dimensional star scheme. We have shown that, in this case, taking into account the functional dependencies has a crucial impact on the efficiency of computing all frequent queries without selection conditions. We are currently implementing the computation of frequent queries with selection conditions.

On the other hand, it is clear that not every rule of the form $q_1 \Rightarrow q_2$ makes sense, when q_1 and q_2 are arbitrary frequent queries. In particular, we must make sure that the confidence of such rules is less than 1 and that q_1 and q_2 refer to the same "objects". We are currently investigating the characterization of relevant rules using the notion of *query key*. This notion is based on the usual notion (although it is a different notion). Future research directions include the following:

1. Considering schemes more sophisticated than star schemes, such as snowflake or constellation schemes. The work reported in [14] provides a suitable theoretical basis for this investigation.
2. Since our work is closely related to [6], we are investigating the relationships between the two approaches.
3. Since data cubes and star schemes both deal with multi dimensional data, the relationships between our work and that of [3] will be investigated further.

Acknowledgements. The authors wish to thank the anonymous referees for their comments that helped improving significantly a previous version of the paper.

References

1. R. Agrawal, H. Mannila, R. Srikant, H. Toivonen, and A.I. Verkamo. Fast discovery of association rules. In *Advances in Knowledge Discovery and Data Mining*, pages 309–328. AAAI-MIT Press, 1996.
2. W.W. Armstrong. Dependency structures of data base relationships. In *IFIP Congress*, pages 580–583. North Holland, 1974.
3. A. Casali, R. Cichetti, and L. Lakhal. Extracting semantics from data cubes using cube transversals and closures. In *ACM KDD*, pages 69–78, 2003.
4. L. Dehaspe and L. De Raedt. Mining association rules in multiple relations. In *7th International Workshop on Inductive Logic Programming*, volume 1297 of *LNCS*, pages 125–132. Springer Verlag, 1997.

5. C. T. Diop. *Etude et mise en oeuvre des aspects itratifs de l'extraction de rgles d'association dans une base de donnes.* PhD thesis, Universit de Tours, France, 2003.

6. C. T. Diop, A. Giacometti, D. Laurent, and N. Spyratos. Composition of mining contexts for efficient extraction of association rules. In *EDBT'02*, volume 2287 of *LNCS*, pages 106–123. Springer Verlag, 2002.

7. A. Faye, A. Giacometti, D. Laurent, and N. Spyratos. Mining rules in databases with multiple tables: Problems and perspectives. In *3rd International Conference on Computing Anticipatory Systems (CASYS)*, 1999.

8. A. Giacometti, D. Laurent, C. T. Diop, and N. Spyratos. Mining from views : An incremental approach. *International Journal Information Theories & Applications*, 9 (See also RR LI/E3i, Univ. de Tours), 2002.

9. B. Goethals. Mining queries, (unpublished paper). In *Workshop on inductive databases and constraint based mining. Available at http://www.informatik.uni-freiburg.de/~ml/IDB/talks/Goethals_slides.pdf.*, 2004.

10. B. Goethals and J. Van den Bussche. Relational association rules: getting warmer. In D. Hand, R. Bolton, and N. Adams, editors, *Proceedings of the ESF Exploratory Workshop on Pattern Detection and Discovery in Data Mining*, volume 2447 of *LNCS*, pages 125–139. Springer-Verlag, 2002.

11. J. Han, Y. Fu, W. Wang, K. Koperski, and O. Zaiane. Dmql : A data mining query language for relational databases. In *SIGMOD-DMKD'96*, pages 27–34, 1996.

12. J. Han, J. Pei, Y. Yin, and R. Mao. Mining frequent patterns without candidate generation: A frequent-pattern tree approach. *Data Mining and Knowledge Discovery*, 8:53–87, 2004.

13. D. Laurent, V. P. Luong, and N. Spyratos. Querying weak instances under extension chase semantics. *Intl Journal of Comp. Mathematics*, 80(5):591–613, 2003.

14. M. Levene and G. Loizou. Why is the snowflake schema a good data warehouse design? *Information Systems*, 28(3):225–240, 2003.

15. R. Meo, G. Psaila, and S. Ceri. An extension to sql for mining association rules. *Data Mining and Knowledge Discovery*, 9:275–300, 1997.

16. T. Turmeaux, A. Salleb, C. Vrain, and D. Cassard. Learning caracteristic rules relying on quantified paths. In *PKDD*, volume 2838 of *LNCS*, pages 471–482. Springer Verlag, 2003.

17. J.D. Ullman. *Principles of Databases and Knowledge-Base Systems*, volume 1. Computer Science Press, 1988.

Inductive Databases in the Relational Model: The Data as the Bridge

Stefan Kramer, Volker Aufschild, Andreas Hapfelmeier, Alexander Jarasch, Kristina Kessler, Stefan Reckow, Jörg Wicker, and Lothar Richter

Technische Universität München, Institut für Informatik, Boltzmannstr 3, 85748 Garching bei München, Germany
kramer@in.tum.de

Abstract. We present a new and comprehensive approach to inductive databases in the relational model. The main contribution is a new inductive query language extending SQL, with the goal of supporting the whole knowledge discovery process, from pre-processing via data mining to post-processing. A prototype system supporting the query language was developed in the SINDBAD (structured inductive database development) project. Setting aside models and focusing on distance-based and instance-based methods, closure can easily be achieved. An example scenario from the area of gene expression data analysis demonstrates the power and simplicity of the concept. We hope that this preliminary work will help to bring the fundamental issues, such as the integration of various pattern domains and data mining techniques, to the attention of the inductive database community.

1 Introduction

Many of the recent proposals for inductive databases and constraint-based data mining focus on single pattern domains (such as itemsets or molecular fragments) or single tasks, such as pattern discovery or decision tree induction [15, 2, 6, 13, 7]. Although the closure property is fulfilled by many of those approaches, the possibilities of combining various techniques in multi-step and compositional data mining are rather limited.

In this paper, we report the first results of a project that explores a different avenue. The SINDBAD (structured inductive database development) project[1] aims at the development of a prototype of an inductive database system that supports the most basic preprocessing and data mining operations such that they can be combined more or less arbitrarily. One explicit goal of the project is to support the complete knowledge discovery process, from pre-processing to post-processing. Since it is at the moment far from clear what the requirements of a full-fledged inductive database will be, it is our belief that we can only find out by building prototype systems.

The research described in this paper follows ideas worked out at the Dagstuhl perspectives workshop "Data Mining: The Next Generation" [1], where a system

---

[1] Structured in the sense of SQL – structured query language.

F. Bonchi and J.-F. Boulicaut (Eds.): KDID 2005, LNCS 3933, pp. 124–138, 2006.

of types and signatures of data manipulation and mining operators was proposed to support compositionality in the knowledge discovery process. At the workshop, the idea of using the data as the bridge between the various operators was explicitly articulated. In this work, the main idea was to use the simplest possible signature (mapping tables onto tables) as a starting point for the exploration of more complex scenarios.

The development of ideas was guided by a concrete use case, the analysis of the NCI DTP human tumor cell line screening data. We started out with concrete scenarios for multi-step, compositional data mining and then identified the building blocks necessary for supporting them. SINDBAD was developed over a period of nine months by a group of six students and recently finished the first iteration of its develoment.

For the development of such a system, various paradigms could have been adopted. In SINDBAD, we chose the relational model, as it possesses several desirable properties. First, closure can easily be achieved. Second, it allows handling collections of tuples conveniently and in a declarative manner. Third, the technology scales up well, and highly optimized implementations are available. Fourth, systems supporting (variants of) SQL are well-known and established, making it easier to get users acquainted with new querying facilities. Thus, we took the same approach as Meo *et al.* [15] and devised an extension of SQL, but for the most basic pre-processing and data mining techniques, discretization, feature selection, pattern discovery, clustering and classification. Similar approaches have been taken by Imielinski and Virmani [12] and Han *et al.* [10]. For a comprehensive discussion of these query languages and the current lack of preprocessing (and postprocessing) primitives, we refer the reader to a survey by Boulicaut and Masson [4].

This paper is organized as follows: After sketching the main ideas of the inductive query language, we present the query operators in some detail. Subsequently, we show how the query language can be used in a typical multi-step data mining scenario. In the following section, details of the SINDBAD implementation, its current limitations and possible extensions are presented. Finally, we touch upon related work and discuss implementation alternatives.

2   Main Ideas of the Inductive Query Language

Adopting the relational model, queries are mappings from relations onto a relation. We designed an extension of SQL (a superset of SQL) to support different kinds of preprocessing and data mining operations. Since every operator returns a table, queries can be arbitrarily nested. If we would like to work with more complex data, e.g., chemical compounds or substructures, we might handle tables of SMILES or SMARTS strings [5]. The mining operators were designed in analogy to relational algebra and SQL: For instance, we made heavy use of the extend-add-as operator and devised a feature-select clause in analogy to the select clause.

To make this approach feasible, we took the design decision to set aside models for the moment and consider distances between objects as more elementary and fundamental than models. That is, we support patterns and clusterings for descriptive mining, but for predictive mining we focus exclusively on instance-based learning. However, distances between instances and the nearest neighbors of an instance can be handled conveniently in the query language (see below).

The results of mining operations applied to tables are again tables. For instance, the discretization and feature selection operators return modified tables. More importantly, the classification from a nearest-neighbor query can be added to a table as a new attribute. Similarly, clustering results (cluster membership) can simply be added to a table as a new attribute.

Since the goal of the project was to explore the power of compositionality in data mining, we consciously chose the most basic building blocks and implemented one fundamental technique per category. For discretization, we implemented: equal-frequency/equal width, for feature selection: a filter approach based on information gain or variance, for pattern discovery: APriori, for clustering: k-Medoids and for classification: k-Nearest Neighbor. The goal is to support the whole knowledge discovery process, including pre-processing steps as discretization and feature selection. However, it is not our ambition to reimplement every technique ourselves, but to make the system extensible by design. External tools can easily be integrated by declaring wrappers for exporting and importing tables as plug-ins. Still, every analysis step can be performed via queries from a command line interface. For instance, once a wrapper for molecular data is written and declared as a plug-in, we might run an external graph mining tool and import the results, e.g., a table of frequent or significant molecular substructures, or a table of the occurrences of substructures in small molecules.

A conceptual issue that still needs to be resolved concerns the notion of views. At this point, it is not clear whether the new tables that are created as a results of preprocessing or mining operations should be considered as (materialized) views in the sense of databases. Conceptually, these derived tables should be treated just as regular tables. However, they are often the product of extensive computations. More sophisticated methods for implementing genuine data mining views are conceivable in the future.

3   Inductive Query Language

Before sketching the main query operators, we briefly present the preliminaries and assumptions of the approach.

3.1   Preliminaries

For every relation, we assume that an attribute heading as well as non-deletable and non-mutable tuple identifiers are given. Since in many of the envisaged applications rows and columns should interchangeable, we included an operator for transposing a table. Table transposition is only possible if all attributes are

Table 1. Main parameters to be set in configure clause

```
<configure-clause>        ::=  configure <group-expression-value>;

<group-expression-value> ::=  knn k=<integer>                    |
                              kmed k=<integer>                   |
                              apriori minSupport=<float>         |
                              discretization <disc-method-value>

<disc-method-value>       ::=  numofintervals=<integer>          |
                              method=(frequency|width|manual)   |
                              classColumn=<string>
```

Table 2. The extend clause as adapted for clustering, sampling and k-Nearest Neighbor prediction. The last two clauses are variants of k-medoids and k-NN that might be useful in practice: The k-medoid clause returns a relation with the medoids only. The k-NN clause retrieves the closest instances from a relation for a given instance.

```
<extend-clause> ::=
        extend <relation> add
            (
                kmedoid membership as <att>                        |
                kmedoid centers as <att>                           |
                knn prediction of <att> from <relation> as <att>  |
                sample membership as <att>                         |
                distances from <relation> [as <prefix-att>]        |
                covered by <relation> [as <prefix-att>]            |
                external <external-program> [<relation>]
                                            [as <prefix-att>]
            )

<kmedoid-clause> ::= kmedoid relation <relation>

<knn-clause> ::= <singleton-relation> knns from <relation>
```

of the same type. If a table is transposed, the tuple identifiers become attributes, and vice versa. If tables are joined, the new tuple identifiers are concatenations of the tuple identifiers of the tuples from the joined tables.

Most of the query operators below can be parameterized. Parameters can be either passed directly, or set in a so-called configure clause (see Table 1). For the sake of simplicity, we did not include the parameters in the following definitions in Backus-Naur Form (BNF), and assume the parameters are set in a configure clause.

3.2 extend add as

We adopted the extend operator to add the results of the various data mining operations as new attributes to a relation. The extend operator, one of the simplest extensions of the original relational algebra proposal, adds computational capabilities to the algebra [5]. It computes a function for each tuple and adds the result as the value of a new attribute. The most general form of an extend clause is given as follows:

<extend-clause> ::= extend <relation> add <function> as <att>

As an example, consider we want to add a new attribute *gmwt* to a table *p*, defined as the attribute *weight* multiplied by 454 [5]:

extend p add (weight*454) as gmwt

In SQL, extending a table by computed attributes can easily be achieved by the first part of a select statement ($SELECT\ AS$). All the data mining operations would then be treated in the same way as aggregate functions (e.g., $SELECT\dots,KMEDOIDS(*)\ AS\ \dots\ FROM\dots$). Somewhat related, but conceptually different, is the ALTER TABLE operator in today's SQL systems that *changes the structure* of existing tables ($ALTER\ TABLE\ \dots\ ADD\ \dots$).

In SINDBAD, the extend operator is modified in several ways and used directly in the query language. The complete syntax of the new operators in BNF is shown in Table 2. Additionally, schema definitions of input and output relations are presented in Table 3 and Table 4. Tables 3 and 4 also highlight the requirements of the operators on schema compatibility. The operators support a variety of pre-processing and data mining operations.

Now we are going to explain some of the extension functions in more detail. *kmedoid* provides distance-based clustering, which can come in two flavors. If combined with *membership*, the new attribute values are the identifiers (integers greater than or equal to one) of the clusters the respective example falls into, whereas in combination with *centers* the value of the attribute indicates whether it is a medoid or not (one for centers, zero otherwise). Another, less space-intensive way is to use the *k-medoid* clause from Table 2, only returning a table of medoids. Even simpler, one could only return a table with the keys of the medoids. Another possibility (not implemented yet) is to return both cluster membership and centers to facilitate the easy reconstruction of clusters.[2]

A simple prediction method is included by *knn prediction of*. The class identified by the first attribute in the clause is predicted on the basis of training examples (the relation specified after the *from* keyword), and the resulting prediction is stored in the new attribute specified following *as*.

Particularly useful for testing purposes is the *sample membership* operation, which allows the user to split the set of examples into test and training set, simply indicated by zero or one values of the added attribute. Cross-validation is currently not supported, but will be integrated into one of the next versions of SINDBAD.

---

[2] Note that the user perspective need not conincide with the implementation perspective. We might use a very compact representation of clusters internally and present them to the user in a seemingly space-intensive way. Further, the main idea of SINDBAD is to transform data successively, and not to create too many extra tables containing results in various forms.

Table 3. Schema definition of input and output relations for the extend-add-as clause: k-Medoids, k-NN and sampling. m denotes the number of attributes in the relation (except for the identifier). Without loss of generality, we assume some order over the attributes.

Operator:
extend REL add kmedoid membership as CLUSTER
Schema of input relation(s):
$REL(ID, X_1, \ldots, X_m)$
Schema of output relation:
$NEWREL(ID, X_1, \ldots, X_m, CLUSTER)$
Operator:
extend REL add kmedoid centers as CENTER
Schema of input relation(s):
$REL(ID, X_1, \ldots, X_m)$
Schema of output relation:
$NEWREL(ID, X_1, \ldots, X_m, CENTER)$
Operator:
extend TESTREL add knn prediction of Y from TRAINREL as Z
Schema of input relation(s):
$TESTREL(ID, X_1, \ldots, X_m, Y)$
$TRAINREL(ID, X_1, \ldots, X_m, Y)$
Schema of output relation:
$NEWREL(ID, X_1, \ldots, X_m, Y, Z)$
Operator:
extend REL add sample membership as SAMPLE
Schema of input relation(s):
$REL(ID, X_1, \ldots, X_m)$
Schema of output relation:
$NEWREL(ID, X_1, \ldots, X_m, SAMPLE)$

If distances to certain examples (one to many) are desired, they can be easily created by the *distances from* operation, which adds the distances from the examples in the given relation as new attributes, either with attribute names generated from the examples' identifiers or with a specified name prefix.

To use the frequent itemsets generated by the APriori algorithm (see below), the *covered by* operation was included, that maps the occurrence of itemsets back to the examples.

The genuine extensibility of the system comes into play with the *external* keyword. This is not merely an operator transforming the data, but rather indicates an external plug-in to the system, whose results are used as input for the new attribute's values.

3.3 feature select

In Table 5, several variants of feature selection are offered, which is an indispensable step in the knowledge discovery process. The schema definition of all input/output tables for feature selection and all remaining operators can be found in Table 6. Fea-

Table 4. Schema definition of input and output relations for the extend-add-as clause: addition of distances and pattern coverage. n_2 denotes the number of rows of the second input table.

Operator:
extend REL_1 add distances from REL_2
Schema of input relation(s):
$REL_1(ID, X_1, \ldots, X_m)$
$REL_2(ID, X_1, \ldots, X_m)$
Schema of output relation:
$NEWREL(ID, X_1, \ldots, X_m, ID_1, \ldots, ID_{n_2})$

Operator:
extend REL_1 add distances from REL_2 as Y
Schema of input relation(s):
$REL_1(ID, X_1, \ldots, X_m)$
$REL_2(ID, X_1, \ldots, X_m)$
Schema of output relation:
$NEWREL(X_1, \ldots, X_m, Y_1, \ldots, Y_{n_2})$

Operator:
extend $DATAREL$ add covered by $PATTERNREL$
Schema of input relation(s):
$DATAREL(ID, X_1, \ldots, X_m)$, $X_1, \ldots, X_m$ being Boolean attributes
$PATTERNREL(ID, X_1, \ldots, X_m)$, $X_1, \ldots, X_m$ being Boolean attributes
Schema of output relation:
$NEWREL(ID, X_1, \ldots, X_m, ID_1, \ldots, ID_{n_2})$

Operator:
extend $DATAREL$ add covered by $PATTERNREL$ as Y
Schema of input relation(s):
$DATAREL(ID, X_1, \ldots, X_m)$, $X_1, \ldots, X_m$ being Boolean attributes
$PATTERNREL(ID, X_1, \ldots, X_m)$, $X_1, \ldots, X_m$ being Boolean attributes
Schema of output relation:
$NEWREL(ID, X_1, \ldots, X_m, Y_1, \ldots, Y_{n_2})$

Table 5. The feature select clause, reminiscent of the select clause in SQL

```
<feature-select-clause> :: =
            feature select <conditions-on-tuples>
            from <relation>
            where <fs-condition>

<fs-condition> ::= ((variance | infogain <att>)
                    (( <|>|=|<=|>=) <real> |
                     in top <integer>)              |
                    <attribute-condition-expression>)
```

ture selection can be done according to various criteria. These criteria are specified in the *<fs-condition>*. Feature selection can be done either by applying hard thresholds for variance or information gain, or by relative thresholds (*in top*). Alter-

Table 6. Schema definition of input and output relations for all remaining operators. n denotes the number of rows of the input table.

Operator:
feature select $*$ *from REL where infogain Y in top P*
Schema of input relation(s):
$REL(ID, X_1, \ldots, X_m, Y)$
Schema of output relation:
$NEWREL(ID, X_{s_1}, \ldots, X_{s_p}, Y)$, where $\{X_{s_1}, \ldots, X_{s_p}\} \subseteq \{X_1, \ldots, X_m\}$
Operator:
discretize $X_{s_1}, \ldots, X_{s_p}$ *in REL*
Schema of input relation(s):
$REL(ID, X_1, \ldots, X_m)$, where $\{X_{s_1}, \ldots, X_{s_p}\} \subseteq \{X_1, \ldots, X_m\}$
$\qquad\qquad\qquad$ a subset of REL's numeric attributes
Schema of output relation:
$NEWREL(ID, X_1, \ldots, X_m)$, with selected numeric attributes
$\qquad\qquad\qquad \{X_{s_1}, \ldots, X_{s_p}\} \subseteq \{X_1, \ldots, X_m\}$ discretized
Operator:
frequent itemsets in REL
Schema of input relation(s):
$REL(ID, X_1, \ldots, X_m)$, X_1 to X_m being Boolean attributes
Schema of output relation:
$NEWREL(ID, X_1, \ldots, X_m)$, $NEWREL$ containing a Boolean representation
$\qquad\qquad\qquad$ of frequent itemsets found
Operator:
transpose REL
Schema of input relation(s):
$REL(ID, X_1, \ldots, X_m)$
Schema of output relation:
$NEWREL(X, ID_1, \ldots, ID_n)$
Operator:
project REL_1 *onto* REL_2 *attributes*
Schema of input relation(s):
$REL_1(ID, X_1, \ldots, X_m, \ldots, X_p)$
$REL_2(ID, X_1, \ldots, X_m)$
Schema of output relation:
$NEWREL(ID, X_1, \ldots, X_m)$

natively, simple string matching over the attributes' names can be applied, where the keyword *attribute* is used to refer to attribute names (see below).

In a way, the feature-select clause resembles the select clause "rotated by 90 degrees". However, in the feature-select clause, we can apply criteria for attributes to be included, and need not specify explicit lists of attributes.[1]

---

[1] In principle, it would be desirable to support arbitrary Boolean expressions (analogously to the select clause [5], pp. 973-976), composed of syntactic criteria regarding the attribute's name as well as criteria regarding the attribute's variance or information gain.

3.4   Other Operators

We complete our list of pre-processing and data mining operators in Table 7. Discretization may be applied either to all numerical attributes in the table, or to a selected subset.

Table 7. Various other operators, for discretization, pattern discovery, table transposition and projection on another table's attributes

```
<disc-clause> ::=          discretize (* | <att-list>)
                           in <relation>

<pattern-disc-clause> ::= frequent itemsets
                           in <relation>

<transpose-clause> ::=     transpose <relation>

<project-onto-clause> ::= project <relation>
                           onto <relation> attributes
```

Moreover, we can compute the frequent itemsets of a table. The resulting table contains the same attributes as the input table. Much as in early proposals for inductive databases, each row in the new table represents one frequent itemset [3]. Finally, we can transpose tables, given that all the attributes are of the same type. The last clause serves the purpose of restricting the set of attributes of one relation to those of another. This is particularly useful for predictive mining, where often the results of class-sensitive feature selection based on a training set has to be transferred to a test set.

4   Worked Example

In the following section, we would like to give an example of the query language at work. In Table 8, a worked example from the field of gene expression data analysis is shown. The leukemia dataset of Golub *et al.* [8] is analyzed step by step. The table shows the input and output of the system without displaying the actual tables and views. In the output we also see the time it takes to answer the queries.

First, the dataset is loaded, discretized and divided into a training and a test set (queries 1 to 4). Note that the discretization and labeling as training or test example is done in the second query. The following two queries simply split the table into two tables based on the previously computed information. Queries 5 and 6 perform class-sensitive feature selection. As a result, we reduce the dataset to the fifty genes with maximal information gain with respect to the tumor subtype to be predicted. Since the test set should have the same attributes as the training set, we project the former onto the attributes of the latter in query 6. Next, we query for frequent itemsets, that is, co-expressed genes. The co-expressed genes are used to transform the data, because individual genes are

Table 8. Example run on leukemia dataset of Golub *et al.*

```
Sindbad [1] > create view expression_profiles as
   >import ../../../ALLAML.arff;
Time needed for query: 12.0 sec.
Sindbad [2] > create view train_test_expression_profiles as
   >extend (discretize * in expression_profiles)
   >add sample membership as train_flag;
Time needed for query: 38.0 sec.
Sindbad [3] > create view train_expression_profiles as
   >select * from train_test_expression_profiles
   >where train_flag = true;
Time needed for query: 59.0 sec.
Sindbad [4] > create view test_expression_profiles as
   >select * from train_test_expression_profiles
   >where train_flag = false;
Time needed for query: 1 min. 8.0 sec.
Sindbad [5] > create view reduced_train_expression_profiles as
   >feature select * from train_expression_profiles
   >where infogain tumor_subtype in top 50;
Time needed for query: 3.0 sec.
Sindbad [6] > create view reduced_test_expression_profiles as
   >project test_expression_profiles
   >onto reduced_train_expression_profiles attributes;
Time needed for query: 0.0 sec.
Sindbad [7] > create view coexpressed_genes as
   >frequent itemsets in reduced_train_expression_profiles;
Time needed for query: 4.0 sec.
Sindbad [8] > create view classified_test_expression_profiles as
   >extend
   >(feature select * from
   >(extend reduced_test_expression_profiles
   >add covered by coexpressed_genes as 'fp1')
   >where attribute like 'fp%' or attribute = 'tumor_subtype')
   >add knn prediction of tumor_subtype from
   >(feature select * from
   >(extend reduced_train_expression_profiles
   >add covered by coexpressed_genes as 'fp2')
   >where attribute like 'fp%' or attribute = 'tumor_subtype')
   >as predicted_tumor_subtype;
Time needed for query: 1.0 sec.
Sindbad > exit;
Have a nice day!
```

usually not very informative for predictive purposes. Query 8 is, by far, the most complex expression listed here. In the query, the training and test data are transformed in terms of the co-expressed genes. Subsequently, the original features representing discretized expression levels of genes are removed (using a feature select clause). The most important part is a *knn* clause, adding the predictions based on instance-based learning to the test table as values for the new attribute *predicted_tumor_subtype*. To simplify query 8, it could be split into three parts:

```
create view train_set as
feature select *
  from
  (extend reduced_train_expression_profiles
    add covered by coexpressed_genes
    as 'fp')
where attribute like 'fp%' or attribute = 'tumor_subtype';

create view test_set as
feature select *
  from
  (extend reduced_test_expression_profiles
    add covered by coexpressed_genes
    as 'fp')
where attribute like 'fp%' or attribute = 'tumor_subtype';

create view classified_test_expression_profiles as
extend test_set
add knn prediction of tumor_subtype
from train_set
as predicted_tumor_subtype;
```

In subsequent steps, the error rate could be determined by comparing the attributes *tumor_subtype* and *predicted_tumor_subtype*.

5   Implementation, Current Limitations and Possible Extensions

In this section, we present details of the implementation and some of the current limitations and discuss possibilities for extending the system.

The SINDBAD prototype is implemented in Java. It should be noted that the current implementation just serves the purpose of proving that the concept is viable. For parsing the queries, we used the lexical analyzer generator JFlex (see http://jflex.sourceforge.net/) and the parser generator Cup (see http://www2.cs.tum.edu/projects/cup/). The implementation supports arbitrarily nested queries. If an operator cannot be applied to an input table, the system stops processing the query (gracefully) and outputs an error message. However, the error message might be output relatively late in query processing, if the error occurs in the outmost part of a nested query. At this point, the implementation is not very "declarative". In the future, we are planning to integrate a full-fledged analysis of parse trees, opening possibilities for query optimization.

The software architecture of SINDBAD is already quite elaborate. The system is built on top of postgreSQL (see `http://www.postgresql.org/`), an open source relational database management system. The operations are mostly performed on tables in memory, but the results can be made persistent at any time. The architecture, in essence, would allow the data to be distributed over various sites. In the implementation we could operate on proxy objects standing for collections of data objects located anywhere in the world. However, no effort has been made to optimize the performance of the system.

At this point, only a small fragment of SQL, namely that of select clauses, is supported by SINDBAD. The processing of select clauses has been (naively) reimplemented in the system and is not delegated to the underlying relational database. Intertwining arbitrary SQL expressions with inductive query operators seems to be out of reach yet. Since reimplementation is obviously not desirable, other implementation strategies may be followed in the development of future prototypes.

Currently, the system works in a single-relational setting, but it could easily be extended towards multi-relational data mining. In fact, the core for multi-relational data mining already exists in SINDBAD, as the select clause can combine an arbitrary number of relations within an inductive query. Aggregate functions [14] could be applied to preprocess the data for further analysis. Another, more appealing approach would be to plug in distance measures for relational data [11, 16].

One of the most important extensions of the system would be to include an elaborate type system with a hierarchy of data types. The present implementation only knows the type of tables (tables in, table out). On a different level, attributes may be of type Boolean, nominal and numeric. Given a type system, operators with type signatures could be defined, paving the way for more complex pre-processing, data mining and post-processing operations [1]. Type signatures define the admissible inputs and outputs of data manipulation and mining operations. Types and signatures would allow for the inclusion of models, which we completely set aside in the current approach. To overcome this limitation, two basic types, that of tables and that of models, and signatures for training, testing and handling collections of models would be required. An open question is whether structures like linear separators or decision trees should be mapped onto relations in some way.

A type system would also be the key to optimizations and extensibility. As mentioned above, our goal was not to reimplement every technique from scratch, but to design an extensible system with a uniform query language supporting the whole knowledge discovery process.

6   Related Work, Discussion and Conclusion

We presented an extension of SQL for inductive databases in the tradition of Imielinski and Virmani [12], Han *et al.* [10] and Meo *et al.* [15]. Our goal was to provide rudimentary support for every data mining operation that is important in practice: discretization, feature selection, frequent patterns, clustering and classification.

A comprehensive SQL-based data mining approach is also taken in MS SQL Server 2005 [17], which was launched in November 2005 after five years of development. In the query language DMX, the user usually creates a so-called "mining structure" first. The mining structure defines the data types of the attributes, but not their usage (e.g., input or output). The usage of attributes is specified in so-called "mining models". The syntax of DMX is quite complex and supports a lot of variants. In contrast, our approach was to focus on the most essential operations, and explore more complex scenarios only in a second step. Overall, the proposal made in this chapter is conceptually much simpler, and therefore hopefully also more amenable to theoretical analysis (e.g., towards an algebra, query optimizations and index structures). SINDBAD should also be viewed as a research prototype to elucidate the requirements for full-fledged inductive databases.

The focus of SQL Server 2005 is clearly on prediction. One of the central concepts is that of a "prediction join" between a data table and a mining model, that adds a prediction and related information. The prediction join seems to perform a similar operation as some of our extend-add-as variants. In particular, various "prediction functions" can be plugged in, interestingly including some for clustering (see [17], p. 56). Therefore, different database concepts (join vs. extend-add-as from a relational algebra extension) served as an inspiration for the various data mining primitives.

Although scale and motivation are quite different and make a comparison hard, there are a number of significant differences in the supported operations. First, the concept of transforming the data on the basis of patterns is not found in SQL Server 2005. Second, the concept of table transposition (motivated by applications in gene expression data analysis) does not have a counterpart in the commercial product. Third, feature selection is done implicitly in SQL Server (see [17], p. 152) and beyond user control, whereas it is one of several data transformation operators in SINDBAD. Fourth, it is possible to extract frequent itemsets in SQL Server, however, it is unclear whether one can also query over them (see [17], p. 242). Therefore, the closure property may not be fulfilled in all cases. Fifth, discretization seems to be tied to the mining model, and is not seen as a data transformation operation (see [17], p. 47). Sixth, multi-relational data mining is mostly dealt with using nested tables and nested keys (see [17], p. 48 and p. 291). In contrast, SINDBAD seems naturally extensible towards a multi-relational setting using recursive descent and set distance functions. Summing up, the focus of SQL Server is on prediction, whereas the focus of SINDBAD is on transforming the data successively.

In the early phases of the project we considered paradigms other than the relational, such as object-orientation or XML, for building an inductive database in the above style. As mentioned in the introduction, we had good reasons for choosing the relational paradigm. Additionally, it has been shown that objects and XML documents can be, to some extent, mapped onto the relational model to support efficient query answering [5, 9]. The idea was that if objects and XML documents can be mapped reasonably onto the relational model, perhaps it can be done successfully for inductive databases as well. It should be noted that scalability was another major motivation for choosing the relational model. However, if an elaborate system of types and signatures should be included, we might have to switch to XML or object-oriented databases.

In summary, we presented a new and comprehensive approach to inductive databases in the relational model. The main contribution of this paper is a new inductive query language in the form of an SQL extension, including pre-processing and data mining operators. We hope that this preliminary work will help to bring fundamental issues in the field of inductive databases, such as the integration of various patterns domains and data mining schemes, to the attention of the research community.

Acknowledgements

We would like to thank the anonymous reviewers for their helpful comments.

References

1. R. Agrawal, T. Bollinger, C.W. Clifton, S. Dzeroski, J.-C. Freytag, J. Gehrke, J. Hipp, D.A. Keim, S. Kramer, H.-P. Kriegel, B. Liu, H. Mannila, R. Meo, S. Morishita, R.T. Ng, J. Pei, P. Raghavan, R. Ramakrishnan, M. Spiliopoulou, J. Srivastava, V. Torra, A. Tuzhilin: *Data Mining: The Next Generation*. Report based on a Dagstuhl perspectives workshop organized by R. Agrawal, J-C. Freytag, and R. Ramakrishnan (see http://www.dagstuhl.de/04292/), 2005.
2. M. Botta, J-F. Boulicaut, C. Masson, R. Meo: Query languages supporting descriptive rule mining: a comparative study. *Database Support for Data Mining Applications – Discovering Knowledge with Inductive Queries*, R. Meo, P.-L. Lanzi, M. Klemettinen (Eds.), 27-56. Springer, Berlin, Germany 2004.
3. J.-F. Boulicaut, M. Klemettinen, H. Mannila: Modeling KDD processes within the inductive database framework. *Proc. of the 1st Int. Conf. on Data Warehousing and Knowledge Discovery (DaWak 1999, Florence, Italy)*, 293-302. Springer, Berlin, Germany 1999.
4. J.-F. Boulicaut, C. Masson: Data mining query languages. *The Data Mining and Knowledge Discovery Handbook*, O. Maimon, L. Rokach (Eds.), 715-727. Springer, Berlin, 2005.
5. C.J. Date: *An introduction to database systems (8th edition)*. Pearson/Addison-Wesley, Boston, USA 2004.
6. L. De Raedt, S. Kramer: The levelwise version space algorithm and its application to molecular fragment finding. *Proc. 17th Int. Joint Conf. on Art. Intell. (IJCAI 2001, Seattle, USA)*, 853-862. Morgan Kaufmann, San Francisco, CA, USA 2001.
7. M.N. Garofalakis, D. Hyun, R. Rastogi, K. Shim: Efficient algorithms for constructing decision trees with constraints. *Proc. 6th ACM SIGKDD Int. Conf. Knowledge Discovery and Data Mining (KDD 2000, Boston, USA)*, 335-339. ACM Press, New York, NY, USA 2000.
8. T.R. Golub, D.K. Slonim, P. Tamayo, C. Huard, M. Gaasenbeek, J. P. Mesirov, H. Coller, M.L. Loh, J.R. Downing, M.A. Caligiuri, C.D. Bloomfield, E.S. Lander: Molecular classification of cancer: class discovery and class prediction by gene expression monitoring. *Science* 286(15):531–537, 1999.

9. T. Grust, M. van Keulen, J. Teubner: Accelerating XPath evaluation in any RDBMS. *ACM Trans. Database Syst.* 29:91-131, 2004.

10. J. Han, Y. Fu, K. Koperski, W. Wang, O. Zaiane: DMQL: A data mining query language for relational databases. *Proc. SIGMOD'96 Workshop. on Research Issues on Data Mining and Knowledge Discovery (DMKD 1996, Montreal, Canada)*, 1996.

11. T. Horvath, S. Wrobel, U. Bohnebeck: Relational instance-based learning with lists and terms. *Machine Learning* 43(1/2):53-80, 2001.

12. T. Imielinski, A. Virmani: MSQL: A query language for database mining. *Data Min. Knowl. Discov.* 3(4):373-408, 1999.

13. S. Kramer, L. De Raedt, C. Helma: Molecular feature mining in HIV data. *Proc. 7th ACM SIGKDD Int. Conf. on Knowledge Discovery and Data Mining (KDD 2001, San Francisco, USA)*, 136-143. ACM Press, New York, NY, USA 2001.

14. M.-A. Krogel, S. Wrobel: Transformation-based learning using multirelational aggregation. *Proc. 11th Int. Conf. on Inductive Logic Programming (ILP 2001, Strasbourg, France)*, Springer, Berlin, Germany, 2001.

15. R. Meo, G. Psaila, S. Ceri: An extension to SQL for mining association rules. *Data Min. Knowl. Discov.* 2(2):195-224, 1998.

16. J. Ramon, M. Bruynooghe: A polynomial time computable metric between point sets. *Acta Informatica* 37(10):765-780, 2001.

17. Z.H. Tang, J. MacLennan: *Data mining with SQL Server 2005*. Wiley, IN, USA 2005.

Transaction Databases, Frequent Itemsets, and Their Condensed Representations

Taneli Mielikäinen

HIIT Basic Research Unit,
Department of Computer Science,
University of Helsinki, Finland

Abstract. Mining frequent itemsets is a fundamental task in data mining. Unfortunately the number of frequent itemsets describing the data is often too large to comprehend. This problem has been attacked by condensed representations of frequent itemsets that are subcollections of frequent itemsets containing only the frequent itemsets that cannot be deduced from other frequent itemsets in the subcollection, using some deduction rules. In this paper we review the most popular condensed representations of frequent itemsets, study their relationship to transaction databases and each other, examine their combinatorial and computational complexity, and describe their relationship to other important concepts in combinatorial data analysis, such as Vapnik-Chervonenkis dimension and hypergraph transversals.

1 Introduction

Mining frequent itemsets from transaction databases has been a very popular research topic in data mining for more than a decade since its introduction [1]. The frequent itemsets themselves describe the co-occurrence of items and they are also an intermediate step in the construction of association rules.

A major problem with frequent itemset mining is that the number of the frequent itemsets is often large. This difficulty has been attacked by the use of condensed representations of frequent itemsets that are typically subcollections of frequent itemsets sufficient together with their frequencies and some simple deduction rules to determine the whole collection of frequent itemsets and their frequencies. The condensed representations of frequent itemsets have been recognized to be promising building blocks of inductive databases [2, 3, 4, 5].

Although most of the condensed representations of frequent itemsets do not address data in any way (apart from the frequencies of the itemsets), their relationship to the data is of highest importance, since the frequent itemsets are aimed to be descriptive models for the data [6]. In this paper we study the correspondence of condensed representations to transaction databases.

The paper is organized as follows. In Section 2 we define the central concepts used in frequent itemset mining. In Section 3 we review the most popular condensed representations and study their properties. Section 4 compares the sizes of the condensed representations on several concrete transaction databases. Section 5 is a short conclusion.

F. Bonchi and J.-F. Boulicaut (Eds.): KDID 2005, LNCS 3933, pp. 139–164, 2006.
© Springer-Verlag Berlin Heidelberg 2006

2   Transaction Databases and Frequent Itemsets

Definition 1 (Items and itemsets). *An* itemset X *is s finite subset of* $\mathcal{I}$, *the set of possible items.*

Definition 2 (Transactions and transaction databases). *A transaction t is a pair $\langle i, X \rangle$ consisting of a transaction identifier $tid(t) = i \in \mathbb{N}$ and an itemset $is(t) = X \subseteq \mathcal{I}$. A transaction database $\mathcal{D}$ is a set of transactions with unique transaction identifiers. The set $\mathcal{S}_{\mathcal{D}}$ of all itemsets in $\mathcal{D}$ is $\mathcal{S}_{\mathcal{D}} = \{X : \langle i, X \rangle \in \mathcal{D}\}$.*

Definition 3 (Occurrences, counts, covers, supports and frequencies). *The* occurrence set *of an itemset X in a transaction database $\mathcal{D}$ is the set of transaction identifiers of the transactions with the itemset X, i.e.,*

$$occ(X, \mathcal{D}) = \{i : \langle i, Y \rangle \in \mathcal{D}, X = Y\}.$$

The count *of X in $\mathcal{D}$ is*

$$count(X, \mathcal{D}) = |occ(X, \mathcal{D})|.$$

The cover *of an itemset X in a transaction database $\mathcal{D}$ is the set of transaction identifiers of the transactions in $\mathcal{D}$ with the itemset containing X, i.e.,*

$$cover(X, \mathcal{D}) = \{i : \langle i, Y \rangle \in \mathcal{D}, X \subseteq Y\} = \bigcup_{Y \supseteq X} occ(Y, \mathcal{D}).$$

The support *of X in $\mathcal{D}$ is*

$$supp(X, \mathcal{D}) = |cover(X, \mathcal{D})| = |\{i : \langle i, Y \rangle \in \mathcal{D}, X \subseteq Y\}|$$

and the frequency *of X in $\mathcal{D}$ is*

$$fr(X, \mathcal{D}) = \frac{supp(X, \mathcal{D})}{|\mathcal{D}|} = \frac{|\{i : \langle i, Y \rangle \in \mathcal{D}, X \subseteq Y\}|}{|\mathcal{D}|}.$$

The projection *of a transaction database $\mathcal{D}$ onto an itemset X, i.e, the intersection of $\mathcal{D}$ and X is*

$$\mathcal{D}|_X = \{\langle i, X \cap Y \rangle : \langle i, Y \rangle \in \mathcal{D}\}.$$

A central task in data mining is to discover itemsets are contained in sufficiently many transactions of the database:

Problem 1 (Frequent itemset mining). Given a transaction database $\mathcal{D}$ and a real value $\sigma \in [0, 1]$, find all σ-frequent itemsets, i.e., determine the collection

$$\mathcal{F}(\sigma, \mathcal{D}) = \{X \subseteq \mathcal{I} : fr(X, \mathcal{D}) \geq \sigma\}$$

of σ-frequent itemsets in $\mathcal{D}$.

The itemsets in $\mathcal{D}$ are the itemsets that have support at least one, i.e., the itemsets in $\mathcal{F}(1/|\mathcal{D}|, \mathcal{D})$. (Another option would be to consider each subset of $\mathcal{I}$ as an itemset in $\mathcal{D}$. Most of the results in this paper are invariant with respect to this choice and also the results that are affected by the choice (Subsection 3.2 in particular) are quite the same for both interpretations of an itemset being in the database.)

There are a couple of alternative views to frequent itemset mining:

1. A transaction database $\mathcal{D}$ can be viewed as a binary matrix such that $\mathcal{D}[i, A] = 1$ if and only if there is $\langle i, X \rangle \in \mathcal{D}$ with $A \in X$, and the itemsets as binary vectors. The binary vector X is σ-frequent in $\mathcal{D}$ if the scalar product between X and at least $\sigma |\mathcal{D}|$ rows of the matrix $\mathcal{D}$ is $|X|$.
2. Items can be interpreted as boolean variables, $\mathcal{D}$ as a multiset of truth value assignments $t : \mathcal{I} \to \{0, 1\}$ and itemsets as monomials. Then the monomial X is σ-frequent in $\mathcal{D}$ if at least $\sigma |\mathcal{D}|$ of the truth value assignments in $\mathcal{D}$ satisfy it.

The total number of itemsets on $\mathcal{I}$ is often prohibitive. Hence the straightforward method to find the frequent itemsets, by computing the frequency for each itemset in $2^{\mathcal{I}} = \{X \subseteq \mathcal{I}\}$, is not feasible in practice. The key to avoid the combinatorial explosions is the anti-monotonicity of frequency:

Proposition 1. $X \subseteq Y \Rightarrow fr(X, \mathcal{D}) \geq fr(Y, \mathcal{D})$

Proof. Recall that

$$fr(X, \mathcal{D}) = \frac{supp(X, \mathcal{D})}{|\mathcal{D}|} = \frac{|cover(X, \mathcal{D})|}{|\mathcal{D}|}.$$

By definition, $cover(X, \mathcal{D}) = \{i : \langle i, Z \rangle \in \mathcal{D}, X \subseteq Z\}$. Hence, $X \subseteq Y$ implies $cover(X, \mathcal{D}) \supseteq cover(Y, \mathcal{D})$. Thus, $X \subseteq Y \Rightarrow fr(X, \mathcal{D}) \geq fr(U, \mathcal{D})$. $\square$

The anti-monotonicity of frequency (Proposition 1) implies the fact that the collection of frequent itemsets is downward closed:

Corollary 1. $X \subseteq Y \in \mathcal{F}(\sigma, \mathcal{D}) \Rightarrow X \in \mathcal{F}(\sigma, \mathcal{D})$

Proof. The corollary follows immediately from Proposition 1 and the definition of $\mathcal{F}(\sigma, \mathcal{D})$. $\square$

Due to Corollary 1, the potential frequent itemsets can be evaluated levelwise, first computing the frequencies for all items occurring in the database, second the frequencies of all 2-itemsets whose all items are frequent, and so on. Most of the frequent itemset mining techniques (including the famous Apriori algorithm [7]) are variations of this idea. The levelwise approach for mining σ-frequent itemsets in $\mathcal{D}$ can be implemented to run in time

$$\mathcal{O}(|\mathcal{I}|^2 |\mathcal{D}| |\mathcal{F}(\sigma, \mathcal{D})|),$$

i.e., in time polynomial in the sum of the sizes of the input and the output.

Finding some σ-frequent itemset in a transaction database is easy, but counting the number of frequent itemsets in the database is #P-hard [8]. Also, given a transaction database $\mathcal{D}$ and a positive integer k, deciding whether or not there is a σ-frequent itemset of cardinality k in $\mathcal{D}$ is NP-complete [8].

3   Condensed Representations

Although the current techniques for discovery of frequent itemsets are able to mine gigabytes of frequent itemsets very quickly (see [9, 10]), such a large number of itemsets is very difficult to query or manipulate. There are many ways how to approach this difficulty. For example, a simple approximation of frequencies of the frequent itemsets can be obtained by taking a random sample of the transactions [11, 12]. However, such a condensed representation is not a subcollection of frequent itemsets. In this paper we focus on the most popular condensed representations that are subcollections of frequent itemsets.

3.1   Condensed Representations Based on Borders

Perhaps the oldest condensed representations of frequent itemsets are the maximal frequent itemsets and the minimal infrequent itemsets [8, 13, 14]:

Definition 4 (Maximal frequent itemsets). *An itemset $X \in \mathcal{F}(\sigma, \mathcal{D})$ is maximal, if $Y \notin \mathcal{F}(\sigma, \mathcal{D})$ for all $Y \supsetneq X$. The collection of maximal σ-frequent itemsets in $\mathcal{D}$ is denoted by $\mathcal{MF}(\sigma, \mathcal{D})$.*

Definition 5 (Minimal infrequent itemsets). *An itemset $X \notin \mathcal{F}(\sigma, \mathcal{D})$ is minimal, if $Y \in \mathcal{F}(\sigma, \mathcal{D})$ for all $Y \subsetneq X$. The collection of minimal σ-infrequent itemsets in $\mathcal{D}$ is denoted by $\mathcal{MI}(\sigma, \mathcal{D})$.*

Maximal frequent and minimal infrequent itemsets are closely related to several important concepts in combinatorics of set collections:

Definition 6 (Chains and antichains). *A set collection $\mathcal{S}$ is a chain if and only if for each $X, Y \in \mathcal{S}$ holds $X \subseteq Y$ or $X \supseteq Y$.*
A set collection $\mathcal{S}$ is an antichain if and only if for each $X, Y \in \mathcal{S}$ holds $X \subseteq Y$ or $X \supseteq Y$ only if $X = Y$.

Proposition 2. *The collections $\mathcal{MF}(\sigma, \mathcal{D})$ and $\mathcal{MI}(\sigma, \mathcal{D})$ are antichains.*

Proof. Let $X, Y \in \mathcal{MF}(\sigma, \mathcal{D}), X \neq Y$. Then $X \not\subseteq Y$, since $X \in \mathcal{MF}(\sigma, \mathcal{D})$ implies that there is no $Z \in \mathcal{F}(\sigma, \mathcal{D}) \supseteq \mathcal{MF}(\sigma, \mathcal{D})$ such that $X \subsetneq Z$.
Similarly, $X, Y \in \mathcal{MI}(\sigma, \mathcal{D}), X \neq Y$, implies that $X \not\subseteq Y$.   □

It follows from the downward closedness of $\mathcal{F}(\sigma, \mathcal{D})$ (Corollary 1) that either of $\mathcal{MF}(\sigma, \mathcal{D})$ and $\mathcal{MI}(\sigma, \mathcal{D})$ determine the collection $\mathcal{F}(\sigma, \mathcal{D})$. Furthermore:

Proposition 3. *$\mathcal{MF}(\sigma, \mathcal{D})$ and $\mathcal{MI}(\sigma, \mathcal{D})$ are minimal collections that determine $\mathcal{F}(\sigma, \mathcal{D})$.*

Proof. The collection $\mathcal{MF}(\sigma, \mathcal{D})$ determines $\mathcal{F}(\sigma, \mathcal{D})$, since

- by Corollary 1, for each $X \in \mathcal{F}(\sigma, \mathcal{D})$ there is $Y \in \mathcal{MF}(\sigma, \mathcal{D})$ such that $X \subseteq Y$ and
- by definition of $\mathcal{MF}(\sigma, \mathcal{D})$, if $Z \subseteq Y \in \mathcal{MF}(\sigma, \mathcal{D})$ then $Z \in \mathcal{F}(\sigma, \mathcal{D})$.

The collection $\mathcal{MF}(\sigma, \mathcal{D})$ is minimal determining $\mathcal{F}(\sigma, \mathcal{D})$, since for any $X \in \mathcal{MF}(\sigma, \mathcal{D})$, there is no $Y \in \mathcal{MF}(\sigma, \mathcal{D}) \setminus \{X\}$ such that $X \subseteq Y$.

Similarly, $\mathcal{MI}(\sigma, \mathcal{D})$ determines $\mathcal{F}(\sigma, \mathcal{D})$ and $\mathcal{MI}(\sigma, \mathcal{D})$ is a minimal collection determining $\mathcal{F}(\sigma, \mathcal{D})$. □

The number of transactions in the database does not have very rigid correspondence to the number of maximal frequent or minimal infrequent itemsets: There are databases with $|\mathcal{S}_\mathcal{D}| = 2^{|\mathcal{I}|}$ different transactions but only one maximal frequent itemset, and databases with the number of maximal frequent and minimal infrequent itemsets exponential in $|\mathcal{S}_\mathcal{D}| = |\mathcal{I}| + 1$:

Proposition 4. *Let $\mathcal{MI}(\sigma, \mathcal{D}) \neq \emptyset$. Then*

$$1 \leq |\mathcal{MF}(\sigma, \mathcal{D})|, |\mathcal{MI}(\sigma, \mathcal{D})| \leq \binom{|\mathcal{I}|}{\lfloor |\mathcal{I}|/2 \rfloor},$$

even when $|\mathcal{I}| = |\mathcal{S}_\mathcal{D}| - 1$ and $\sigma \in [0, 1)$.

Proof. As $\mathcal{F}(\sigma, \mathcal{D})$ is always non-empty and for each $X \in \mathcal{F}(\sigma, \mathcal{D})$ there is $Y \in \mathcal{MF}(\sigma, \mathcal{D})$ such that $X \subseteq Y$, we have $1 \leq |\mathcal{MF}(\sigma, \mathcal{D})|$.

The number of maximal frequent (or the number of minimal infrequent itemsets) is at most $\binom{|\mathcal{I}|}{\lfloor |\mathcal{I}|/2 \rfloor}$ because $\mathcal{MF}(\sigma, \mathcal{D})$ and $\mathcal{MI}(\sigma, \mathcal{D})$ are antichains and the largest antichain in $2^{\mathcal{I}}$ consists of all subsets of $\mathcal{I}$ of cardinality $\binom{|\mathcal{I}|}{\lfloor |\mathcal{I}|/2 \rfloor} = \binom{|\mathcal{I}|}{\lceil |\mathcal{I}|/2 \rceil}$.

The collections with exactly $\binom{|\mathcal{I}|}{\lfloor |\mathcal{I}|/2 \rfloor}$ itemsets can be obtained by the database $\mathcal{D}$ consisting of one transaction for each itemset $\mathcal{I} \setminus \{A\}$, $A \in \mathcal{I}$, and c transactions with itemset Y, where $Y = \mathcal{I}$ if $\sigma \geq 1/2$ and $Y = \emptyset$ otherwise. The number c is a positive integer such that for each $X \subseteq \mathcal{I}$ such that $|X| = \lfloor |\mathcal{I}|/2 \rfloor$ holds $fr(X, \mathcal{D}) \geq \sigma$ and $fr(X \cup \{A\}, \mathcal{D}) < \sigma$, $A \in \mathcal{I} \setminus X$. □

Neither of $\mathcal{MF}(\sigma, \mathcal{D})$ and $\mathcal{MI}(\sigma, \mathcal{D})$ is always the winner with respect to the cardinality. Sometimes $\mathcal{MF}(\sigma, \mathcal{D})$ is smaller than $\mathcal{MI}(\sigma, \mathcal{D})$ and sometimes $\mathcal{MI}(\sigma, \mathcal{D})$ is smaller than $\mathcal{MF}(\sigma, \mathcal{D})$.

Proposition 5 ([15]). *Let $\mathcal{MI}(\sigma, \mathcal{D}) \neq \emptyset$. Then*

$$|\mathcal{MF}(\sigma, \mathcal{D})| \leq ((1 - \sigma)|\mathcal{D}| + 1)|\mathcal{MI}(\sigma, \mathcal{D})|.$$

In practice, the smaller of the collections can be chosen. Furthermore, it is possible to describe $\mathcal{F}(\sigma, \mathcal{D})$ by a subcollection $\mathcal{MF}(\sigma, \mathcal{D}) \cup \mathcal{MI}(\sigma, \mathcal{D})$ containing some maximal frequent and some minimal infrequent itemsets [11]. (Furthermore, it is possible to show that the smallest subcollection determining the collection of frequent itemsets is necessarily a subset of $\mathcal{MF}(\sigma, \mathcal{D}) \cup \mathcal{MI}(\sigma, \mathcal{D})$.)

The maximal frequent and minimal infrequent itemsets are closely related to minimal hypergraph transversals:

Definition 7 (Minimal hypergraph transversals). *A hypergraph is a pair* $\langle \mathcal{I}, \mathcal{S} \rangle$ *where* $\mathcal{I}$ *is a set of elements and* $\mathcal{S}$ *is an antichain of subsets of* $\mathcal{I}$.

A transversal *in a hypergraph* $\langle \mathcal{I}, \mathcal{S} \rangle$ *is a set* $X \subseteq \mathcal{I}$ *such that* $X \cap Y \neq \emptyset$ *for each* $Y \in \mathcal{S}$. *A hypergraph transversal is often called a* hitting set.

A transversal X *is* minimal *in a hypergraph* $\langle \mathcal{I}, \mathcal{S} \rangle$ *if none of the proper subsets of* X *is a transversal in* $\langle \mathcal{I}, \mathcal{S} \rangle$.

Namely, $\mathcal{MI}(\sigma, \mathcal{D})$ can be obtained from $\mathcal{MF}(\sigma, \mathcal{D})$ by minimal hypergraph transversals [14] and vice versa:

Proposition 6. *The collection* $\mathcal{MI}(\sigma, \mathcal{D})$ *consists of minimal hypergraph transversals in* $\langle \mathcal{I}, \{\mathcal{I} \setminus X : X \in \mathcal{MF}(\sigma, \mathcal{D})\} \rangle$ *and the collection* $\mathcal{MF}(\sigma, \mathcal{D})$ *consists of complements minimal hitting sets in* $\langle \mathcal{I}, \mathcal{MI}(\sigma, \mathcal{D}) \rangle$.

Proof. Each frequent itemset is a subset of some maximal frequent itemset. A hypergraph transversal $Y \subseteq \mathcal{I}$ in $\langle \mathcal{I}, \{\mathcal{I} \setminus X : X \in \mathcal{MF}(\sigma, \mathcal{D})\} \rangle$ contains for each $X \in \mathcal{MF}(\sigma, \mathcal{D})$ an item $A_X \in Y$ such that $A_X \notin Y$. Thus, such Y is an infrequent itemset. If an itemset Z is not a hypergraph transversal in $\langle \mathcal{I}, \{\mathcal{I} \setminus X : X \in \mathcal{MF}(\sigma, \mathcal{D})\} \rangle$, then it is contained in at least one maximal frequent itemset and thus it is frequent. Hence, minimal hypergraph transversals are minimal infrequent itemsets. Furthermore all minimal infrequent itemsets are minimal transversals in $\langle \mathcal{I}, \{\mathcal{I} \setminus X : X \in \mathcal{MF}(\sigma, \mathcal{D})\} \rangle$.

All supersets of minimal infrequent itemsets are infrequent. The complement of any proper superset of a complement of a minimal infrequent itemset is frequent. Thus, the complements of the minimal hypergraph transversals of $\langle \mathcal{I}, \mathcal{MI}(\sigma, \mathcal{D}) \rangle$ are maximal frequent itemsets. Furthermore, all maximal frequent itemsets are complements of minimal hypergraph transversals in the hypergraph $\langle \mathcal{I}, \mathcal{MI}(\sigma, \mathcal{D}) \rangle$.   □

Also the computational complexity of finding maximal frequent itemsets (or minimal infrequent itemsets) is closely related to minimal hypergraph transversals. Namely, the incremental complexity of generating the collection $\mathcal{MF}(\sigma, \mathcal{D}) \cup \mathcal{MI}(\sigma, \mathcal{D})$ is equivalent to generating minimal hypergraph transversals, which implies that k itemsets from $\mathcal{MF}(\sigma, \mathcal{D}) \cup \mathcal{MI}(\sigma, \mathcal{D})$ can be generated in time $|\mathcal{I}|^{\mathcal{O}(1)} |\mathcal{D}|^{\mathcal{O}(1)} + k^{o(k)}$ [15].

A maximal σ-frequent itemset in $\mathcal{D}$ can be found in time $\mathcal{O}(|\mathcal{I}| |\mathcal{D}|)$ by Algorithm 1.

Given a transaction database $\mathcal{D}$, counting the number of maximal frequent itemsets in $\mathcal{D}$ is #P-hard [16] and deciding, for a given positive integer k, whether there is a σ-frequent itemset of cardinality at least k in $\mathcal{D}$ is NP-complete [8].

Furthermore, it is NP-complete to decide, given a transaction database $\mathcal{D}$ and minimum frequency threshold σ and a collection $\mathcal{S} \subseteq \mathcal{MF}(\sigma, \mathcal{D})$, whether or not $\mathcal{S} \neq \mathcal{MF}(\sigma, \mathcal{D})$, even if $|\mathcal{S}| = \mathcal{O}(|\mathcal{D}|^\epsilon)$ and $|\mathcal{MF}(\sigma, \mathcal{D})|$ is exponentially large in $|\mathcal{D}|$, where $\epsilon > 0$ can be arbitrary small [15]. Also finding a subcollection of maximal frequent itemsets that approximate the frequent itemsets well is NP-hard [17].

Algorithm 1. An algorithm for finding a maximal itemset in $\mathcal{D}$

Input: A set $\mathcal{I}$ of items, a transaction database $\mathcal{D}$ over $\mathcal{I}$ and a minimum frequency threshold $\sigma \in (0, 1]$.

Output: A pair $\langle X, fr(X, \mathcal{D}) \rangle$ consisting of a maximal σ-frequent itemset X in $\mathcal{D}$ and its frequency $fr(X, \mathcal{D})$.

1: **function** FINDMAXIMAL($\mathcal{I}, \mathcal{D}, \sigma$)
2:     $X \leftarrow \emptyset; T \leftarrow \{i : \langle i, X \rangle \in \mathcal{D}\}$
3:     **for all** $A \in \mathcal{I}$ **do**
4:         $T_A \leftarrow \{i : \langle i, X \rangle \in \mathcal{D}, A \in X\}$
5:         **if** $|T \cap T_A| \geq \sigma |\mathcal{D}|$ **then**
6:             $X \leftarrow X \cup \{A\}; T \leftarrow T \cap T_A$
7:         **end if**
8:     **end for**
9:     **return** $\langle X, |T| / |\mathcal{D}| \rangle$
10: **end function**

Observe that σ-frequent itemsets in $\mathcal{D}$ correspond to the satisfying truth value assignments for the boolean formula

$$\bigvee_{X \in \mathcal{MF}(\sigma, \mathcal{D})} \bigwedge_{A \in \mathcal{I} \setminus X} \neg A$$

that is in disjunctive normal form. The number of satisfying truth value assignments of a boolean formula in disjunctive normal form can be approximated well [18]. Thus, the cardinality of $\mathcal{F}(\sigma, \mathcal{D})$ can be approximated from $\mathcal{MF}(\sigma, \mathcal{D})$. (See [17] for a direct construction.)

Sometimes the collection of frequent itemsets is not sufficient alone but also the frequencies are needed. Even in that case some of the frequent itemsets can be omitted. For example, based on the anti-monotonicity of frequency (Proposition 1), the frequency of an itemset is at least as large as the largest frequency of any of its supersets. Thus, the frequent itemsets with frequency equal to the maximum frequency of its supersets can be considered as redundant. Such irredundant frequent itemsets are called then the frequent closed itemsets [19]:

Definition 8 (Closed frequent itemsets). *An itemset $X \in \mathcal{F}(\sigma, \mathcal{D})$ is closed, if $fr(X, \mathcal{D}) > fr(Y, \mathcal{D})$ for all $Y \supsetneq X$. The collection of closed σ-frequent itemsets in $\mathcal{D}$ is denoted by $\mathcal{C}(\sigma, \mathcal{D})$.*

Note that a closed itemset X in $\mathcal{D}$ is a maximal σ-frequent itemset in $\mathcal{D}$ for $\sigma = [fr(X, \mathcal{D}), \min \{fr(Y, \mathcal{D}) : Y \subsetneq X, fr(X, \mathcal{D}) < fr(Y, \mathcal{D})\})$. The frequency of a frequent itemset $X \in \mathcal{F}(\sigma, \mathcal{D})$ is obtained by taking the maximum of the frequencies of the closed supersets of X, i.e.,

$$fr(X, \mathcal{D}) = \max \{fr(Y, \mathcal{D}) : X \subseteq Y \in \mathcal{C}(\sigma, \mathcal{D})\}.$$

In addition to the ease of frequency estimation, the closed itemsets have a beautiful characterization as intersections of transactions [19, 20, 21]:

Proposition 7. *An itemset $X \subseteq \mathcal{I}$ is closed in $\mathcal{D}$ if and only if X is its own closure, i.e.,*

$$X = cl(X, \mathcal{D}) = \bigcap_{\langle i, Z \rangle \in \mathcal{D}, Z \supseteq X} Z.$$

Proof. If $X \neq cl(X, \mathcal{D})$, then there is $Y = cl(X, \mathcal{D})$ such that $X \subsetneq Y$ and $fr(X, \mathcal{D}) = fr(Y, \mathcal{D})$.

If $X = cl(X, \mathcal{D})$ then for each $Y \subseteq \mathcal{I}, Y \supsetneq X$, there is $\langle i, Z \rangle \in \mathcal{D}$ such that $X \subseteq Z$ but $Y \not\subseteq Z$ and hence $fr(X, \mathcal{D}) > fr(Y, \mathcal{D})$.   □

Based on Proposition 7, it is possible to show the following relationship between the closed and maximal σ-frequent itemsets and transaction databases:

Proposition 8. *Let $\mathcal{D}'$ be a transaction database consisting of (at least) one transaction for the intersection of each $\lceil \sigma |\mathcal{D}| \rceil$-subset of transactions of $\mathcal{D}$. Then $\mathcal{MF}(\sigma, \mathcal{D}) = \mathcal{MF}(1/|\mathcal{D}'|, \mathcal{D}')$ and $\mathcal{C}(\sigma, \mathcal{D}) = \mathcal{C}(1/|\mathcal{D}'|, \mathcal{D}')$.*

Proof. $\mathcal{D}'$ contains a transaction for each itemset $X \in \mathcal{C}(\sigma, \mathcal{D})$ no other transactions. Thus, $\mathcal{MF}(1/|\mathcal{D}'|, \mathcal{D}') = \mathcal{MF}(\sigma, \mathcal{D})$.

Because the intersection of closed itemsets is closed, we have $\mathcal{C}(1/|\mathcal{D}'|, \mathcal{D}') = \mathcal{C}(\sigma, \mathcal{D})$.   □

The number of closed frequent itemsets is at least the number of maximal frequent itemsets and at most the number of all frequent itemsets, whereas $|\mathcal{C}(\sigma, \mathcal{D})|$ can be exponentially larger than $|\mathcal{MF}(\sigma, \mathcal{D})|$ and exponentially smaller than $|\mathcal{F}(\sigma, \mathcal{D})|$:

Proposition 9. $2^{-|\mathcal{I}|} |\mathcal{C}(\sigma, \mathcal{D})| \leq |\mathcal{MF}(\sigma, \mathcal{D})| \leq |\mathcal{C}(\sigma, \mathcal{D})| \leq 2^{\mathcal{I}} |\mathcal{MF}(\sigma, \mathcal{D})|$
$2^{-|\mathcal{I}|} |Fr\sigma, \mathcal{D}| \leq |\mathcal{C}(\sigma, \mathcal{D})| \leq |\mathcal{F}(\sigma, \mathcal{D})| \leq 2^{|\mathcal{I}|} |\mathcal{C}(\sigma, \mathcal{D})|$

Proof. Observe that there are $2^{|\mathcal{I}|}$ subsets of $\mathcal{I}$. This gives the upper and the lower bounds. We shall now show that the bounds are also tight.

Let $\mathcal{D} = \{\langle 1, \mathcal{I} \rangle\}$. Then $|\mathcal{F}(\sigma, \mathcal{D})| = 2^{|\mathcal{I}|} |\mathcal{C}(\sigma, \mathcal{D})|$.

Let $\mathcal{D}$ consists of one transaction for each $\mathcal{I} \setminus \{A\}, A \in \mathcal{I}$, and $|\mathcal{I}| \sigma / (1 - \sigma)$ transactions with the itemset $\mathcal{I}$. Then $\mathcal{C}(\sigma, \mathcal{D}) = 2^{\mathcal{I}}$ whereas $\mathcal{MF}(\sigma, \mathcal{D}) = \{\mathcal{I}\}$.   □

The computational complexity of mining closed frequent itemsets is understood quite well. Some closed frequent itemset can be obviously found in polynomial time in the size of the database by computing the intersection of any sufficiently large subset of transactions. Furthermore, closed σ-frequent itemsets in a transaction database $\mathcal{D}$ can be found in polynomial time in $|\mathcal{C}(\sigma, \mathcal{D})|$, $|\mathcal{D}|$ and $|\mathcal{I}|$ [22] and all closed itemsets can be found in polynomial time with only one pass over the database [20].

There are methods for approximating the frequencies of the frequent itemsets by subcollections of closed frequent itemsets by expressing the frequencies inaccurately [23, 24, 25, 26, 27, 28].

Given a transaction database $\mathcal{D}$ and a positive integer k, deciding whether there is a closed σ-frequent itemset of cardinality at least k in $\mathcal{D}$ is NP-complete [8] and counting the number of closed σ-frequent itemsets in $\mathcal{D}$ is #P-hard [16, 29].

Closed frequent itemsets $X \in \mathcal{C}(\sigma, \mathcal{D})$ partition frequent itemsets into equivalence classes $\mathcal{S}_X = \{Y \in \mathcal{F}(\sigma, \mathcal{D}) : Y \subseteq X, cover(Y, \mathcal{D}) = cover(X, \mathcal{D})\}$. The itemset $X \in \mathcal{C}(\sigma, \mathcal{D})$ is the maximal itemset in the equivalence class $\mathcal{S}_X$ and contains all other itemsets in $\mathcal{S}_X$.

Instead of representing the frequencies of the itemsets using the maximal itemsets in the equivalence classes, the frequencies can be represented using the minimal itemsets in the classes. Such itemsets are called free itemsets [30] (or key patterns [31] or generators [19]):

Definition 9 (Free frequent itemsets). *An itemset $X \in \mathcal{F}(\sigma, \mathcal{D})$ is free, if $fr(X, \mathcal{D}) < fr(Y, \mathcal{D})$ for all $Y \subsetneq X$. The collection of free σ-frequent itemsets in $\mathcal{D}$ is denoted by $\mathcal{G}(\sigma, \mathcal{D})$.*

The free frequent itemsets have the advantage that any collection $\mathcal{G}(\sigma, \mathcal{D})$ is downward closed:

Proposition 10. $X \in \mathcal{G}(\sigma, \mathcal{D}), Y \subseteq X \Rightarrow Y \in \mathcal{G}(\sigma, \mathcal{D})$

Proof. Assume that there is $Y \notin \mathcal{G}(\sigma, \mathcal{D})$ such that $Y \subsetneq X \in \mathcal{G}(\sigma, \mathcal{D})$. However, then there is $Z \subsetneq Y$ such that $cover(Y, \mathcal{D}) = cover(Z, \mathcal{D})$. Hence, $supp(Y \cup W, \mathcal{D}) = supp(Z \cup W, \mathcal{D})$ for any $W \subseteq \mathcal{I} \setminus Y$, which means that no superset $Y \cup W$ of Y can be free, since there is always its proper subset $Z \cup (W \setminus Y)$ such that $supp(Y \cup W, \mathcal{D}) = supp(Z \cup (W \setminus Y), \mathcal{D})$. This contradicts with our assumption. Thus the proposition holds. $\square$

This implies that virtually all frequent itemset mining algorithms can be adapted to mine free frequent itemsets. Thus, similarly to all frequent itemsets, the free frequent itemsets can be found in time polynomial in the sum of the sizes of the input and the output.

The free frequent itemsets do not seem to have such a clean characterization by the properties of the transaction databases as closed frequent itemsets (Proposition 7) but still their relationship to transactions is relatively simple:

Proposition 11. *An itemset X is free in $\mathcal{D}$ if and only if for each $A \in X$ there is $\langle i, Z \rangle \in \mathcal{D}$ such that $X \cap Z = X \setminus \{A\}$.*

Proof. If for each $A \in X$ there is $\langle i, Z \rangle \in \mathcal{D}$ such that $X \cap Z = X \setminus \{A\}$, then $supp(X, \mathcal{D}) < supp(X \setminus \{A\}, \mathcal{D})$ for each $A \in X$.

If there is such a $A \in X$ that there is no $\langle i, Z \rangle$ such that $X \cap Z = X \setminus \{A\}$, then $supp(X, \mathcal{D}) = supp(X \setminus \{A\}, \mathcal{D})$ for that $A \in X$, and thus X is not free. $\square$

A major drawback of free frequent itemsets is that they are not sufficient to determine the collection of all frequent itemsets. Given only the free frequent itemsets, it is not known which of the other itemsets are frequent and which are not. Thus, in addition to free frequent itemsets, also minimal free infrequent itemsets are needed:

Definition 10 (Minimal free infrequent itemsets). *An itemset $X \notin \mathcal{F}(\sigma, \mathcal{D})$ is minimal free, if $fr(X, \mathcal{D}) < fr(Y, \mathcal{D}) Y \in \mathcal{G}(\sigma, \mathcal{D})$ for all $Y \subsetneq X$. The collection of minimal free σ-infrequent itemsets in $\mathcal{D}$ is denoted by $\mathcal{GI}(\sigma, \mathcal{D})$.*

Apparently, the collection of minimal free infrequent itemsets coincides with the collection of all minimal infrequent itemsets:

Proposition 12. $\mathcal{GI}(\sigma, \mathcal{D}) = \mathcal{MI}(\sigma, \mathcal{D})$

Proof. By definition, $\mathcal{GI}(\sigma, \mathcal{D}) \subseteq \mathcal{MI}(\sigma, \mathcal{D})$. Thus, it suffices to show that $\mathcal{GI}(\sigma, \mathcal{D}) \supseteq \mathcal{MI}(\sigma, \mathcal{D})$. To see that, let $X \in \mathcal{MI}(\sigma, \mathcal{D})$. Clearly $fr(X, \mathcal{D}) < fr(X \setminus \{A\}, \mathcal{D})$ for all $A \in X$. Thus X is free infrequent itemset. As all of the subsets if X are frequent, X must also be minimal infrequent free itemset.   □

Note that finding both free frequent and minimal free infrequent itemsets does not affect most of the mining algorithms since they usually discover also the minimal (free) infrequent itemsets (to ensure that the collection of free frequent itemsets is indeed complete).

It is easy to see that the number of free frequent itemsets is at least as large as the number of closed frequent itemsets:

Proposition 13. $|\mathcal{C}(\sigma, \mathcal{D})| \leq |\mathcal{G}(\sigma, \mathcal{D})|$

Proof. Each each itemset $X \in \mathcal{G}(\sigma, \mathcal{D})$ has a unique closure $cl(X, \mathcal{D})$. Thus, for each closed frequent itemset, there is at least one free frequent itemset.   □

3.2   Condensed Representations Based on Frequencies

Maximal, minimal, closed and free itemsets are based on bounding the frequencies from above and below. However, also quantitative relationships between the frequencies contain valuable information about the underlying database. For example, not all syntactically valid collections of frequent itemsets have a transaction database with the corresponding frequencies [32, 33].

A natural next step is to strengthen the upper and the lower bounds, i.e., to decrease the uncertainty in the frequencies as much as possible [34]. One approach to obtain bounds can be observed by rewriting the support of X in $\mathcal{D}$ as follows. Let X be any superset of Y. Then

$$supp(Y, \mathcal{D}) = |occ(Y, \mathcal{D}|_X)| + \left| \bigcup_{A \in X \setminus Y} cover(Y \cup \{A\}, \mathcal{D}) \right|$$

$$= |occ(Y, \mathcal{D}|_X)| + \sum_{Y \subsetneq Z \subseteq X} (-1)^{|Z \setminus Y| + 1} |cover(Z, DB)|$$

$$= count(Y, \mathcal{D}|_X) + \sum_{Y \subsetneq Z \subseteq X} (-1)^{|Z \setminus Y| + 1} supp(Z, DB)$$

(the last equality being obtained using the inclusion exclusion principle [35]). By noticing that $count(X, \mathcal{D}|_Y) \geq 0$ and by reordering the terms of , we get

$$(-1)^{|X \setminus Y|} supp(X, \mathcal{D}) \geq \sum_{Y \subseteq Z \subsetneq X} (-1)^{|Z \setminus Y| + 1} supp(Z, \mathcal{D}).$$

That is, for all $X \subseteq \mathcal{I}$ and $Y \subseteq X$, we get an upper bound

$$\overline{supp}(X, Y, \mathcal{D}) = \sum_{Y \subseteq Z \subsetneq X} (-1)^{|Z \setminus Y|} supp(Z, \mathcal{D}) = \sum_{Y \subseteq Z \subsetneq X} (-1)^{|X \setminus Z|+1} supp(Z, \mathcal{D})$$

for odd $|X \setminus Y|$ and a lower bound

$$\underline{supp}(X, Y, \mathcal{D}) = \sum_{Y \subseteq Z \subsetneq X} (-1)^{|Z \setminus Y|+1} supp(Z, \mathcal{D}) = \sum_{Y \subseteq Z \subsetneq X} (-1)^{|X \setminus Z|+1} supp(Z, \mathcal{D})$$

for even $|X \setminus Y|$. Thus, the frequency of X in $\mathcal{D}$ is bounded between

$$\overline{supp}(X, \mathcal{D}) = \min_{Y \subset X} \overline{supp}(X, Y, \mathcal{D}) \quad \text{and}$$

$$\underline{supp}(X, \mathcal{D}) = \max_{Y \subset X} \underline{supp}(X, Y, \mathcal{D}).$$

These bounds are worst-case optimal for bounding the frequency of X by the frequencies of its subsets [36] and they give rise of the non-derivable frequent itemsets [37]:

Definition 11 (Non-derivable frequent itemsets). *An itemset $X \in \mathcal{F}(\sigma, \mathcal{D})$ is non-derivable, if $\underline{supp}(X, \mathcal{D}) < \overline{supp}(X, \mathcal{D})$. The collection of non-derivable σ-frequent itemsets is denoted by $\mathcal{N}(\sigma, \mathcal{D})$.*

Also non-derivable frequent itemsets have the advantage of forming a downward closed collection [37] and they can be characterized by transactions:

Proposition 14. $X \in \mathcal{N}(\sigma, \mathcal{D}), Y \subseteq X \Rightarrow Y \in \mathcal{N}(\sigma, \mathcal{D})$

Proof. If an itemset X is derivable in $\mathcal{D}$, then $\overline{supp}(X, \mathcal{D}) = \underline{supp}(X, \mathcal{D})$, i.e., there are itemsets $Y_l \subset X$ and $Y_u \subset X$ such that $\underline{supp}(X, Y_l, \mathcal{D}) = \overline{supp}(X, Y_u, \mathcal{D})$. Hence, $count(Y_l, \mathcal{D}) = 0$ and $count(Y_u, \mathcal{D}) = 0$. Furthermore, we have $\overline{supp}(X \cup \{A\}, Y_u, \mathcal{D}) = \underline{supp}(X \cup \{A\}, Y_l, \mathcal{D})$ for any $X \cup \{A\}, A \in \mathcal{I} \setminus X$, since if $|X \setminus Z|$ is odd (even), then $|(X \cup \{A\}) \setminus Z|$ is even (odd). □

Proposition 15. *An itemset X is non-derivable in $\mathcal{D}$ if and only if there are no two itemsets $Y, Z \subseteq X$ such that $|Y|$ is odd, $|Z|$ is even and $Y, Z \notin \mathcal{S}_{\mathcal{D}}|_X$.*

Proof. If $Y = X$ or $Z = X$, then X in not in $\mathcal{D}$. Thus, we can assume that Y and Z are proper subsets of X.

If there are two proper subsets Y and Z of X such that $Y, Z \notin \mathcal{S}_{\mathcal{D}}|_X$ with $|Y|$ being odd and $|Z|$ even, then one of $|X \setminus Y|$ and $|X \setminus Z|$ is odd and one is even. Hence, $\underline{supp}(X, \mathcal{D}) = \overline{supp}(X, \mathcal{D})$.

If there is no proper subset Y of X such that $Y \notin \mathcal{S}_{\mathcal{D}}|_X$ and $|X \setminus Y|$ is odd (even), then $\underline{supp}(X, \mathcal{D}) < \overline{supp}(X, \mathcal{D})$ ($\underline{supp}(X, \mathcal{D}) < \overline{supp}(X, \mathcal{D})$). □

Evaluating the the upper and lower bounds completely can be quite time-consuming. One simple approach to relieve the computational burden is to consider the inclusion-exclusion formulas only up to certain depth:

$$\overline{supp}_k(X, \mathcal{D}) = \min_{Y \subset X, |X \setminus Y| \leq k} \overline{supp}(X, Y, \mathcal{D}) \quad \text{and}$$

$$\underline{supp}_k(X, \mathcal{D}) = \max_{Y \subset X, |X \setminus Y| \leq k} \underline{supp}(X, Y, \mathcal{D}).$$

Itemsets irredundant with respect to such bounds are called k-free [38, 39]:

Definition 12 (k-free frequent itemsets). *An itemset* $X \in \mathcal{F}(\sigma, \mathcal{D})$ *is* k-free *if* $\overline{supp}_k(X, \mathcal{D}) > supp(X, \mathcal{D})$ *and* $\underline{supp}_k(X, \mathcal{D}) < supp(X, \mathcal{D})$. *The collection of* k-free σ-frequent itemsets in $\mathcal{D}$ is denoted by $\mathcal{G}_k(\sigma, \mathcal{D})$.

With $k = 1$, k-free frequent itemsets are the same as free frequent itemsets. Thus, it is not surprising that, similarly to free itemsets, k-free frequent itemsets are not sufficient to determine all frequent itemsets, but some additional itemsets are needed:

Definition 13 (Minimal non-k-free frequent itemsets). *An itemset* $X \subseteq \mathcal{I}$ *is* minimal non-k-free, *if* X *is not* k-free, *but all* $Y \subsetneq X$ *are* k-free *and* $\underline{supp}_k(X, \mathcal{D}) < \overline{supp}_k(X, \mathcal{D})$. *The collection of minimal non-k-free σ-frequent itemsets in $\mathcal{D}$ is denoted by* $\mathcal{GI}_k(\sigma, \mathcal{D})$.

This representation coincides with non-derivable frequent itemsets when k is sufficiently large, for example $k = |\mathcal{I}|$:

Proposition 16. $\mathcal{N}(\sigma, \mathcal{D}) = \mathcal{G}_{|\mathcal{I}|}(\sigma, \mathcal{D}) \cup \mathcal{GI}_{|\mathcal{I}|}(\sigma, \mathcal{D})$.

Proof. If $X \in \mathcal{N}(\sigma, \mathcal{D})$, then $X \setminus \{A\} \in \mathcal{G}_{|\mathcal{I}|}(\sigma, \mathcal{D})$ for all $A \in X$. Hence, $X \in \mathcal{G}_{|\mathcal{I}|}(\sigma, \mathcal{D})$ or $X \in \mathcal{GI}_{|\mathcal{I}|}(\sigma, \mathcal{D})$.
　If $X \notin \mathcal{N}(\sigma, \mathcal{D})$, then $\underline{supp}_{|\mathcal{I}|}(X, \mathcal{D}) = \underline{supp}(X, \mathcal{D}) = supp(X, \mathcal{D}) = \overline{supp}(X, \mathcal{D}) = \overline{supp}_{|\mathcal{I}|}(X, \mathcal{D})$ and thus $X \notin \mathcal{G}_{|\mathcal{I}|}(X, \mathcal{D}) \cup \mathcal{GI}_{|\mathcal{I}|}(X, \mathcal{D})$. □

Also k-free itemsets have a nice characterization by the transactions of the database, generalizing the characterization of free itemsets [39]:

Proposition 17. *An itemset* X *is* k-free *in* $\mathcal{D}$ *if if and only if* $Y \in \mathcal{S}_\mathcal{D}|_X$ *for all* $Y \subseteq X$ *such that* $|X \setminus Y| \leq k$.

Proof. If X is k-free, then $Y \in \mathcal{S}_\mathcal{D}|_X$ for all $Y \subseteq X$ such that $|X \setminus Y| \leq k$.
　If X is not k-free, then there is $Y \subseteq X$ such that $Y \notin \mathcal{S}_\mathcal{D}|_X$ and $|X \setminus Y| \leq k$. □

Proposition 17 implies that the cardinality of the largest k-free itemset is at most l such that $|\mathcal{S}_\mathcal{D}| \geq \sum_{i=0}^{k} \binom{l}{i}$. For example, the largest $|\mathcal{I}|$-free itemset is of cardinality at most $\log |\mathcal{S}_\mathcal{D}|$.
　The characterization reveals also that k-free itemsets are strongly connected to some fundamental concepts of the combinatorics of set systems [35]:

Definition 14 (universality and density of transaction databases). *Let* $supp(\{A\}, \mathcal{D}) > 0$ *for all* $A \in \mathcal{I}$. *A transaction database* $\mathcal{D}$ *is* k-dense *if there is a subset* $X \subseteq \mathcal{I}$ *of cardinality* k *such that* $|\mathcal{S}_\mathcal{D}|_X| = 2^{|X|} = 2^k$. $\mathcal{D}$ *is* k-universal *if for all* $X \subseteq \mathcal{I}$ *of cardinality* k *holds* $|\mathcal{S}_\mathcal{D}|_X| = 2^k$.

Proposition 18. *A transaction database* $\mathcal{D}$ *is* k-dense *if and only if there are* k-free *itemsets of cardinality* k *in* $\mathcal{D}$. *A transaction database* $\mathcal{D}$ *is* k-universal *if and only if all itemsets* $X \subseteq \mathcal{I}$ *with* $|X| = k$ *are* k-free *in* $\mathcal{D}$.

Proof. A transaction database $\mathcal{D}$ is k-dense if and only if there is $X \subseteq \mathcal{I}, |X| = k$ such that $Y \in \mathcal{S}_{\mathcal{D}}|_X$ for all $Y \subseteq X$. Thus, $\mathcal{D}$ is k-dense if and only if there is at least one k-free itemset of cardinality k in $\mathcal{D}$.

A transaction databases $\mathcal{D}$ is k-universal if and only if for all itemsets $X \subseteq \mathcal{I}, |X| = k$, the collection $\mathcal{S}_{\mathcal{D}}|_X$ consists of all subsets of X. That is, all itemsets $X \subseteq \mathcal{I}$ of cardinality k are k-free in $\mathcal{D}$.   □

The density of a transaction database is closely related to Vapnik-Chervonenkis dimension that is an important measure of the complexity of data in machine learning [40] and computational geometry [41] to name a few:

Definition 15 (VC-dimension). *The* Vapnik-Chervonenkis dimension *of a transaction database is equal to the largest k such that the database is k-dense.*

Thus, the cardinality of the largest $|\mathcal{I}|$-free itemset in $\mathcal{D}$ is closely related to the VC-dimension of $\mathcal{D}$:

Proposition 19. *The cardinality of the largest $|\mathcal{I}|$-free itemset in a transaction database $\mathcal{D}$ is equal to the* VC*-dimension of $\mathcal{D}$.*

Proof. On one hand, the VC-dimension of $\mathcal{D}$ is at least as large as the cardinality of the largest $|\mathcal{I}|$-free itemset X in $\mathcal{D}$, because $\mathcal{S}_{\mathcal{D}}|_X = 2^X$.

On the other hand, the VC-dimension of $\mathcal{D}$ cannot be strictly larger than the cardinality of the largest $|\mathcal{I}|$-free itemset in $\mathcal{D}$, since for any non-k-free itemset X, there is $Y \subsetneq X$ such that $Y \notin \mathcal{S}_{\mathcal{D}}|_X$.   □

This relationship sheds much light to k-free itemsets. For example, the upper bounds for the cardinalities of k-free itemsets given in [39] are implied Sauer's Lemma (see [40]) using the VC-dimension of the database $\mathcal{D}$ (or equivalently the cardinality of the largest $|\mathcal{I}|$-free itemset in $\mathcal{D}$).

In addition to providing combinatorial insights to the relationship between k-free itemsets and transaction databases, the VC-dimension implies important computational complexity results for mining k-free itemsets.

Namely, deciding whether the VC-dimension of the database is at least l is LOGNP-complete problem [42]. (Class LOGNP contains the problems that can be in polynomial time using $\log^2 n$ nondeterministic bits [42]. Note that it is very unlikely that the problem of computing the VC-dimension is NP-hard since the problem can be solved in time proportional to $n^{\log n}$.)

The problem is believed to be difficult to solve also for a constant l. More specifically, deciding whether VC-dimension of a given binary matrix is at least l for a constant l is known to be W[1]-complete [43, 44]. (A problem being W[1]-complete means that the problem cannot be solved in time $f(l)n^{\mathcal{O}(1)}$ for *any* function f unless the parameterized complexity hierarchy collapses and thus a large number of other problems that believed to be difficult to solve could be solved efficiently [43].) Furthermore, it is possible to show the following hardness results for non-derivable frequent itemsets:

Proposition 20. *It is* LOGNP-*complete to decide, given a transaction database $\mathcal{D}$, a minimum frequency threshold $\sigma \in [0, 1]$ and a positive integer l, whether* *or not there is a non-derivable σ-frequent itemset of cardinality at least l in $\mathcal{D}$. Furthermore, the problem is $W[1]$-complete for constant l.*

Proof (Sketch). The proof for this can be obtained by adapting the LOGNP-completeness proof VC-dimension as given in [42]. The proof gives a construction to encode an instance of an arbitrary problem in LOGNP as a binary matrix C in such a way that the instance is a positive one if and only if the VC-dimension of the matrix C is at least (and, in fact, exactly) $(3 + p + q) \log n$. Furthermore, the VC-dimension of C is $(3 + p + q) \log n$ if and only if C has the row $1^{\log n} 0^{(2+p+q) \log n}$ (where p and q are constants, and n is the size of the input).

Let C' be a matrix consisting of rows $r0$ and $r1$ for each row r in C. Then VC-dimension of C' is $1 + (3+p+q) \log n$ if and only if there is a non-derivable itemset of cardinality $1 + (3 + p + q) \log n$ in the transaction database corresponding to C'. □

The complexities of counting the number of k-free frequent itemsets and counting the number of k-free itemsets of certain cardinality are still unknown. The latter of the problems is also of independent interest as a measure of the stability of VC-dimension and thus having some relevance for many problems in learning theory and algorithmics.

4 Experiments

As the worst-case bounds for the number of frequent itemsets and their condensed representations are quite loose and the generative models of real transaction data is still quite unclear (although some interesting progress have been made recently, see [39, 45]), we computed frequent itemsets and their condensed

Table 1. The transaction databases used in the experiments. The columns are the name of the database, the number of transactions, the number of items, the total number of items in the database, and the density of the database.

$\mathcal{D}$	$|\mathcal{D}|$	$|\mathcal{I}|$	$||\mathcal{D}||$	$||\mathcal{D}||/(|\mathcal{D}| |\mathcal{I}|)$
accidents	340183	468	11500870	0.0722390846897362
chess	3196	75	118252	0.493333333333333
connect	67557	129	2904951	0.333333333333333
kosarak	990002	41270	8019015	0.00019626844652002
mushroom	8124	119	186852	0.19327731092437
retail	88162	16470	908576	0.000625728920102058
BMS-WebView-1	59601	497	149638	0.00505163495528295
BMS-WebView-2	77511	3340	358277	0.00138391406218797
pumsb	49046	2113	3629404	0.0350212967345007
pumsb_star	49046	2088	2475947	0.0241772697395814
T10I4D100K	100000	870	1010228	0.011611816091954
T40I10D100K	100000	942	3960507	0.0420435987261146

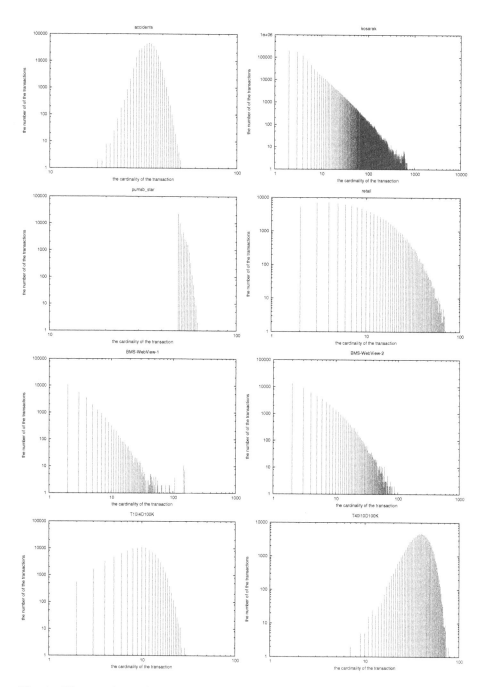

Fig. 1. The number of transactions of different cardinalities in the transaction databases from left to right, top to bottom: accidents, kosarak, pumsb_star, retail, BMS-WebView-1, BMS-WebView-2, T10I4D100K and T40I10D100K

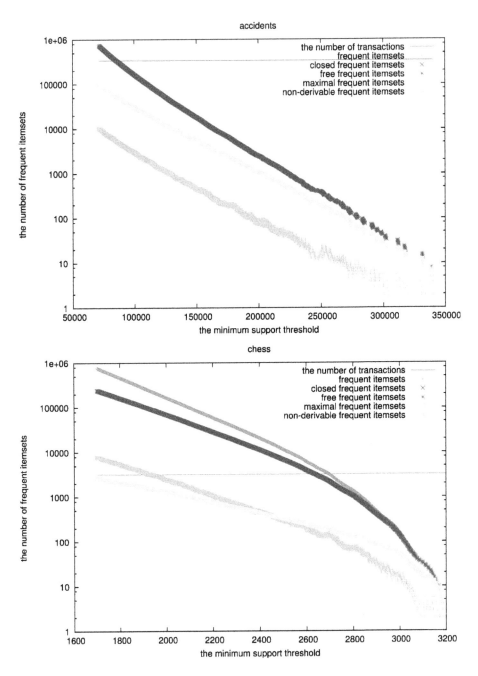

Fig. 2. The number of all, closed, free, maximal and non-derivable frequent itemsets for several minimum support thresholds in the transaction databases accidents (top) and chess (bottom)

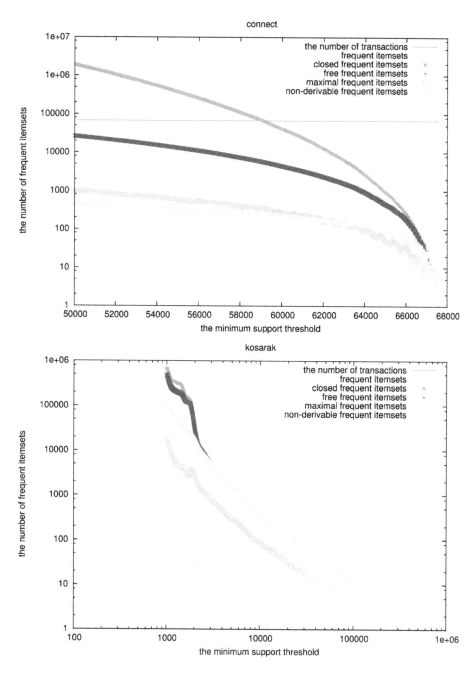

Fig. 3. The number of all, closed, free, maximal and non-derivable frequent itemsets for several minimum support thresholds in the transaction databases `connect` (top) and `kosarak` (bottom)

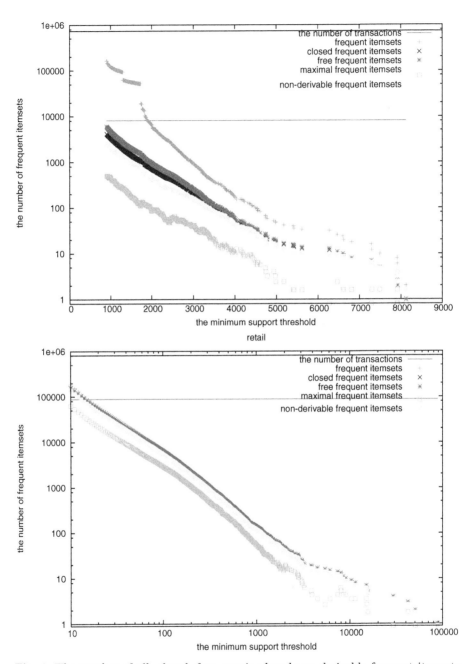

Fig. 4. The number of all, closed, free, maximal and non-derivable frequent itemsets for several minimum support thresholds in the transaction databases `mushroom` (top) and `retail` (bottom)

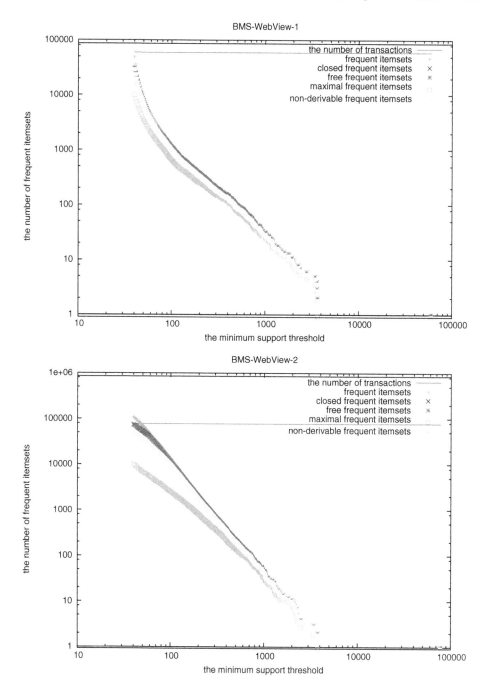

Fig. 5. The number of all, closed, free, maximal and non-derivable frequent itemsets for several minimum support thresholds in the transaction databases BMS-WebView-1 (top) and BMS-WebView-2 (bottom)

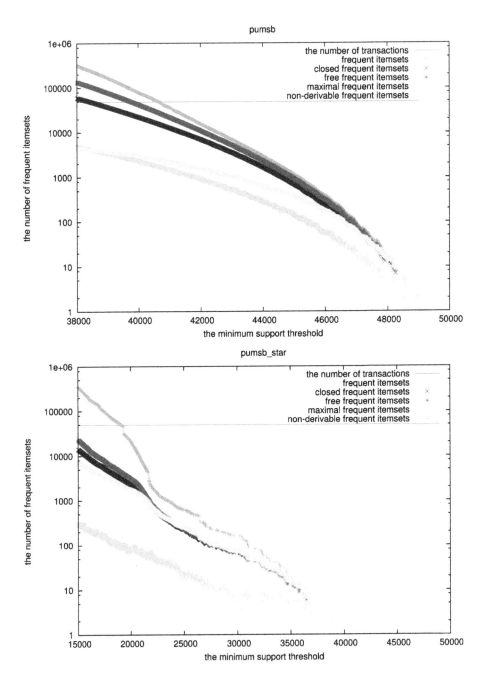

Fig. 6. The number of all, closed, free, maximal and non-derivable frequent itemsets for several minimum support thresholds in the transaction databases `pumsb` (top) and `pumsb_star` (bottom)

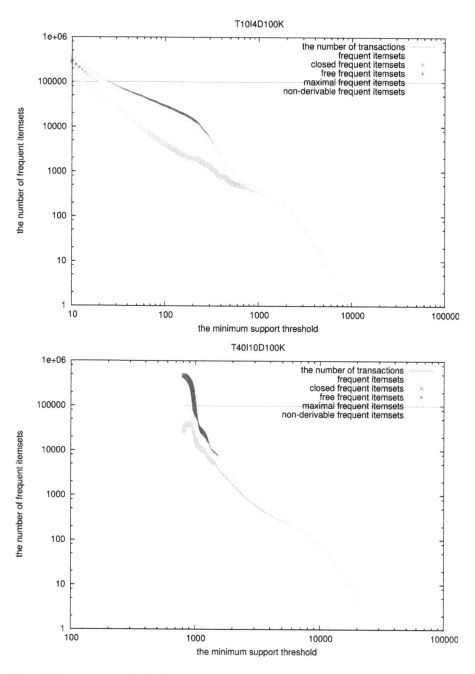

Fig. 7. The number of all, closed, free, maximal and non-derivable frequent itemsets for several minimum support thresholds in the transaction databases T10I4D100K (top) and T40I10D100K (bottom)

representations for a few transaction databases available at FIMI repository[1]. The transaction databases used in the experiments are summarized in Table 1. To get further insights to the transaction databases, the cardinality distributions of the transaction databases accidents, kosarak, pumsb_star, retail, BMS-WebView-1, BMS-WebView-2, T10I4D100K and T40I10D100K are shown in Figure 1. The cardinality distributions of transaction databases chess, connect, mushroom and pumsb are not shown, since all transaction in them are 37, 43, 23 and 74, respectively.

More specifically, we computed all, closed, free, maximal, and non-derivable frequent itemsets for the transaction databases of Table 1. The results are shown in Figures 2–7. Each figure also contains a line showing the number of transaction of the corresponding transaction database. The number of transactions in the database can be used as a baseline of whether the frequent itemset collection is more concise representation. It is worth recalling that the frequent free itemsets are not themselves sufficient representation but also the collection of minimal infrequent itemsets (or the transaction database, for computing the closures of the free itemsets) is needed.

The figures show that 1) the condensed representations provide sometimes considerable reduction in the space consumption and 2) the non-derivable itemsets provide compact representations, especially for small transaction databases. Neither of these are very surprising and both in fact have quite similar possible explanations. First, all condensed representations use the frequency structure of the frequent itemset collection to detect redundant frequent itemsets. Second, non-derivable itemsets use much stronger operations to detect the redundancy: free and closed itemsets are determined only by the minimums and maximums of frequencies in very small neighborhoods whereas non-derivable itemsets are based on deducing quite complicated upper and lower bounds for the frequencies and in addition to the fact that they can exploit much larger neighborhoods.

5   Conclusions and Future Work

There are many interesting connections between transaction databases, frequent itemsets and their condensed representations. Many condensed representations show relevance also at the level of data. The computational complexity of mining frequent itemsets is quite well understood, but there are still important open problems. In general, relating the complexity measures for data to the complexity measures for patterns and pattern collections seems to have great potential in increasing our understanding on pattern discovery, both conceptually and algorithmically. Also studying the relationships between mining the condensed representations of pattern collections and related problems, such as minimal hypergraph transversals and the stability of VC-dimension, seem to be tasks worth looking at. Especially, the fact that many related problems can be solved in polynomial time using $\log^2 n$ nondeterministic bits [42, 46] should be pondered carefully. Finally, more emphasis should be put on identifying and analyzing the

---

[1] http://fimi.cs.helsinki.fi

most important use cases of frequent itemsets (and interesting patterns in general) and how the applications affect the way the frequent itemsets are actually represented [11, 34, 47]. For example, the need for efficient frequency queries pose very different requirements for the inductive database than representing frequent itemsets to the user as a concise summary of the data.

Acknowledgments. I wish to thank Francesco Bonchi, Toon Calders, Floris Geerts, Bart Goethals, Heikki Mannila, and Ari Rantanen for valuable discussions and constructive comments. I am most thankful to the anonymous reviewers for useful suggestions.

The experiments could not have been done without data. Therefore I wish to thank Blue Martini Software for contributing the KDD Cup 2000 data [48] as BMS-WebView-1 and BMS-WebView-2 were part of the KDD Cup 2000 data. I wish to thank also Tom Brijs for providing the transaction database retail. The FIMI data repository was also very valuable for the experiments. Thus, I wish to thank Roberto Bayardo, Bart Goethals and Mohammed Zaki.

References

1. Agrawal, R., Imielinski, T., Swami, A.N.: Mining association rules between sets of items in large databases. In Buneman, P., Jajodia, S., eds.: Proceedings of the 1993 ACM SIGMOD International Conference on Management of Data, Washington, D.C., May 26-28, 1993. ACM Press (1993) 207–216
2. Boulicaut, J.F.: Inductive databases and multiple uses of frequent itemsets: The cInQ approach. [49] 1–23
3. De Raedt, L.: A perspective on inductive databases. SIGKDD Explorations **4** (2003) 69–77
4. Imielinski, T., Mannila, H.: A database perspective on knowledge discovery. Communications of The ACM **39** (1996) 58–64
5. Mannila, H.: Inductive databases and condensed representations for data mining. In Maluszynski, J., ed.: Logic Programming, Proceedings of the 1997 International Symposium, Port Jefferson, Long Island, N.Y., October 13-16, 1997. MIT Press (1997) 21–30
6. Mannila, H., Toivonen, H.: Multiple uses of frequent sets and condensed representations. In Simoudis, E., Han, J., Fayyad, U.M., eds.: Proceedings of the Second International Conference on Knowledge Discovery and Data Mining (KDD-96). AAAI Press (1996) 189–194
7. Agrawal, R., Mannila, H., Srikant, R., Toivonen, H., Verkamo, A.I.: Fast discovery of association rules. In Fayyad, U.M., Piatetsky-Shapiro, G., Smyth, P., Uthurusamy, R., eds.: Advances in Knowledge Discovery and Data Mining. AAAI/MIT Press (1996) 307–328
8. Gunopulos, D., Khardon, R., Mannila, H., Saluja, S., Toivonen, H., Sharma, R.S.: Discovering all most specific sentences. ACM Transactions on Database Systems **28** (2003) 140–174
9. Goethals, B., Zaki, M.J., eds.: Proceedings of the Workshop on Frequent Itemset Mining Implementations (FIMI-03), Melbourne Florida, USA, November 19, 2003. Volume 90 of CEUR Workshop Proceedings. (2003) http://CEUR-WS.org/Vol-90/.

10. Bayardo, R., Goethals, B., Zaki, M.J., eds.: Proceedings of the Workshop on Frequent Itemset Mining Implementations (FIMI-04), Brighton, UK, November 1, 2004. Volume 126 of CEUR Workshop Proceedings. (2004) `http://CEUR-WS.org/Vol-126/`.

11. Mielikäinen, T.: Separating structure from interestingness. In Dai, H., Srikant, R., Zhang, C., eds.: Advances in Knowledge Discovery and Data Mining, 8th Pacific-Asia Conference, PAKDD 2004, Sydney, Australia, May 26-28, 2004, Proceedings. Volume 3056 of Lecture Notes in Artificial Intelligence. Springer (2004) 476–485

12. Toivonen, H.: Sampling large databases for association rules. In Vijayaraman, T.M., Buchmann, A.P., Mohan, C., Sarda, N.L., eds.: VLDB'96, Proceedings of 22th International Conference on Very Large Data Bases, September 3-6, 1996, Mumbai (Bombay), India. Morgan Kaufmann (1996) 134–145

13. Bayardo Jr., R.J.: Efficiently mining long patterns from databases. In Haas, L.M., Tiwary, A., eds.: SIGMOD 1998, Proceedings ACM SIGMOD International Conference on Management of Data, June 2-4, 1998, Seattle, Washington, USA. ACM Press (1998) 85–93

14. Mannila, H., Toivonen, H.: Levelwise search and borders of theories in knowledge discovery. Data Mining and Knowledge Discovery 1 (1997) 241–258

15. Boros, E., Gurvich, V., Khachiyan, L., Makino, K.: On the complexity of generating maximal frequent and minimal infrequent sets. In Alt, H., Ferreira, A., eds.: STACS 2002, 19th Annual Symposium on Theoretical Aspects of Computer Science, Antibes - Juan les Pins, France, March 14-16, 2002, Proceedings. Volume 2285 of Lecture Notes in Computer Science. Springer (2002) 133–141

16. Yang, G.: The complexity of mining maximal frequent itemsets and maximal frequent patterns. [50] 344–353

17. Afrati, F.N., Gionis, A., Mannila, H.: Approximating a collection of frequent sets. [50] 12–19

18. Karp, R.M., Luby, M., Madras, N.: Monte-Carlo approximation algorithms for enumeration problems. Journal of Algorithms 10 (1989) 429–448

19. Pasquier, N., Bastide, Y., Taouil, R., Lakhal, L.: Discovering frequent closed itemsets for association rules. In Beeri, C., Buneman, P., eds.: Database Theory - ICDT '99, 7th International Conference, Jerusalem, Israel, January 10-12, 1999, Proceedings. Volume 1540 of Lecture Notes in Computer Science. Springer (1999) 398–416

20. Mielikäinen, T.: Finding all occurring sets of interest. In Boulicaut, J.F., Džeroski, S., eds.: 2nd International Workshop on Knowledge Discovery in Inductive Databases. (2003) 97–106

21. Kryszkiewicz, M.: Concise representation of frequent patterns based on disjunction-free generators. In Cercone, N., Lin, T.Y., Wu, X., eds.: Proceedings of the 2001 IEEE International Conference on Data Mining, 29 November - 2 December 2001, San Jose, California, USA. IEEE Computer Society (2001) 305–312

22. Uno, T., Asai, T., Uchida, Y., Arimura, H.: An efficient algorithm for enumerating closed patterns in transaction databases. In Arikawa, S., Suzuki, E., eds.: Discovery Science, 7th International Conference, DS 2004, Padova, Italy, October 2–5, 2004, Proceedings. Volume 3245 of Lecture Notes in Computer Science. Springer (2004) 16–31

23. Boulicaut, J.F., Bykowski, A.: Frequent closures as a concise representation for binary data mining. In Terano, T., Liu, H., Chen, A.L.P., eds.: Knowledge Discovery and Data Mining, Current Issues and New Applications, 4th Pacific-Asia Conference, PAKDD 2000, Kyoto, Japan, April 18-20, 2000, Proceedings. Volume 1805 of Lecture Notes in Computer Science. Springer (2000) 62–73

24. Mielikäinen, T.: Frequency-based views to pattern collections. In Hammer, P.L., ed.: Proceedings of the IFIP/SIAM Workshop on Discrete Mathematics and Data Mining, SIAM International Conference on Data Mining (2003), May 1-3, 2003, San Francisco, CA, USA. SIAM (2003)
25. Mielikäinen, T., Mannila, H.: The pattern ordering problem. [51] 327–338
26. Pei, J., Dong, G., Zou, W., Han, J.: On computing condensed pattern bases. In Kumar, V., Tsumoto, S., eds.: Proceedings of the 2002 IEEE International Conference on Data Mining (ICDM 2002), 9-12 December 2002, Maebashi City, Japan. IEEE Computer Society (2002) 378–385
27. Xin, D., Han, J., Yan, X., Cheng, H.: Mining compressed frequent-pattern sets. In Böhm, K., Jensen, C.S., Haas, L.M., Kersten, M.L., Larson, P.Å., Ooi, B.C., eds.: Proceedings of the 31st International Conference on Very Large Data Bases, Trondheim, Norway, August 30 - September 2, 2005. ACM (2005) 709–720
28. Yan, X., Cheng, H., Han, J., Xin, D.: Summarizing itemset patterns: a profile-based approach. In Grossman, R., Bayardo, R., Bennett, K.P., eds.: Proceedings of the Eleventh ACM SIGKDD International Conference on Knowledge Discovery and Data Mining, Chicago, Illinois, USA, August 21-24, 2005. ACM (2005) 314–323
29. Zaki, M.J., Ogihara, M.: Theoretical foundations of association rules. In: SIGMOD'98 Workshop on Research Issues in Data Mining and Knowledge Discovery. (1998)
30. Boulicaut, J.F., Bykowski, A., Rigotti, C.: Free-sets: a condensed representation of Boolean data for the approximation of frequency queries. Data Mining and Knowledge Discovery **7** (2003) 5–22
31. Bastide, Y., Taouil, R., Pasquier, N., Stumme, G., Lakhai, L.: Mining frequent patterns with counting inference. SIGKDD Explorations **2** (2000) 66–75
32. Calders, T.: Computational complexity of itemset frequency satisfiability. In: Proceedings of the Twenty-Third ACM SIGACT-SIGMOD-SIGART Symposium on Principles of Database Systems, June 13-18, 2004, Maison de la Chimie, Paris, France. ACM (2004)
33. Mielikäinen, T.: On inverse frequent set mining. In Du, W., Clifton, C.W., eds.: Proceedings of the 2nd Workshop on Privacy Preserving Data Mining (PPDM), November 19, 2003, Melbourne, Florida, USA. IEEE Computer Society (2003) 18–23
34. Mielikäinen, T.: Implicit enumeration of patterns. [52]
35. Jukna, S.: Extremal Combinatorics: With Applications in Computer Science. EATCS Texts in Theoretical Computer Science. Springer-Verlag (2001)
36. Calders, T.: Deducing bounds on the supports of itemsets. [49] 214–233
37. Calders, T., Goethals, B.: Mining all non-derivable frequent itemsets. In Elomaa, T., Mannila, H., Toivonen, H., eds.: Principles of Data Mining and Knowledge Discovery, 6th European Conference, PKDD 2002, Helsinki, Finland, August 19-23, 2002, Proceedings. Volume 2431 of Lecture Notes in Artificial Intelligence. Springer (2002) 74–865
38. Calders, T., Goethals, B.: Minimal k-free representations of frequent sets. [51] 71–82
39. Dexters, N., Calders, T.: Theoretical bounds on the size of condensed representations. [52] 46–65
40. Anthony, M., Biggs, N.: Computational Learning Theory: An Introduction. Paperback edn. Cambridge University Press (1997)
41. Chazelle, B.: The Discrepancy Method: Randomness and Complexity. Paperback edn. Cambridge University Press (2001)

42. Papadimitriou, C.H., Yannakakis, M.: On limited nondeterminism and the complexity of V-C dimension. Journal of Computer and System Sciences **53** (1996) 161–170
43. Downey, R.G., Fellows, M.R.: Parameterized Complexity. Monographs in Computer Science. Springer-Verlag (1999)
44. Flum, J., Grohe, M., Weyer, M.: Bounded fixed-parameter tractability and $\log^2 n$ nondeterministic bits. In Diaz, J., Karhumäki, J., Sannella, D., eds.: Automata, Languages and Programming: 31st International Colloquium, ICALP 2004, Turku, Finland, July 12-16, 2004. Proceedings. Volume 3142 of Lecture Notes in Computer Science. Springer (2004) 555–567
45. Ramesh, G., Maniatty, W.A., Zaki, M.J.: Feasible itemset distributions in data mining: Theory and application. In: Proceedings of the Twenty-Second ACM SIGACT-SIGMOD-SIGART Symposium on Principles of Database Systems, June 9-12, 2003, San Diego, CA, USA. ACM (2003) 284–295
46. Eiter, T., Gottlob, G., Makino, K.: New results on monotone dualization and generating hypergraph transversals. In: Proceedings on 34th Annual ACM Symposium on Theory of Computing, May 19-21, 2002, Montréal, Québec, Canada. ACM (2002) 14–22
47. Mielikäinen, T.: An automata approach to pattern collections. [52]
48. Kohavi, R., Brodley, C., Frasca, B., Mason, L., Zheng, Z.: KDD-Cup 2000 organizers' report: Peeling the onion. SIGKDD Explorations **2** (2000) 86–98 http://www.ecn.purdue.edu/KDDCUP.
49. Meo, R., Lanzi, P.L., Klemettinen, M., eds.: Database Support for Data Mining Applications: Discovering Knowledge with Inductive Queries. Volume 2682 of Lecture Notes in Computer Science. Springer (2004)
50. Kim, W., Kohavi, R., Gehrke, J., DuMouchel, W., eds.: Proceedings of the Tenth ACM SIGKDD International Conference on Knowledge Discovery and Data Mining, Seattle, Washington, USA, August 22-25, 2004. ACM (2004)
51. Lavrač, N., Gamberger, D., Blockeel, H., Todorovski, L., eds.: Knowledge Discovery in Databases: PKDD 2003, 7th European Conference on Principles and Practice of Knowledge Discovery in Databases, Cavtat-Dubrovnik, Croatia, September 22-26, 2003, Proceedings. Volume 2838 of Lecture Notes in Artificial Intelligence. Springer (2003)
52. Goethals, B., Siebes, A., eds.: KDID 2004, Knowledge Discovery in Inductive Databases, Proceedings of the Third International Workshop on Knowledge Discovery in Inductive Databases, Pisa, Italy, September 20, 2004, Revised Selected and Invited Papers. Volume 3377 of Lecture Notes in Computer Science. Springer (2005)

Multi-class Correlated Pattern Mining

Siegfried Nijssen[1] and Joost N. Kok[2]

[1] Albert-Ludwidgs-Universität, Georges-Köhler-Allee,
Gebäude 097, D-79110, Freiburg im Breisgau, Germany
[2] LIACS, Leiden University, Niels Bohrweg 1, 2333 CA, Leiden, The Netherlands
snijssen@informatik.uni-freiburg.de

Abstract. To mine databases in which examples are tagged with class labels, the minimum correlation constraint has been studied as an alternative to the minimum frequency constraint. We reformulate previous approaches and show that a minimum correlation constraint can be transformed into a disjunction of minimum frequency constraints. We prove that this observation extends to the multi-class χ^2 correlation measure, and thus obtain an efficient new $O(n)$ prune test. We illustrate how the relation between correlation measures and minimum support thresholds allows for the reuse of previously discovered pattern sets, thus avoiding unneccessary database evaluations. We conclude with experimental results to assess the effectivity of algorithms based on our observations.

1 Introduction

One of the oldest and most popular problems in machine learning is that of classification. Classification algorithms are applicable to all databases in which examples are tagged with class labels. Surprisingly, within inductive database theory the problem of classification has received little attention. In this paper we study a problem related to classification, which was first proposed by Bay and Pazzani [2, 3] and later by Morishita and Sese [10]. These authors studied the problem of mining *contrast sets* (name proposed by Bay and Pazzani) or *correlated itemsets* (name proposed by Morishita and Sese). Both terms refer to the same straightforward problem: given a database and a function which computes a measure of correlation between a pattern and a target attribute in the database, can we find all patterns that satisfy a minimum *correlation* constraint? Clearly, from a conceptual point of view this problem is very similar to the frequent itemset mining problem, which is to find all patterns that satisfy a minimum *support* constraint. Compared to the minimum support constraint, the minimum correlation constraint is however computationally more difficult as it is neither monotonic nor anti-monotonic. Given that highly correlated patterns can be useful features for classification algorithms, it can be argued that minimum correlation is a constraint that should be supported by inductive databases. This point was observed earlier, and besides Bay, Pazzani, Morishita and Sese, also other authors have proposed algorithms to mine correlated patterns, for example Zimmermann and De Raedt [12], or the closely related *class association rules* of Liu et al. [9] and *subgroups* of Kavšek et al. [8].

F. Bonchi and J.-F. Boulicaut (Eds.): KDID 2005, LNCS 3933, pp. 165–187, 2006.

In comparison with these previous approaches, this paper introduces one fundamentally new idea: that there is a relation between disjunctions of minimum frequency constraints and minimum correlation constraints. This simple, but important observation allows us to improve previous results and provide deeper insight in the use of correlation constraints in inductive databases:

- In previous research [12] it was implied that to prune branches in a search for correlated patterns, an $O(2^d)$ test for each node in this tree would be required, where d is the number of class values. We show that an $O(d)$ test is sufficient.
- One of the supposed key features of inductive databases is that they treat patterns as data, and that queries can also be defined on sets of patterns. We show that many searches for highly correlated patterns can be reformulated as filtering operations over sets of frequent patterns. Thus, once we have built a set of frequent patterns, our observations show which different kinds of correlation queries can be formulated over these patterns, without accessing the data from which the patterns were obtained. This allows for the reuse of pattern sets for multiple purposes.

The paper is organized as follows. In Section 2 we recall the problem of correlated pattern mining and the notion of ROC spaces. We introduce the basic idea of linking minimum frequency to minimum correlation. In Section 3 we consider the more complex χ^2 and information gain correlation measures, for the case of two classes. In Section 4 we extend this approach to multiple classes. Section 5 discusses how to compute minimum support thresholds, and illustrates how sets of patterns can be reused. Section 6 compares our approach to the work of Bay, Pazzani, Morishita and Sese. Section 7 lists several ways of using our observations in APRIORI-like algorithms, and provides experimental results. Section 8 concludes.

2   Plotting Frequent Patterns in ROC Space

In classification problems we consider databases $\mathcal{D}$ of examples, where each example is labeled by one class in a domain of classes $\mathcal{C}$ through a function $f : \mathcal{D} \to \mathcal{C}$; we denote by $\mathcal{D}_c$ the set of examples for which the class label is c. Rule learners repeatedly search for rules of the form $x \to c$, where c is a class label in $\mathcal{C}$, x is a pattern in a pattern language $\mathcal{X}$ and a cover relation $\succeq$ is defined between patterns in $\mathcal{X}$ and examples in $\mathcal{D}$. Rule learners search rules for which $\rho(x \to c)$ is maximized or minimized, for a measure ρ such as accuracy, weighted accuracy, gain, or χ^2. The measure is computed from the *contingency table*. In binary classification problems this table can be represented as follows:

$a_1(x)n_1$	$(1 - a_1(x))n_1$	n_1
$a_2(x)n_2$	$(1 - a_2(x))n_2$	n_2
$a_1(x)n_1 + a_2(x)n_1$	$n_1 + n_2 - a_1(x)n_1 - a_2(x)n_2$	$n_1 + n_2$

Here n_1 is the number of examples in class 1, n_2 is the number of examples in class 2 and $a_i(x)$ is the fraction of examples of class i that is covered by the body of rule $x \to c$. We call $a_i(x)$ the *frequency* of pattern x in class i. When this is clear of the context we do not denote the argument x of the a function. For convenience we furthermore denote $N = \sum_{i=1}^{d} n_i$.

When inducing a classifier from a dataset the sizes of the classes (n_i) can be considered to be fixed. Here we furthermore assume that the head of the rule is fixed to class 1. In *Receiver Operating Characteristic curve (ROC) analysis* $a_1(x)$ is known as the *true positive rate* (TPR) and $a_2(x)$ is the *false positive rate* (FPR). A *ROC graph* is a graph in which rules are depicted in the FPR-TPR plane [6]. Ideally a rule has a FPR of zero and a TPR of one; the corresponding point, which is depicted in the upper left corner of the ROC graph, is known as *ROC heaven*. Heuristics of classification algorithms can be conceived as measures that determine how far from ROC heaven a classifier is.

We will start our investigation by considering the very simple *accuracy* measure, which can be formalized as $(a_1(x)n_1 + (1 - a_2(x))n_2)/N$, and is a function of the vector $\boldsymbol{a}(x) = (a_1(x), a_2(x))$, so we can write

$$\rho_{acc}(x \to c) = \rho_{acc}(\boldsymbol{a}(x)) = \rho_{acc}(a_1(x), a_2(x)) = (a_1(x)n_1 + (1 - a_2(x))n_2)/N.$$

Adapting terminology proposed by [10], we call vector $\boldsymbol{a}(x)$ the stamp point of pattern x. In this paper for patterns the only property of importance is their stamp point. Usually we therefore unify a pattern with its stamp point and drop the x from our notation. If we solve the equation $\rho_{acc}(\boldsymbol{a}) = \theta$ for an accuracy value θ, we obtain the following *isometric* of possible stamp points that achieve this accuracy:

$$\frac{a_1 n_1 + (1 - a_2)n_2}{N} = \theta \qquad \Longleftrightarrow \qquad a_1 n_1 - a_2 n_2 = \theta N - n_2$$

$$\Longleftrightarrow \qquad a_1 = \frac{\theta N - n_2}{n_1} + a_2 \frac{n_2}{n_1}, \quad (1)$$

which is a straight line in the ROC graph. An example for this isometric with $n_1 = 20$, $n_2 = 40$ and $\theta = \frac{44}{60}$ is given in Figure 1.

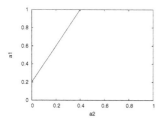

Fig. 1. An isometric for the accuracy measure

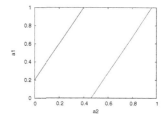

Fig. 2. An isometric for the class neutral accuracy measure

The essential observation is the following. If we consider *all* rules for which the accuracy is higher than $\frac{44}{60}$, then *all* these rules also have a frequency in class 1 which is higher than $\frac{2}{10}$ (enter $a_2 = 0$ into equation 1 to verify this).

The minimum accuracy constraint can therefore be transformed into a tight *minimum frequency* constraint on one class.

More formally, let $\boldsymbol{b}(i)$ denote the vector $(b_1, \ldots, b_d)$ where $b_i = 1$ and $b_j = 0$ for $j \neq i$. Then to find the threshold θ_1 on the frequency of class 1 we need to solve the equation

$$\rho(\theta_1 \boldsymbol{b}(1)) = \theta.$$

For accuracy we have that

$$\theta_1 = \frac{\theta N - n_2}{n_1}.$$

1. Transform minimum accuracy θ into minimum support θ_1 for class 1;
2. Mine all frequent patterns $\mathcal{F}$ in $\mathcal{D}_1$ with minimum support θ_1;
3. Determine the support in $\mathcal{D}_2$ of all frequent patterns in $\mathcal{F}$;
4. Prune all patterns from $\mathcal{F}$ for which accuracy is lower than θ;

Fig. 3. A simple algorithm for mining patterns with high accuracy

At this point we wish to give an example of the consequences of this observation. Consider the algorithm of Figure 3. Then the observation shows that this algorithm is correct: to mine patterns with high accuracy we can use any frequent pattern mining algorithm and postprocess its results.

The algorithm in the figure first determines the *entire* set of frequent patterns; their frequencies in the other part of the data are evaluated second, thus *postprocessing* results. A different approach is to evaluate each frequent pattern *immediately* in the second part of the data (thus *mixing* the evaluation). We will return later in more detail to these different approaches.

Given these observations on the *2 dimensional* case of two target classes, the question is how this applies to higher numbers of classes and other correlation measures. This is what we study in the rest of the paper.

3   Class Neutral Measures

In the previous section we assumed that we only search for rules that have a fixed class in the head of the rule. Usually, one is interested in patterns that correlate with one of the target classes, independent of which class this is. In that case, a *class neutral* measure should be used. A simple class neutral measure is $\max\{\rho_{acc}(x \rightarrow 1), \rho_{acc}(x \rightarrow 2)\}$, which maximizes the correlation over all possible consequences. For some threshold value θ the isometric is depicted in Figure 2. In comparison with the original accuracy measure there is now a 'second ROC heaven'. To find all patterns that achieve a certain accuracy, a single minimum frequency no longer suffices. A second minimum frequency is necessary, this time for the second class. Thus we have to solve two equations:

$$\rho(\theta_1 \boldsymbol{b}(1)) = \theta \qquad \text{and} \qquad \rho(\theta_2 \boldsymbol{b}(2)) = \theta. \qquad (2)$$

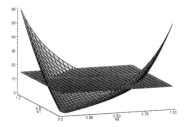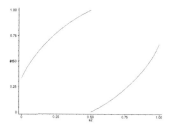

Fig. 4. The χ^2 correlation measure and the plane corresponding to a threshold value (left) and its isometric (right)

Then, we have to find all patterns for which the frequency exceeds a minimum threshold value, either on the first class, or on the second class, or on both; the minimum frequency constraint on $\boldsymbol{a}(x)$ is thus

$$a_1(x) \geq \theta_1 \quad \vee \quad a_2(x) \geq \theta_2. \tag{3}$$

Besides accuracy many other correlation measures are in common used. One of these is the χ^2 statistic, which is the main focus of this work. The χ^2 statistic is computed as follows. Let $E_{i1} = (a_1 n_1 + a_2 n_2) n_i / N$, $E_{i2} = ((1 - a_1)n_1 + (1 - a_2)n_2)n_i/N$, $O_{i1} = a_i n_i$ and $O_{i2} = (1 - a_i)n_i$, then

$$\chi^2(\boldsymbol{a}) = \frac{(O_{11} - E_{11})^2}{E_{11}} + \frac{(O_{12} - E_{12})^2}{E_{12}} + \frac{(O_{21} - E_{21})^2}{E_{21}} + \frac{(O_{22} - E_{22})^2}{E_{22}}.$$

The χ^2 measure and an isometric are depicted in Figure 4, for $n_1 = 20$, $n_2 = 40$ and $\theta = 15$. Therefore also for χ^2 we can obtain thresholds by solving equation (2) and using equation (3) as pruning constraint; again the minimum frequency thresholds of the classes are determined by the points where the χ^2 statistic crosses the a_1 and a_2 axis, respectively.

Just like for accuracy, there is a simple expression to compute the θ_i values. We postpone this computation however to Section 5, at which point we have introduced χ^2 for higher numbers of classes.

More-or-less similar in shape to the χ^2 measure is information gain:

$$\rho_{gain}(\boldsymbol{a}) = -\frac{n_1}{N} \log \frac{n_1}{N} \log - \frac{n_2}{N} \log \frac{n_2}{N} + \frac{a_1 n_1 + a_2 n_2}{N} (P_{11} \log P_{11} + P_{21} \log P_{21})$$
$$+ \frac{(1 - a_1)n_1 + (1 - a_2)n_2}{N} (P_{12} \log P_{12} + P_{22} \log P_{22}),$$

where $P_{i1} = \frac{a_i n_i}{a_1 n_1 + a_2 n_2}$ and $P_{i2} = \frac{(1 - a_i)n_i}{(1 - a_1)n_1 + (1 - a_2)n_2}$. The gain measure can be treated similar as the χ^2 measure: the points where the gain isometric crosses the a_1 and a_2 axes, respectively, determine the minimum frequency thresholds for each of the two classes.

4   More Than Two Classes

Until now only situations were considered in which there are two target classes. In general, however, there may be multiple target classes. To measure whether there is a correlation between a pattern and the target classes, we will consider the χ^2 and information gain measures here; in the next section we will consider accuracy. The contingency table is easily extended to the multi-class case:

$a_1 n_1$	$(1-a_1)n_1$	n_1
$a_2 n_2$	$(1-a_2)n_2$	n_2
$\vdots$	$\vdots$	$\vdots$
$a_d n_d$	$(1-a_d)n_d$	n_d
$\sum_{i=1}^{d} a_i n_i$	$\sum_{i=1}^{d}(1-a_i)n_i$	N

The definitions of E_{i1}, E_{i2}, O_{i1} and O_{i2}, are straightforwardly extended to define χ^2 as $\chi^2(\boldsymbol{a}) = \sum_{i=1}^{d} \frac{(O_{i1}-E_{i1})^2}{E_{i1}} + \frac{(O_{i2}-E_{i2})^2}{E_{i2}}$. Similarly, also the definition of gain ratio is extended. To give an impression of the shape of higher dimensional χ^2 and information gain measures, isometrics for three-class classification problems are given in Figure 5 and Figure 7.

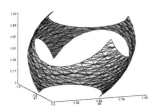

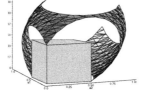

Fig. 5. Isometric for χ^2 in a three-class classification problem

Fig. 6. Isometric for χ^2 in a three-class classification problem; can a box be fitted within the isometric?

Fig. 7. Isometric for information gain in a three-class classification problem

One of the main contributions of this paper is to anwer this question: suppose that we want to find all itemsets for which χ^2 or information gain exceeds a predefined threshold value, is it possible to define a minimum frequency threshold on each of the classes, similar to the two dimensional case? Intuitively, this means that we want to prove that it is possible to put a 'box' completely inside the isometric body, such that the corners of the box are determined by the points where the isometric crosses the axes, as illustrated in Figure 6. In this section we provide an outline of our proof. Details are given in the Appendix.

First, we introduce some notation. Let us denote by $\mathcal{B}_d$ the set of all vectors $(b_1, b_2, \ldots, b_d)$ such that $b_i \in \{0, 1\}$. These vectors can be considered to be the corners of a higher dimensional unit rectangle. For example, $\mathcal{B}_2 = \{(0,0), (1,0),$

$(0, 1), (1, 1)\}$. By $\mathcal{B}_{d, \geq k}$ we denote the subset of vectors in $\mathcal{B}_d$ for which the sum of b_i components is higher than k. As an example, $\mathcal{B}_{2, \geq 1} = \{(1, 0), (0, 1), (1, 1)\}$ and $\mathcal{B}_{2, \geq 2} = \{(1, 1)\}$.

Definition 1. *A $d-$dimensional function ρ is a* suitable correlation function *iff it satisfies the following two properties:*

- *$\rho(a_1, a_2, \ldots, a_d)$ is convex;*
- *for every $\boldsymbol{b} \in \mathcal{B}_{d, \geq 2}$, every $0 \leq \alpha \leq 1$ and every $1 \leq k \leq d$ it must hold that:*

$$\rho(\alpha \cdot b_1, \ldots, \alpha \cdot b_{k-1}, \alpha \cdot b_k, \alpha \cdot b_{k+1}, \ldots, \alpha \cdot b_d) \leq \rho(\alpha \cdot b_1, \ldots, \alpha \cdot b_{k-1}, 0, \alpha \cdot b_{k+1}, \ldots, \alpha \cdot b_d).$$

As an example, consider the χ^2 test for two classes. Among others, in [10] it was shown that χ^2 defines a convex function. The same can be shown for our χ^2 function. The set $\mathcal{B}_{2, \geq 2}$ consists of one single vector $\{(1, 1)\}$. As $\chi^2(\alpha, \alpha) = 0$ it is clearly true that $\chi^2(\alpha, \alpha) \leq \chi^2(\alpha, 0)$ and $\chi^2(\alpha, \alpha) \leq \chi^2(0, \alpha)$, for all $0 \leq \alpha \leq 1$. This shows that the χ^2 test for two classes defines a suitable correlation function. Note that the χ^2 function has several peculiar properties ($\chi^2(1, 0) = \chi^2(0, 1) = n_1 + n_2$ and $\chi^2(\alpha, \alpha) = 0$), but that correlation functions are not required to have these properties within our framework. We have the following theorem.

Theorem 1. *Let ρ be a suitable correlation function. Consider a stamp point $\boldsymbol{a} = (a_1, a_2, \ldots, a_d)$ and let $S_{\boldsymbol{a}}$ be the set of all stamp points $(a'_1, a'_2, \ldots, a'_d)$ with $0 \leq a'_i \leq a_i$. Then*

$$\max_{\boldsymbol{a}' \in S_{\boldsymbol{a}}} \rho(\boldsymbol{a}') = \max\{\rho(a_1, 0, \ldots, 0), \rho(0, a_2, 0, \ldots, 0), \ldots, \rho(0, 0, \ldots, a_d)\}.$$

Proof. See Appendix.

From this theorem it follows that to compute an upper bound on the highest achievable correlation value for a given pattern, it suffices to compute a correlation value for each of the classes separately, or —equivalently— to consider only d thresholds in the case of d classes. To show that this theorem is also usable in practice, we also prove the following.

Theorem 2. *The χ^2 test on a contingency table of d classes defines a suitable correlation function.*

Proof. See Appendix.

These observations have the following consequences. Assume that we solve the following equations

$$\chi^2(\theta_1 \boldsymbol{b}(1)) = \theta, \quad \chi^2(\theta_2 \boldsymbol{b}(2)) = \theta, \quad \ldots \quad \chi^2(\theta_d \boldsymbol{b}(d)) = \theta,$$

similar to equation (2); then we can use the following as frequency constraint:

$$a_1 \geq \theta_1 \quad \vee \quad a_2 \geq \theta_2 \quad \vee \quad \ldots \quad \vee \quad a_d \geq \theta_d,$$

similar to equation (3). Thus, we have a frequency constraint which can be computed in linear time. In the next sectiom we consider how to compute θ_i for the χ^2 contraint.

We wish to conclude this section with an observation for another correlation measure: information gain. We can show that the nice properties of χ^2 do not apply to information gain. Consider a database with three target classes of sizes $n_1 = 30$, $n_2 = 40$ and $n_3 = 50$. Then $\rho_{gain}(0.9 \times 30, 0.9 \times 40, 0) > \rho_{gain}(0.9 \times 30, 0, 0)$. We can therefore not determine minimum frequency thresholds for each of the classes by considering the points on the $a_1, \ldots, a_d$ axes through which the iso-information gain body crosses. Still, intuitively, one should be able to determine a largest possible hyper-rectangle that fits within an iso-information gain body, and thus a set of minimum threshold values. We leave that issue as future work.

5   Choosing Thresholds for χ^2

In this section, we first show how thresholds can be computed for χ^2. It appears that this formula is remarkably simple and that we can draw several further conclusions; the remainder of the section is devoted to listing some of these consequences.

Theorem 3. *Given a stamp point* $\boldsymbol{a} = a_j \boldsymbol{b}(j)$. *Then*

$$\chi^2(\boldsymbol{a}) = \frac{(N - n_j)a_j N}{N - a_j n_j}.$$

Proof. Without loss of generality we can assume that $j = 1$. Then we can split the χ^2 sum into two parts: the 1th row, and the other rows. For the first row the contribution to χ^2 is:

$$N\frac{(n_1 a_1 - \frac{n_1 a_1 n_1}{N})^2}{n_1 a_1 n_1} + N\frac{((1 - a_1)n_1 - \frac{n_1(N - a_1 n_1)}{N})^2}{N(N - a_1 n_1)} = \frac{a_1(N - n_1)^2}{N - a_1 n_1}.$$

For a row $i > 1$ the contribution to χ^2 is:

$$N\frac{(-\frac{n_i a_1 n_1}{N})^2}{n_i a_1 n_1} + N\frac{(n_i - \frac{n_i(N - a_1 n_1)}{N})^2}{n_i(N - a_1 n_1)} = \frac{a_1 n_i n_1}{N} + \frac{a_1^2 n_1^2 n_i}{N(N - a_1 n_1)} = \frac{a_1 n_1 n_i}{N - a_1 n_1}.$$

If we sum all rows $i > 1$, the contribution of all these rows together is $\frac{(N - n_1)a_1 n_1}{N - a_1 n_1}$. Summing this term and the term for the first row, we obtain $\frac{(N - n_1)a_1 N}{N - a_1 n_1}$.   □

From this theorem follows a simple closed formula for computing the threshold minimum support for every class, starting from the χ^2 threshold.

Theorem 4. *Given a threshold* χ^2 *value* θ, *the solution of* $\chi^2(\theta_i \boldsymbol{b}(i)) = \theta$ *is*

$$\theta_i = \frac{\theta N}{N^2 - n_i N + \theta n_i}.$$

Proof. This follows immediately from Theorem 3.   □

Until now we studied the use of a multi-dimensional χ^2 statistic to measure correlation when multiple target classes are involved. A different, perhaps more straightforward way to deal with multiple classes is not to use a more complex correlation function, but to repeatedly solve 2 dimensional search problems: assume that we have d classes, then we can also build a database in which all examples for an original class $1 \leq i \leq d$ are put into a new class 'A' and all examples which are *not* in class i are put into class 'B'. By searching for correlated patterns in this newly labeled database, one would discover patterns that achieve the highest correlation with class i, or its complement; by repeating this procedure for each class one finds correlated patterns for each original class. A natural question is how this approach compares to the approach of the previous section.

To study this different setup we require some additional notation. Similar to the symbols a_i, n_i, N, let us introduce the symbols a_i^j, n_i^j and N^j for the two-class contingency table for class j:

$a_1^j n_1^j$	$(1-a_1^j)n_1^j$	n_1^j
$a_2^j n_2^j$	$(1-a_2^j)n_2^j$	n_2^j
$\sum_{i=1}^d a_i^j n_i^j$	$\sum_{i=1}^d (1-a_i^j)n_i^j$	N^j

The entries are computed from the entries of the original contingency table: $a_1^j = a_j$, $a_2^j = (\sum_{k=1}^d a_k n_k - a_j n_j)/n_2^j$, $n_1^j = n_j$, $n_2^j = \sum_{k=1}^d n_k - n_j = N - n_j$ and $N^j = N$. We can also compute χ^2 for this new contingency table; let us denote this value by $\chi_j^2(\boldsymbol{a}^j)$. Then one can show that the following is not generally true:

$$\chi_j^2(\boldsymbol{a}^j) = \chi^2(\boldsymbol{a});$$

the correlation computed over the 2 class table does not equal the correlation computed over the table with multiple classes. As an example, for $n_1 = 30$, $n_2 = 40$ and $n_5 = 50$ it does not hold that $\chi_1^2(0.9, 0.9 \times 40/90) = \chi^2(0.9, 0.9, 0)$.

Of interest is now to study how the minimum support thresholds for the two-class search problems compare to the thresholds for the single (original) higher dimensional correlated pattern search. From Theorem 3 follows the following:

Theorem 5. *Given a stamp point* $\boldsymbol{a} = a_j \boldsymbol{b}(j)$ *for the* d *dimensional search problem. Then*

$$\chi_j^2(a_j, 0) = \chi^2(\boldsymbol{a}).$$

Proof. If we consider the formula of Theorem 3, we note that the χ^2 value only depends on the total number of examples and the number of examples in the given class j. In the multi-class situation and the constructed two-class situation these are the same, and therefore also the threshold χ^2 values.   □

This theorem has a practical consequence. Assume that we have determined all frequent patterns for all two-class search problems (for both classes of each problem), then it follows that we have also computed all necessary candidate patterns for the higher dimensional correlation measure. We only need to post-process the results of the two-class search problems to fill in missing support values and obtain exact χ^2 values; although therefore access to the database is required, a new frequent pattern search is not necessary.

A natural question is then whether the reverse is also true: assume that we have determined all frequent patterns for each of the classes of the multi-dimensional χ^2 statistic, have we then also determined all patterns that achieve a high correlation in each of the two-dimensional correlation problems?

Summarizing, for a class j we are interested in patterns for which $\chi_j^2(a_1^j, a_2^j) \geq \theta$. We assume that we have all patterns for which $a_1 \boldsymbol{b}(1) \geq \theta_1 \vee \ldots \vee a_d \boldsymbol{b}(d) \geq \theta_d$. Then it is clear from Theorem 5 that we have also determined all patterns for which $a_1^j = a_j \geq \theta_j = \theta_1^j$. However, we require an additional theorem to prove that we also find all patterns for which $a_2^j \theta_2^j$ (and thus all patterns are found for which $a_1^j \geq \theta_1^j \vee a_2^j \geq \theta_2^j$, which is the necessary condition to find all patterns for which $\chi_j^2(a_1^j, a_2^j) \geq \theta$).

Theorem 6. *If for a stamp point $\boldsymbol{a}$ we have $a_2^j \geq \frac{N\theta}{N^2-(N-n_j)(N-\theta)}$ then for at least one $1 \leq i \leq d$, $i \neq j$:*

$$a_i \geq \frac{N\theta}{N^2 - n_i(N - \theta)}.$$

Proof. Without loss of generality we can assume that $j = 1$. Then from the assumption follows that

$$\sum_{i=2}^{d} a_i n_i \geq \frac{N\theta(N - n_1)}{N^2 - (N - n_1)(N - \theta)}.$$

Now let us assume that $a_i < \frac{N\theta}{N^2 - n_i(N-\theta)}$, for all $1 < i < d$. Then we have that

$$\begin{aligned}
a_d n_d &\geq \frac{N\theta(N - n_1)}{N^2 - (N - n_1)(N - \theta)} - \sum_{i=2}^{d-1} a_i n_i \\
&\geq \frac{N\theta(N - n_1)}{N^2 - (N - n_1)(N - \theta)} - \sum_{i=2}^{d-1} \frac{N\theta n_i}{N^2 - n_i(N - \theta)} \\
&\geq \frac{N\theta(N - n_1)}{N^2 - (N - n_1)(N - \theta)} - \frac{N\theta(N - n_1 - n_d)}{N^2 - (N - n_1)(N - \theta)} \\
&\geq \frac{N\theta n_d}{N^2 - (N - n_1)(N - \theta)} \\
&\geq \frac{N\theta n_d}{N^2 - n_d(N - \theta)};
\end{aligned} \tag{4}$$

this shows that at least one term in the logical or must satisfy the given constraint. $\qquad\square$

From this theorem follows that to find correlated patterns for two-class patterns, it suffices to postprocess the result from a multi-dimensional correlation search; access to the database is not even required.

The advantage of these observations is that they provide insight in the ways that sets of frequent patterns can be reused for different purposes. They show that if we search patterns that are frequent in individual classes, we can use these patterns both for multi-dimensional correlation measures as for more simplistic two-dimensional correlation measures.

At this point we can also ask ourselves how the two-way χ^2 correlation measure compares to the accuracy measure of Section 3. Assume that were first interested in finding all patterns for which $\chi^2(a) \geq \theta_{\chi^2}$, then we had to find all patterns for which $a_1 \geq \theta_{\chi^2,1} = \frac{N\theta}{N^2 - n_1(N-\theta)} \vee a_2 \geq \theta_{\chi^2,2} = \frac{N\theta}{N^2 - n_2(N-\theta)}$. Now assume that we want to find all patterns which satisfy a minimum accuracy constraint, then we can observe the following. If we solve the equation

$$\frac{\theta_{acc,i} N - (N - n_i)}{n_i} = \theta_{\chi^2,i},$$

we obtain

$$\theta_{acc,i} = \frac{N\theta_{\chi^2,i} n_i}{N(N^2 - n_i(N - \theta))} + \frac{N - n_i}{N};$$

Then for minimum accuracy thresholds $\theta_{acc} \geq \max_i \theta_{acc,i}$ we can compute all patterns with high accuracy simply by postprocessing the results of the previous search; this follows from the comparison of class thresholds.

The same approach extends to many other situations. For example, assume that we want to contrast two classes against each other, disregarding examples of all other classes. If we already know the frequent patterns for the multi-class case, we can compute for which threshold on minimum χ^2 correlation between two classes we do not need to recompute the frequent patterns.

To conclude this section, let us sketch a possible scenario in which these observations can be exploited. Assume that we have a table with $d > 2$ classes, and the user is first interested in finding patterns that are highly correlated according to a higher dimensional χ^2 statistic. Then we showed that we can transform this minimum correlation threshold into minimum frequency thresholds, and perform a pattern search for these thresholds; then we will find all patterns that achieve high correlation, but also some additional patterns. To answer the user's query, we postprocess the patterns. Assume that we store all patterns that achieve a high frequency in at least one of the classes, and that we also store the supports in all classes.

Then if the user changes her mind, and becomes interested in another kind of question, we showed how we can exploit the previously stored pattern set: if the user wants to find all patterns which have a high accuracy with respect to one class, we can exactly compute for which thresholds we can reuse the previously stored pattern set, and thus, we showed how a second access to the data for this second question can be avoided.

6   Related Work

From our point of view these results are a more simple and more efficient formulation of the methodology of Bay and Pazzani [2, 3], Morishita and Sese [10] and Zimmermann and De Raedt [12]. To show this, we will briefly review this method. By these authors the contingency table is denoted as follows:

y	$m - y$	m
$x - y$	$n - m - (x - y)$	$n - m$
x	$n - x$	n

The χ^2 statistic is defined as a function from (x, y). If a pattern with stamp point (x, y) is refined, it is shown by Morishita and Sese that an upper bound for the χ^2 value of refined patterns is $\max\{\chi^2(y, y), \chi^2(x - y, 0)\}$. Clearly, this notation is a transformation of ours. The claim of Morishita and Sese can be specified equivalently in our notation. Assume that we are given a minimum χ^2 threshold. In our notation Morishita and Sese use the upper bound to stop refining if $\max\{\chi^2(0, a_2), \chi^2(a_1, 0)\} < \theta$. From Figure 4 we can conclude that an equivalent way to specify this test is $a_2 < \theta_2 \wedge a_1 < \theta_1$, where θ_1 and θ_2 are chosen such that $\chi^2(0, \theta_2) = \theta$ and $\chi^2(\theta_1, 0) = \theta$, where θ is the given threshold on χ^2. We can thus conclude that the algorithm of Morishita and Sese which finds all correlated patterns, is a frequent itemset mining algorithm with multiple minimum support constraints.

By Zimmermann et al. [12] it was implied that an exponential number of χ^2 evaluations would be required to compute a reliable upperbound on the highest achievable χ^2 value. Extending to multiple classes the correspondence between Morishita and Sese's approach and ours, we can prove that a linear number of thresholds is sufficient and equally strong pruning power is obtained.

Our observation also provides additional insight in the work of Bay and Pazzani [2]. They propose to prune branches in a search tree using both minimum support constraints and bounds on the highest achievable correlation (similar to Morishita and Sese). We can see now that explicit pruning on class frequencies may not be required, as the correlation constraint transforms into a minimum frequency constraint. Thus, our observation makes it possible to compare the pruning power of several constraints. Additionally, our pruning strategy for multiple classes can be shown to be more tight than Bay and Pazzani's.

Much work has been done on class association rules, which are rules with high confidence and support, and a fixed attribute in the rule head. Using ROC spaces, it can be seen that the confidence constraint transforms into a maximum support constraint, but not in a minimum support constraint. If separate supports for each class are specified, such as by Liu et al. in [9], we can see now that the amount of search tree pruning is the same as for the other algorithms.

7   Algorithms and Experimental Results

The observations of the previous sections can be exploited in algorithms in several ways. In this section, we provide some details of algorithms that exploit our theory, where we restrict ourselves to integrating correlated pattern mining in the well-known trie based APRIORI algorithm [1]; integration in other kinds of algorithms is left as possible future work, but is expected to deliver similar results. To test the performance of our proposed algorithms, we implemented several of them; this section also contains experimental results obtained from running these implementations.

All our experiments were run on an Intel Pentium(R) 4 CPU 2.80GHz with 2GB main memory. We used datasets that we obtained from the UCI (see Figure 8). Datasets with small and large numbers of target classes were used; furthermore the datasets vary in size and number of attributes.

To implement our algorithms, we extended the APRIORI implementation of Ferenc Bodon [4]. Although this implementation is not the fastest, it has the advantage that it is small and clean; thus, we could easily change settings and compare them to each other. Unless pointed out otherwise we use the optimisation of this algorithm which loads the dataset in main memory.

Name	N	d	Comments
Internet Advertisements	3279	2	Class sizes: 2821, 458; numeric attributes not used
Mushroom	8124	2	Class sizes: 4208, 3916
Chess (KRKPA7)	3196	2	Class sizes: 1669, 1527
Chess (KRK)	28056	18	Largest class sizes: 4553, 4194; smallest: 27
Covertype	581012	7	Largest class sizes: 283301, 211840, 35754; smallest: 2747; 8 discretized numeric attributes

Fig. 8. UCI datasets that we used in our experiments [5]

Choosing thresholds in practice. The first topic that we wish to study in practice is the choice of threshold values. In statistics there are some rules of thumb for the choice of χ^2 thresholds. The most commonly used rule is that the p-value of the test should be 5%. The p-value is the probability of obtaining a given statistic, or a better statistic, if no association between the attributes of an instance and its class is assumed. A parameter for computing the p-value is the number of degrees of freedom of the test (which is $d - 1$ in our case). For a given number degrees of freedom, a threshold p-value can be transformed into a threshold on χ^2. Some values are illustrated in Figure 9.

In practice it turns out to be hard to transform this rule of thumb into viable minimum support thresholds. On the chess dataset (KRKPA7) a minimum support of 4 would be required on the first class for a minimum χ^2 threshold of 3.84. On most datasets such a support value is much too low; on this particular dataset if we use a χ^2 threshold of 418, which results in an (absolute) support threshold of 400 in this first class, we already obtain $> 2.000.000$ patterns that are frequent in at least one of the two classes.

Thus, computable minimum support thresholds correspond to very low p-values, which is desirable. There are however more issues involved in the determination of good thresholds. One of the advantages of using relatively high

	Degrees of freedom		
p-value	1	6	16
0.05	3.84	12.59	26.30
0.01	6.64	16.81	32.00
0.001	10.83	22.46	39.25
10^{-300}	36.00	51.62	73.39

Fig. 9. The correspondence between χ^2 values and p-values for the degrees of freedom relevant for the databases in the experiments

minimum support thresholds is that it reduces the risk that expected values in the contingency table become very low. A typical rule which statisticians use to estimate the reliability of the χ^2 test is

χ^2 can be used if no more than 20% of the expected frequencies are less than 5 and none is less than 1.

For example, in the KRKPA7 dataset, in which 52% of the examples are in class 'won', we would require a minimum support threshold of 10 on this class to avoid getting expected values which are lower than 5.

We could also transform this statistician's rule differently into combinations of minimum frequency constraints. In this paper we will not study this possibility further.

As for a database of size N the highest achievable χ^2 value is N, we will choose χ^2 thresholds which are percentages of N.

Linear vs Exponential search space pruning. Our second experiment involves a comparison of pruning algorithms. The setup of the experiment is as follows: we modify the original APRIORI algorithm such that with every pattern in the trie not one support, but multiple supports are stored — for each class one. When we pass an example through the trie, like in the original APRIORI algorithm, we only increase counters of the class to which the example belongs. Thus we obtain a simple mixing approach (see Section 2). When we have to determine whether an itemset should be pruned we consider two alternatives:

- our linear disjunction of minimum frequency tests;
- a generalization of the approach of Morishita and Sese which is exponential in d [10, 12].

The exponential generalization of Morishita and Sese (as also implied in [12]) works as follows. Let $\boldsymbol{a}$ be a stamp point, and consider all a_i which are not zero. Then by setting a subset of these a_i's to zero, we obtain a new stamp point which may be an upperbound on χ^2. By computing χ^2 for all these new stamp points, and determining the maximum, we obtain the upper bound.

Results which compare these approaches for several datasets are given in Figure 10. It is clear that only if the number of target classes grows larger, the linear pruning test becomes interesting. At first sight it may seem strange that a decrease in threshold does not always result in much longer runtimes. This

Dataset	d	θ	Lin.	Exp.	# Cand.	# Freq.	# Corr.
Mushroom	2	12.0%	15.1s	15.1s	158021	157243	141953
Mushroom	2	10.0%	36.1s	36.1s	284590	283699	255037
Cover type	7	1.0%	19.9s	33.7s	208246	150610	42784
Cover type	7	0.5%	33.0s	63.3s	550169	433807	151952
Chess (KRK)	18	1.0%	0.8s	108.3s	13220	8029	2637
Chess (KRK)	18	0.5%	0.9s	111.3s	23246	13760	6610

Fig. 10. Experiments with a linear (Lin.) and an exponential (Exp.) test for pruning the search space. Given are run times (Lin. and Exp.); number of candidates (# Cand.), number of frequent patterns (# Freq.) and number of correlated patterns exceeding the θ threshold (# Corr.).

can be explained by the fact that the exponential approach only generates all subsets for coordinates which are non-zero. Although the number of candidates that is evaluated is much larger for a lower threshold, many of the additional candidates have zeros in many coordinates, and require less evaluation time than the patterns which have high support values in all classes.

Postprocessing Sets of Patterns. We showed that in stead of recomputing all frequent patterns, it is often possible to reuse the same set of frequent patterns for different kinds of correlation queries. In this section we provide a short investigation of this idea. To this purpose we use the Cover type dataset, which consists of 7 target classes. We are interested in two kind of correlated patterns: patterns that correlate with all classes according to a 7-dimensional χ^2 statistic, and patterns that correlate with the first (largest) class according to a 2-dimensional χ^2 statistic that compares the first class with the aggregation of all other classes. For both correlated statistics we wish to use the same threshold value.

We use 2 kinds of algorithms. First, we have the basic *mixing* algorithm that we used earlier this section. We can start this algorithm two times to answer both questions (see Figure 11, rows 'Search 7 dimensional' and 'Search 2 dimensional'). Another possibility is to run the 7 dimensional correlation query first, and to store all frequent patterns in an additional trie during the run of the algorithm[1]. We answer the second query by scanning the previously constructed trie.

To obtain more insight in the run time behavior of the implementations we also include in Figure 11 the run times of an implementation which does not load the database in memory, but rescans the data from disc, like the original APRIORI algorithm.

In the experiment we can see that the time to answer a query form a constructed trie is much shorter than to compute the same result from data. Most queries can be answered within 2 seconds.

On the other hand, we also see that our implementation requires more time to construct a trie of all patterns in main memory. In some cases the additional

---

[1] We require an additional trie as the APRIORI implementation removes unnecessary short patterns from the trie when generating longer candidates.

χ^2 Threshold	Memory		From disc	
	1.0%	0.5%	1.0%	0.5%
Search 7 dimensional	19.9s	33.3s	82.6s	129.9s
Search 2 dimensional	7.9s	10.6s	27.7s	40.4s
Search 7 dim., store, query once	34.9s	66.3s	99.2s	164.9s
Search 7 dim., store, query twice	35.3s	67.6s	99.8s	166.6s

Fig. 11. A comparison between algorithms that compute patterns from data and from pattern sets

time required for this construction is longer than the time required to perform an additional search for correlated patterns with a lower dimensional χ^2 statistic.

It can be expected that 2 dimensional χ^2 searches require less time than 7 dimensional ones, as for the 7 dimensional case some classes have rather low minimum threshold values. In the 2 dimensional case the small classes are summed together.

Some differences in run time are most likely a consequence of implementation issues and side effects of the architecture of modern computers. For example, we cannot otherwise explain that the run time for building the additional trie is larger when loading the data from disc, while in our implementation both the trie datastructures and the trie algorithms used during the construction of the second trie are exactly the same.

Dataset θ	Mushroom 10%		Mushroom 12%		Internet 3.5%		Cover t. 0.5%	
	Memory	Disc	Memory	Disc	Memory	Disc	Memory	Disc
Mixing	36.1s	47.0s	15.5s	25.0s	33.1s	37.4s	10.7s	40.6s
Class 1 search	10.4s	17.5s	10.0s	16.5s	<0.1s	<0.1s	4.3s	16.1s
Class 2 search	10.4s	22.3s	1.2s	3.9s	17.9s	20.5s	5.1s	15.6s
Cl. 1 search + Cl. 2 count	18.3s	39.5s	17.5s	29.8s	<0.1s	<0.1s	16.2s	29.6s
Cl. 2 search + Cl. 1 count	18.7s	31.1s	3.5s	10.1s	35.0s	41.7s	8.6s	20.5s

Fig. 12. Comparison of evaluation strategies

Evaluation Strategies. In our previous experiment we used a *mixing approach*, in which all patterns are evaluated in all classes. Another approach is to *postprocess* results. The simplest way is to proceed is illustrated in Figure 13; first one performs a search for frequent patterns in class 1, and stores these into a new trie; then we evaluate these frequent patterns in the part of the database correponding to the second class. Finally, we repeat the procedure with the classes reversed.

An overview of some experimental results is given in Figure 12. What is immediately remarkable in this table is the rather long additional time required to evaluate frequent patterns for the second class of examples. We investigated this phenomenon in detail, and found that the additional run time is *not* caused by scanning the examples of the second class; this scan is performed in < 2s in all cases. Furthermore, the additional run time is *not* (entirely) spent building

1. Transform minimum χ^2 into minimum supports θ_1 and θ_2;
2. Mine all frequent patterns $\mathcal{F}_1$ in $\mathcal{D}_1$ with minimum support θ_1;
3. Determine all supports of patterns in $\mathcal{F}_1$ in $\mathcal{D}_2$; 4. Prune all patterns from $\mathcal{F}_1$ for which χ^2 is lower than θ;
5. Mine all frequent patterns $\mathcal{F}_2$ in $\mathcal{D}_2$ with minimum support θ_2;
6. Determine all supports of patterns in $\mathcal{F}_2$ in $\mathcal{D}_1$; 7. Prune all patterns from $\mathcal{F}_1$ for which χ^2 is lower than θ;
8. (Optional) Merge the sets $\mathcal{F}_1$ and $\mathcal{F}_2$.

Fig. 13. A simple algorithm for mining patterns with high χ^2 value

the second trie, as the additional run time is dependent on the evaluation strategy (from memory or from disk). The main slow down seems to be caused by the mere allocation of additional main memory, and a resulting memory inefficiency of evaluating patterns in the first class. Thus, we can assume that most differences in this table are rather hardware dependent, or within margins of implementation details. We tried several further variations — including using different item orders for both classes, evaluating tries in the second class during the search in the first class, and so on, but in all cases the results do not seem to improve significantly. Thus, we can conclude that there are some differences in run time behavior of the several evaluation strategies, but that these differences are not very significant.

8   Conclusions

In this paper we showed that to find all patterns that correlate with a target attribute, it is sufficient to search for all patterns that satisfy a set of frequency thresholds, where these thresholds can be computed exactly by filling in a minimum correlation threshold in a correlation measure, such as information gain, accuracy, weighted accuracy or χ^2. For the χ^2 measure we showed that this approach can even be used even if the target attribute has multiple values. We illustrated that a major consequence of this observation is that we can reuse pattern bases: if we know all patterns that satisfy a given disjunction of minimum frequency constraints, we can reuse these patterns to answer many kinds of correlation queries.

To illustrate the use of our theory, we gave several algorithms that exploit it. Although several algorithmic variations follow from our theory that are not significantly better in terms of efficiency, we showed that the main contributions of the paper do make sense:

- for large numbers of target attribute values, the reduction in run time for the $O(d)$ prune test is significant;
- to reuse existing sets of patterns is more efficient than to recompute corrated patterns from data.

Much further research can be considered in this direction. In this paper we studied only a small amount of correlation measures, and showed only for a few of them how they relate to each other. Future inductive databases should provide a wide range of correlation measures and should be able to relate them to each other to reuse existing pattern bases efficiently. We already gave some attention to the reliability of the χ^2 test, but more work could be done in this direction. For example, for small expected values in the contingency table Fischer's exact test is considered to be more reliable than the χ^2 test. To 'automatically' switch to a more reliable test and still find all patterns, we require a further theory on the differences between the tests.

In our experiments we showed how correlated pattern mining can be performed on top of an implementation of the traditional APRIORI frequent itemset mining algorithm. There are many kinds of algorithms, such as FP GROWTH [7] or ECLAT [11], which could incorporate the same ideas. Finally, condensed representations for answering correlated pattern mining queries have not been studied yet.

Acknowledgements. This work was partly supported by the EU FET IST project IQ ("Inductive Querying"), contract number FP6-516169.

References

1. R. Agrawal, H. Mannila, R. Srikant, H. Toivonen, and A. I. Verkamo. Fast discovery of association rules. In *Advances in knowledge discovery and data mining*, pages 307–328, 1996.
2. S. D. Bay and M. J. Pazzani. Detecting change in categorical data: Mining contrast sets. In *Proceedings of the 5th International Conference on Knowledge Discovery and Data Mining (KDD)*, pages 302–306. ACM Press, 1999.
3. S. D. Bay and M. J. Pazzani. Detecting group differences: Mining contrast sets. In *Data Mining and Knowledge Discovery*, volume 5, pages 213–246. Kluwer Academic Publishers, 2001.
4. F. Bodon. Surprising results of trie-based FIM algorithms. In *Proceedings of the Workshop on Frequent Itemset Mining Implementations (FIMI)*, volume 90 of *CEUR Workshop Proceedings*, 2004.
5. C.L. Blake D.J. Newman, S. Hettich and C.J. Merz. UCI repository of machine learning databases, 1998.
6. J. Fürnkranz and P. Flach. ROC 'n' rule learning – towards a better understanding of covering algorithms. In *Machine Learning*, volume 58, pages 39–77, 2005.
7. J. Han, J. Pei, and Y. Yin. Mining frequent patterns without candidate generation. In *Proceedings of the ACM SIGMOD International Conference on Management of Data*, pages 1–12, 2000.
8. B. Kavšek, N. Lavrač, and V. Jovanoski. APRIORI-SD: Adapting association rule learning to subgroup discovery. In *Proceedings of the Fifth International Symposium on Intelligent Data Analysis*, volume 2810 of *Lecture Notes in Computer Science*, pages 230–241. Springer-Verlag, 2003.
9. B. Liu, Y. Ma, and C.-K.Wong. Improving an exhaustive search based rule learner. In *Proceedings of the 4th European Conference on Principles and Practice of Knowledge Discovery in Databases (PKDD)*, volume 1910 of *Lecture Notes in Artificial Intelligence*, pages 504–509, 2000.

10. S. Morishita and J. Sese. Traversing itemset lattices with statistical metric pruning. In *Proceedings of the Nineteenth ACM SIGACT-SIGMOD-SIGART Symposium on Database Systems (PODS)*, pages 226–236, 2000.
11. M. J. Zaki, S. Parthasarathy, M. Ogihara, and W. Li. New algorithms for fast discovery of association rules. In *Proceedings of the Third International Conference on Knowledge Di scovery and Data Mining (KDD)*, pages 283–286, 1997.
12. A. Zimmermann and L. De Raedt. Cluster-grouping: From subgroup discovery to clustering. In *Proceedings of the 15th European Conference on Machine Learning (ECML)*, volume 3201 of *Lecture Notes in Computer Science*, pages 575–577, 2004.

A   Proof Outlines

In this Appendix we provide some short outlines of the proofs of Theorems 1 and 2. We will illustrate our argumentation in the case of a target attribute with 3 classes. First, however, we require the following lemma.

Lemma 1. *Let ρ be a suitable correlation function. Given a binary vector $\boldsymbol{b} \in \mathcal{B}_{d,\geq 2}$, then for every k in this vector for which $b_k = 1$ it holds that:*

$$\rho(\alpha \boldsymbol{b}) \leq \rho(\alpha \boldsymbol{b}'), \text{ where } \boldsymbol{b}' \text{ is a vector such that } b_k' = 1 \text{ and } b_i' = 0 \text{ for } i \neq k.$$

Proof. This follows from the second constraint on suitable correlation functions, which states that by setting one coordinate to zero the correlation value can only increase. More formally, the vector $\boldsymbol{b}$ consists of ones at positions $i_1, \ldots, i_k$, while other bits are zero. By setting first i_1 to zero, than i_2, and so on, until i_{k-1} is zero, a sequence of bit vectors results, for which the correlation values increase monotonically. As we did not assume any order on the indexes in $\boldsymbol{i}$, we can conclude that we can construct a sequence which reduces every bit vector $\boldsymbol{b}$ to a bit vector in which only one bit is one.   □

In Figure 14 this is illustrated for the three-dimensional case. Consider the vector $\alpha \cdot (1,1,1) = (\alpha, \alpha, \alpha)$. According to the second constraint on correlation functions, $\rho(\alpha, \alpha, \alpha) \leq \rho(0, \alpha, \alpha) \leq \rho(0, 0, \alpha)$. Furthermore, among others, $\rho(\alpha, 0, \alpha) \leq \rho(\alpha, 0, 0)$. The theorem does not claim that $\rho(\alpha, 0, \alpha) \leq \rho(0, \alpha, 0)$ holds.

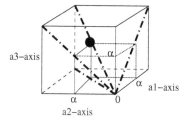

Fig. 14. Illustration of Lemma 1

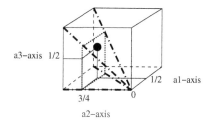

Fig. 15. An example stamp point

Proof. (**Theorem 1**). As the function ρ is assumed to be convex the following must hold:

$$\max_{a' \in S_a} \rho(a') = \max_{b \in \mathcal{B}_d} \rho(a_1 \cdot b_1, a_2 \cdot b_2, \ldots, a_d \cdot b_d).$$

This follows from the property that for convex functions any domain that can be characterized by a bounding polygon is maximized on one of the vertexes of the polygon. We now have to show that we can discard all elements of $\mathcal{B}_{d,\geq 2}$.

Consider the given stamp point $a = (a_1, \ldots, a_d)$ and consider one of its dimensions k such that $a_k = \max_{1 \leq j \leq d} a_j$. Then the following points define a $d-1$ dimensional rectangle:

$$\{a_k \cdot b \mid b \in \mathcal{B}_d, b_k = 1\}$$

The stamp point a is an element of this rectangle, as for all a_i it holds that $0 \leq a_i \leq a_k$. Please note that a rectangle in any dimension can be defined by giving two points 'opposite' from each other. The rectangle here is defined by the two points $(0, \ldots, a_k, \ldots, 0)$ and $(a_k, \ldots, a_k)$.

From the convexity of ρ it follows that for a given a with $a_k = \max_{1 \leq j \leq d} a_j$:

$$\max_{b \in \mathcal{B}_d, b_k = 1} \rho(a_k \cdot b) \geq \rho(a).$$

From Lemma 1 it follows that $\max_{b \in \mathcal{B}_d, b_k = 1} \rho(a_k \cdot b) = \rho(a_k \cdot b)$, where b is the vector in which all elements are zero except b_k. For any given stamp point a we may therefore conclude that $\rho(a) \leq \rho(a_k \cdot b)$, where $a_k = \max_{1 \leq i \leq d} a_i$ and b is a vector that is zero in all coordinates except for the kth, which is 1.   □

As an example consider the following stamp point: $(\frac{1}{2}, \frac{3}{4}, \frac{1}{2})$. This stamp point is illustrated in Figure 15. What we wish to show is that we do not need to consider this stamp point, as its correlation value is always lower than that of one of the points in $\{(\frac{1}{2}, 0, 0), (0, \frac{3}{4}, 0), (0, 0, \frac{1}{2})\}$. This would show that the only points that we need to consider are in $\{(\frac{1}{2}, 0, 0), (0, \frac{3}{4}, 0), (0, 0, \frac{1}{2})\}$.

As $a_2 = \frac{3}{4} \geq \frac{1}{2} = a_1 = a_3$ the binary vectors of importance are $\{b \mid b \in \mathcal{B}_d, b_2 = 1\} = \{(0, 1, 0), (0, 1, 1), (1, 1, 0), (1, 1, 1)\}$. After multiplication with $\frac{3}{4}$ the rectangle $\{(0, \frac{3}{4}, 0), (0, \frac{3}{4}, \frac{3}{4}), (\frac{3}{4}, \frac{3}{4}, 0), (\frac{3}{4}, \frac{3}{4}, \frac{3}{4})\}$ is obtained. This rectangle is highlighted in the Figure. The original stamp point is part of this rectangle.

From Lemma 1 it follows that $\max\{\rho(0, \frac{3}{4}, 0), \rho(0, \frac{3}{4}, \frac{3}{4}), \rho(\frac{3}{4}, \frac{3}{4}, 0), \rho(\frac{3}{4}, \frac{3}{4}, \frac{3}{4})\} = \rho(0, \frac{3}{4}, 0)$. Due to convexity all points within the rectangle are lower than the highest point on the bounding polygon, therefore also $\rho(\frac{1}{2}, \frac{3}{4}, \frac{1}{2}) \leq \rho(0, \frac{3}{4}, 0)$. This proves that we do not need to consider the given stamp point. Similar arguments apply to the points in $\{(\frac{1}{2}, \frac{3}{4}, 0), (0, \frac{3}{4}, \frac{1}{2}), (\frac{1}{2}, 0, \frac{1}{2})\}$.

What remains to be shown is that suitable correlation functions indeed exist. We will show this in the proof of the following theorem.

Proof. (**Theorem 2**). It was already observed in other work that the χ^2 function for multiple classes is convex [12]. Here we concentrate on the second constraint. As one can always change the order of arguments of ρ without loss of generality we may state that we consider the following change in a contingency table:

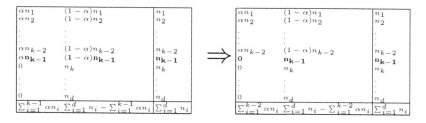

We denote the χ^2 value of the contingency table before the change as $\chi_n^2(\alpha, k)$; after the change the χ^2 value is $\chi_n^2(\alpha, k-1)$. We show the following:

$$\chi_n^2(\alpha, k) - \chi_n^2(\alpha, k-1) =$$

$$\frac{\alpha(\alpha - 1)n_{k-1}\left(\sum_{i=1}^{d} n_i\right)^2}{\left(\sum_{i=1}^{k-2}(1-\alpha)n_i + \sum_{i=k-1}^{d} n_i\right)\left(\sum_{i=1}^{k-1}(1-\alpha)n_i + \sum_{i=k}^{d} n_i\right)}. \quad (5)$$

Clearly, for $0 \leq \alpha \leq 1$ it holds that $\chi_n^2(\alpha, k) - \chi_n^2(\alpha, k-1) \leq 0$ and therefore that $\chi_n^2(\alpha, k) \leq \chi_n^2(\alpha, k-1)$. We show now how the first term of equation (5) can be rewritten into the second term. The right term is defined as

$$\sum_{i=1}^{d} \frac{(E_{i1} - O_{i1})^2}{E_{i1}} + \frac{(E_{i2} - O_{i2})^2}{E_{i2}} - \frac{(E_{i1}' - O_{i1}')^2}{E_{i1}'} - \frac{(E_{i2}' - O_{i2}')^2}{E_{i2}'}, \quad (6)$$

where

$$E_{i1} = \frac{\alpha(n_1 + \cdots + n_{k-1})n_i}{N}, \qquad O_{i1} = \begin{cases} \alpha n_i & \text{if } i \leq k - 1; \\ 0 & \text{otherwise}; \end{cases}$$

furthermore, $E_{i2} = n_i - E_{i1}$, $O_{i2} = n_i - O_{i1}$, O_{ij}' is defined similar to O_{ij}, and

$$E_{i1}' = E_{i1} - \frac{\alpha n_{k-1} n_i}{N}, \qquad E_{i2}' = E_{i2} + \frac{\alpha n_{k-1} n_i}{N}.$$

Equation (6) can then be rewritten as

$$\sum_{i=1}^{d}(E_{i1} - 2O_{i1} + \frac{O_{i1}^2}{E_{i1}}) + (E_{i2} - 2O_{i2} + \frac{O_{i2}^2}{E_{i2}})$$

$$- (E_{i1} - \frac{\alpha n_{k-1} n_i}{N} - 2O_{i1}' + \frac{(O_{i1}')^2}{E_{i1}'}) - (E_{i2} + \frac{\alpha n_{k-1} n_i}{N} - 2O_{i2}' + \frac{(O_{i2}')^2}{E_{i2}'}),$$

which reduces to

$$\sum_{i=1}^{d} 2(O_{i1}' - O_{i1} + O_{i2}' - O_{i2}) + \frac{O_{i1}^2}{E_{i1}} + \frac{O_{i2}^2}{E_{i2}} - \frac{(O_{i1}')^2}{E_{i1}'} - \frac{(O_{i2}')^2}{E_{i2}'}. \quad (7)$$

It is easy to see that $\sum_{i=1}^{d} 2(O'_{i1} - O_{i1} + O'_{i2} - O_{i2}) = 0$, as the O elements only sum over all observations, and this number does not change. Therefore we rewrite equation (7) to:

$$\sum_{i=1}^{d} \frac{O_{i1}^2}{E_{i1}} + \frac{O_{i2}^2}{E_{i2}} - \frac{(O'_{i1})^2}{E'_{i1}} - \frac{(O'_{i2})^2}{E'_{i2}},$$

which reduces to:

$$\left(\sum_{i=1}^{d} \frac{O_{i1}^2}{E_{i1}} + \frac{O_{i2}^2}{E_{i2}} - \frac{O_{i1}^2}{E'_{i1}} - \frac{O_{i2}^2}{E'_{i2}} \right) + \frac{(\alpha n_{k-1})^2}{E'_{(k-1)1}} - \frac{(1 - (1-\alpha)^2)n_{k-1}^2}{E'_{(k-1)2}}.$$

or, equivalently:

$$\left(\sum_{i=1}^{d} \frac{O_{i1}^2}{E_{i1}} - \frac{O_{i1}^2}{E'_{i1}} \right) + \left(\sum_{i=1}^{d} \frac{O_{i2}^2}{E_{i2}} - \frac{O_{i2}^2}{E'_{i2}} \right) + \frac{(\alpha n_{k-1})^2}{E'_{(k-1)1}} + \frac{\alpha(\alpha - 2)n_{k-1}^2}{E'_{(k-1)2}}. \quad (8)$$

We first rewrite the first term:

$$\sum_{i=1}^{d} \frac{O_{i1}^2}{E_{i1}} - \frac{O_{i1}^2}{E'_{i1}} = \sum_{i=1}^{k-1} \frac{\alpha^2 n_i^2 N}{\alpha(n_1 + \cdots + n_{k-1})n_i} - \frac{\alpha^2 n_i^2 N}{\alpha(n_1 + \cdots + n_{k-2})n_i}$$

$$= \sum_{i=1}^{k-1} \frac{\alpha^2 n_i^2 (n_1 + \cdots + n_{k-2})N - \alpha^2 n_i^2 (n_1 + \cdots + n_{k-1})N}{\alpha(n_1 + \cdots + n_{k-1})(n_1 + \cdots + n_{k-2})n_i}$$

$$= \sum_{i=1}^{k-1} \frac{-\alpha n_i n_{k-1} N}{(n_1 + \cdots + n_{k-1})(n_1 + \cdots + n_{k-2})}$$

$$= \frac{-\alpha \left(\sum_{i=1}^{k-1} n_i \right) n_{k-1} N}{(n_1 + \cdots + n_{k-1})(n_1 + \cdots + n_{k-2})} = \frac{-\alpha n_{k-1} N}{n_1 + \cdots + n_{k-2}}$$

Furthermore, we have that:

$$\frac{(\alpha n_{k-1})^2}{E'_{(k-1)1}} = \frac{(\alpha n_{k-1})^2 N}{\alpha(n_1 + \cdots + n_{k-2})n_{k-1}} = \frac{\alpha n_{k-1} N}{n_1 + \cdots + n_{k-2}},$$

therefore two of the terms in equation (8) cancel out. Next we consider:

$$\sum_{i=1}^{d} \frac{O_{i2}^2}{E_{i2}} - \frac{O_{i2}^2}{E'_{i2}} = \sum_{i=1}^{k-1} \frac{(1-\alpha)^2 n_i^2 N}{(N - \alpha(n_1 + \cdots + n_{k-1}))n_i} - \frac{(1-\alpha)^2 n_i^2 N}{(N - \alpha(n_1 + \cdots + n_{k-2}))n_i} +$$

$$\sum_{i=k}^{d} \frac{n_i^2 N}{(N - \alpha(n_1 + \cdots + n_{k-1}))n_i} - \frac{n_i^2 N}{(N - \alpha(n_1 + \cdots + n_{k-2}))n_i}$$

$$= \sum_{i=1}^{k-1} \frac{\alpha(1-\alpha)^2 n_i N n_{k-1}}{(N - \alpha(n_1 + \cdots + n_{k-1}))(N - \alpha(n_1 + \cdots + n_{k-2}))} +$$

$$\sum_{i=k}^{d} \frac{\alpha n_i N n_{k-1}}{(N - \alpha(n_1 + \cdots + n_{k-1}))(N - \alpha(n_1 + \cdots + n_{k-2}))}$$

$$= \frac{\alpha(\sum_{i=1}^{k-1}(1-\alpha)^2 n_i + \sum_{i=k}^{d} n_i) N n_{k-1}}{(N - \alpha(n_1 + \cdots + n_{k-1}))(N - \alpha(n_1 + \cdots + n_{k-2}))}$$

Summing the remaining terms we have that:

$$\left(\sum_{i=1}^{d} \frac{O_{i2}^2}{E_{i2}} - \frac{O_{i2}^2}{E'_{i2}} \right) + \frac{\alpha(\alpha - 2) n_{k-1}^2}{E'_{(k-1)2}} =$$

$$\frac{\alpha(\sum_{i=1}^{k-1}(1-\alpha)^2 n_i + \sum_{i=k}^{d} n_i) N n_{k-1} + \alpha(\alpha - 2) n_{k-1} N (N - \alpha(n_1 + \cdots + n_{k-1}))}{(N - \alpha(n_1 + \cdots + n_{k-1}))(N - \alpha(n_1 + \cdots + n_{k-2}))}.$$

This simplifies to

$$\frac{\alpha(\alpha - 1) N^2 n_{k-1}}{(N - \alpha(n_1 + \cdots + n_{k-1}))(N - \alpha(n_1 + \cdots + n_{k-2}))},$$

which is the final rewritten term that we were searching. Clearly, for $0 \leq \alpha \leq 1$ this term is negative, and χ^2 measure is therefore suitable. $\qquad \square$

Shaping SQL-Based Frequent Pattern Mining Algorithms*

Csaba István Sidló[1] and András Lukács[2]

[1] Eötvös Loránd University, Faculty of Informatics,
Pázmány Péter sétány 1/c, 1117 Budapest, Hungary
scs@elte.hu
[2] Computer and Automation Research Institute,
Hungarian Academy of Sciences, Kende u. 13-17., 1111 Budapest, Hungary
alukacs@sztaki.hu
http://informatika.ilab.sztaki.hu/websearch/

Abstract. Integration of data mining and database management systems could significantly ease the process of knowledge discovery in large databases. We consider implementations of frequent itemset mining algorithms, in particular pattern-growth algorithms similar to the top-down FP-growth variations, tightly coupled to relational database management systems. Our implementations remain within the confines of the conventional relational database facilities like tables, indices, and SQL operations. We compare our algorithm to the most promising previously proposed SQL-based FIM algorithm. Experiments show that our method performs better in many cases, but still has severe limitations compared to the traditional stand-alone pattern-growth method implementations. We identify the bottlenecks of our SQL-based pattern-growth methods and investigate the applicability of tightly coupled algorithms in practice.

1 Introduction

Frequent itemset mining (FIM) is a central exercise of data mining. FIM is a base to solve several further tasks like association rule, sequential and other frequent pattern mining. Although algorithms for FIM were studied exhaustively (see e.g. [1]), much fewer results and solutions are known about FIM algorithms implemented in and for relational database management systems. On the other hand the demand for integration of data mining tools into the existing database management systems is tangible. An obvious next step solution is the extension of the existing database query languages with new functions supporting FIM algorithms.

* Research was partially supported from the grant *Data Riddle* NKFP-2/0017/2002 (Ministry of Education, Hungary). The research of the first author was partially supported by Inter-University Telecommunication Center (ETIK, http://www.etik.hu). The research of the second author was partially supported by Hungarian Scientific Research Fund (OTKA) grant T042706.

F. Bonchi and J.-F. Boulicaut (Eds.): KDID 2005, LNCS 3933, pp. 188–201, 2006.

Comparing the SQL-based implementations to the stand-alone FIM algorithms one can notice that the second class contains the very well performing pattern-growth algorithms [10, 19], while the idea of pattern-growth is poorly represented among the available SQL-based FIM algorithms [25]. The main proposal of this paper is to eliminate this flaw by suggesting a new pattern-growth FIM algorithm tightly coupled to relational database management systems. Therefore we examine SQL-based FP-growth algorithms in a performance perspective, that is whether they are usable in practice. The main result is the efficient implementation of the sophisticated FP-growth algorithm. We expect that our algorithms do the data processing inside the database. We identify the bottlenecks of the algorithms in order to determine the promising directions for development of data mining enabled database systems.

2   Integrating Data Mining and Databases, Related Work

Data mining addresses extraction of interesting knowledge from large databases. However, this complements the goals of the data warehouse and on-line analytical processing technologies, the chasm between the existing *data mining* and the *database* world is rather wide. Most data mining solutions include fully database-independent applications for the data mining tasks. We belive that coupling data mining with relational databases would remarkably improve the efficiency in the knowledge discovery process and simplify the construction of decision support systems.

Inductive databases [12, 7] are databases that integrate data with knowledge. The main goal of an inductive database is to allow the user not only to query the data that resides in the database, but also to query and mine generalizations, patterns of interest. The knowledge discovery process should be supported by an integrated framework, the user should be allowed to perform different operations on both data and patterns. The interaction takes place through inductive query languages supporting data mining, which are often extensions of SQL. A good comparison between languages supporting descriptive rule mining can be found in [6]. Other directions allowing data mining-like queries are data mining query interfaces and APIs [18]. From the analyst point of view the usability of OLAP (on-line analytical processing) systems could also be significantly increased by the integration of data mining methods. This viewpoint of inductive databases is the on-line analytical mining (OLAM) [9].

Despite the probable usefulness we are still far away from a general theory and practical realizations of full value of inductive databases, however, there are promising partial results, and also RDBMS vendors try to integrate more and more knowledge discovery support in their systems, turning them into decision support platforms (see [14] and [15]).

The accomplishment of integration from the architectural point of view is still an open question. In case of the fully separated systems, the required data is read from the DBMS, the mining is performed on a file system-cached version, and the results are written back to the database. The advantage here is the possibility to use special memory structures and buffer strategies. The loosely coupled architectures access the data through some standard interface too, but push parts of the data mining tasks in the DBMS. The tightly coupled variants use only facilities of the DBMS. A tightly coupled architecture is introduced in [16].

Nonetheless, SQL-based tightly coupled algorithms are considered bearing significantly inferior in terms of running times compared to stand-alone implementations, there exist advantages of tightly coupled data mining. Since data appears mostly in data warehouses and other databases in practice, in the case of tightly coupled data mining applications no additional data mining system is needed. Databases have already solved the problem of efficient and safe storing and querying large datasets reliably. Therefore, DBMSs can facilitate data mining to become an online, robust, scalable and concurrent process by complementing the existing querying and analytical functions. A relevant example is that of the caching problem. When data structures are too large to fit in memory, we can try to entrust caching to the database engine.

The first attempt to the particular problem of integrated frequent itemset mining was the SETM algorithm [11], expressed as SQL queries working on relational tables. The Apriori algorithm [2] opened up new prospects for FIM. The database-coupled variations of the Apriori algorithm were carefully examined in [22]. The SQL-92 based implementations were too slow, but the SQL implementations enhanced with object-relational extensions (SQL-OR) performed acceptable. The so-called Cache-Mine implementation had the best overall performance, where the database-independent mining algorithm cached the relevant data in a local disk cache. The optimization of the key operation, the join queries was studied in [26], and a new SQL-92-based method, Set-oriented Apriori was introduced. Further performance evaluations on commercial RDBMS can be found in [28], evaluations of the SQL-OR option in [17]. An interesting SQL-92 algorithm based on universal quantification is discussed in [20] and [21].

Since the introduction of the FP-growth method [10], a few attempts were made to implement pattern-growth methods inside the RDBMS [25]. [3] presents a novel, FP-tree-based indexing method, which provides a complete and compact representation of the dataset for frequent itemset mining, and collaborates efficiently with the relational database kernel. [8] deals with database-independent frequent itemset mining from secondary memory.

FIM is investigated most intensively among the problems of data mining in DBMS, but other classical data mining tasks are also studied, e.g. building and applying decision tree classifiers [23, 5].

3   Association Rule and Frequent Itemset Mining

Several data mining tasks, including identification of joint distribution, compression, and fast counting can be reduced to association rules mining.

Let us consider the set of *items* $I = \{item_1, item_2, \ldots item_m\}$. A setsystem $D \subseteq P(I)$ of I is called *database* and the elements of D are the *baskets* of items.

The *support* of an *itemset* $A \subset I$ is the number of baskets that have all of the items from A. We call an itemset A *frequent* if A has a support greater than some fix threshold s. Finding all frequent itemsets is the goal of the *frequent itemset mining* (FIM).

Association rules are binary relations between itemsets. An *association rule* $A \rightarrow B$ is an ordered pair of two disjoint itemset, here A and B. The support of the rule $A \rightarrow B$ is the support of $A \cup B$, the number of baskets containing $A \cup B$. The confidence of this rule is defined by the ratio of the support of the set $A \cup B$ to the support of the set A. The aim of association rule mining is to find all the rules that have a support and confidence greater than or equal to some previously given s and c, respectively. Practically association rule mining can be derived to the frequent itemsets mining problem.

To solve the FIM problem one can observe that frequent itemsets satisfy the *antimonotonicity property* (or Apriori principle), for a subset A of itemset B the support of A is greater or equal to the support of B. This property is the base of the multi-pass algorithm called *Apriori* [2]. Further algorithms solving the FIM problem are based on pattern-growth [10, 19].

4   Apriori-Based Methods

The Apriori algorithm iterates two basic phases to find frequent itemsets. In the nth iteration step it generates at first candidates for frequent itemsets having size n, which can be done utilizing the Apriori principle: the nth candidate set C_n can be produced from the $(n-1)$th set of frequent itemsets F_{n-1}. Next it tests the candidate set against the database, by counting support values for the candidates. The process iterates until the candidate itemset becomes empty. We don not have to materialize C_1, all items in the database are candidates, and in all other cases we materialize C_n and F_n. Next we discuss the SQL-92 methods briefly.

The SQL implementations differ in data representation. Two basic variations to represent these sets in relations are the horizontal approach, where C_n and F_n have the schema $(item_1, item_2, ...item_n)$, and the vertical approach with $(set\_id, item)$ schema. The horizontal approach have the disadvantage that the item count is limited by the possible count of table attributes, but can be beneficial in the performance view. The input database table has always $(transaction\_id, item)$ schema, because of the unknown number of items per transaction, and fits mostly to the star schema in relational data warehouses.

The implementations also differ in the SQL commands for candidate generation and support counting. Since the support counting phase is the most time consuming part of the computing, most algorithms share the candidate generation operation, using a k-way join to generate C_n from F_{n-1}. The support counting commands like K-Way-Join, Subquery and 2-Way-Join utilize join operations, or rely on group by computations like Two-Group-Bys [22]. The basic K-Way-Join support counting joins the data table n times in the nth step:

insert into F_n select $item_1$ ... $item_n$ $count(*)$
from C_n, F_{n-1} as I_1, ... F_{n-1} as I_n

where $I_1.item < C_n.item_1$ and ... and $I_n.item < C_n.item_n$ and
          $I_1.tid = I_2.tid$ and ... and $I_{n-1}.tid = I_n.tid$
group by $item_1, ... item_n$
having $count(*) \geq minsup.$

Subquery is an optimization of the K-Way-Join, which makes use of the common prefixes between the itemsets in the candidate set. We developed different versions of Subquery to apply the divide-and-conquer idea of [24]: if we divide the database into distinct partitions, then an itemset can only be frequent, if it is frequent on at least one partition. It is possible therefore to partition the input table, find the frequent itemsets over the partitions, then test all partition-wise valid frequent itemsets over the whole input table. Unfortunately, as depicted on Figure 3, the execution times against the size of the input table don not allow to efficiently apply the partition trick. However, the method could be used to mine data stored on multiple databases, as shown in [13].

5   Pattern-Growth Methods

Pattern-growth methods, first published in [10], represent the database in a compact data structure, called Frequent-Pattern-tree (FP-tree) to avoid repeated database scans and large candidate sets. The FP-tree stores items having greater support than the minimum support in a tree structure. Given an ordering of the items, transactions are represented as paths from the root node, sharing the same upper path if their first few frequent items are the same. The FP-tree is searched recursively to find the frequent itemsets with the FP-growth method.

Figure 1 shows an FP-tree built for an example database with minimum support 2. Each node is labelled by an item, which has a count value and a sidelink to its siblings. The count value refers to the support of the itemset represented by the path from the root to the given node. An additional header table stores the initial sidelinks and the total supports for the items.

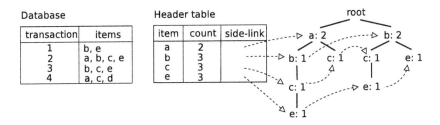

Fig. 1. FP-tree for a given database, built with minimum support 2

5.1   Constructing the FP-tree

A table having the schema

$$node : (node\_id, parent\_id, item, count, sidelink)$$

represents the FP-tree in a natural fashion. In a particular state of the processing of the tree the attribute *sidelink* shows, whether a node is part of the processed subtree or not (Y/N). On the first level of the tree attributes *parent_id* are null. An alternative approach can be found in [25], where instead of a reference for the parents, a not fully discussed path type is used as attribute for all nodes.

The FP-tree can be built by reading the database once, inserting a new path into the tree per transaction if the set of its frequent items has not been represented yet, or else increasing the values of counts. This method expressed as SQL queries is not efficient enough, because of the high cost of the *node* table accesses individually for all items. Instead of that, we build the FP-tree level by level, inserting all nodes on a particular level of the tree by one SQL query.

Our first version uses the subset of the original input table containing only parts of transactions formed by frequent items, and a table containing elements (*node_id*, *item*), representing the prefix we have processed. We delete the processed rows from the filtered input table. We get the next item per transaction by a minimum search, and insert new rows in *node*. Assuming that input table is $tdb\_filtered : (tid, item)$, the prefix table is $prefix : (tid, node\_id)$, and $node\_seq.nextval$ is used to generate the unique identifiers, the key step is:

```
insert into node
    select      node_seq.nextval, min.minitem,
                prefix.node_id, count(min.tid)
    from        ( select    tid, min(item) minitem
                  from      tdb_filtered
                  group by  tid ) min, prefix
    where       min.tid = prefix.tid
    group by    min.item, prefix.node_id.
```

Our second version uses an analytic function called *dense rank* to produce a sorted and filtered version of the input table. We create groups according to the *tid* attribute with the help of this function, and the items in the group are ranked based on the given ordering (supposing that $tdb:(tid, item)$ is the input table):

```
select tid, item, dense_rank() over ( partition by tid order by item ) rank
from  tdb.
```

In this case the filtered input table is $tdb\_filtered : (tid, item, rank)$. Building *node* is similar to the previous version, but we eliminate the minimum search and the deletion step by referring to all levels by the rank value.

Items in the input table are represented by identifiers. A natural ordering is given for these identifiers, but that is not suitable for building the FP-tree. Accordingly we use an additional table for items, in which they are assigned to exactly one new identifier. The new identifiers are given so that their natural ordering will be the same as the descending ordering of the original items based on the support. This ordering promises an optimal size of the tree. This step can be solved by a simple sorting query, and the results can be used initially for filling up the header table described later.

5.2   FP-tree Evaluation

To avoid the combinatorial problem of evaluating the FP-tree, we use a method similar to the top-down FP-growth described in [27], which finds all frequent itemsets without materializing conditional subtrees. The core of the algorithm is a recursive procedure utilizing SQL operations and some additional tables. The *header* : (*header_id, item, count*) table stores counting information for items coming up in stages of the recursion, and the table also serves as a recursion heap. Identifiers of the header table are analogous to the separate header tables in the original FP-growth concept. All those itemsets are considered in a recursion step, which end up with a given item sequence $\bar{x}$. An other table *header_postfix* : (*header_id, item*) stores the postfixes of $\bar{x}$ for the header identifiers. The **mine** procedure recursively produces all frequent itemsets above a given minimal support value *minsup*. The procedure starts with **mine(0)** after the FP-tree creation phase, when the table *header* is already filled up with frequent items and their counts, having the initial *header_id* **0**.

Procedure mine(*h_id***)**
1 **for** *h_rec* in (select *header_id, item, count* from *header*
                    where *header_id* = *h_id*)
2   **if** *h_rec.count* ≥ *minsup* **then**
3   output long pattern: (*h_rec.item*, postfix) using *header_postfix* ;
4   *new_header* ← generate new header id ;
5   **for** each *n* node from *node* located on paths
                        upwards from *h_rec.item*-s, having *sidelink* = *Y*
6   *n.count* ← sum of counts of leaves ;
7   *n.sidelink* ← *Y* ;
8   **if** (*new_header, n.item*) exists in *header* **then**
9   add *n.count* to header row identified by (*new_header, n.item*)
10   **else** insert (*new_header, n.item, n.count*) into *header*;
11   **for** each *n* node from *node* not located on paths upwards from
                        h_rec.item-s, having *sidelink* = *Y* and *item* < *h_rec.item*
12   *n.sidelink* ← *N* ;
13   **mine(***new_header***)** ;

We implemented the steps of the above algorithms as SQL queries, with the help of auxiliary tables. Frequent sets are put in the table *result* : (*set_id, item*), and absolute support values of frequent itemsets in the table *result_support*: (*set_id, support*).

Application of the top-down FP-growth method was motivated by the main observation discussed in the following. If we process the tree in a top-down fashion, then the counts of the nodes above the actual leaf are no longer needed, therefore they can be reused for counting. We use further temporary tables for the purpose of climbing up the paths and setting sidelinks and counts (rows 5-12). Table *path* : (*node_id, count*) stores the nodes found on the paths with the actual *count* value. We climb up the paths level by level, accumulating the counts of the leaves. The required information (original node, actual node, count value of the original node) for these steps are stored in a subsequent auxiliary table. This step can be also solved by the use of a recursive query (assuming the syntax of Oracle):

select   *node_id* from *node*
start with *node_id* = (actual node) connect by prior *parent_id* = *node_id*.

Processing the nodes on the paths leaf by leaf with the use of a recursive query instead of processing level by level was found less effective in our tests.

5.3   Indices and Further Optimization

After implementing the first versions of the algorithm it became clear, that the main cost arises from the *node* table accesses, especially from updates (steps 6, 7 and 12). These accesses refer to more and more node by the end of the processing, when processed nodes are near to the leaves. We can optimize the updates, for example updating only those sidelinks of the nodes which do not have the right value yet, but after all without the use of indices these steps require full scans of the table *node*, which typically costs lot of block reads and writes.

The values of the attributes *node_id*, *parent_id* and *item* do not change after building the *node* table. Therefore it is profitable using standard B-tree indices on them, like (*item, node_id*) index for searching *node_id*-s by *item*, or (*node_id, parent_id*) to find parent nodes efficiently. The values of *sidelink* and *count* are changed frequently. We do not want to access the table by the attribute *count*, but using some index on the attribute *sidelink* can be profitable. We can use regular or bitmap indices since the attribute *sidelink* has only two distinct attributes. We tested both the regular and bitmap versions for *sidelink*. Bitmap indices were found good for selecting by attributes of low cardinality, and we found the access times were really lower in the tests. Hereafter we refer to the indexed version of the above described algorithm as FP-TDG.

We implemented several alternatives of FP-TDG. We experienced, that denormalizing the *node* table is beneficial: the database schema

$$node : (node\_id, parent\_id, item)$$
$$sidelink : (node\_id)$$
$$count : (node\_id, count)$$

enables us to manage the frequently changed information apart from the permanent tree-structure information. In this case we store the binary "header" information as a set of *node_id*. The "count" values for nodes are stored in a smaller and separate table. Instead of building separate indices on these two tables we store them as B-trees with the help of the so-called "index-organized table" facility of the database server. We refer this version as FP-TDG2.

6   Experiments

Our experiments were performed on Oracle9i Release 2 DBMS, installed on a PC server with a 3 GHz Intel Pentium processor, 2 GB memory, RAID 5 with

IDE disks and Debian Linux operating system. Memory usage of the database server was limited to 1 GB, because of other background services on the server. Redo logging was reduced for all tables, and parallel processing functions of the database were not enabled.

Our algorithms was implemented using PL/SQL procedures. This method could be exchanged to any other programming environment, in which we can connect to the database server through a standard database API. The algorithms can be executed on an arbitrary client, because the main part of the data processing remains inside the database server. The client generates the adequagte SQL statements only, which requires only little computing and networking capacity.

We used the public FIMI datasets [1] for our tests. Table 1 shows the properties of the six selected datasets.

Table 1. Dataset properties

Dataset	Num. of records (K)	Num. of transactions	Num. of items	Avg. num. of items per transaction
ACCIDENTS	11,500	340,183	468	33.8
BMS-WebView-1	149.6	59,602	497	2.5
BMS-WebView-2	358.3	77,512	3,340	4.6
KOSARAK	8,019	990,002	41,270	8.1
RETAIL	908.6	88,162	16,469	10.3
T10I4D100K	1010	100,000	870	10.1

We have chosen the Subquery method to compare our algorithms to, because - as suggested in [22] - Subquery had the best overall performance (although this is in fact opposed to the result in [21], where K-Way-Join is superior in this category). We implemented our version with the so-called second-pass optimization: we don not materialize the candidates of size two, it is replaced by a 2-way join between frequent item tables of size one.

The other algorithm we have chosen for comparison is the algorithm *nonordfp* [1] implemented in C++, as a fully database-independent application. The algorithm *nonordfp* handles an FP-tree-like structure, and the algorithm can efficiently evaluate the tree without materializing subtrees. We made up a tiny cache-mine system, where *nonordfp* runs on the same server as the database, but connects to the database only to read out the input data and to write back the results through standard JDBC interface. The algorithm *nonordfp* caches the data in the filesystem for processing. Its memory usage was not limited. We refer hereinafter this implementation as NFP-CACHE.

The main part of the total execution times of *nonordfp* came from reading and writing the database. The response time goes up only below low minimum support values, when the result set becomes large. The algorithm *nonordfp* outperforms the SQL-based methods for low minimum support, however as being in-memory algorithm, the input size is limited by the available memory.

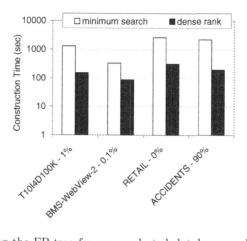

Fig. 2. Constructing the FP-tree for some selected databases and minimum support values

Figure 2 shows execution times of our two methods for FP-tree construction. Figure 3 (left) shows execution times on different sized samples of the RETAIL database with the minimum support value of 0.5 %. Figures 3 (right), 4, 5 and 6 (left) compare the total execution times of our algorithms.

FP-TDG and FP-TDG2 mostly outperform Subquery, but in case of the generated dataset T10I4D100K they do not perform well. This dataset is rather sparse, and most FP-growth methods work less efficiently on sparse datasets. This can be seen here as well. The FP-tree becomes too large, it does not compress the database efficiently, and this causes a leap in the aggregated node-access times. On the other hand the sparsity of the database is advantageous for the join-based Apriori methods, when the size of the candidate sets shrink fast.

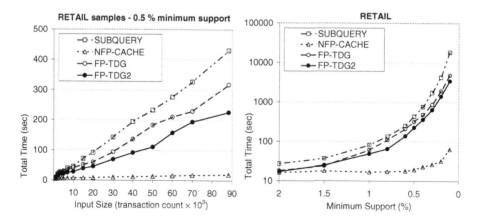

Fig. 3. Execution times on the RETAIL dataset

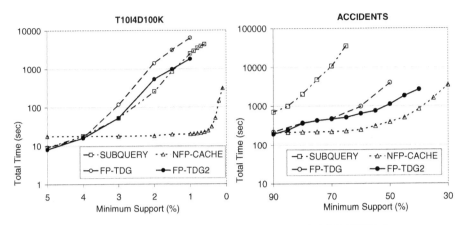

Fig. 4. Execution times on the T10I4D100K and ACCIDENTS datasets

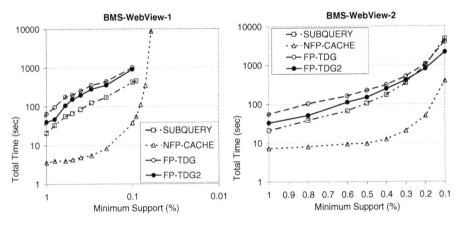

Fig. 5. Execution times on the BMS-WebView datasets

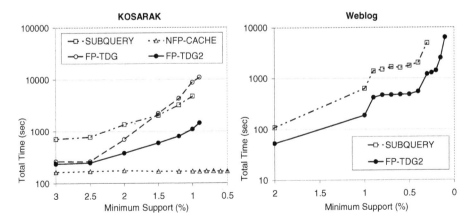

Fig. 6. Execution times on the KOSARAK dataset, and on real-life weblog data

We have also tested Subquery and FP-TDG2 in a real-life environment, over logs of the largest Hungarian web portal (www.origo.hu). The site produces 7,000,000 page hits on a typical workday, which is processed by an experimental weblog mining architecture (see [4] for details). The preprocessed data is stored in an Oracle 9i database component of the architecture. The task is identifying set of pages accessed together by a large fraction of the users on a given day. Execution times of the algorithms on a typical workday can be seen on Figure 6 (right side), where 767,663 identified user accessed 57,911 different pages during the day, which resulted in 2,395,146 records of hits. The average number of downloaded pages per user was 3.12.

In the weblog mining architecture the results can be analysed by a statististical analysis framework. It can be reached through a webserver with dynamic web pages, connected to the database. Users can discover frequent sets of pages by extending the frequent sets one-by-one, starting with an empty, or with a directly given set of pages. The possible extensions can be choosen from a toplist. This simple method is suitable in our case, where we have 1 to 47 thousand frequent sets with a maximum size of 13 for the different minimum supports measured and appeared on Figure 6.

In this real-life application of the SQL-based FP-TDG2 we eliminated the need for a separate FIM system producing duplicated data. Frequent sets are produced by only the use of the common database facilities. The execution times are acceptable, they are comparable to the computation times of some complex statistical aggregations in the database.

Implementations of the algorithms and the used sample datasets can be downloaded from `http://scs.web.elte.hu/sqlfim/`.

7   Conclusion

In this paper an FP-tree based algorithm for frequent itemset mining is proposed. Variants for both constructing and evaluating the FP-tree is discussed. Our best algorithm performed well in its category, but it has severe limitations compared to stand-alone FIM algorithms. We found that the common buffer management and indexing technics do not provide enough support for the task of efficient storing and accessing the FP-tree by relations and relational operators. However, practical application of our algorithm seems possible, especially for high support thresholds, where the result set still has a manageable size.

References

1. Frequent itemset mining implementations repository. http://fimi.cs.helsinki.fi/.
2. R. Agrawal and R. Srikant. Fast algorithms for mining association rules in large databases. In *VLDB '94: Proceedings of the 20th International Conference on Very Large Data Bases*, pages 487–499, San Francisco, CA, USA, 1994. Morgan Kaufmann Publishers Inc.
3. E. Baralis, T. Cerquitelli, and S. Chiusano. Index support for frequent itemset mining in a relational DBMS. In *ICDE '05: Proceedings of the 21st International Conference on Data Engineering (ICDE'05)*, pages 754–765. IEEE Computer Society, 2005.

4. A. A. Benczúr, K. Csalogány, K. Hum, A. Lukács, B. Rácz, C. Sidló, and M. Uher. Architecture for mining massive web logs with experiments. In *Proceedings of the HUBUSKA Open Workshop on Generic Issues of Knowledge Technologies*, 2005.

5. F. Bentayeb and J. Darmont. Decision tree modeling with relational views. In *ISMIS '02: Proceedings of the 13th International Symposium on Foundations of Intelligent Systems*, pages 423–431. Springer-Verlag, 2002.

6. M. Botta, J.-F. Boulicaut, C. Masson, and R. Meo. Query languages supporting descriptive rule mining: A comparative study. In *Database Support for Data Mining Applications*, volume 2682/2004 of *Lecture Notes in Computer Science*, pages 24–51. Springer-Verlag, 2004.

7. J.-F. Boulicaut, M. Klemettinen, and H. Mannila. Modeling KDD processes within the inductive database framework. In *DaWaK '99: Proceedings of the First International Conference on Data Warehousing and Knowledge Discovery*, pages 293–302. Springer-Verlag, 1999.

8. G. Grahne and J. Zhu. Mining frequent itemsets from secondary memory. In *ICDM '04: Proceedings of the Fourth IEEE International Conference on Data Mining (ICDM'04)*, pages 91–98, Washington, DC, USA, 2004. IEEE Computer Society.

9. J. Han. Towards on-line analytical mining in large databases. *SIGMOD Rec.*, 27(1):97–107, 1998.

10. J. Han, J. Pei, and Y. Yin. Mining frequent patterns without candidate generation. In *Proceedings of the 2000 ACM SIGMOD international conference on Management of data*, pages 1–12. ACM Press, 2000.

11. M. Houtsma and A. Swami. Set-oriented data mining in relational databases. *Data Knowl. Eng.*, 17(3):245–262, 1995.

12. T. Imielinski and H. Mannila. A database perspective on knowledge discovery. *Commun. ACM*, 39(11):58–64, 1996.

13. H. Kona and S. Chakravarthy. Partitioned approach to association rule mining over multiple databases. pages 320–330, 2004.

14. W. Li and A. Mozes. Computing frequent itemsets inside Oracle 10g. In *VLDB'04*, pages 1253–1256, 2004.

15. J. MacLennan. SQL Server 2005: Unearth the new data mining features of analysis services 2005. *MSDN Magazine*, 19(9), 2004.

16. R. Meo, G. Psaila, and S. Ceri. A tightly-coupled architecture for data mining. In *ICDE '98: Proceedings of the Fourteenth International Conference on Data Engineering*, pages 316–323, Washington, DC, USA, 1998. IEEE Computer Society.

17. P. Mishra and S. Chakravarthy. Performance evaluation of SQL-OR variants for association rule mining. *Lecture Notes in Computer Science*, 2737/2003:288–298, 2003.

18. A. Netz, S. Chaudhuri, U. M. Fayyad, and J. Bernhardt. Integrating data mining with SQL databases: OLE DB for data mining. In *Proceedings of the 17th International Conference on Data Engineering*, pages 379–387. IEEE Computer Society, 2001.

19. J. Pei, J. Han, H. Lu, S. Nishio, S. Tang, and D. Yang. H-Mine: Hyper-structure mining of frequent patterns in large databases. In *Proceedings of the 2001 IEEE International Conference on Data Mining*, pages 441–448. IEEE Computer Society, 2001.

20. R. Rantzau. Processing frequent itemset discovery queries by division and set containment join operators. In *Proceedings of the 8th ACM SIGMOD workshop on Research issues in data mining and knowledge discovery*, pages 20–27. ACM Press, 2003.

21. R. Rantzau. Frequent itemset discovery with SQL using universal quantification. In *Database Support for Data Mining Applications*, pages 194–213, 2004.
22. S. Sarawagi, S. Thomas, and R. Agrawal. Integrating association rule mining with relational database systems: alternatives and implications. In *SIGMOD '98: Proceedings of the 1998 ACM SIGMOD international conference on Management of data*, pages 343–354. ACM Press, 1998.
23. K.-U. Sattler and O. Dunemann. SQL database primitives for decision tree classifiers. In *CIKM '01: Proceedings of the tenth international conference on Information and knowledge management*, pages 379–386. ACM Press, 2001.
24. A. Savasere, E. Omiecinski, and S. B. Navathe. An efficient algorithm for mining association rules in large databases. In *Proceedings of the 21th International Conference on Very Large Data Bases*, pages 432–444. Morgan Kaufmann Publishers Inc., 1995.
25. X. Shang, K.-U. Sattler, and I. Geist. SQL based frequent pattern mining with fp-growth. In *INAP/WLP*, pages 32–46, 2004.
26. S. Thomas and S. Chakravarthy. Performance evaluation and optimization of join queries for association rule mining. In *Proceedings of the First International Conference on Data Warehousing and Knowledge Discovery*, pages 241–250. Springer-Verlag, 1999.
27. K. Wang, L. Tang, J. Han, and J. Liu. Top down FP-growth for association rule mining. In *PAKDD '02: Proceedings of the 6th Pacific-Asia Conference on Advances in Knowledge Discovery and Data Mining*, pages 334–340, London, UK, 2002. Springer-Verlag.
28. T. Yoshizawa, I. Pramudiono, and M. Kitsuregawa. SQL based association rule mining using commercial RDBMS (IBM DB2 UBD EEE). In *Proceedings of the Second International Conference on Data Warehousing and Knowledge Discovery*, pages 301–306. Springer-Verlag, 2000.

Exploiting Virtual Patterns for Automatically Pruning the Search Space

Arnaud Soulet and Bruno Crémilleux

GREYC, CNRS - UMR 6072,
Université de Caen, Campus Côte de Nacre,
F-14032 Caen Cédex, France
{Forename.Surname}@info.unicaen.fr

Abstract. A lot of works address the mining of patterns under constraints. The search space is reduced by taking advantage of pruning conditions on patterns, typically by using anti-monotone and monotone properties. In this paper, we introduce two virtual patterns in order to automatically deduce pruning conditions from *any* constraint coming from the primitive-based framework which gathers a large set of varied constraints. These virtual patterns enable us to provide negative and positive pruning conditions according to the generalization and the specialization of patterns. We show that these pruning conditions are monotone or anti-monotone and can be pushed into usual constraint mining algorithms. Experiments carried on several contexts show that our proposals improve the mining.

Keywords: constraint-based mining, virtual patterns, pruning conditions.

1 Introduction

The constraint-based pattern discovery is a significant field of the Knowledge Discovery in Databases (KDD). A constraint expresses the viewpoint of the analyst and guarantees the interest of the extracted patterns. The soundness and completeness of the extraction ensure that the collection of patterns is respectively correct and exhaustive. Constraint-based mining remains a challenge due to the huge size of the search space which has to be explored. This task is hard to automate because there is a broad spectrum of constraints requiring their own pruning strategies to prune the search space.

In practice, most of the algorithms take advantage of *pruning conditions* depending on the constraint in order to reduce the search space. Typically, whenever a pattern satisfies a pruning condition, the algorithm safely discards all its subsets or supersets. Introduced in [1], the anti-monotonicity offers the outstandingly useful pruning condition according to the specialization of patterns and we have efficient algorithms to extract them. There is also a dual kind of pruning condition according to the generalization of patterns with the monotone constraints [19]. We will see in Section 2 that such pruning conditions are called *negative pruning conditions* (i.e., the pruned patterns do not

F. Bonchi and J.-F. Boulicaut (Eds.): KDID 2005, LNCS 3933, pp. 202–221, 2006.

satisfy the constraint). Contrary to the negative pruning conditions, other approaches [16] benefit from a *positive pruning condition* (i.e., the pruned patterns satisfy the constraint). Combined with the generalization or specialization of patterns, we get four pruning conditions (i.e., negative/positive according to the generalization/specialization) and numerous efficient algorithms use them individually [1, 19] or simultaneously [7, 9]. Unfortunately, most of constraints are neither monotone nor anti-monotone and pruning conditions are not easy to infer. To the best of our knowledge, there is no work which makes the most of the pruning conditions for any constraint. This observation motivates us to automatically deduce these pruning conditions for a lot of varied constraints and, in this paper, we focus on constraints defined by the primitive-based framework [24] (such constraints are called *primitive-based constraints*). This framework enables us to define in a flexible way a large set of varied constraints such as monotone, anti-monotone, convertible and tougher ones [25].

The key idea of this paper is to use two *virtual patterns* in order to automatically achieve the pruning conditions from any primitive-based constraint. By focussing on the patterns present at least once in the data, the virtual patterns synthesize the specificities of the data mining context to get powerful pruning conditions. The bottom (resp. top) virtual pattern enables to consider all the subsets (resp. the supersets) of a given pattern. These virtual patterns are only linked to the data (they do not change if the constraint varies). The use of the primitive-based framework is important because its relies on monotone primitives whose properties are needed to automatically deduce the pruning conditions.

This paper proposes two main contributions. First, we introduce the concept of *virtual patterns* and detail the definition of the *bottom* and *top* virtual patterns. They are elegant tricks to adequately manipulate constraints by taking into account the specificities of the mining context. Furthermore, we show that they stem from the minimal and the maximal patterns present in the dataset, which enables an efficient computation of these patterns. Second, by exploiting these virtual patterns in conjunction with the primitive-based framework, we provide negative and positive pruning conditions according to the generalization and the specialization for the primitive-based constraints. These efficient pruning conditions, which preserve the soundness and the completeness, are automatically obtained. We prove that they verify suitable properties of monotonicity. Thereby, they can easily be pushed by usual algorithms. Furthermore, performance study shows that they improve the mining task (with different mining algorithms and several constraints). In many cases, they allow us to mine constraints intractable until now.

This paper is organized in the following way. Section 2 introduces the basic definitions and related work. It highlights the difficulties of finding pruning conditions and the main principles of our approach. Section 3 depicts the primitive-based framework and its properties which are necessary for understanding the rest of the paper. Section 4 defines the notion of virtual patterns and links it to the primitive-based framework. Section 5 indicates how to find pruning conditions by using virtual patterns. Finally, Section 6 shows the practical uses of these pruning conditions and experiments them.

2   Preliminaries

We start by describing the task of mining all patterns satisfying a constraint. Then, we define the notion of pruning conditions and we give the key ideas of our paper.

2.1   Notations and Definitions

A transactional dataset $\mathcal{D}$ is a triplet $(\mathcal{A}, \mathcal{O}, R)$ where $\mathcal{A}$ is a set of attributes, $\mathcal{O}$ is a set of objects and $R \subseteq \mathcal{A} \times \mathcal{O}$ is a binary relation between the attributes and the objects. $(a, o) \in R$ expresses that the object o contains the attribute a (see for instance, the dataset $\mathcal{D}$ in Table 1 where $A, \ldots, F$ denote the attributes and $o_1, \ldots, o_7$ denote the objects). Finally, a mining context is a transactional dataset completed with additional information (e.g., a table of attribute values, see Table 1).

Table 1. Example of a mining context (a transactional dataset $\mathcal{D}$ and a table of values)

$\mathcal{D}$

Objects	Attributes
o_1	A B E F
o_2	A E
o_3	A B C D
o_4	A B C
o_5	D E
o_6	C F
o_7	A E

Attribute	A	B	C	D	E	F
val	55	30	70	10	30	15

The aim of constraint-based mining is to extract all the patterns[1] present in $\mathcal{D}$ and satisfying a predicate q (also called query or constraint). A pattern X is present in $\mathcal{D}$ whenever it is at least included in one object of $\mathcal{D}$. Let us consider an example by assuming that we are interested in all patterns having an *area* greater than 6: these patterns can be mined with the constraint $count(X) \times length(X) \geq 6$ (where $count(X)$ denotes the number of objects in $\mathcal{D}$ that contain the pattern X and $length(X)$ is the cardinality of X).

The property of monotonicity has a great role in constraint-based mining to efficiently prune the search space. A constraint q is anti-monotone (resp. monotone) with respect to the specialization of the patterns[2] iff whenever $X \subseteq Y$ then $q(Y) \Rightarrow q(X)$ (resp. $q(X) \Rightarrow q(Y)$). The minimal frequency constraint (i.e., $count(X) \geq \gamma$ where γ is a threshold) is probably the most usual among the anti-monotone constraints. Unfortunately, like the area constraint, a lot of constraints do not satisfy the monotonicity properties: this one is neither monotone

---

[1] This paper only focuses on non-empty itemsets (i.e., a pattern is a subset of $\mathcal{A}$). Nevertheless, by using an other partially ordered language than $\mathcal{L}_\mathcal{A}$, all the definitions can be extended to other kinds of patterns like graphs, sequences, trees and so on.

[2] A *specialization relation* [20] is a partial order on the patterns in $\mathcal{L}_\mathcal{A}$.

($area(ABC) \geq 6$ but $area(ABCD) < 6$), nor anti-monotone ($area(BC) < 6$ but $area(ABC) \geq 6$) and there is no trivial pruning condition.

2.2   Pruning Conditions

A *pruning condition* is a property which enables the algorithms to reduce the search space. Most of the algorithms (based on breadth-first search [1, 19], depth-first search [5] or particular data structures [13]) use them to eliminate candidate patterns during the generation step. The pruning conditions are also used to perform data reductions [6]. Moreover, other kinds of patterns (like sequences [2], graph [17] and so on) are extracted by benefiting from the principle of the pruning conditions. When a pattern satisfies a pruning condition, the result of the constraint is known for all its *generalizations* (i.e., subsets) or all its *specializations* (i.e, supersets). Then we can prune them. If the pruned patterns satisfy the constraint, the pruning is called *positive*. If none of the pruned patterns satisfies the constraint, the pruning is named *negative*. Combined with the generalization or specialization of patterns, we get four pruning conditions (i.e., negative/positive w.r.t. the generalization/specialization). These pruning conditions are extensively used in the literature as seen now.

The most common negative pruning conditions according to the specialization stem from monotonicity [1, 19]. Once we know that a pattern does not satisfy an anti-monotone constraint, any superset of this pattern does not satisfy the constraint anymore. Dually, the monotone constraints provide negative pruning conditions according to the generalization. Many algorithms rely on one of these monotone prunings [1, 19]. There are also specific algorithms devoted to combine both negative prunings in order to mine a conjunction of one monotone constraint and one anti-monotone constraint [7, 9].

Other classes of constraints (e.g. *succinct* [21], *convertible* [23], *loose anti-monotone* [8] or *primitive-based constraints* [24]) have their own pruning properties. For instance, by using a particular specialization relation based on prefixes, the convertibility provides negative pruning w.r.t. this relation. The *inductive databases* framework [15] proposes to decompose complex constraints into several constraints having suitable properties like monotonicity. Thereby, it is again possible to exploit monotone pruning conditions. For example, the mining of emerging patterns can be expressed as a disjunction of conjunctions of such constraints [10]. Based on version spaces [20], an algebra is proposed to evaluate and optimize such inductive queries [18]. Introduced in [16], the concept of *witness* simultaneously allows pruning patterns according to different kinds of specialization (e.g., coming from monotonicity or convertibility). This pruning strategy has the originality to take into account the positive pruning. Nevertheless, given a constraint without monotone property, the authors do not propose a method to automatically obtain witnesses.

2.3   Problem Statement and Key Ideas

As indicated in the introduction, in this paper, we automatically deduce positive and negative pruning conditions for any primitive-based constraint. This is achieved thanks to the characteristics of the constraint. By using the running example of the area constraint, we give now the main idea of our approach. Let us note that many works mine closed patterns [22], fault-tolerant bi-sets [4], tiles [12] and blocks [11]. Constrained closed patterns are a subset of the patterns satisfying the area constraint and mining the closed patterns do not provide the complete collection of patterns satisfying the area constraint. In our approach, we preserve the completeness for the area constraint and more generally for any primitive-based constraint.

A key point is to observe the area behavior with the shortest and the longest patterns. Given a constant l, we notice that $count(X) \times l \geq \gamma$ is anti-monotone. The difficulty is to fix l such that $count(X) \times l < \gamma$ implies $area(X) < \gamma$. This is checked as soon as l is greater than or equal to the length of each pattern. As the mined patterns are present at least once in $\mathcal{D}$, the longest pattern has a size equal to the longest object. Thus in our mining context (see Table 1), l can be fixed to 4 and $count(X) < 6/4$ becomes a valid negative pruning condition w.r.t. the specialization. Thereby, as $count(CD) = 1$ is lower than $6/4$, CD satisfies the pruning condition and its supersets do not satisfy the constraint. Then, we can negatively prune the patterns ACD, BCD and so on. Similarly, as all the patterns in $\mathcal{D}$ have a frequency lower than or equal to 5, we obtain that $length(X) < 6/5$ is a negative pruning of $area(X) \geq 6$ w.r.t. the generalization. Note that the relevant values (4 for the negative pruning condition w.r.t. the specialization and 5 for the negative pruning condition w.r.t. the generalization) are only deduced from the specificities of $\mathcal{D}$ (properties coming from the longest and shortest patterns present at least once in $\mathcal{D}$). In Section 4.1, we will see that these features are embedded in the two virtual patterns. In the following, we generalize these principles to the primitive-based constraints.

3   Scope of the Primitive-Based Framework

The next sections deal with the primitive-based constraints and the bounding operators. We give here a more general definition than in [24] to easily extend the primitive-based framework to virtual patterns.

3.1   The Primitive-Based Constraints

Contrary to the usual classes of constraints, the primitive-based constraints are based on a set of primitives. The primitive-based constraints depicted in [24], are only restricted to a particular set of primitives. In this paper, we extend them by defining the notion of primitive:

Definition 1 (primitive). *Let* $S_{i_1}, \ldots, S_{i_n}$ *and* S_j *be posets. A function* $p :$ $S_{i_1} \times \cdots \times S_{i_n} \to S_j$ *is a primitive iff for each variable, p is a monotone function (when the others remain constant).*

The set of primitives is denoted by $\mathcal{P}$. Let us note that *count* and *length* are primitives of our framework because they are respectively a decreasing and an increasing functions. Given a function $val : \mathcal{A} \to \Re^+$, we extend it to a pattern X and note $X.val$ the multiset $\{val(a)|a \in X\}$. This kind of function is used with the usual SQL-like primitives sum, min and max. For instance, $sum(X.val)$ is the sum of val of each attribute of X. The considered primitives are based on three spaces: the booleans $\mathfrak{B}$ (i.e., $true$ or $false$), the positive reals $\Re^+$ and the patterns of $\mathcal{L}_\mathcal{A}$, where $\mathcal{L}_\mathcal{A}$ denotes the language associated with the attributes $\mathcal{A}$ (i.e., the power-set $2^\mathcal{A}$ without the empty set). These different spaces are ordered sets: $false < true$ for booleans, the usual ordering relation for reals and the inclusion operator for sets. The latter is only a partial order relation.

In practice, more complex primitives are useful to the user. For instance, the area function is not monotone, but it is a combination of several primitives of $\mathcal{P}$: the $area$ is decomposed into $count(X) \times length(X)$. This kind of combination can be seen as a high-level primitive. The next definition provides the set of all the possible high-level primitives starting from $\mathcal{P}$:

Definition 2 (high-level primitive). *The set of high-level primitives of degree n, denoted by $\mathcal{H}_n$, is recursively defined by:*

- *if $n = 0$: $\mathcal{H}_0$ is the set of the primitives $\mathcal{P}$ defined on $\mathcal{L}_\mathcal{A}$.*
- *if $n > 0$: $\mathcal{H}_n$ is the set of functions h such that $h = p(h_1, \dots, h_k)$ where $p \in \mathcal{P}$ of arity k and $\forall i \in \{1, \dots, k\}$, $h_i \in \mathcal{H}_{n_i}$, with $max_{i \in \{1, \dots, k\}} n_i = n - 1$. $p(h_1, \dots, h_k)$ is named the decomposition of h.*

Following on, the set of whole high-level primitives is noted $\mathcal{H}$ i.e., $\mathcal{H} = \bigcup_{i=0}^{\infty} \mathcal{H}_i$. For instance, as $count$ and $length$ are monotone primitives from $\mathcal{L}_\mathcal{A}$ to $\Re^+$, they belong to $\mathcal{H}_0$. Thus, the $area$ belongs to $\mathcal{H}_1$ (and then, $\deg area = 1$) because its affix decomposition is $\times (count, length)$ and $\mathcal{P}$ contains $\times$.

A primitive-based constraint is a constraint which is a high-level primitive of $\mathcal{H}$:

Definition 3 (primitive-based constraint). *A constraint $q : \mathcal{L}_\mathcal{A} \to \mathfrak{B}$ is a primitive-based constraint iff q is a high-level primitive of $\mathcal{H}$.*

A primitive-based constraint is a combination of monotone primitives, defined from $\mathcal{L}_\mathcal{A}$ to $\mathfrak{B}$. The set of such constraints is denoted by $\mathcal{Q}$. Then, we have $\mathcal{Q} = \{q : \mathcal{L}_\mathcal{A} \to \mathfrak{B} | q \in \mathcal{H}\}$. Table 2 recursively defines the subset of $\mathcal{Q}$ corresponding to the particular primitives seen above.

We give now some examples of constraints belonging to $\mathcal{Q}$ and highlighting the generality of our framework (more examples are given in [24]).

$$
\begin{cases}
count(X) \times length(X) \geq 6 & \text{minimal area (nothing)} \\
(min(X.val) + max(X.val))/2 \leq 50 & \text{maximal mean (loose anti-monotone)} \\
sum(X.val)/length(X) \geq 25 & \text{minimal average (convertible)} \\
AE \subseteq X & \text{having } AE \text{ (monotone)} \\
count(X) \geq 2 & \text{minimal frequency (anti-monotone)}
\end{cases}
$$

We proved that the primitive-based constraints constitute a superclass of monotone and anti-monotone constraints [25]. Furthermore, the primitive-based

Table 2. A subset of the primitive-based constraints $\mathcal{Q}$

Constraint $q \in \mathcal{Q}$	Primitive(s)	Operand(s)
$q_1 \theta q_2$	$\theta \in \{\wedge, \vee\}$	$(q_1, q_2) \in \mathcal{Q}^2$
θq_1	$\theta \in \{\neg\}$	$q_1 \in \mathcal{Q}$
$e_1 \theta e_2$	$\theta \in \{<, \leq\}$	$(e_1, e_2) \in \mathcal{E}^2$
$s_1 \theta s_2$	$\theta \in \{\subset, \subseteq\}$	$(s_1, s_2) \in \mathcal{S}^2$
constant $b \in \mathfrak{B}$	-	-
Aggregate expression $e \in \mathcal{E}$	**Primitive(s)**	**Operand(s)**
$e_1 \theta e_2$	$\theta \in \{+, -, \times, /\}$	$(e_1, e_2) \in \mathcal{E}^2$
$\theta(s)$	$\theta \in \{count, length\}$	$s \in \mathcal{S}$
$\theta(s.val)$	$\theta \in \{sum, max, min\}$	$s \in \mathcal{S}$
constant $r \in \Re^+$	-	-
Syntactic expression $s \in \mathcal{S}$	**Primitive(s)**	**Operand(s)**
$s_1 \theta s_2$	$\theta \in \{\cup, \cap, \backslash\}$	$(s_1, s_2) \in \mathcal{S}^2$
variable $X \in \mathcal{L}_\mathcal{A}$	-	-
constant $l \in \mathcal{L}_\mathcal{A}$	-	-

constraint is closed under boolean combinations [25]. These two properties highlight the generality of the operators defined in the next sections because they can be applied to numerous and varied constraints.

3.2   The Lower and Upper Bounding Operators

This section briefly recalls a key result which is necessary to understand the rest of this paper. This result has been introduced in [24], but we extend it to any high-level primitive (see Definition 2).

Let X and Y be two patterns. The interval between these patterns (denoted $[X, Y]$) corresponds to the set $\{Z \in \mathcal{L}_\mathcal{A} | X \subseteq Z \subseteq Y\}$. We start by giving the definition of the bounding operators denoted $\lfloor . \rfloor$ and $\lceil . \rceil$[3]:

Definition 4 (bounding operators). *Let h be a high-level primitive and $[X, Y]$ be an interval, $\lfloor h \rfloor \langle X, Y \rangle$ and $\lceil h \rceil \langle X, Y \rangle$ are defined as below:*

- *if $\deg h = 0$: $\lfloor h \rfloor \langle X, Y \rangle = h(X)$ and $\lceil h \rceil \langle X, Y \rangle = h(Y)$ iff h is an increasing function. Otherwise h decreases, $\lfloor h \rfloor \langle X, Y \rangle = h(Y)$ and $\lceil h \rceil \langle X, Y \rangle = h(X)$.*
- *if $\deg h \geq 1$: $\lfloor h \rfloor \langle X, Y \rangle = p(h'_1, \ldots, h'_k)$ and $\lceil h \rceil \langle X, Y \rangle = p(H'_1, \ldots, H'_k)$ where $p(h_1, \ldots, h_k)$ is the decomposition of h and for each variable $i \in \{1, \ldots, k\}$:*

$$\begin{cases} h'_i = \lfloor h_i \rfloor \langle X, Y \rangle \text{ and } H'_i = \lceil h_i \rceil \langle X, Y \rangle \text{ if } p \text{ increases with} \\ \qquad\qquad\qquad\qquad\qquad\qquad\qquad\qquad \text{the } i^{th} \text{ variable} \\ h'_i = \lceil h_i \rceil \langle X, Y \rangle \text{ and } H'_i = \lfloor h_i \rfloor \langle X, Y \rangle \text{ otherwise} \end{cases}$$

Starting from h and $[X, Y]$, these operators are recursively applied and lead to automatically compute a lower and an upper bounds of $[X, Y]$ for h. Table 3 gives

---

[3] To alleviate the notations, we replace $\lfloor . \rfloor([X, Y])$ by $\lfloor . \rfloor \langle X, Y \rangle$.

Table 3. The definitions of $\lfloor . \rfloor$ and $\lceil . \rceil$ with particular primitives

$e \in \mathcal{E}_i$	Primitive(s)	$\lfloor e \rfloor \langle X,Y \rangle$	$\lceil e \rceil \langle X,Y \rangle$
$e_1 \theta e_2$	$\theta \in \{\wedge, \vee, +, \times, \cup, \cap\}$	$\lfloor e_1 \rfloor \langle X,Y \rangle \theta \lfloor e_2 \rfloor \langle X,Y \rangle$	$\lceil e_1 \rceil \langle X,Y \rangle \theta \lceil e_2 \rceil \langle X,Y \rangle$
$e_1 \theta e_2$	$\theta \in \{>, \geq, \supset, \supseteq, -, /, \backslash\}$	$\lfloor e_1 \rfloor \langle X,Y \rangle \theta \lceil e_2 \rceil \langle X,Y \rangle$	$\lceil e_1 \rceil \langle X,Y \rangle \theta \lfloor e_2 \rfloor \langle X,Y \rangle$
θe_1	$\theta \in \{\neg, count, \}$	$\theta \lceil e_1 \rceil \langle X,Y \rangle$	$\theta \lfloor e_1 \rfloor \langle X,Y \rangle$
$\theta(e_1.val)$	$\theta \in \{min\}$	$\theta(\lceil e_1 \rceil \langle X,Y \rangle.val)$	$\theta(\lfloor e_1 \rfloor \langle X,Y \rangle.val)$
$\theta(e_1)$	$\theta \in \{length\}$	$\theta \lfloor e_1 \rfloor \langle X,Y \rangle$	$\theta \lceil e_1 \rceil \langle X,Y \rangle$
$\theta(e_1.val)$	$\theta \in \{sum, max\}$	$\theta(\lfloor e_1 \rfloor \langle X,Y \rangle.val)$	$\theta(\lceil e_1 \rceil \langle X,Y \rangle.val)$
$c \in E_i$	-	c	c
$X \in \mathcal{L}_A$	-	X	Y

the description of the lower and upper bounding operators corresponding to the subset of the primitives $\mathcal{P}$ given in Table 2. In Table 3, the general notation E_i designates one space among $\mathfrak{B}$, $\Re^+$ or $\mathcal{L}_A$ and $\mathcal{E}_i$ the associated expressions (for instance, the set of constraints $\mathcal{Q}$ for the booleans $\mathfrak{B}$).

Let us illustrate $\lfloor . \rfloor$ and $\lceil . \rceil$ on the area constraint: as $\geq$ increases in $\mathfrak{B}$ according to the first variable and decreases according to the second one, we have $\lfloor area(X) \geq 6 \rfloor \langle X,Y \rangle = \lfloor area(X) \rfloor \langle X,Y \rangle \geq \lceil 6 \rceil \langle X,Y \rangle$ (this is illustrated by the second line in Table 3). As 6 is a constant and $\times$ increases with each variable, we obtain respectively that $\lceil 6 \rceil \langle X,Y \rangle = 6$ (line 7) and $\lfloor area(X) \rfloor \langle X,Y \rangle = \lfloor count(X) \rfloor \langle X,Y \rangle \times \lfloor length(X) \rfloor \langle X,Y \rangle$ (line 1). Finally, $\lfloor area(X) \geq 6 \rfloor \langle X,Y \rangle$ is equal to $count(Y) \times length(X) \geq 6$ because $count$ decreases (line 3) and $length$ increases (line 5). In the same way, $\lceil area(X) \geq 6 \rceil \langle X,Y \rangle$ is equal to $count(X) \times length(Y) \geq 6$.

The following property justifies that the operators $\lfloor . \rfloor$ and $\lceil . \rceil$ are respectively named the lower and upper bounding operators:

Property 1 (bounds of an interval [24]). *Let q be a primitive-based constraint, $\lfloor q \rfloor$ and $\lceil q \rceil$ are respectively a lower bound and an upper bound of q i.e., given an interval $[X,Y]$ and a pattern $Z \in [X,Y]$, we have $\lfloor q \rfloor \langle X,Y \rangle \leq q(Z) \leq \lceil q \rceil \langle X,Y \rangle$.*

These top-level operators are useful to obtain efficient pruning conditions of a primitive-based constraint on an interval [24]. For instance, $\lceil area(X) \geq 6 \rceil$ $\langle CD, ABCD \rangle = count(CD) \times length(ABCD) \geq 6$ is false. Then, any pattern included in $[CD, ABCD]$ has an area smaller than 6 and we can negatively prune this interval.

In this paper, we re-use these bounding operators on intervals delimited by a virtual pattern and a pattern X of the search space. Such intervals are in fact all the generalizations or all the specializations of X.

4   Virtual Patterns

This section introduces the bottom and top virtual patterns and links them to the primitive-based framework.

4.1   Definition of Virtual Patterns

A virtual pattern dissents from a usual pattern of $\mathcal{L}_A$ because its properties, by embedding specificities of the mining context, differ from those of the usual patterns. This behavior constitutes its great interest.

We recall that by definition (see Section 2.1), the extracted patterns have to be present in the dataset. The collection of present patterns in the dataset is denoted by $\mathcal{C}$, i.e., $\mathcal{C} = \{X \in \mathcal{L}_A | count(X) \geq 1\}$. Our example dealing with the area constraint (Section 2.3) has shown the usefulness of the information (e.g., length, frequency) concerning the smallest and longest patterns of collection $\mathcal{C}$. The bottom and top virtual patterns are an elegant way to bring together the information. We start by giving their definition:

Definition 5 (bottom and top virtual patterns). *The bottom virtual pattern $\perp$ and the top virtual pattern $\top$ are respectively defined as $\emptyset$ and A, which have for each function $p : \mathcal{L}_A \rightarrow \Re^+$ the following properties:*

$$p(\perp) = \begin{cases} \min_{X \in \mathcal{C}} p(X), & \text{if } p \text{ is an increasing function} \\ \max_{X \in \mathcal{C}} p(X), & \text{if } p \text{ is a decreasing function} \end{cases}$$

$$p(\top) = \begin{cases} \max_{X \in \mathcal{C}} p(X), & \text{if } p \text{ is an increasing function} \\ \min_{X \in \mathcal{C}} p(X), & \text{if } p \text{ is a decreasing function} \end{cases}$$

The bottom virtual pattern $\perp$ is clearly an imaginary pattern. For instance, even if it is defined as $\emptyset$ (its cardinality (or length) of which is zero in reality), Definition 5 fixes its length equal to 1. Indeed, we have $length(\perp) = \min_{X \in \mathcal{C}} length(X)$ because the length is an increasing function on $\mathcal{L}_A$. As the length of the shortest patterns is equal to 1, we obtain that $length(\perp) = 1$. The top virtual pattern $\top$ is an imaginary pattern whenever all the objects of $\mathcal{D}$ are different from A and, in this case, it does not belong to the collection $\mathcal{C}$.

Let us note that according to Definition 5, the virtual patterns are the same for any constraint. In fact, the virtual patterns $\perp$ and $\top$ only depend on the mining context (i.e., the dataset and the additional information). For instance, the values of sum, min or max for each virtual pattern is linked to those of the tables of values. The left part of Table 4 formulates their definition according to the particular mining context given by Table 1. The right part gives the definition of the patterns $\emptyset$ and A.

Table 4 highlights a twofold advantage of the bottom and top virtual patterns compared to the real patterns $\emptyset$ and A. First, the empty set is not defined for all the primitives used in constraints. Second, the virtual pattern $\perp$ (resp. $\top$) is more refined than the pattern $\emptyset$ (resp. A). For instance, the pattern ABC is included in both A and $\top$ (since the latter is defined as A). But, $length(\top) = 4$ is a better approximation of $length(ABC) = 3$ than $length(A) = 6$. Section 5.3 shows that the pruning conditions resulting from these virtual patterns would be ineffective with the patterns $\emptyset$ and A. Thereby, virtual patterns are useful tricks to manipulate constraints and then, speed-up computations.

Thanks to Property 2 (see below), we focus now on the patterns which are at the core of the properties of $\perp$ and $\top$. In the rest of the paper, the sets $\mathcal{M}in$

Table 4. Definition of the virtual patterns $\perp$ and $\top$ (in our particular mining context) and comparison with the patterns $\emptyset$ and $\mathcal{A}$

Primitive p	$p(\perp)$	$p(\top)$
count	5	1
length	1	4
sum	10	165
min	70	10
max	10	70

Primitive p	$p(\emptyset)$	$p(\mathcal{A})$
count	7	0
length	0	6
sum	-	210
min	-	10
max	-	70

and $\mathcal{M}ax$ respectively denote the minimal patterns and the maximal patterns of $\mathcal{C}$ with respect to the partial order $\subseteq$ (i.e., $\mathcal{M}in = \{X \in \mathcal{C} | \nexists Y \in \mathcal{C}, Y \subset X\}$ and $\mathcal{M}ax = \{X \in \mathcal{C} | \nexists Y \in \mathcal{C}, X \subset Y\}$). These two sets of extreme patterns present in $\mathcal{D}$ allow us to directly compute the virtual patterns:

Property 2. *The virtual patterns $\perp$ and $\top$ check the following relations for each function* $p : \mathcal{L}_\mathcal{A} \mapsto \Re^+$:

$$p(\perp) = \begin{cases} \min_{X \in \mathcal{M}in} p(X), & \text{if } p \text{ is an increasing function} \\ \max_{X \in \mathcal{M}in} p(X), & \text{if } p \text{ is a decreasing function} \end{cases}$$

$$p(\top) = \begin{cases} \max_{X \in \mathcal{M}ax} p(X), & \text{if } p \text{ is an increasing function} \\ \min_{X \in \mathcal{M}ax} p(X), & \text{if } p \text{ is a decreasing function} \end{cases}$$

Proof. Let $p : \mathcal{L}_\mathcal{A} \mapsto \Re^+$ be an increasing function. For each pattern $X \in \mathcal{C}$, there exists $Y \in \mathcal{M}in$ such that $Y \subseteq X$. As p increases, we obtain that $p(Y) \leq p(X)$ and $\min_{Y \in \mathcal{M}in} p(X) \leq \min_{X \in \mathcal{C}} p(X)$. As $\mathcal{M}in \subseteq \mathcal{C}$, we conclude that $\min_{X \in \mathcal{C}} p(X) = \min_{Y \in \mathcal{M}in} p(X)$. The three other relations are proven with a similar reasoning. $\square$

Property 2 highlights that the bottom (resp. top) virtual patterns summarizes the knowledge about the shortest (resp. longest) patterns w.r.t. $\subseteq$. This property shows that $\perp$ and $\top$ can be efficiently computed. For instance, with the attribute language $\mathcal{L}_\mathcal{A}$, the only attributes (resp. objects) allow us to define the virtual pattern $\perp$ (resp. $\top$).

Even if we have defined the virtual patterns separately from the primitive-based framework, they can naturally be integrated in this framework.

4.2 Extension of the Primitive-Based Framework to Virtual Patterns

This section introduces a new language based on virtual patterns. Property 3 proves that the language $\mathcal{L}_\mathcal{A}$ can be replaced by this new one in the primitive-based framework.

We consider the virtual language $\mathcal{L}_\mathcal{V} = \mathcal{C} \cup \{\perp, \top\}$. The usual partial order $\subseteq$ on $\mathcal{L}_\mathcal{A}$ is again a partial order on $\mathcal{L}_\mathcal{V}$. As for the language $\mathcal{L}_\mathcal{A}$, if $X \in \mathcal{L}_\mathcal{V}$ is included in $Y \in \mathcal{L}_\mathcal{V}$, the interval $[X, Y]$ corresponds to the patterns included

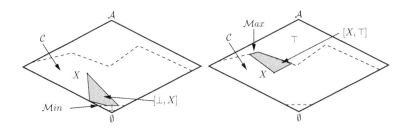

Fig. 1. Representation of the intervals $[\perp, X]$ and $[X, \top]$ on virtual lattices

between X and Y. In particular, we can note that for each pattern X of $\mathcal{L}_\mathcal{V}$, we have $\perp \subseteq X \subseteq \top$. Then, the intervals $[\perp, X]$ and $[X, \top]$ have a meaning and contain respectively all the subsets and all the supersets of X. Figure 1 represents two virtual lattices corresponding to the virtual language $\mathcal{L}_\mathcal{V}$. In both lattices, the bottom (resp. top) dashed line indicates the minimal patterns $\mathcal{M}in$ (resp. maximal patterns $\mathcal{M}ax$) present in $\mathcal{D}$. The gray shape illustrates the interval $[\perp, X]$ (resp. $[X, \top]$) on the left (resp. right) lattice.

The poset $(\mathcal{L}_\mathcal{V}, \subseteq)$ is easy to exploit in the primitive-based framework. Indeed, as all the definitions and the properties of primitive-based framework are based on its primitives, we extend this framework to the virtual language by proving that its primitives deal again with this new language:

Property 3. *A monotone primitive p on $\mathcal{L}_\mathcal{A}$ is a monotone primitive on $\mathcal{L}_\mathcal{V}$.*

Proof. Let p be a monotone primitive on $\mathcal{L}_\mathcal{A}$. p is monotone (Definition 1) and we distinguish two cases. First, if p increases on $\mathcal{L}_\mathcal{A}$, p is also an increasing function on $\mathcal{C}$ because $\mathcal{C} \subseteq \mathcal{L}_\mathcal{A}$. Besides, let $X \in \mathcal{C}$, as $p(\perp) = \min_{Y \in \mathcal{C}} p(Y)$, we obtain that $p(\perp) \leq p(X)$. Similarly, let $X \in \mathcal{C}$, Definition 5 shows that $p(\top) = \max_{Y \in \mathcal{C}} p(Y) \geq p(X)$. Thus, p is an increasing function on $\mathcal{L}_\mathcal{V}$. Second, if p decreases on $\mathcal{L}_\mathcal{A}$, a similar approach allows us to conclude that p remains a decreasing function on $\mathcal{L}_\mathcal{V}$ and then, a monotone primitive from $\mathcal{L}_\mathcal{V}$ to $\Re^+$.   □

This property expresses that the virtual language $\mathcal{L}_\mathcal{V}$ can replace the usual language $\mathcal{L}_\mathcal{A}$ in the primitive-based framework. In other words, Definition 3 can be extended to a primitive-based constraint from $\mathcal{L}_\mathcal{V}$ to $\mathfrak{B}$ and Property 1 deals with intervals of the virtual language $\mathcal{L}_\mathcal{V}$.

5   Pruning Conditions

This section shows how to exploit the virtual patterns to automatically obtain pruning conditions through the primitive-based framework. Furthermore, Theorem 2 shows that the pruning conditions have properties of monotonicity.

5.1   Automatically Deducing Pruning Conditions

We have noticed (Section 2.3) that whenever a pattern $X \subseteq Y$, we have $(count(Y) \times length(Y) \geq 6) \leq (count(X) \times 4 \geq 6)$ in $\mathcal{D}$ because $length(Y) \leq 4$

and *count* is a decreasing function. In fact, $count(X) \times 4 \geq 6$ is an upper bound of the area constraint on the supersets of X corresponding to $[X, \top]$. As for the area constraint, if an upper bound of q on $[X, \top]$ is equal to *false*, any superset of X does not satisfy the constraint because its constraint value is less than or equal to *false*. In this case, we can perform a negative pruning according to the specialization. Similarly, assuming that a lower bound of q on $[X, \top]$ is *true*, we are sure that all the supersets of X satisfy the constraint and we positively prune w.r.t. the specialization. The same reasoning with the interval $[\bot, X]$ enables to obtain negative and positive pruning conditions on the subsets of X.

Logically, we want to use the bounding operators $\lfloor . \rfloor$ and $\lceil . \rceil$ (see Definition 4) in order to bound the value of the constraint on $[\bot, X]$ and $[X, \top]$. Property 3 allows us to manipulate virtual patterns with upper and lower bounding operators. Then, let q be a constraint and X be a pattern of $\mathcal{L}_\mathcal{V}$, we introduce the following notations:

$$\begin{cases} \lfloor q \rfloor^\bot \langle X \rangle \equiv \lfloor q \rfloor \langle \bot, X \rangle \\ \lceil q \rceil^\bot \langle X \rangle \equiv \lceil q \rceil \langle \bot, X \rangle \\ \lfloor q \rfloor^\top \langle X \rangle \equiv \lfloor q \rfloor \langle X, \top \rangle \\ \lceil q \rceil^\top \langle X \rangle \equiv \lceil q \rceil \langle X, \top \rangle \end{cases}$$

Let us come back on our example of the area constraint by applying the operator $\lceil . \rceil^\top$ to this constraint. We have $\lceil area(X) \geq 6 \rceil \langle X, Y \rangle = count(X) \times length(\top) \geq 6$ because $\lceil area(X) \geq 6 \rceil^\top = count(X) \times length(Y) \geq 6$ (see Section 3.2) and $\lceil q \rceil^\top \langle X \rangle \equiv \lceil q \rceil \langle X, \top \rangle$. As $length(\top) = 4$, we obtain that $count(X) \geq 6/4$ which gives the negative pruning condition $count(X) < 6/4$ w.r.t. the specialization. Symmetrically, we also deduce the pruning condition $length(X) < 6/5$ given in Section 2.3 stemming from $\lceil area(X) \geq 6 \rceil^\bot \langle \bot, X \rangle = count(\bot) \times length(X) \geq 6 = 5 \times length(X) \geq 6$.

Now, we link the pruning conditions to the bounding operators by giving the following key theorem:

Theorem 1 (pruning conditions). *Let q be a primitive-based constraint, the primitive-based constraints $\lfloor q \rfloor^\bot$, $\lfloor q \rfloor^\top$, $\neg \lceil q \rceil^\bot$ and $\neg \lceil q \rceil^\top$ are pruning conditions i.e., for each pattern X of $\mathcal{L}_\mathcal{V}$, one has the following relations:*

$$\begin{cases} \lfloor q \rfloor^\bot \langle X \rangle = true \Rightarrow \forall Y \subseteq X, \; q(Y) = true & \text{(positive/generalization)} \\ \lfloor q \rfloor^\top \langle X \rangle = true \Rightarrow \forall Y \supseteq X, \; q(Y) = true & \text{(positive/specialization)} \\ \lceil q \rceil^\bot \langle X \rangle = false \Rightarrow \forall Y \subseteq X, \; q(Y) = false & \text{(negative/generalization)} \\ \lceil q \rceil^\top \langle X \rangle = false \Rightarrow \forall Y \supseteq X, \; q(Y) = false & \text{(negative/specialization)} \end{cases}$$

Proof. Let q be a constraint and $X \in \mathcal{L}_\mathcal{V}$ such that $\lfloor q \rfloor^\bot \langle X \rangle$ is satisfied i.e., $\lfloor q \rfloor \langle \bot, X \rangle = true$. Let $Y \subseteq X$, we can notice that $Y \in [\bot, X]$ by definition of the poset $(\mathcal{L}_\mathcal{V}, \subseteq)$ (see Section 4.2). Then, Property 1 ensures that $\lfloor q \rfloor \langle \bot, X \rangle \leq q(Y)$. Thus, as the lower bound is *true*, we obtain that $q(Y)$ equals *true*. The other assertions are proven by the same way and we conclude that Theorem 1 is correct.

□

Whenever a pruning condition is *true* for a pattern, we know the value of the constraint for each subset and superset of this pattern. Thereby, many patterns can be pruned without having to satisfy the constraint on the whole set of patterns. For instance, $\neg\lceil area(X) \geq 6 \rceil^\top \langle CD \rangle = count(CD) < 6/4 = true$ expresses that all the supersets of CD can be negatively pruned (see Section 6.2 for the practical use of this pruning). Let us note that the converse of each assertion given by Theorem 1 is false.

5.2   Properties of Monotonicity of the Pruning Conditions

We show now that the pruning conditions satisfy the properties of monotonicity:

Theorem 2 (monotonicity of pruning conditions). *Let q be a primitive-based constraint, the pruning conditions $\neg\lceil q \rceil^\top$ and $\lfloor q \rfloor^\top$ (resp. $\neg\lceil q \rceil^\perp$ and $\lfloor q \rfloor^\perp$) are anti-monotone (resp. monotone) according to the specialization of the patterns.*

We start by giving Lemma 1 which facilitates the understanding of this theorem. This lemma expresses that the accuracy of the bounding operators increases when the size of the interval decreases.

Lemma 1. *Let $h \in \mathcal{H}$ and $[X_1, Y_1] \subseteq [X_2, Y_2]$, we have $\lfloor h \rfloor \langle X_1, Y_1 \rangle \geq \lfloor h \rfloor \langle X_2, Y_2 \rangle$ and $\lceil h \rceil \langle X_1, Y_1 \rangle \leq \lceil h \rceil \langle X_2, Y_2 \rangle$.*

Proof. Let $h \in \mathcal{H}$ and let $[X_1, Y_1] \subseteq [X_2, Y_2]$ be two intervals. First, if $\deg h = 0$, we can distinguish two cases. If h is an increasing function, as we have $\lfloor h \rfloor \langle X, Y \rangle = h(X)$ and $\lceil h \rceil \langle X, Y \rangle = h(Y)$, we check that $h(X_1) \geq h(X_2)$ and $h(Y_1) \leq h(Y_2)$. With a decreasing function, we can also conclude that the hypothesis is true. Second, if $\deg h = n$, we fix the decomposition of h is $p(h_1, \ldots, h_k)$. Suppose that for all the h' such that $\deg h' < n$, we have $\lfloor h' \rfloor \langle X_1, Y_1 \rangle \geq \lfloor h' \rfloor \langle X_2, Y_2 \rangle$ and $\lceil h' \rceil \langle X_1, Y_1 \rangle \leq \lceil h' \rceil \langle X_2, Y_2 \rangle$. If p is an increasing function with the ith variable, Definition 4 ensures that the lower bounding operator is again applied on the ith operand in order to compute $\lfloor h \rfloor$. As we have $\lfloor h_i \rfloor \langle X_1, Y_1 \rangle \geq \lfloor h_i \rfloor \langle X_2, Y_2 \rangle$ by hypothesis, p is greater on $[X_1, Y_1]$ than on $[X_2, Y_2]$. On the contrary, when p decreases with the ith variable, the upper bounding operator is applied to compute $\lfloor h \rfloor$. Thus, p is greater on $[X_1, Y_1]$ than on $[X_2, Y_2]$ because $\lceil h_i \rceil \langle X_1, Y_1 \rangle \leq \lceil h_i \rceil \langle X_2, Y_2 \rangle$. Finally, by applying this approach for all the $i \in \{1, \ldots, k\}$, we obtain that $\lfloor h \rfloor \langle X_1, Y_1 \rangle \geq \lfloor h \rfloor \langle X_2, Y_2 \rangle$. Dually, we have also $\lceil h \rceil \langle X_1, Y_1 \rangle \leq \lceil h \rceil \langle X_2, Y_2 \rangle$. Thus, by induction, we conclude that Lemma 1 is right.   □

We prove now Theorem 2:

Proof. Let $q \in \mathcal{Q}$ and X be a pattern such that $\lfloor q \rfloor^\top \langle X \rangle$ is *true*. Let Y be a pattern such that $X \subseteq Y$. As we have $\lfloor q \rfloor^\top \langle X \rangle = \lfloor q \rfloor \langle X, \top \rangle$ and $[Y, \top] \subseteq [X, \top]$, we obtain that $\lfloor q \rfloor \langle Y, \top \rangle \geq \lfloor q \rfloor \langle X, \top \rangle = true$ (Lemma 1). Thus, $\lfloor q \rfloor^\top$ is anti-monotone. The other properties about monotonicity are proven by the same method and we conclude that Theorem 2 is correct.   □

Theorem 2 clearly highlights the link between the pruning conditions and the monotonicity. In practice, the usual algorithms which mine monotone or/and anti-monotone constraints, can naturally push the negative pruning conditions

Table 5. Pruning conditions corresponding to our examples of constraints

Constraint	Pruning conditions	
$count(X) \times length(X) \geq 6$	$count(X) \geq 6$	(pos./gen.)
	$length(X) \geq 6$	(pos./spec.)
	$length(X) < 6/5$	(neg./gen.)
	$count(X) < 6/4$	(neg./spec.)
$(min(X.val) + max(X.val))/2 \leq 50$	$max(X.val) \leq 30$	(pos./gen.)
	$min(X.val) \leq 30$	(pos./spec.)
	$min(X.val) > 90$	(neg./gen.)
	$max(X.val) > 90$	(neg./spec.)
$sum(X.val)/length(X) \geq 25$	$10/length(X) \geq 25$	(pos./gen.)
	$sum(X.val)/4 \geq 25$	(pos./spec.)
	$sum(X.val) < 25$	(neg./gen.)
	$165/length(X) < 25$	(neg./spec.)
$AE \subseteq X$	$false$	(pos./gen.)
	$AE \subseteq X$	(pos./spec.)
	$AE \not\subseteq X$	(neg./gen.)
	$false$	(neg./spec.)
$count(X) \geq 2$	$count(X) \geq 2$	(pos./gen.)
	$false$	(pos./spec.)
	$false$	(neg./gen.)
	$count(X) < 2$	(neg./spec.)

(see Section 6.1). Table 5 gives the four pruning conditions for each constraint introduced in Section 3.1. We can note that each pruning condition is monotone or anti-monotone.

In Table 5, many pruning conditions are very efficient. For instance, the minimal average constraint can be efficiently mined with the positive pruning condition according to the specialization (i.e., $sum(X.val)/4 \geq 25$). In particular, as $sum(AC.val)$ equals 135, all the supersets of the pattern AC (i.e., ABC, ACD and $ABCD$ in our data mining context) can be positively pruned. However, for one constraint, all the pruning conditions are not effective in a given context. For instance, the positive pruning condition according to the generalization is useless with the minimal frequency constraint (due to the fact that this constraint is anti-monotone). Indeed, we get $false$ for this positive pruning condition, which means that there is no pruning. Nevertheless, we can observe a good complementarity between the pruning conditions, especially between the positive and negative ones. Finally, let us note that the monotone and anti-monotone constraints are well treated by our operators. They allow us to deduce the usual negative pruning condition with the "having AE" and the minimal frequency constraint, which are respectively $AE \not\subseteq X$ and $count(X) < 2$. In this case, we get the optimal pruning conditions.

5.3 Relevance of the Definition of the Virtual Patterns

Now we provide a comment about the definition of the virtual patterns compared to the empty set and the set of attributes. Let us assume that we would like to use

$\emptyset$ and $\mathcal{A}$ instead of the virtual patterns $\bot$ and $\top$. Even if the generalizations and the specializations of X respectively correspond to the intervals $[\emptyset, X]$ and $[X, \mathcal{A}]$, the bounding operators provide a poor interest for such intervals. For instance, $\lceil area(X) \geq 6 \rceil \langle X, \mathcal{A} \rangle = count(X) \times length(\mathcal{A}) \geq 6 = count(X) \times 6 \geq 6$ only expresses that the mined patterns have to be present in the dataset. Similarly, $\lceil area(X) \geq 6 \rceil \langle \emptyset, X \rangle = count(\emptyset) \times length(X) \geq 6 = 7 \times length(X) \geq 6$ offers the useless pruning condition $length(X) < 0.86$ which is never satisfied by any pattern. Section 6.2 clearly points and quantifies the assets of the virtual pattern $\top$ compared to the pattern $\mathcal{A}$. Thus, the concept of virtual patterns is a key point of our method.

6 Experimental Results

This section illustrates how to take advantage of the pruning conditions and reports our performance analysis.

6.1 Practical Uses of Pruning Conditions

In these experiments, we focus on the negative pruning conditions according to the specialization. We use two approaches (MUSIC-$\top$ and APRIORI-$\top$ processes) in order to mine patterns satisfying a primitive-based constraint q. These two mining processes are sound and complete.

MUSIC-$\top$ *mining process.* Based on the primitive-based framework, we have proposed a constraint solver named MUSIC [24] which mines soundly and completely patterns under a primitive-based constraint q. It benefits from a negative pruning condition according to the specialization (which is discovery preserving [3]) to improve the extraction. The proposed approach (see Figure 2) exploits the *constraint handler* implementing $\lceil . \rceil^{\top}$ which provides the anti-monotone constraint q_{AM}.

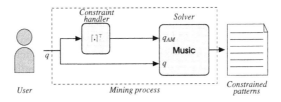

Fig. 2. Illustration of MUSIC-$\top$ process

APRIORI-$\top$ *mining process.* This process is based on an APRIORI-like algorithm [1, 19]. We use this process to demonstrate contribution of the virtual patterns even for this simple method. At first, we mine all the patterns satisfying $\lceil q \rceil^{\top}$ i.e., we push the negative pruning condition w.r.t. the specialization as an anti-monotone constraint. As previously, the constraint handler (i.e., the box denoted by $\lceil . \rceil^{\top}$) automatically computes the anti-monotone constraint.

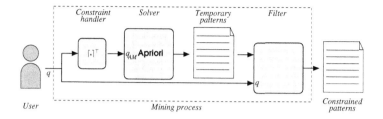

Fig. 3. Illustration of APRIORI-⊤ process

Secondly, the extracted patterns are post-processed to only select the patterns which satisfy q. Figure 3 depicts this mining process.

Let us note that many existing algorithms (see Section 2.2) can also benefit from these pruning conditions. For instance, the framework [16] enables to simultaneously take advantage of the negative and positive pruning conditions w.r.t. the specialization. Indeed, given a primitive-based constraint, the patterns which satisfy $\lfloor q \rfloor^\top$ or $\neg \lceil q \rceil^\top$, are respectively positive and negative witnesses. Besides, DUALMINER [9] and EXANTE [6] can use the two negative pruning conditions automatically computed by applying $\lceil . \rceil^\perp$ and $\lceil . \rceil^\top$.

6.2   Performance Analysis

The aim of our experiments is to measure the runtime benefit brought by the negative pruning condition according to the specialization obtained thanks to the virtual patterns. We compare MUSIC-⊤ and APRIORI-⊤ (see previous section) to four following approaches:

- MUSIC: in this approach, we use MUSIC without taking into account any optimization due to the upper bounding operator. In particular, the pruning conditions are not exploited.
- APRIORI: in this approach, the original algorithm is used at first to mine the collection $\mathcal{C}$. Then, the patterns satisfying the constraint are achieved by a post-processing step.
- MUSIC-$\mathcal{A}$: this approach is briefly described at Section 5.3. It exploits the upper bounding operator with the interval $[X, \mathcal{A}]$ instead of considering $[X, \top]$, with the use of MUSIC.
- APRIORI-$\mathcal{A}$: this approach is similar to the previous one, except that APRIORI is used instead of MUSIC.

All the experiments were conducted on a 2.2 GHz Pentium IV processor with Linux operating system and 3GB of RAM memory. The used dataset is mushroom coming from the FIMI repository[4]. The constraints using numeric values were applied on a table of values randomly generated within the range [1,100]. Table 6 provides the definition of the virtual patterns $\perp$ and $\top$ with the used table of values.

---

[4] http://fimi.cs.helsinki.fi/data/

Table 6. The bottom and top virtual patterns with mushroom

Primitive p	$p(\bot)$	$p(\top)$
count	8124	1
length	1	23
sum	0	1166
min	97	0
max	0	97

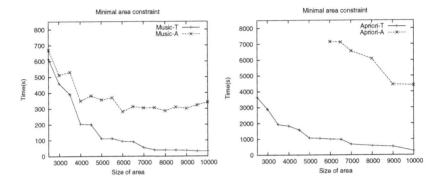

Fig. 4. Runtime performances with the minimal area constraint

Figure 4 reports the runtime performances for mining the minimal area constraint according to the size of the area. The results have been split into two parts because there is an order of magnitude between Music-like and Apriori-like approaches. The left and right charts respectively plot the comparison between Music-$\mathcal{A}$ and Music-$\top$, and the comparison between Apriori-$\mathcal{A}$ and Apriori-$\top$. Results with Apriori and Music are not drawn: these approaches fail for all the area thresholds. Apriori-$\mathcal{A}$ fails whenever the area size diminishes (i.e., less than 6000).

First, we can observe that the improvement brought by the primitive-based framework and the lower bounding operator: Music-$\mathcal{A}$ (resp. Apriori-$\mathcal{A}$) is better than Music (resp. Apriori). In particular, due to the selectivity of the constraint, the efficiency of the Apriori-like and Music-like approaches increases with the area size. Second, the best performances (in their own category) are achieved by Apriori-$\top$ and Music-$\top$. This result underlines the usefulness of the virtual patterns with the area constraint.

Figure 5 plots the runtime performances for the minimal average constraint on the mushroom dataset. We use here an additional minimal frequency constraint with a threshold fixed at 2% in order to make feasible Apriori. With such a frequency threshold, the impact of pruning condition is weak on Music. Thus, all the Music-like approaches are comparable. The right chart shows that Apriori-$\mathcal{A}$ and Apriori have the same results. Besides, Apriori-$\top$ outperforms Apriori and Apriori-$\mathcal{A}$ whenever the minimal average exeeds 70.

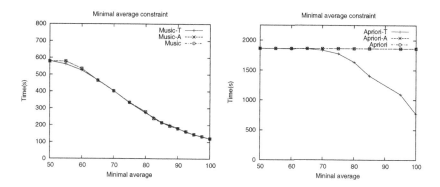

Fig. 5. Runtime performances with the minimal average constraint

The efficiency of the pruning depends on the selectivity of the constraint. As we only use the negative pruning, the more selective the constraint, the faster the mining. Even if MUSIC-T clearly outperforms APRIORI-T, the negative pruning condition w.r.t. specialization has a good impact on both algorithms. Thus, the mining is always improved and extractions intractable until now become feasible.

7   Conclusion

In this paper, we have proposed the use of virtual patterns to automatically compute positive and negative pruning conditions for *any* primitive-based constraint. Virtual patterns are elegant tricks to take into account the specificities of the data mining context. More precisely, the bottom and top virtual patterns enable to consider respectively all the subsets and all the supersets of a given pattern. These virtual patterns lead to automatically obtain four different pruning conditions for a primitive-based constraint. These pruning conditions have suitable properties of monotonicity which improve the extraction step. In practice, many existing algorithms can use them to mine varied constraints. Besides, experimental results on different mining contexts underline the efficiency of the negative pruning conditions according to the specialization.

Further work addresses the implementation and the experimentation of virtual patterns with other kinds of patterns. Secondly we would refine the bottom and top virtual patterns to take into account more accurately the contiguous subsets and supersets. In the same way, we would like to revisit mining problems by introducing other virtual patterns. Finally, another way is to achieve pruning conditions concerning convertibility.

Acknowledgements. This work has been partially funded by the ACI "masse de données" (MD 46, 2004-2007) BINGO (Bases de données INductives pour la GénOmique).

References

[1] R. Agrawal and R. Srikant. Fast algorithms for mining association rules in large databases. In J. B. Bocca, M. Jarke, and C. Zaniolo, editors, *VLDB*, pages 487–499. Morgan Kaufmann, 1994.

[2] R. Agrawal and R. Srikant. Mining sequential patterns. In P. S. Yu and A. L. P. Chen, editors, *ICDE*, pages 3–14. IEEE Computer Society, 1995.

[3] R. J. Bayardo. The hows, whys, and whens of constraints in itemset and rule discovery. In *Proceedings of the Workshop on Inductive Databases and Constraint Based Mining*, 2005.

[4] J. Besson, R. Pensa, C. Robardet, and J.-F. Boulicaut. Constraint-based mining of fault-tolerant patterns from boolean data . In *4th International Workshop on Knowledge Discovery in Inductive Databases (KDID'05) co-located with the 9th European Conference on Principles and Practice of Knowledge Discovery in Databases PKDD'05* , pages 13–26, Porto, Portugal, 10 2005.

[5] K. S. Beyer and R. Ramakrishnan. Bottom-up computation of sparse and iceberg cubes. In A. Delis, C. Faloutsos, and S. Ghandeharizadeh, editors, *SIGMOD Conference*, pages 359–370. ACM Press, 1999.

[6] F. Bonchi, F. Giannotti, A. Mazzanti, and D. Pedreschi. Exante: Anticipated data reduction in constrained pattern mining. In N. Lavrac, D. Gamberger, H. Blockeel, and L. Todorovski, editors, *PKDD*, volume 2838 of *Lecture Notes in Computer Science*, pages 59–70. Springer, 2003.

[7] F. Bonchi and C. Lucchese. On closed constrained frequent pattern mining. In *ICDM*, pages 35–42. IEEE Computer Society, 2004.

[8] F. Bonchi and C. Lucchese. Pushing tougher constraints in frequent pattern mining. In Ho et al. [14], pages 114–124.

[9] C. Bucila, J. Gehrke, D. Kifer, and W. M. White. Dualminer: a dual-pruning algorithm for itemsets with constraints. In *KDD*, pages 42–51. ACM, 2002.

[10] G. Dong and J. Li. Efficient mining of emerging patterns: discovering trends and differences. In *Proceedings of the fifth ACM SIGKDD international conference on Knowledge discovery and data mining (KDD'99)*, pages 43–52, New York, NY, USA, 1999. ACM Press.

[11] K. Gade, J. Wang, and G. Karypis. Efficient closed pattern mining in the presence of tough block constraints. In W. Kim, R. Kohavi, J. Gehrke, and W. DuMouchel, editors, *KDD*, pages 138–147. ACM, 2004.

[12] F. Geerts, B. Goethals, and T. Mielikäinen. Tiling databases. In E. Suzuki and S. Arikawa, editors, *Discovery Science*, volume 3245 of *Lecture Notes in Computer Science*, pages 278–289. Springer, 2004.

[13] J. Han, J. Pei, and Y. Yin. Mining frequent patterns without candidate generation. In W. Chen, J. F. Naughton, and P. A. Bernstein, editors, *SIGMOD Conference*, pages 1–12. ACM, 2000.

[14] T. B. Ho, D. Cheung, and H. Liu, editors. *Advances in Knowledge Discovery and Data Mining, 9th Pacific-Asia Conference, PAKDD 2005, Hanoi, Vietnam, May 18-20, 2005, Proceedings*, volume 3518 of *Lecture Notes in Computer Science*. Springer, 2005.

[15] T. Imielinski and H. Mannila. A database perspective on knowledge discovery. *Commun. ACM*, 39(11):58–64, 1996.

[16] D. Kifer, J. Gehrke, C. Bucila, and W. M. White. How to quickly find a witness. In *PODS*, pages 272–283. ACM, 2003.

[17] M. Kuramochi and G. Karypis. Frequent subgraph discovery. In N. Cercone, T. Y. Lin, and X. Wu, editors, *ICDM*, pages 313–320. IEEE Computer Society, 2001.

[18] S. D. Lee and L. D. Raedt. An algebra for inductive query evaluation. In *Proceedings of the Second International Workshop on Inductive Databases (KDID'03)*, pages 80–96. Rudjer Boskovic Institute, Zagreb, Croatia, september 2003.

[19] H. Mannila and H. Toivonen. Levelwise search and borders of theories in knowledge discovery. *Data Min. Knowl. Discov.*, 1(3):241–258, 1997.

[20] T. M. Mitchell. Generalization as search. *Artif. Intell.*, 18(2):203–226, 1982.

[21] R. T. Ng, L. V. S. Lakshmanan, J. Han, and A. Pang. Exploratory mining and pruning optimizations of constrained association rules. In L. M. Haas and A. Tiwary, editors, *SIGMOD Conference*, pages 13–24. ACM Press, 1998.

[22] N. Pasquier, Y. Bastide, R. Taouil, and L. Lakhal. Discovering frequent closed itemsets for association rules. In C. Beeri and P. Buneman, editors, *ICDT*, volume 1540 of *Lecture Notes in Computer Science*, pages 398–416. Springer, 1999.

[23] J. Pei, J. Han, and L. V. S. Lakshmanan. Mining frequent item sets with convertible constraints. In *ICDE*, pages 433–442. IEEE Computer Society, 2001.

[24] A. Soulet and B. Crémilleux. An efficient framework for mining flexible constraints. In Ho et al. [14], pages 661–671.

[25] A. Soulet and B. Crémilleux. Optimizing constraint-based mining by automatically relaxing constraints. In *Proceedings of The Fifth IEEE International Conference on Data Mining (ICDM'05)*, 2005.

Constraint Based Induction of Multi-objective Regression Trees

Jan Struyf[1] and Sašo Džeroski[2]

[1] Katholieke Universiteit Leuven, Dept. of Computer Science,
Celestijnenlaan 200A, B-3001 Leuven, Belgium
`Jan.Struyf@cs.kuleuven.be`
[2] Jozef Stefan Institute, Dept. of Knowledge Technologies,
Jamova 39, 1000 Ljubljana, Slovenia
`Saso.Dzeroski@ijs.si`

Abstract. Constrained based inductive systems are a key component of inductive databases and responsible for building the models that satisfy the constraints in the inductive queries. In this paper, we propose a constraint based system for building multi-objective regression trees. A multi-objective regression tree is a decision tree capable of predicting several numeric variables at once. We focus on size and accuracy constraints. By either specifying maximum size or minimum accuracy, the user can trade-off size (and thus interpretability) for accuracy. Our approach is to first build a large tree based on the training data and to prune it in a second step to satisfy the user constraints. This has the advantage that the tree can be stored in the inductive database and used for answering inductive queries with different constraints. Besides size and accuracy constraints, we also briefly discuss syntactic constraints. We evaluate our system on a number of real world data sets and measure the size versus accuracy trade-off.

1 Introduction

The idea behind inductive databases [13, 7] is to tightly integrate databases with data mining. An inductive database not only stores data, but also models that have been obtained by running mining algorithms on the data. By means of a query language, the end user can retrieve particular models. For example, the user could query the system for a decision tree that is smaller than 20 nodes, has an accuracy above 80%, and with a particular attribute in the top node. If the database does not include a model satisfying the constraints, then an induction algorithm is called to construct it.

In this paper we propose a constraint based induction algorithm for multi-objective regression trees (MORTs). MORTs are regression trees [6] capable of predicting several numeric variables at once [2]. This has two main advantages over building a separate regression tree for each target: (1) a single MORT is usually much smaller than the total size of the individual trees for all variables, and (2) a MORT explicitates dependencies between the different target variables.

F. Bonchi and J.-F. Boulicaut (Eds.): KDID 2005, LNCS 3933, pp. 222–233, 2006.

The approach that we propose is to first build a large tree based on the training data and then to prune it in a second step to satisfy the user constraints. This has the advantage that the tree can be stored in the inductive database and used for answering inductive queries with different constraints. The pruning algorithm that we propose is an extension to MORTs of the pruning algorithm for classification trees developed by Garofalakis et al. [12], which in turn is based on earlier work by Bohanec and Bratko [3] and Almuallim [1]. It is a dynamic programming algorithm that searches for a subtree of the given tree that satisfies the size and accuracy constraints. It can either minimize tree size and return the smallest tree satisfying a minimum accuracy constraint or maximize accuracy and return the most accurate tree satisfying a maximum size constraint.

After extending the pruning algorithm to MORTs, we present an extensive empirical evaluation measuring the size versus accuracy trade-off of MORTs on several real world data sets. Our evaluation shows (1) that the accuracy of MORTs is close to that of a set of single-objective regression trees of the same size, and (2) that in many cases tree size can be reduced significantly (thereby increasing interpretability) at the expense of only a small accuracy loss.

The rest of this paper is organized as follows. In Section 2, we briefly discuss MORTs and their induction algorithm. Section 3 reviews the pruning algorithm by Garofalakis et al. and Section 4 extends it to MORTs. Accuracy and syntactic constraints are discussed in Section 5. The empirical evaluation follows in Section 6. Future work is discussed in Section 7 and Section 8 states the main conclusions.

2 Multi-objective Regression Trees (MORTs)

MORTs are regression trees [6] capable of predicting several numeric target variables at once. An example of a MORT is depicted in Fig. 1. Each leaf stores a vector with as components the predictions for the different target variables.

MORTs have been introduced as a special instance of predictive clustering trees [2]. In this framework, a tree is viewed as a hierarchy of clusters: the top-node corresponds to one cluster containing all data, which is recursively partitioned into smaller clusters while moving down the tree. MORTs are constructed with a standard top-down induction algorithm similar to that of CART [6] or C4.5 [15]. The heuristic used in this algorithm for selecting the attribute tests in the internal nodes is intra-cluster variation summed over the subsets induced by the test. Intra-cluster variation is defined as $N \cdot \sum_{t=1}^{T} \text{Var}[y_t]$, with N the

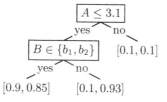

Fig. 1. A MORT predicting two numeric variables

number of examples in the cluster, T the number of target variables, and Var$[y_t]$ the variance of target variable t in the cluster. Minimizing intra-cluster variation results in homogeneous leaves, which in turn results in accurate predictions (the predicted vector in a leaf is the vector mean of the target vectors of the training examples belonging to it). More details about MORTs can be found in [2].

3   Constraint-Based Decision Tree Pruning

Fig. 2 defines the pruning method proposed by Garofalakis et al. [12] for computing for a given maximum tree size k a subtree of the given tree (rooted at node N) with maximum accuracy (minimum error). First ComputeError is called to find out which nodes are to be included in the solution and then PruneRecursive is called to remove the other nodes.

ComputeError employs dynamic programming to compute in Tree$[N, k]$.error the error of the minimum-error subtree rooted at N containing at most k nodes. This subtree is either the tree in which N is pruned to a leaf or a tree in which N has two children (we only consider binary trees) N_1 and N_2 such that N_1 (N_2) is a minimum error subtree of size at most k_1 (k_2) and $k_1 + k_2 = k - 1$. The algorithm computes the minimum over these possibilities in the for-loop starting on line 6. The possibility that N is pruned to a leaf is taken into account by initializing the error to leaf_error(N) in line 4. The flag Tree$[N, k]$.computed is used to avoid repeated computation of the same information.

After ComputeError completes, Tree$[N, k].k_1$ stores the maximum size of the left subtree in the minimum-error subtree of at most k nodes rooted at N. Note that if Tree$[N, k].k_1 = -1$, then this subtree consists of only the node N. PruneRecursive is called next to prune nodes that do not belong to the minimum-error subtree.

The time and space complexity of the algorithm(s) are both $\mathcal{O}(nk)$ with n the size of the tree and k the maximum tree size parameter [12].

procedure ComputeError(N, k)
1: **if** Tree$[N, k]$.computed
2:     **return** Tree$[N, k]$.error
3: Tree$[N, k].k_1 := -1$
4: Tree$[N, k]$.error := leaf_error(N)
5: **if** $k \geq 3$ **and** N is no leaf
6:     **for** $k_1 := 1$ **to** $k - 2$
7:         $k_2 := k - k_1 - 1$
8:         $e :=$ ComputeError(N_1, k_1)
9:             $+$ComputeError(N_2, k_2)
10:         **if** $e <$ Tree$[N, k]$.error
11:             Tree$[N, k]$.error := e
12:             Tree$[N, k].k_1 := k_1$
13: Tree$[N, k]$.computed := true
14: **return** Tree$[N, k]$.error

procedure PruneToSizeK(N, k)
1: ComputeError(N, k)
2: PruneRecursive(N, k)

procedure PruneRecursive(N, k)
1: **if** N is a leaf
2:     **return**
3: **if** $k < 3$ **or** Tree$[N, k].k_1 = -1$
4:     remove children of N
5: **else**
6:     $k_1 :=$ Tree$[N, k].k_1$
7:     $k_2 := k - k_1 - 1$
8:     PruneRecursive(N_1, k_1)
9:     PruneRecursive(N_2, k_2)

Fig. 2. The constraint-based decision tree pruning algorithm

4   Size Constraints for MORTs

The pruning algorithm discussed in the previous section was originally developed in a classification setting with as error measure the number of misclassified examples or the minimum description length cost. It is however not difficult to see that the algorithm can be used in combination with any error measure that is *additive*, i.e., a measure for which it holds that if a data set is partitioned into a number of subsets, the error computed on the whole set is equal to the sum of the errors computed on the subsets in the partition.

Definition 1 (Additive error measure). *An error measure f is additive iff for any data set D and for any partition of D into subsets D_i it holds that $f(D) = \sum_i f(D_i)$.*

The additivity property of the error measure is used in lines 8-9 of the ComputeError algorithm.

Examples of error measures in the multi-objective regression setting that satisfy the additivity property are squared error and absolute error.

Definition 2 (Squared and absolute error). *Given a data set with N examples and T targets, squared error is defined as* $\mathrm{SE} = \sum_{i=1}^{N} \sum_{t=1}^{T} (y_{t,i} - y_{t,i}^{p})^2$ *and absolute error as* $\mathrm{AE} = \sum_{i=1}^{N} \sum_{t=1}^{T} |y_{t,i} - y_{t,i}^{p}|$, *with $y_{t,i}$ the actual and $y_{t,i}^{p}$ the predicted value for target variable t of example i.*

Obviously, the pruning algorithm can also be used to minimize these error measures by just plugging them in at line 4. Note that minimizing squared error implicitly also minimizes error measures that are a monotonically increasing function of the former, such as mean squared error (MSE) and root mean squared error (RMSE). The same holds for absolute error and mean absolute error (MAE)[1]. Therefore, the pruning algorithm can be trivially extended to all these error measures. In the empirical evaluation (Section 6), we will use the pruning algorithm in combination with squared error (Definition 2).

We end this section with a number of remarks.

- To obtain good results, it is required that the heuristic used for building the tree is "compatible" with the error measure, i.e., the heuristic should be designed to optimize the same error measure as is used in the pruning algorithm. In our case, one might say that this requirement holds because the intra-cluster variation heuristic locally optimizes squared error. Locally optimizing the error measure is however not always the best choice, e.g., in the context of classification trees, one should use information gain as heuristic and not accuracy [6].
- Some error measures that are used in regression tasks, such as Pearson correlation, are neither additive nor a monotonically increasing function of an additive measure. These error measures cannot be minimized with the pruning algorithm of Fig. 2.

---

[1] Or for any error measure based on a Minkowski distance $d(x, y) = \left(\sum |x_k - y_k|^p \right)^{\frac{1}{p}}$.

– Garofalakis et al. [12] also propose a method for pushing the constraints into the tree building phase. While this makes tree building more efficient, it has the disadvantage that the resulting tree is specific to the constraints in the given query and that it cannot be used anymore for answering queries with other constraints.

  Pushing constraints in the case of MORTs is more difficult than in the case of classification trees. The reason is that the constraint pushing algorithm requires the computation of a lower bound on the error of a partially built tree. To our knowledge, such a lower bound has not yet been defined for regression trees or MORTs.

– In this paper, we focus on MORTs, but a similar approach is also possible for predictive clustering trees [2] in general, as long as the error measure has the additivity property. For example, one could consider multi-objective classification trees (MOCTs) with as error measure the number of misclassified examples summed over the different target variables. For multi-objective trees with both numeric and nominal target variables one could define an additive error measure as the (weighted) sum of the measure on the nominal variables and that on the numeric variables.

5 Maximum Error and Syntactic Constraints

The pruning algorithm can be used to find a subtree with minimum error given a maximum size constraint. The same algorithm can also be used for solving the following, dual problem: given a maximum error constraint, find the smallest tree that satisfies this constraint. To accomplish this, one constructs a sequence of pruned trees using the algorithm of Fig. 2 for increasing values of the size constraint k, i.e., $k_1 = 1$, $k_2 = 3$, ..., $k_m = 2m - 1$, until a tree that satisfies the maximum error constraint is found. The resulting tree is the smallest tree having an error less than the maximum error constraint. (Computing the sequence of trees is computationally cheap because the pruning algorithm does not access the data; leaf_error(N) can be computed and stored for each node before running the pruning algorithm. Moreover, the Tree$[N, k]$ values of small trees can be reused when constructing larger trees.)

  In the multi-objective regression setting, one approach is to specify the maximum error summed over all target variables. Another approach is to specify a bound for each individual target variable. The latter can be useful if an application demands that some target variables are predicted more accurately than others.

  Besides size and error constraints, syntactic constraints are also important in practice. Although they are not the focus of this paper, we discuss them briefly. Syntactic constraints can be used as follows in the context of decision trees. Suppose that a domain expert knows which attributes are important for a given application. A syntactic constraint can then be used to mine for a decision tree with such an attribute in the top node. Although other trees with different attributes in the top node might be equally accurate, the one with the attribute selected by the expert will probably be more easy to interpret.

CLUS, the system that we will use in the empirical evaluation, supports this type of syntactic constraints. The idea is that the user can specify a partial tree (a subtree including the root node) in the inductive query. The induction algorithm is then initialized with this partial tree and the regular top-down induction method is used to complete it.

The ability to use syntactic (partial tree) constraints allows for a greater involvement of the user in the construction of the decision tree and a greater user influence on the final result. Some domain knowledge of the user can be taken into account in this way.

6   Empirical Evaluation

The goal of our empirical evaluation is two-fold. First we would like to evaluate the size versus error trade-off that is possible by using the size constraints in real world applications. Second, we compare single-objective and multi-objective regression. The hypothesis that we test is that a single multi-objective tree of size s is equally accurate as a set of single-objective trees, one for each target variable, each one of the same size s. Having one single small multi-objective model that is equally accurate is advantageous because it is easier to interpret than a set of trees. Moreover, it can explicitly represent dependencies between the different targets. E.g., the tree in Fig. 1 shows that $A > 3.1$ has a negative influence on both targets, while $(A \leq 3.1) \wedge (B \notin \{b_1, b_2\})$ has a negative influence on the first target, but a positive effect on the second.

6.1   Experimental Setup

The size, error and syntactic constraints have been implemented in CLUS[2]. CLUS is a system for building clustering trees [2] in general and MORTs in particular.

The data sets that we use are listed, together with their properties, in Table 1. Most data sets are of ecological nature. Each data set represents a multi-objective regression problem and the number of target variables T varies from 2 to 39. A detailed description of the data sets can be found in the references included in Table 1.

For each data set, we run CLUS in single-objective mode for each target variable and in multi-objective mode. We use 10-fold cross-validation to estimate the performance of the resulting trees. For each run, we build one large tree, store it, and then generate subtrees of this tree using the pruning algorithm discussed in Section 3 for different values of the size constraint k. We set the pruning algorithm to minimize squared error on the training set. (I.e., we follow the approach proposed in [12]. Note that the algorithm can also be used in combination with a separate validation set.)

We also include results obtained with the M5' system from the Weka toolkit [17]. Note that M5' only supports single-objective regression.

---

[2] CLUS is available from the authors upon request.

Table 1. Data set properties: domain, number of instances (N), number of input attributes (Attr), and number of target attributes ($|T|$)

	Domain	Task	N	Attr	$|T|$
E_1	Sigmea real [8]		817	4	2
E_2	Sigmea simulated [11]		10368	11	2
E_3	Soil quality 1 [9]	Acari/Coll./Biodiv.	1944	139	3
E_4		Acari groups	"	"	4
E_5		Coll. groups	"	"	5
E_6		Coll. species	"	"	39
E_7	Soil quality 2 [14]		393	48	3
E_8	Water quality [10]	Plants	1060	16	7
E_9		Animals	"	"	7
E_{10}		Chemical	1060	836	16

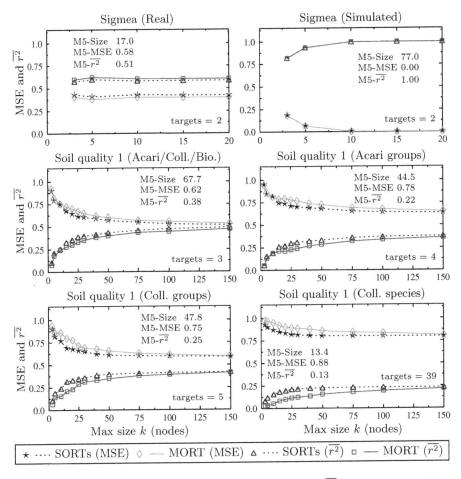

Fig. 3. Comparing the MSE and average squared correlation $\overline{r^2}$ of SORTs and MORTs for different values of the size constraint k

6.2   Results

Fig. 3 and Fig. 4 present the results. For each experiment, the mean squared error (MSE) and the average squared Pearson correlation $\overline{r^2}$ (averaged over the T target variables) is reported. For most data sets, the results for the multi-objective tree are close to these of the set of single-objective trees (SORTs), especially for large tree sizes. Most results are slightly in favor of the SORTs. Hence, the increased interpretability offered by MORTs comes at the price of a small increase in error. One exception is Soil quality 2, where MORTs perform a little better than SORTs. This effect can be explained by the fact that the target variables are highly correlated in this data set.

The largest performance difference is obtained on Soil quality 1, Collembola species. Here SORTs perform clearly better than MORTs. But the number of target variables (39) is also high. Note that this also implies that the total size of the SORTs is 39 times the size of the MORT. To investigate this effect further, we have plotted the results with total model size on the horizontal axis in Fig. 5 and Fig. 6. These results show that for a given total size, the error obtained with a MORT is in 6 out of 10 data sets clearly smaller than that of the set of SORTs. (For the other 4, the measured error is similar.)

Observe that the error curves are typically flat for a large size-interval. Therefore, tree size can in most cases be kept small without loosing much accuracy.

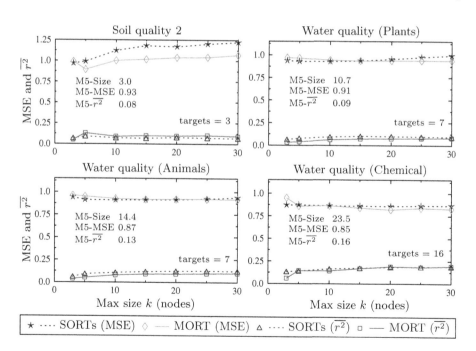

Fig. 4. Comparing the MSE and average squared correlation $\overline{r^2}$ of SORTs and MORTs for different values of the size constraint k

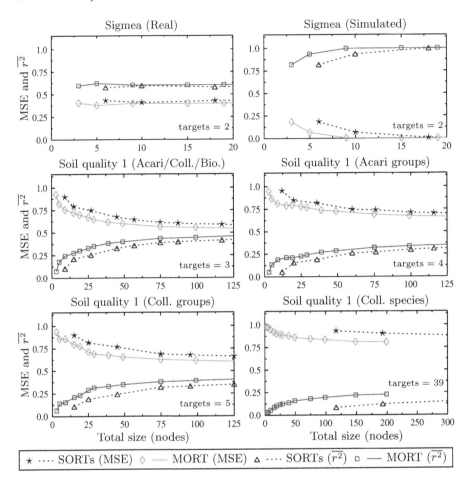

Fig. 5. MSE and average squared correlation $\overline{r^2}$ versus total model size

Based on graphs as in Fig. 3 and Fig. 4 the domain expert can easily select a tree that has a good trade-off between size (and thus interpretability) and accuracy.

It is interesting to note that no overfitting occurs, except in Soil quality 2. I.e., for most data sets, the error decreases with tree size to a constant value and does not increase again for larger trees.

The graphs also include results for M5' in regression tree mode. Accuracy-wise, the results of M5' are close to the results obtained with CLUS. The size of the M5' trees is always situated in the flat part of the error curve. For some data sets M5' generates trees that are rather large. The most extreme case is Sigmea Simulated where it generates a tree with 77 nodes. By setting a size constraint, unnecessarily large trees can be easily avoided.

To summarize, MORTs together with size constraints are a good choice if interpretability is important and a small loss in accuracy can be tolerated. If accuracy is more important, then a larger MORT might still be preferable over a set of SORTs, of which the total size will be even larger.

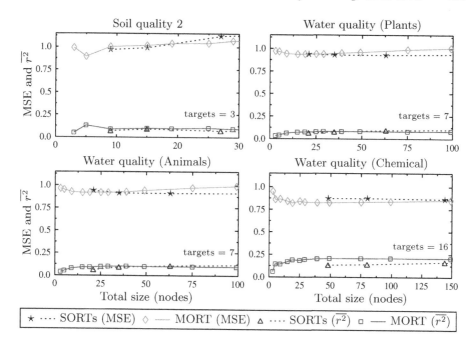

Fig. 6. MSE and average squared correlation $\overline{r^2}$ versus total model size

7   Further Work

As we already noted in Section 4, the size and error constraints can also be extended to multi-objective classification and multi-objective prediction with both nominal and numeric targets. We would like to experimentally evaluate these settings as well.

We are also planning to compare the MORT and SORT settings in more detail. Currently, we have compared the extreme case where each target attribute is predicted by a single regression tree to the other extreme case where all target attributes are predicted by one single MORT. An in-between approach could be to partition the target attributes into subsets and construct a MORT for each subset. Target attributes that depend in a similar way on the input attributes should be combined in the same subset. Clearly, constructing sets of MORTs for all possible partitions and picking the partition that minimizes a given trade-off between error and complexity would be too expensive. Therefore, we would like to investigate heuristic approaches. One method could be to construct the partition by clustering the attributes using correlation as similarity measure, i.e., to put highly correlated attributes in the same cluster. Note that we already observed in the experiments in Section 6 that MORTs perform good if the target attributes are highly correlated.

We would also like to investigate the effect of several parameters of the input data on the relative performance of a MORT compared to a set of SORTs, such as training set size or the effect of noise.

Furthermore, we would like investigate the use of MORTs in ensemble methods. This has already been explored to some extent by Sain and Carmack [16], who propose a boosting approach with MORTs. Similarly, MORTs could be used for bagging [4] and in random forests [5].

8   Conclusion

In this paper, we have proposed a system for constrained based induction of multi-objective regression trees (MORTs). It supports size, error and syntactic constraints and works in two steps. In a first step, a large tree is built that satisfies the syntactic constraints. This tree is stored in the inductive database and used in a second step to generate trees that satisfy particular size or error constraints. To accomplish this, we have extended the pruning algorithm introduced by Garofalakis et al. to MORTs. Two modes of operation are supported: (1) given a maximum size constraint, return a subtree with the smallest error, and (2) given a maximum error constraint, return the smallest subtree that satisfies this constraint.

While we have focused on MORTs, the pruning algorithm can also be extended to predictive clustering trees in general. E.g., it can also be used for multi-objective classification and multi-objective prediction with both nominal and numeric targets.

In an empirical evaluation, we have tested our approach on a number of real world data sets. Our evaluation shows (1) that the accuracy of MORTs is close to that of a set of single-objective regression trees, each of the same size, and (2) that in many cases tree size can be reduced significantly (thereby increasing interpretability) at the expense of only a small accuracy loss. MORTs together with size constraints are thus a good choice if interpretability is important and a small loss in accuracy can be tolerated. Moreover, if we consider total size instead of average tree size, we observe that for a given total size, the error obtained with a MORT is smaller than or similar to that of a set of SORTs.

Acknowledgments

The authors are grateful to Hendrik Blockeel who provided valuable comments on the text and the empirical evaluation. Jan Struyf is a postdoctoral fellow of the Fund for Scientific Research of Flanders (FWO-Vlaanderen).

References

1. H. Almuallim. An efficient algorithm for optimal pruning of decision trees. *Artificial Intelligence*, 83(2):347–362, 1996.
2. H. Blockeel, L. De Raedt, and J. Ramon. Top-down induction of clustering trees. In *Proceedings of the 15th International Conference on Machine Learning*, pages 55–63, 1998.
3. M. Bohanec and I. Bratko. Trading accuracy for simplicity in decision trees. *Machine Learning*, 15(3):223–250, 1994.

4. L. Breiman. Bagging predictors. *Machine Learning*, 24(2):123–140, 1996.
5. L. Breiman. Random forests. *Machine Learning*, 45(1):5–32, 2001.
6. L. Breiman, J.H. Friedman, R.A. Olshen, and C.J. Stone. *Classification and Regression Trees*. Wadsworth, Belmont, 1984.
7. L. De Raedt. A perspective on inductive databases. *SIGKDD Explorations*, 4(2):69–77, 2002.
8. D. Demšar, M. Debeljak, C. Lavigne, and S. Džeroski. Modelling pollen dispersal of genetically modified oilseed rape within the field, 2005. Abstract presented at The Annual Meeting of the Ecological Society of America, Montreal, Canada, 7-12 August 2005.
9. D. Demšar, S. Džeroski, P. Henning Krogh, T. Larsen, and J. Struyf. Using multiobjective classification to model communities of soil microarthropods. *Ecological Modelling*, 2005. To appear.
10. S. Džeroski, D. Demšar, and J. Grbović. Predicting chemical parameters of river water quality from bioindicator data. *Applied Intelligence*, 13(1):7–17, 2000.
11. S. Džeroski, N. Colbach, and A. Messean. Analysing the effect of field characteristics on gene flow between oilseed rape varieties and volunteers with regression trees, 2005. Submitted to the The Second International Conference on Co-existence between GM and non-GM based agricultural supply chains (GMCC-05). Montpellier, France, 14-15 November 2005.
12. M. Garofalakis, D. Hyun, R. Rastogi, and K. Shim. Building decision trees with constraints. *Data Mining and Knowledge Discovery*, 7(2):187–214, 2003.
13. T. Imielinski and H. Mannila. A database perspective on knowledge discovery. *Communications of the ACM*, 39(11):58–64, 1996.
14. C. Kampichler, S. Džeroski, and R. Wieland. The application of machine learning techniques to the analysis of soil ecological data bases: Relationships between habitat features and collembola community characteristics. *Soil Biology and Biochemistry*, 32:197–209, 2000.
15. J. R. Quinlan. *C4.5: Programs for Machine Learning*. Morgan Kaufmann series in Machine Learning. Morgan Kaufmann, 1993.
16. R. S. Sain and P. S. Carmack. Boosting multi-objective regression trees. *Computing Science and Statistics*, 34:232–241, 2002.
17. I. Witten and E. Frank. *Data Mining: Practical machine learning tools and techniques*. Morgan Kaufmann, 2005. 2nd Edition.

Learning Predictive Clustering Rules

Bernard Ženko[1], Sašo Džeroski[1], and Jan Struyf[2]

[1] Department of Knowledge Technologies, Jožef Stefan Institute, Slovenia
Bernard.Zenko@ijs.si, Saso.Dzeroski@ijs.si
[2] Department of Computer Science, Katholieke Universiteit Leuven, Belgium
Jan.Struyf@cs.kuleuven.be

Abstract. The two most commonly addressed data mining tasks are predictive modelling and clustering. Here we address the task of predictive clustering, which contains elements of both and generalizes them to some extent. Predictive clustering has been mainly evaluated in the context of trees. In this paper, we extend predictive clustering toward rules. Each cluster is described by a rule and different clusters are allowed to overlap since the sets of examples covered by different rules do not need to be disjoint. We propose a system for learning these predictive clustering rules, which is based on a heuristic sequential covering algorithm. The heuristic takes into account both the precision of the rules (compactness w.r.t. the target space) and the compactness w.r.t. the input space, and the two can be traded-off by means of a parameter. We evaluate our system in the context of several multi-objective classification problems.

1 Introduction

Predictive modeling or supervised learning aims at constructing models that can predict the value of a target attribute (dependent variable) from the known values for a set of input attributes (independent variables). A wide array of predictive modeling methods exist, which produce more or less (or not at all) interpretable models. Typical representatives of the group of methods that result in understandable and interpretable models are decision tree learning [14] and rule learning [7].

Clustering [9], on the other hand, is an unsupervised learning method. It tries to find subgroups of examples or clusters with homogeneous values for all attributes, not just the target attribute. In fact, the target attribute is usually not even defined in a clustering task. The result is a set of clusters and not necessarily their descriptions or models; usually we can link new examples to the constructed clusters based on e.g., proximity in the attribute space.

Predictive modeling and clustering are therefore regarded as quite different techniques. Nevertheless, different viewpoints also exist [10] which stress the many similarities that some predictive modeling techniques, most notably techniques that partition the example space, such as decision trees, share with clustering. Decision trees partition the set of examples into subsets with homogeneous values for *the target attribute*, while clustering methods search for subsets in which the examples have homogeneous values for *all the attributes*.

F. Bonchi and J.-F. Boulicaut (Eds.): KDID 2005, LNCS 3933, pp. 234–250, 2006.
© Springer-Verlag Berlin Heidelberg 2006

In this paper, we consider the task of predictive clustering [1, 2], which contains elements of both predictive modelling and clustering and generalizes them to some extent. In predictive clustering, one can simultaneously consider homogeneity along the target attribute and the input attributes, and trade-off one for the other. It has been argued [1] that predictive clustering is useful in noisy domains and in domains with missing values for the target attribute. Furthermore, predictive clustering has been proven useful in applications with non-trivial targets such as multi-objective classification and regression [2, 17], ranking [20], and hierarchical multi-classification [18].

Predictive clustering has been evaluated mainly in the context of trees. In this paper we extend predictive clustering toward rules. We call the resulting framework predictive clustering rules (PCRs). The task of learning PCRs generalizes the task of rule induction, on one hand, and clustering, and in particular item set constrained clustering [15, 16], on the other.

Since learning PCRs is a form of constrained clustering, it is directly related to constraint-based data mining and inductive databases (IDBs). Constraint-based clustering is an under-researched topic in constraint-based data mining and the present research is a step towards rectifying this. Bringing the two most common data mining tasks closer together (as done in predictive clustering) moves us towards finding a general framework for data mining, which is also the main goal of IDBs.

The rest of this paper is organized as follows. In the next section, we discuss prediction, clustering and predictive clustering in more detail. Section 3 extends predictive clustering toward rules and proposes the first system for building predictive clustering rules. The algorithm used in the system is a heuristic sequential covering algorithm and the heuristic trades-off homogeneity w.r.t. the target attributes and homogeneity w.r.t. the input attributes. We compare our system to related approaches in Section 4. Section 5 evaluates the system on a number of multi-objective classification and regression data sets. The paper ends with a discussion of further work and a conclusion.

2   Prediction, Clustering, and Predictive Clustering

The tasks of predictive modelling and clustering are two of the oldest and most commonly addressed tasks in data analysis and data mining. Here we briefly introduce each of them and discuss predictive clustering, a task that combines elements of both prediction and clustering.

2.1   Predictive Modelling

Predictive modeling aims at constructing models that can predict a target property of an object from a description of the object. Predictive models are learned from sets of examples, where each example has the form (D, T), with D being an object description and T a target property value. While a variety of languages ranging from propositional to first order logic have been used for D, T is almost always considered to consist of a single target attribute called the class:

if this attribute is discrete we are dealing with a classification problem and if continuous with a regression problem.

In practice, D is most commonly a vector and each element of this vector is the value for a particular attribute (attribute-value representation). In the remainder of the paper, we will consider both D and T to be vectors of attribute values (discrete or real-valued). If T is a vector with several target attributes, then we call the prediction task multi-objective prediction. If T only contains discrete attributes we speak of multi-objective classification. If T only contains continuous attributes we speak of multi-objective regression.

Predictive models can take many different forms that range from linear equations to logic programs. Two commonly used types of models are decision trees [14] and rules [7]. Unlike (regression) equations that provide a single predictive model for the entire example space, trees and rules divide the space of examples into subspaces and provide a simple prediction or predictive model for each of these.

2.2   Clustering and Clustering Trees

Clustering [9] in general is concerned with grouping objects into classes of similar objects. Given a set of examples (object descriptions), the task of clustering is to partition these examples into subsets, called clusters. Note that examples do not contain a target property to be predicted, but only an object description (which is typically a vector of attribute-values D). The goal of clustering is to achieve high similarity between objects within individual clusters and low similarity between objects that belong to different clusters.

Conventional clustering focuses on distance-based cluster analysis. The notion of a distance (or conversely, similarity) is crucial here: examples are considered to be points in a metric space (a space with a distance measure). A prototype (or prototypical example) may be used as a representative for a cluster. Usually, the prototype is the point with the lowest average distance to all the examples in the cluster, i.e., the mean or the medoid of the examples.

In conceptual clustering [12], a symbolic representation of the resulting clusters is produced in addition to the partition into clusters: we can thus consider each cluster to be a concept (much like a class in classification). In this context, a decision tree structure may be used to represent a hierarchical clustering: such a tree is called a clustering tree [1]. In a clustering tree each node represents a cluster. The conjunction of conditions on the path from the root to that node gives a symbolic representation of the cluster. Essentially, each cluster has a symbolic description in the form of a rule (IF conjunction of conditions THEN cluster), while the tree structure represents the hierarchy of clusters. Clusters that are not on the same branch of a tree do not overlap.

Given the above, predictive modelling approaches which divide the set of examples into subsets, such as decision tree and rule induction, are in a sense very similar to clustering. A major difference is that they partition the space of examples into subsets with homogeneous values of the *target attribute*, while (distance-based) clustering methods seek subsets with homogeneous values of

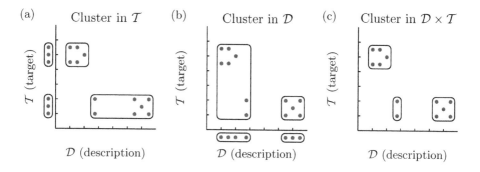

Fig. 1. Predictive modelling (a), clustering (b), and predictive clustering (c)

the *descriptive attributes*. This is illustrated in Fig. 1. Assume that each example has a description $D \in \mathcal{D}$ and is labeled with a target value $T \in \mathcal{T}$. A predictive tree learner will build a tree with leaves that are as pure as possible w.r.t. the target value, i.e., it will form clusters that are homogeneous in $\mathcal{T}$, as shown in Fig. 1.a. The reason is that the quality criterion that is used to build the tree (e.g., information gain [14]) is based on the target attributes only[1]. In unsupervised clustering, on the other hand, there is no target value defined and the clusters that are generated will be homogeneous w.r.t. $\mathcal{D}$, as shown in Fig. 1.b. In the next section, we will consider predictive clustering, which in general searches for clusters that are homogeneous w.r.t. to both $\mathcal{D}$ and $\mathcal{T}$ (Fig. 1.c).

2.3   Predictive Clustering

The task of predictive clustering [2] combines elements from both prediction and clustering. As is common in clustering, we seek clusters of examples that are similar to each other (and dissimilar to examples in other clusters), but in general taking both the descriptive and the target attributes into account. In addition, a predictive model must be associated with each cluster; the model gives a prediction of the target variables T in terms of the attributes D for all examples that are established to belong to that cluster.

In the simplest and most common case, the predictive model associated to a cluster would be the projection on T of the prototype of the examples that belong to that cluster. This would be a simple average when T is a single continuous variable. In the discrete case, it would be a probability distribution across the discrete values or the mode thereof. When T is a vector, the prototype would be a vector of averages and distributions/modes.

To summarize, in predictive clustering, each cluster has both a symbolic description (in terms of a language bias over D) and a predictive model (a prototype

---

[1] Because the leaves of a decision tree have conjunctive descriptions in $\mathcal{D}$, the corresponding clusters will also have some homogeneity w.r.t. $\mathcal{D}$, but the latter is not optimized by the system.

in T) associated to it, i.e., the resulting clustering is defined by a symbolic model. If we consider a tree based representation, then this model is called a predictive clustering tree. Predictive clustering trees have been proposed by Blockeel et al. [2]. In the next section, we will propose predictive clustering rules, a framework in which the clustering model is represented as a rule set.

3   Predictive Clustering Rules (PCRs)

This section presents the main contribution of this paper, which is the predictive clustering rules (PCRs) framework. We start with a general definition of PCRs. Then we apply this general definition to the multi-objective prediction setting. Finally, we propose a system for learning PCRs in this setting.

3.1   Definition

The task of learning a set of PCRs is defined as follows.

Given:

  - a target space $\mathcal{T}$
  - a description space $\mathcal{D}$
  - a set of examples $E = \{e_i\}$, with $e_i \in \mathcal{D} \times \mathcal{T}$
  - a declarative language bias B over $\mathcal{D}$
  - a distance measure d that computes the distance between two examples
  - a prototype function p that computes the prototype of a set of examples

Find a set of clusters, where

  - each cluster is associated with a description expressed in B
  - each cluster has an associated prediction expressed as a prototype
  - within-cluster distance is low (similarity is high) and
  - between-cluster distance is high (similarity is low)

Each cluster can thus be represented as a so-called predictive clustering rule, which is a rule of the form "IF cluster description THEN cluster prototype".

Example 1. Consider the data set shown in Fig 2.a. It has two numeric attributes: a is a descriptive attribute and b is the target attribute, i.e., $\mathcal{D} = \mathcal{T} = \mathbb{R}$. Suppose that the distance metric is the Euclidean distance over $\mathbb{R}^2$. The corresponding prototype is the vector average. If the language bias B allows conjunctions of tests comparing a to a particular constant, then a possible set of PCRs for this data set is shown in Fig 2.b.

Note that the description in the conditional part of a PCR only takes D into account and not T. The reason is that it must be possible to apply the rule to unseen examples later on for which T is not defined.

    There are two main differences between PCRs and predictive clustering trees. The first difference is that predictive clustering trees represent a hierarchical

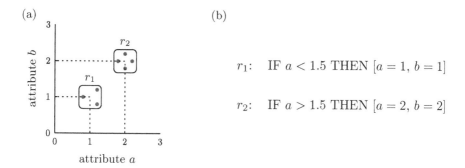

(a)

(b)

r_1:   IF $a < 1.5$ THEN $[a = 1, b = 1]$

r_2:   IF $a > 1.5$ THEN $[a = 2, b = 2]$

Fig. 2. A data set (left) and the corresponding set of predictive clustering rules (right)

clustering of the data whereas the clustering corresponding to a set of PCRs is flat. The other difference is that the clusters defined by a set of PCRs may overlap. In fact, there are two possible interpretations of a set of PCRs: the rules can be ordered and treated as a decision list. In that case, a given example belongs to the cluster of the first rule in the list that fires and the resulting clustering is disjoint. On the other hand, if the rules are considered unordered, then the clusters may overlap as several rules may apply to a given example. If in the latter case a set of rules fire for a given example, then a method is required for combining the predictions of the different rules. Such a method is not required in predictive clustering trees since in that case the clusters are guaranteed to be disjoint. We will propose a suitable combining method later in the paper.

3.2   PCRs for Multi-objective Prediction (MOP)

In this section, we discuss the PCR framework in the context of multi-objective prediction (MOP) tasks. This includes multi-objective classification and multi-objective regression as discussed before. As a result, the examples will be of the form (D, T) with D and T both vectors of attribute-values. MOP has two main advantages over using a separate model for each target attribute: (1) a single MOP model is usually much smaller than the total size of the individual models for all attributes, and (2) a MOP model may explicitate dependencies between the different target variables [17].

The distance metric that we will use in the clustering process takes both D and T into account and is defined as follows.

$$d = (1 - \tau)d_D + \tau d_T. \tag{1}$$

It has two components, one for the descriptive part d_D and a second one for the target part d_T and the relative contribution of the two components can be changed by means of the parameter τ.

In our rule induction algorithm, we will estimate the quality of a (partial) rule that covers a set of examples S as the average distance of an example in S

to the prototype of S. We will call this the "compactness" of the rule. Because the attributes can in general be nominal or numeric, different measures for each type are needed which are then combined (added) into a single measure.

For nominal attributes, the prototype is a vector with as components the frequencies of each of the attribute's values in the given set of examples S, i.e., for an attribute with k possible values (v_1 to v_k), the prototype is of the form $[f_1, f_2, \ldots, f_k]$, with f_i the frequency of v_i in S. The distance between an example and the prototype is defined as follows: if the attribute value for the example is v_i, then the distance to the prototype is defined as $(1 - f_i)$. For numeric attributes, the prototype is the mean of the attribute's values and the distance between an example and the prototype is computed as the absolute difference. Numeric attributes are normalized during a preprocessing step such that their mean is zero and their variance is one.

Example 2. Consider a data set with a nominal attribute a with possible values $\oplus$ and $\ominus$ and a numeric attribute b. There are three examples in S: $[\oplus, 1]$, $[\oplus, 2]$, and $[\ominus, 1]$. The prototype for a is the vector $[2/3, 1/3]$ and the prototype for b is 2. The compactness of a is $4/9$ and the compactness of b is $2/3$. The combined compactness is $2/3 + 4/9 = 10/9$.

Note that our compactness measure is actually an "incompactness" measure, since smaller values mean more compact sets of examples.

The declarative bias will restrict our hypothesis language to rules consisting of conjunctions of attribute-value conditions over the attributes D. In particular, we consider subset tests for nominal attributes and inequality tests for numeric attributes. Additional language constraints are planned for consideration.

3.3 Learning Predictive Clustering Rules

This section describes our system for learning PCRs. The majority of rule induction methods are based on a sequential covering algorithm and among these the CN2 algorithm [4] is well known. Our system is based on this algorithm, but several important parts are modified. In this section we first briefly describe the original CN2 algorithm, and then we present our modifications.

Rule Induction with CN2. The CN2 algorithm iteratively constructs rules that cover examples with homogeneous target variable values. The heuristic used to guide the search is simply the accuracy of the rule under construction. After a rule has been constructed, the examples covered by this rule are removed from the training set, and the procedure is repeated on the new data set until the data set is empty or no new rules are found. The rules constructed in this way are ordered, meaning that they can be used for prediction as a decision list; we test rules on a new example one by one and the first rule that fires is used for prediction of the target value of this example. Alternatively, CN2 can also construct unordered rules if only correctly classified examples are removed from the training set after finding each rule and if rules are built for each class in turn. When using unordered rules for prediction, several rules can fire on each example and a combining method is required as discussed before.

The Search Heuristic: Compactness. The main difference between CN2 and the approach presented in this paper is the heuristic that is used for guiding the search for rules. The purpose of the heuristic is to evaluate different rules; it should measure the quality of each rule separately and/or the quality of the whole rule set.

One of the most important properties of rules (and other models) is their accuracy, and standard CN2 simply uses this as a heuristic. Accuracy is only connected to the target attribute. Our goal when developing predictive clustering rules was (besides accuracy) that the induced rules should cover compact subsets of examples, just as clustering does. For this purpose we need a heuristic which takes into account the target attributes as well as the descriptive attributes.

As explained above, we will use the compactness (average distance of an example covered by a rule to the prototype of this set of examples). The compactness takes into account both the descriptive and the target attributes and is a weighted sum of the compactness along each of the dimensions (the latter are normalized to be between 0 and 1). At present only a general weight τ is applied for putting the emphasis on the targets attributes ($\tau = 1$) or the input attributes ($\tau = 0$): target attributes should in general have higher weights in order to guide the search toward accurate rules.

Weighted Covering. The standard covering algorithm removes the examples covered by a rule from the training set in each iteration. As a consequence, subsequent rules are constructed on smaller example subsets which can be improperly biased and can have small coverage. To overcome these shortages we employ the weighted covering algorithm [11]. The difference is that once an example is covered by a new rule, it is not removed from the training set but instead, its weight is decreased. As a result, the already covered example will be less likely covered in the next iterations. We use the additive weighting scheme, which means that the weight of an example after being covered m times is equal to $\frac{1}{1+m}$. Finally, when the example is covered more than a predefined number of times (in our experiments five), the example is completely removed from the training set.

Probabilistic Classification. As already mentioned, the original CN2 algorithm can induce ordered or unordered rules. In case of ordered rules (i.e., a decision list) the classification is straightforward. We scan the rules one by one and whichever rule fires first on a given example is used for prediction. If no rule fires, the default rule is used. When classifying with unordered rules, CN2 collects class distributions of all rules that fire on an example and uses them for weighted voting. We use the same probabilistic classification scheme even though our unordered rules are not induced for each possible class value separately.

4   Related Work

Predictive modeling and clustering are regarded as quite different tasks. While there are many approaches addressing each of predictive modelling and clustering, few approaches look at both or try to relate them. A different viewpoint is taken by Langley [10]: predictive modeling and clustering have many similarities and this has motivated some recent research on combining prediction and clustering.

The approach presented in this paper is closely related to predictive clustering trees [2], which also address the task of predictive clustering. The systems TILDE [2] and CLUS [3] use a modified top-down induction of decision trees algorithm to construct clustering trees (which can predict values of more than one target variables simultaneously). So far, however, distances used in TILDE and CLUS systems have considered attributes or classes separately, but not both together, even though the idea was presented in [1].

Our approach uses a rule-based representation for predictive clustering. As such, it is closely related to approaches for rule induction, and among these in particular CN2 [4]. However, it extends rule induction to the more general task of multi-objective prediction. While some work exists on multi-objective classification with decision trees (e.g., [19]), the authors are not aware of any work on rule-induction for multi-objective classification. Also, little work exists on rule-based regression (e.g., R2 [21] for propositional learning and FORS [8] for first order logic learning), let alone rule-based multi-objective regression (or multi-objective prediction in general, with mixed continuous and discrete targets).

Related to rule induction is subgroup discovery [11], which tries to find and describe interesting groups of examples. While subgroup discovery algorithms are similar to rule induction ones, they have introduced interesting innovations, including the weighted covering approach used in our system.

Another related approach to combining clustering and classification is *itemset constrained clustering* [15, 16]. Here the attributes describing each example are separated in two groups, called feature items and objective attributes. Clustering is done on the objective attributes, but only clusters which can be described in terms of frequent item sets (using the feature items attributes) are constructed. As a result each cluster can be classified by a corresponding frequent item set.

As in our approach, itemset classified clustering tries to find groups of examples with small variance of the objective attributes. As compared to itemset classified clustering, our approach allows both discrete (and not only binary attributes / items) and continuous variables on the feature/attribute side, as well as the objective/target side. Itemset constrained clustering is also related to subgroup discovery, as it tries to find interesting groups of examples, rather than a set of (overlapping) clusters that cover all examples. A second important difference is that in itemset classified clustering the distance metric takes only the objective attributes into account, whereas the rules constructed by our approach are also compact w.r.t. the descriptive space.

5   Experiments

The current implementation of predictive clustering rules has been tested on several classification problems with multiple target attributes. For each data set two sets of experiments have been performed. First, we tried to test the performance of our method when predicting multiple target attributes at once in comparison to single target attribute prediction task. In the second set of experiments we investigated the influence of the target weighting parameter (τ) on the accuracy and compactness of induced rules.

5.1   Data Sets

There are not a lot of publicly available data sets suitable for multi-target classification. However, some of the data sets from the UCI repository [13] can also be used for this purpose, namely the data sets *monks, solar-flare,* and *thyroid*. The first two data sets have three target attributes each, while the third has seven.

In addition to these UCI data sets we have also used Slovenian rivers water quality data set (*water-quality*). The data set comprises biological and chemical data that were collected through regular monitoring of rivers in Slovenia. The data come from the Environmental Agency of the Republic of Slovenia that performs water quality monitoring for most Slovenian rivers and maintains a database of water quality samples. The data cover a six year period, from 1990 to 1995 and have been previously used in [5].

Biological samples are taken twice a year, once in summer and once in winter, while physical and chemical analysis are performed several times a year for each sampling site. The physical and chemical samples include the measured values of 15 different parameters. The biological samples include a list of all taxa (plant and animal species) present at the sampling site. All the attributes of the data set are listed in Table 1. In total, 1060 water samples are available in the data

Table 1. The attributes of the river water quality data set

Independent attributes physical & chemical properties numeric type	Target attributes taxa – presences/absences nominal type (0,1)
water temperature	Cladophora sp.
alkalinity (pH)	Gongrosira incrustans
electrical conductivity	Oedogonium sp.
dissolved O_2	Stigeoclonium tenue
O_2 saturation	Melosira varians
CO_2 conc.	Nitzschia palea
total hardness	Audouinella(Chantransia) chalybea
NO_2 conc.	Erpobdella octoculata
NO_3 conc.	Gammarus fossarum
NH_4 conc.	Baetis rhodani
PO_4 conc.	Hydropsyche sp.
Cl conc.	Rhyacophila sp.
SiO_2 conc.	Simulium sp.
chemical oxygen demand – $KMnO_4$	Tubifex sp.
chemical oxygen demand – $K_2Cr_2O_7$	
biological oxygen demand (BOD)	

set. In our experiments we have considered the physical and chemical properties as independent attributes, and presences/absences of taxa as target attributes.

5.2 Results

The first set of experiments was performed in order to test the appropriateness of predictive clustering rules for multiple target prediction. In all experiments the minimal number of examples covered by a rule was 20, and the weight of target attributes (τ) was set to 1. The results of 10-fold cross validation can be seen for each data set separately in Tables 2, 3, 4, and 5. The first columns in tables are the accuracies for each target attribute as predicted by the PCR multi-target models and in the second columns are accuracies as predicted by the PCR single-target models. Third and fourth columns are accuracies for predictive clustering trees (PCT). The last rows in the tables give the average accuracies across all target attributes.

Looking at these average accuracies we can see that the performance of models predicting all classes together is comparable to the performance of single target models. There are no significant differences for the monks, solar-flare and thyroid data sets, while the multi-target model is somewhat worse than single-target models on the water quality data set. When comparing predictive clustering rules to predictive clustering trees, the performance of the latter is somewhat better on the thyroid and water quality data set but a little worse on the monks data set; there are no differences on the solar-flare data set.

Table 2. Monks data set. Accuracies of predictive clustering rules (PCR) and predictive clustering trees (PCT) used for multi-objective prediction of all target attributes together and for single target prediction of each target attribute separately.

Target attribute	PCR All	Indiv.	PCT All	Indiv.
monk–1	0.803	0.810	0.711	0.764
monk–2	0.671	0.669	0.664	0.627
monk–3	0.935	0.935	0.972	0.972
Average accuracy	0.803	0.805	0.782	0.788

Table 3. Solar-flare data set. Accuracies of predictive clustering rules (PCR) and predictive clustering trees (PCT) used for multi-objective prediction of all target attributes together and for single target prediction of each target attribute separately.

Target attribute	PCR All	Indiv.	PCT All	Indiv.
class–c	0.828	0.829	0.829	0.826
class–m	0.966	0.966	0.966	0.966
class–x	0.995	0.995	0.995	0.995
Average accuracy	0.930	0.930	0.930	0.929

Table 4. Thyroid data set. Accuracies of predictive clustering rules (PCR) and predictive clustering trees (PCT) used for multi-objective prediction of all target attributes together and for single target prediction of each target attribute separately.

Target attribute	PCR All	Indiv.	PCT All	Indiv.
hyperthyroid	0.974	0.975	0.983	0.984
hypothyroid	0.941	0.947	0.989	0.989
binding protein	0.955	0.961	0.974	0.975
general health	0.970	0.972	0.984	0.985
replacement theory	0.961	0.963	0.985	0.990
antithyroid treatment	0.996	0.996	0.996	0.996
discordant results	0.979	0.979	0.987	0.989
Average accuracy	0.968	0.971	0.986	0.987

Table 5. Water quality data set. Accuracies of predictive clustering rules (PCR) and predictive clustering trees (PCT) used for multi-objective prediction of all target attributes together and for single target prediction of each target attribute separately.

Target attribute	PCR All	Indiv.	PCT All	Indiv.
Cladophora sp.	0.594	0.629	0.630	0.648
Gongrosira incrustans	0.733	0.729	0.722	0.665
Oedogonium sp.	0.713	0.717	0.723	0.710
Stigeoclonium tenue	0.795	0.790	0.796	0.771
Melosira varians	0.569	0.611	0.638	0.643
Nitzschia palea	0.688	0.662	0.714	0.708
Audouinella chalybea	0.751	0.756	0.747	0.712
Erpobdella octoculata	0.721	0.741	0.712	0.691
Gammarus fossarum	0.628	0.654	0.664	0.688
Baetis rhodani	0.676	0.723	0.686	0.700
Hydropsyche sp.	0.584	0.604	0.614	0.630
Rhyacophila sp.	0.686	0.710	0.708	0.709
Simulium sp.	0.633	0.635	0.593	0.642
Tubifex sp.	0.728	0.745	0.735	0.739
Average accuracy	0.679	0.693	0.692	0.690

The task of the second set of experiments was to evaluate the influence of the target weighting parameter (τ) on the accuracy and cluster compactness of induced rules (Tables 6, 7, 8, and 9). Rules were induced for predicting all target attributes together with six different values of the τ parameter. At the bottom of each table are the average accuracies of 10-fold cross-validation and average compactness of subsets of examples (clusters) covered by rules in each model.

Table 6. Monks data set. The accuracy and cluster compactness of predictive clustering rules used for multiple target prediction of all target attributes together with different target attributes weightings (τ).

| Target attribute | τ | | | | | |
	0.5	0.7	0.8	0.9	0.95	1
monk–1	0.843	0.840	0.806	0.833	0.831	0.803
monk–2	0.671	0.671	0.671	0.671	0.671	0.671
monk–3	0.949	0.965	0.975	0.958	0.938	0.935
Average accuracy	0.821	0.826	0.817	0.821	0.813	0.803
Average compactness	0.487	0.486	0.486	0.495	0.506	0.516

Table 7. Solar flare data set. The accuracy and cluster compactness of predictive clustering rules used for multiple target prediction of all target attributes together with different target attributes weightings (τ).

| Target attribute | τ | | | | | |
	0.5	0.7	0.8	0.9	0.95	1
class–c	0.829	0.829	0.829	0.829	0.829	0.828
class–m	0.966	0.966	0.966	0.966	0.966	0.966
class–x	0.995	0.995	0.995	0.995	0.995	0.995
Average accuracy	0.930	0.930	0.930	0.930	0.930	0.930
Average compactness	0.158	0.159	0.161	0.181	0.207	0.239

Table 8. Thyroid data set. The accuracy and cluster compactness of predictive clustering rules used for multiple target prediction of all target attributes together with different target attributes weightings (τ).

| Target attribute | τ | | | | | |
	0.5	0.7	0.8	0.9	0.95	1
hyperthyroid	0.974	0.974	0.974	0.974	0.974	0.974
hypothyroid	0.927	0.927	0.927	0.927	0.928	0.941
binding protein	0.955	0.955	0.955	0.955	0.955	0.955
general health	0.938	0.938	0.938	0.938	0.939	0.970
replacement theory	0.961	0.961	0.961	0.961	0.961	0.961
antithyroid treatment	0.996	0.996	0.996	0.996	0.996	0.996
discordant results	0.979	0.979	0.979	0.979	0.979	0.979
Average accuracy	0.961	0.961	0.961	0.961	0.962	0.968
Average compompactness	1739	1797	1705	1591	1603	1605

The rules induced with larger weighting of the non-target attributes (smaller τ) are on average more compact on the monks and solar-flare data sets (smaller number for compactness means more compact subsets) while there is no clear trend for the thyroid data set and no influence at all on the water quality data

Table 9. Water quality data set. The accuracy and cluster compactness of predictive clustering rules used for multiple target prediction of all target attributes together with different target attributes weightings (τ).

Target attribute	τ					
	0.5	0.7	0.8	0.9	0.95	1
Cladophora sp.	0.586	0.593	0.597	0.599	0.600	0.594
Gongrosira incrustans	0.733	0.733	0.733	0.733	0.733	0.733
Oedogonium sp.	0.716	0.719	0.716	0.717	0.718	0.713
Stigeoclonium tenue	0.792	0.793	0.793	0.793	0.793	0.795
Melosira varians	0.580	0.584	0.578	0.581	0.575	0.569
Nitzschia palea	0.656	0.664	0.657	0.655	0.661	0.688
Audouinella chalybea	0.753	0.753	0.753	0.753	0.753	0.751
Erpobdella octoculata	0.738	0.742	0.742	0.741	0.742	0.721
Gammarus fossarum	0.628	0.641	0.629	0.630	0.632	0.628
Baetis rhodani	0.676	0.676	0.676	0.676	0.676	0.676
Hydropsyche sp.	0.566	0.564	0.568	0.567	0.565	0.584
Rhyacophila sp.	0.684	0.685	0.685	0.685	0.685	0.686
Simulium sp.	0.639	0.640	0.640	0.640	0.646	0.633
Tubifex sp.	0.732	0.729	0.725	0.730	0.731	0.728
Average accuracy	0.677	0.680	0.678	0.679	0.679	0.679
Average compactness	0.348	0.348	0.348	0.348	0.348	0.350

set. Larger weighting of the non-target attributes has very little effect on the accuracy of the models except in case of the monks data set, where it improves accuracy.

6   Conclusions and Further Work

In this paper, we have considered the data mining task of predictive clustering. This is a very general task that contains many features of (and thus to a large extent generalizes over) the tasks of predictive modelling and clustering. While this task has been considered before, we have defined it both more precisely and in a more general form (i.e., to consider distances on both target and attribute variables and to consider clustering rules in addition to trees).

We have introduced the notion of clustering rules and focused on the task of learning predictive clustering rules for multi-objective prediction. The task of inducing PCRs generalizes the task of rule induction, extending it to multi-objective classification, regression and in general prediction. It also generalizes some forms of distance-based clustering and in particular itemset constrained clustering (e.g., it allows both discrete and continuous variables on the feature/attribute side, as well as the objective/target side).

Learning PCRs and predictive clustering in general can be viewed as constrained clustering, where clusters that have an explicit representation in a language of constraints are sought. At present PCR clusters are arbitrary rectangles in the attribute space, as arbitrary conjunctions of conditions are allowed in the rule antecedents. However, one can easily imagine additional language constraints being imposed on rule antecedents.

Viewing precitive clustering as constrained clustering makes it directly related to constraint-based data mining and inductive databases (IDBs). Constraint-based clustering is an under-researched topic in constraint-based data mining and the present research is a step towards rectifying this. Bringing the two most common data mining tasks closer together (as done in predictive clustering) moves us towards finding a general framework for data mining, which is also the main goal of IDBs.

We have implemented a preliminary version of a system for learning PCRs for multi-objective classification. We have also performed some preliminary experiments on several data sets. The results show that a single rule-set for MOC can be as accurate as the collection of rule-sets for individual prediction of each target. The accuracies are also comparable to those of predictive clustering trees. Experiments in varying the weight of target vs. non-target attributes in the compactness heuristic used in the search for rules show that non-zero weights for non-targets increase overall compactness and sometimes also accuracy.

Note, however, that many more experiments are necessary to evaluate the proposed paradigm and implementation. These would include experiments on additional data sets for multi-objective prediction, where classification, regression and a mixture thereof should be considered. Also, a comparison to other approaches to constrained clustering would be in order.

Other directions for further work concern further development of the PCR paradigm and its implementation. At present, our implementation only considers multi-objective classification, but can be easily extended to regression problems, and also to mixed, classification/regression problems. Currently, the heuristic guiding the search for rules does not take the number of covered examples in consideration. Consequently, construction of overly specific rules can only be prevented by means of setting the minimum number of examples covered by a rule. Adding a coverage dependent part to the heuristic would enable the induction of compact rules with sufficient coverage. Another possibility is the use of some sort of significance testing analogous to significance testing of the target variable distribution employed by CN2.

Finally, the selection of weights for calculating the distance measure (and the compactness heuristic) is an open issue. One side of this is the weighting of target vs. non-target variables. Another side is the assignment of relevance-based weights to the attributes: while this has been considered for single-objective classification, we need to extend it to multi-objective prediction.

Acknowledgements

This work was supported by the EU project *Inductive Queries for Mining Patterns and Models (IQ)*, contract 516169. Jan Struyf is a post-doctoral fellow of the Fund for Scientific Research of Flanders (FWO-Vlaanderen). Many thanks to Hendrick Blockeel for his useful comments on an earlier draft of this paper.

References

1. Blockeel, H. (1998): *Top-down induction of first order logical decision trees.* PhD thesis, Department of Computer Science, Katholieke Universiteit, Leuven.
2. Blockeel, H., De Raedt, L., and Ramon, J. (1998): Top-down induction of clustering trees. *Proceedings of the 15th International Conference on Machine Learning,* pages 55–63, Morgan Kaufmann.
3. Blockeel, H. and Struyf, J. (2002): Efficient algorithms for decision tree cross-validation, *Journal of Machine Learning Research,* 3(Dec):621–650, Microtome Publishing.
4. Clark, P. and Niblett, T. (1989): The CN2 Induction Algorithm, *Machine Learning,* 3:261–283, Kluwer.
5. Džeroski, S., Demšar, D., and Grbović, J. (2000): Predicting chemical parameters of river water quality from bioindicator data. *Applied Intelligence,* 13(1): 7–17.
6. Džeroski, S., Blockeel, H., and Grbović. (2001): Predicting river water communities with logical decision trees. Presented at the Third European Ecological Modelling Conference, Zagreb, Croatia.
7. Flach, P. and Lavrač, N. (1999): Rule induction. In *Intelligent Data Analysis,* eds. Berthold, M. and Hand, D. J., pages 229–267, Springer.
8. Karalič, A. and Bratko, I. (1997): First Order Regression. *Machine Learning,* 26:147–176, Kluwer.
9. Kaufman, L. and Rousseeuw, P. J. (1990): *Finding groups in data: An introduction to cluster analysis,* John Wiley & Sons.
10. Langley, P. (1996): *Elements of Machine Learning.* Morgan Kaufman.
11. Lavrač, N., Kavšek, B., Flach, P., and Todorovski, L. (2004): Subgroup discovery with CN2-SD, *Journal of Machine Learning Research,* 5(Feb):153–188, Microtome Publishing.
12. Michalski, R. S. (1980): Knowledge acquisition through conceptual clustering: A theoretical framework and algorithm for partitioning data into conjunctive concepts. *International Journal of Policy Analysis and Information Systems,* 4:219–243.
13. Newman, D. J., Hettich, S., Blake, C. L., and Merz, C. J. (1998): *UCI Repository of machine learning databases.* University of California, Irvine, CA.
14. Quinlan, J. R. (1993): *C4.5: Programs for Machine Learning.* Morgan Kaufmann.
15. Sese, J. and Morishita, S. (2004): Itemset Classified Clustering. *Proceedings of the Eighth European Conference on Principles and Practice of Knowledge Discovery in Databases (PKDD'04),* pages 398–409, Springer.
16. Sese, J., Kurokawa, Y., Kato, K., Monden, M., and Morishita, S. (2004) Constrained clusters of gene expression profiles with pathological features. *Bioinformatics.*
17. Struyf, J., and Dzeroski, S. (2005): Constraint based induction of multi-objective regression trees. *Proceedings of the 4th International Workshop on Knowledge Discovery in Inductive Databases (KDID 2005),* pages 110-121.
18. Struyf, J., Dzeroski, S., Blockeel, H., and Clare, A. (2005): Hierarchical multi-classification with predictive clustering trees in functional genomics. *Proceedings of Workshop on Computational Methods in Bioinformatics as part of the 12th Portuguese Conference on Artificial Intelligence,* pages 272-283, Springer.

19. Suzuki, E., Gotoh,M., and Choki, Y. (2001): Bloomy Decision Tree for Multi-objective Classification. *Proceedings of the Fifth European Conference on Principles and Practice of Knowledge Discovery in Databases (PKDD'01)*, pages 436-447, Springer.

20. Todorovski, L., Blockeel, H., and Dzeroski, S. (2002): Ranking with predictive clustering trees. *Machine Learning: 13th European Conferende on Machine Learning, Proceedings*, pages 444-456, Springer.

21. Torgo, L. (1995): Data Fitting with Rule-based Regression. *Proceedings of the workshop on Artificial Intelligence Techniques (AIT'95)*, Zizka, J. and Brazdil, P. (eds.), Brno, Czech Republic.

Author Index

Lecture Notes in Computer Science

For information about Vols. 1–3824

please contact your bookseller or Springer

Vol. 3875: S. Ur, E. Bin, Y. Wolfsthal (Eds.), Hardware and Software, Verification and Testing. X, 265 pages. 2006.

Vol. 3874: R. Missaoui, J. Schmidt (Eds.), Formal Concept Analysis. X, 309 pages. 2006. (Sublibrary LNAI).

Vol. 3873: L. Maicher, J. Park (Eds.), Charting the Topic Maps Research and Applications Landscape. VIII, 281 pages. 2006. (Sublibrary LNAI).

Vol. 3872: H. Bunke, A. L. Spitz (Eds.), Document Analysis Systems VII. XIII, 630 pages. 2006.

Vol. 3870: S. Spaccapietra, P. Atzeni, W.W. Chu, T. Catarci, K.P. Sycara (Eds.), Journal on Data Semantics V. XIII, 237 pages. 2006.

Vol. 3869: S. Renals, S. Bengio (Eds.), Machine Learning for Multimodal Interaction. XIII, 490 pages. 2006.

Vol. 3868: K. Römer, H. Karl, F. Mattern (Eds.), Wireless Sensor Networks. XI, 342 pages. 2006.

Vol. 3866: T. Dimitrakos, F. Martinelli, P.Y.A. Ryan, S. Schneider (Eds.), Formal Aspects in Security and Trust. X, 259 pages. 2006.

Vol. 3865: W. Shen, K.-M. Chao, Z. Lin, J.-P.A. Barthès, A. James (Eds.), Computer Supported Cooperative Work in Design II. XII, 659 pages. 2006.

Vol. 3863: M. Kohlhase (Ed.), Mathematical Knowledge Management. XI, 405 pages. 2006. (Sublibrary LNAI).

Vol. 3862: R.H. Bordini, M. Dastani, J. Dix, A.E.F. Seghrouchni (Eds.), Programming Multi-Agent Systems. XIV, 267 pages. 2006. (Sublibrary LNAI).

Vol. 3861: J. Dix, S.J. Hegner (Eds.), Foundations of Information and Knowledge Systems. X, 331 pages. 2006.

Vol. 3860: D. Pointcheval (Ed.), Topics in Cryptology – CT-RSA 2006. XI, 365 pages. 2006.

Vol. 3858: A. Valdes, D. Zamboni (Eds.), Recent Advances in Intrusion Detection. X, 351 pages. 2006.

Vol. 3857: M.P.C. Fossorier, H. Imai, S. Lin, A. Poli (Eds.), Applied Algebra, Algebraic Algorithms and Error-Correcting Codes. XI, 350 pages. 2006.

Vol. 3855: E. A. Emerson, K.S. Namjoshi (Eds.), Verification, Model Checking, and Abstract Interpretation. XI, 443 pages. 2005.

Vol. 3854: I. Stavrakakis, M. Smirnov (Eds.), Autonomic Communication. XIII, 303 pages. 2006.

Vol. 3853: A.J. Ijspeert, T. Masuzawa, S. Kusumoto (Eds.), Biologically Inspired Approaches to Advanced Information Technology. XIV, 388 pages. 2006.

Vol. 3852: P.J. Narayanan, S.K. Nayar, H.-Y. Shum (Eds.), Computer Vision – ACCV 2006, Part II. XXXI, 977 pages. 2006.

Vol. 3851: P.J. Narayanan, S.K. Nayar, H.-Y. Shum (Eds.), Computer Vision – ACCV 2006, Part I. XXXI, 973 pages. 2006.

Vol. 3850: R. Freund, G. Păun, G. Rozenberg, A. Salomaa (Eds.), Membrane Computing. IX, 371 pages. 2006.

Vol. 3849: I. Bloch, A. Petrosino, A.G.B. Tettamanzi (Eds.), Fuzzy Logic and Applications. XIV, 438 pages. 2006. (Sublibrary LNAI).

Vol. 3848: J.-F. Boulicaut, L. De Raedt, H. Mannila (Eds.), Constraint-Based Mining and Inductive Databases. X, 401 pages. 2006. (Sublibrary LNAI).

Vol. 3847: K.P. Jantke, A. Lunzer, N. Spyratos, Y. Tanaka (Eds.), Federation over the Web. X, 215 pages. 2006. (Sublibrary LNAI).

Vol. 3846: H. J. van den Herik, Y. Björnsson, N.S. Netanyahu (Eds.), Computers and Games. XIV, 333 pages. 2006.

Vol. 3845: J. Farré, I. Litovsky, S. Schmitz (Eds.), Implementation and Application of Automata. XIII, 360 pages. 2006.

Vol. 3844: J.-M. Bruel (Ed.), Satellite Events at the MoDELS 2005 Conference. XIII, 360 pages. 2006.

Vol. 3843: P. Healy, N.S. Nikolov (Eds.), Graph Drawing. XVII, 536 pages. 2006.

Vol. 3842: H.T. Shen, J. Li, M. Li, J. Ni, W. Wang (Eds.), Advanced Web and Network Technologies, and Applications. XXVII, 1057 pages. 2006.

Vol. 3841: X. Zhou, J. Li, H.T. Shen, M. Kitsuregawa, Y. Zhang (Eds.), Frontiers of WWW Research and Development - APWeb 2006. XXIV, 1223 pages. 2006.

Vol. 3840: M. Li, B. Boehm, L.J. Osterweil (Eds.), Unifying the Software Process Spectrum. XVI, 522 pages. 2006.

Vol. 3839: J.-C. Filliâtre, C. Paulin-Mohring, B. Werner (Eds.), Types for Proofs and Programs. VIII, 275 pages. 2006.

Vol. 3838: A. Middeldorp, V. van Oostrom, F. van Raamsdonk, R. de Vrijer (Eds.), Processes, Terms and Cycles: Steps on the Road to Infinity. XVIII, 639 pages. 2005.

Vol. 3837: K. Cho, P. Jacquet (Eds.), Technologies for Advanced Heterogeneous Networks. IX, 307 pages. 2005.

Vol. 3836: J.-M. Pierson (Ed.), Data Management in Grids. X, 143 pages. 2006.

Vol. 3835: G. Sutcliffe, A. Voronkov (Eds.), Logic for Programming, Artificial Intelligence, and Reasoning. XIV, 744 pages. 2005. (Sublibrary LNAI).

Vol. 3834: D.G. Feitelson, E. Frachtenberg, L. Rudolph, U. Schwiegelshohn (Eds.), Job Scheduling Strategies for Parallel Processing. VIII, 283 pages. 2005.

Vol. 3833: K.-J. Li, C. Vangenot (Eds.), Web and Wireless Geographical Information Systems. XI, 309 pages. 2005.

Vol. 3832: D. Zhang, A.K. Jain (Eds.), Advances in Biometrics. XX, 796 pages. 2005.

Vol. 3831: J. Wiedermann, G. Tel, J. Pokorný, M. Bieliková, J. Štuller (Eds.), SOFSEM 2006: Theory and Practice of Computer Science. XV, 576 pages. 2006.

Vol. 3830: D. Weyns, H. V.D. Parunak, F. Michel (Eds.), Environments for Multi-Agent Systems II. VIII, 291 pages. 2006. (Sublibrary LNAI).

Vol. 3829: P. Pettersson, W. Yi (Eds.), Formal Modeling and Analysis of Timed Systems. IX, 305 pages. 2005.

Vol. 3828: X. Deng, Y. Ye (Eds.), Internet and Network Economics. XVII, 1106 pages. 2005.

Vol. 3827: X. Deng, D.-Z. Du (Eds.), Algorithms and Computation. XX, 1190 pages. 2005.

Vol. 3826: B. Benatallah, F. Casati, P. Traverso (Eds.), Service-Oriented Computing - ICSOC 2005. XVIII, 597 pages. 2005.